AF764372

THE LEGEND OF CHINA

The History of Pudong Development

THE LEGEND OF CHINA

The History of Pudong Development

Guoping Xie

Translated by Li Zhang

World Scientific

NEW JERSEY • LONDON • SINGAPORE • BEIJING • SHANGHAI • HONG KONG • TAIPEI • CHENNAI • TOKYO

Published by

World Scientific Publishing Co. Pte. Ltd.
5 Toh Tuck Link, Singapore 596224
USA office: 27 Warren Street, Suite 401-402, Hackensack, NJ 07601
UK office: 57 Shelton Street, Covent Garden, London WC2H 9HE

Library of Congress Cataloging-in-Publication Data
Names: Xie, Guoping, author. | Li, Zhang, 1965– translator.
Title: The legend of China : the history of Pudong development / Guoping Xie ;
translated by Li Zhang.
Other titles: Zhongguo chuan qi. English | History of Pudong development
Description: New Jersey : World Scientific, [2021]
Identifiers: LCCN 2020041561 | ISBN 9789811221699 (hardcover) |
ISBN 9789811222450 (ebook) | ISBN 9789811222467 (ebook other)
Subjects: LCSH: Pudong Xinqu (Shanghai, China)--Economic conditions. | Shanghai (China)--
Economic conditions. | Pudong (Shanghai, China)--History. | Shanghai (China)--
History--20th century. | Economic development projects--China--Shanghai.
Classification: LCC HC428.P8 X54513 2021 | DDC 338.951/132--dc23
LC record available at https://lccn.loc.gov/2020041561

British Library Cataloguing-in-Publication Data
A catalogue record for this book is available from the British Library.

中国传奇: 浦东开发史
Originally published in Chinese by Shanghai People's Publishing House
Copyright © Shanghai People's Publishing House 2017

Copyright © 2021 by World Scientific Publishing Co. Pte. Ltd.

All rights reserved. This book, or parts thereof, may not be reproduced in any form or by any means, electronic or mechanical, including photocopying, recording or any information storage and retrieval system now known or to be invented, without written permission from the publisher.

For photocopying of material in this volume, please pay a copying fee through the Copyright Clearance Center, Inc., 222 Rosewood Drive, Danvers, MA 01923, USA. In this case permission to photocopy is not required from the publisher.

For any available supplementary material, please visit
https://www.worldscientific.com/worldscibooks/10.1142/11861#t=suppl

Desk Editor: Lai Ann

Typeset by Stallion Press
Email: enquiries@stallionpress.com

Foreword 1

I received Xie Guoping's manuscript for *The Legend of China: The History of Pudong Development* after the National Day of the People's Republic of China in 2016. This is his third masterpiece on the theme of Pudong as a symbol of China's reform and opening-up. Reading this rich, in-depth, and well-written manuscript, I felt happy for him, and happy for Pudong with this book as the first to record the history of her development. Pudong, underdeveloped and enclosed in the past, had witnessed so few changes for hundreds of years that one picture was almost enough to depict her. But for Pudong at present, which is undergoing changes with each passing day, a huge database is needed to record her development.

Xie Guoping is currently based in Pudong and has been writing about Pudong. Over the years, he, as both a journalist of news and a "journalist of old news", not only records reality but also studies history. As he once said, he aims to explore why history can ultimately give Pudong a chance to create new history and the Shanghai people are so smart and diligent to take full advantage of this opportunity. Writing and studying Pudong history requires a general view, that is, not only down-to-earth thinking, but also viewing Pudong from a wider perspective, just as viewing the world from satellite. Therefore, such a book about the "original history" of Pudong development comes into being, written by the "contemporary correspondent" of Pudong development. This book provides follow-up researchers a reliable original basis for the "history of introspection" and "the history of philosophy".

Today, there is a strange phenomenon that the international image of China is far different from that of the real China. Although there is a deviation in international media coverage of China, there is another reason why when we explain China to the world and tell China's stories, our narration is not timely, clear, and specific, with an apparent lack of accuracy concerning cross-cultural issues. In the early days of the development of Pudong, Milton Friedman, a Nobel Laureate in Economics and an Economist of the monetary school of thought, came to Shanghai. He said the Pudong development plan might be a "Potemkin village". Friedman was knowledgeable, but he could not read Chinese, he could not understand Pudong, so what he said is not true. There are a lot of people in the world like Friedman, so it is our duty to tell the true story of China, and to present the true picture of Pudong.

The author has kept in close contact with me for many years and whenever we met, we talked all about Pudong — the plans, the progresses, the difficulties, the achievements, and the prospects. So I know that the author has been working hard to tell the story of Pudong well. Hard work pays off. With all due respect, he handed in yet another historical work. It is written fluently, easy to read, and has a story. And I think that the story is closest to the truth, most affectionate, and most touching. The story can prompt China to be well-accepted all over the world.

This book is written about Pudong, but the author puts the development and opening of Pudong in a broader context to reflect the ups and downs of China's reform and opening-up, just like looking at the sun in a drop of water. For example, the book tells the dispute between planned economy and market economy, the big dispute of "socialism and capitalism", as well as the minor dispute for the English translation of the name of Waigaoqiao Free Trade Zone in that year. Indeed, if the broader context of these debates is not made clear, not only are the young people unable to understand, but also it is more incomprehensible to foreigners. They may wonder why Chinese spend so much time getting obsessed with several concepts. Thus, with the help of history and a broader global context, we may be able to face the future better.

Xie Guoping is a man with persistence. He has published two books, *An Experiment of Wealth Growth: Pudong as the Example* and *The Story of Pudong: A Dream Come True*. The latter has been translated into

English by the National Foreign Language Bureau for global distribution. From a historical point of view, this new book by Xie Guoping tells the story of Pudong more comprehensively and more accurately, so it can be regarded as a sub-volume in the series of *The History of China's Reform and Opening-up*. I would like to share with other readers the moving music for the march of Pudong's development.

Zhao Qizheng
January 1, 2017

Foreword 2

Shanghai was gradually formed into land from the west to the east, and the development also took place from the west to the east. In the Tianbao era of the Tang Dynasty when Huating County was set up, a considerable part of Pudong (east side of the Huangpu River) was still in the vast sea. In the Yuan Dynasty when Shanghai County was set up with the government in Puxi (west side of the Huangpu River), many wharves were located in Puxi. In the late Qing Dynasty, concessions were also set up in Puxi. Although the Nanhui County and Chuansha Fumin Hall were set up in Pudong in the Qing Dynasty and there were already a number of towns that had taken shape in Pudong since the era of the Republic of China before her development and opening-up, the differences between Pudong and Puxi were always remarkably obvious. Comparing both sides of the Huangpu River, Puxi was more developed with towns and heavy industry, while Pudong was underdeveloped with countryside and light industry. A widely spread saying that "it is better to have a bed in Puxi than a room in Pudong" was a vivid reflection of this situation.

With the development and opening-up of Pudong in 1990, like the spring breeze coming overnight, Pudong transformed greatly in a very short time. A new modern Pudong with high-rise buildings, lined-up shops, colorful and beautiful streets rose magically and echoed with Puxi across the river, developing side by side. Pudong, with its rapid development, excellent quality and beautiful environment, is regarded as a miracle in the history of the development of cities in the world.

Like facing a star suddenly gaining popularity, a rookie rising from the horizon, people appreciated him and wanted to know more about his background and information about him. This is both a matter of curiosity and a necessity for a comprehensive understanding of him. In Pudong, when people bought houses, opened factories, investigated Pudong, strolled the parks, enjoyed the beautiful scenery, and visited Disneyland, on the go or at leisure, they always wanted to know more relevant information about the hot soil at their feet, such as the process of land formation, administrative evolution, scenic resorts, humanistic quality, anecdotes, and so on. *The Legend of China: The History of Pudong Development* written by Xie Guoping is such a wonderful work to meet people's need to understand Pudong.

The boundary of Pudong and Puxi is the Huangpu River. The direction of the Huangpu River varies from section to section. When the river body is in the east-west direction, the two sides are divided into south and north; in the north-south direction, it is divided into east and west. On the two sides, there is no fundamental difference in natural endowments such as geology, geomorphology, climate, and products. In the course of the development and evolution of the two sides of the river, the larger resource allocation system resulted in the division of a rise and a fall, and the difference in reliance on heavy industry and light industry. In the agricultural era, especially when the imperial court implemented the policy of enclosure, inland China was the center of development, not on the coast. In the Yangtze River Delta, the center of development was in Suzhou, Hangzhou, Nanjing, and other regional political centers. In Songjiang Prefecture, the political and cultural center was in Songjiang. The rise of Shanghai Town and the establishment of Shanghai County were all related to the functioning of Shanghai as a port. For a long time, especially during the Ming and Qing Dynasties, Shanghai Port existed as an outer port of Suzhou, the gateway port that led Suzhou to the vast ocean. The goods at Shanghai Port, coming in or going out, were mainly connected with Puxi. Therefore, the port, the port-related institutions, and the Municipal Department of Tax Administration were all located in Puxi. As a result, Shanghai City, which sprung up on this basis, was naturally located in Puxi. The simple reason is that in the larger and higher resource allocation system, the transaction cost in Puxi was lower than that in Pudong. The old map of

Shanghai, published before modern times, showed how many miles "west to Suzhou" and "west to Songjiang", because at that time coastal people looked inland, and in Shanghai people looked west. After the opening of Shanghai port, foreigners named Wusong River, which connected Suzhou and Shanghai, as "Suzhou River" instead of "Shanghai River", because though they stayed in Shanghai, they looked at Suzhou, which was regarded as the richest and most cultural place in China, the paradise on Earth that they most yearned for.

When China's awareness of the oceans grew and it no longer saw itself as a purely landlocked country but also as a maritime country, and when it implemented its policy of opening to the outside world, in other words, when people looked at Shanghai from a larger system, from the Asia-Pacific region or the entire East-West system, Shanghai changed from the margin to the frontier. When the technology of building bridges and laying tunnels developed to a certain extent, and when the transportation entered the age of aircraft and high-speed rail, there was hardly any difference in transaction costs between Pudong and Puxi. Therefore, when the Central Government, as part of China's development strategy, launched the plan of developing and opening Pudong, Pudong embarked on a process of rapid development.

Of course, for a long time before the reform and opening-up, both Pudong and Puxi belonged to Songjiang Prefecture, Shanghai County, or Shanghai City at the same time, and the Huangpu River was not wide enough, so cross-river exchanges were relatively convenient and the economic and cultural links were quite close. The economy in Pudong was unique in its own way and rich in culture.

Pudong as the coastal land, after the era of the Five Dynasty (907 to 960 A.D.), was very developed in salt industry. There were many saltworks. At that time, coastal people mainly lived on "salt boiled from seawater, firewood made of reeds". In the mid- and late-Ming Dynasty, due to the southward movement of fresh water and the decline of the salt industry, costal people began to return to agriculture, mainly planting cotton. Only in modern times did they gradually take cotton, grain, and oil as the main crops. After Shanghai opened its port, the city developed rapidly, and Pudong, relying on Puxi, gradually developed its own characteristics and advantages. There were four major industries. The first was towel.

In 1900, the towel industry rose in Pudong. Before 1937, there had been 202 towel factories in Chuansha County, with many families making weaving a business and weaving machines ran even at night. Therefore, it was called "the hometown of towels". The second one was the construction industry. In 1880, Yang Sisheng opened the first construction plant in Shanghai, Yang Ruitai Construction Plant. After that, nearly 10 construction plants started in Shanghai successively, including Zhou Ruiji, Tao Guiji, Gu Lanji, and so on. Many famous buildings were built by Pudong people, such as Jianghai Beiguan Office, Yangshupu Power Plant, Bank of China Building, Xianshi Company Building, and Municipal Government Auditorium. The third one was the flower-planting industry. Pudong was named as flower township because of its 300 years of flower-planting history. During the Guangxu period of the Qing Dynasty, the "God of Flower Meeting" was organized by the flower farmers in Pudong. After the meeting, they joined the Shanghai Flower and Tree Trade Association. They opened shops in Shanghai to sell flowers, took on contracts to plant flowers, and designed parks and rebuilt gardens. The fourth was the cow-breeding industry. In the Pudong coastal area, Tangjiao cows began to be bred very early. The cows usually served as labor, and after calving, they were milked for self-use. In the early Guangxu period, a Dutch bull was introduced to breed a unique black-and-white cow by hybridization and reproduction. After that, they made profit by selling calves. In 1932, more than a thousand cows were sold to the Huashang Ranch in Shanghai. The towel industry, construction industry, flower-planting industry, and cow-breeding industry are all necessary for mega-cities like Shanghai. Therefore, the industries of Pudong in modern times have become inseparable organic components in the economic system of Shanghai.

Before modern times, there had been many active and open-minded figures in Pudong. In the Song and Yuan Dynasties, Zhang Qi, a native of Gaoqiao, and Zhu Qing, a native of Chongming in Pudong, built a large number of flat-bottomed sea vessels, namely sand vessels, with the maximum load of 8000 or 9000 shi and the minimum load of 2000 or 3000 shi (1 shi = 59.2 kilogram). These vessels solved the problem of sea transportation of grains. As a result, the Yuan government conferred them the official titles of Wanhu in sea transportation and Youcheng of Jiangnan province. Zhang Xuan and Zhu Qing made important contributions to the development of Shanghai and Taicang areas.

In the Ming Dynasty, Lujiazui of Pudong was a place with many scholars. Lujiazui was named after the Lu family, a big family who lived in the South Yangtze River. Lu Shen and his father Lu Ji were temporary prominent individuals. Lu Shen was the first person in the history of Shanghai County to get high positions through the imperial examination, such as Jinshi in the 18th year of Hongzhi as the emperor (1505 A.D.), compiler and editor, governor of Sichuan Province, and Head of the Zhanshi Province. He was a famous writer and calligrapher. He owned real estate in both Puxi and Pudong. The Houshan Garden built in Lujiazui was well known in scale and scenery, with miles of hillocks with twists and turns, just like a mountain. Lu Ji was a very original thinker. He believed that luxury consumption had a positive significance, while the traditional concept of advocating thrift and combating extravagance was not entirely correct. Banning extravagance and advocating thrift could not enrich people, while luxury could promote economic prosperity and the circulation of wealth and increase employment, thus playing a positive role in social development. This notion takes a very important position in Chinese economic history. His famous book, *Debate on Hua Yi*, proposed that the criterion for distinguishing Chinese people did not lie in the difference of races, but the level of civilization, which at that time was an extraordinarily surprising idea put forward a hundred years earlier than Wang Fuzhi's similar view. Huang Tianren, Xu Guangqi's teacher, serving as Jinshi and then Chief of Penalty Ministry in the Wanli period of Ming, was an open-minded, well-known prolific scholar. He lived in Pudong for a long time. Sun Yuanhua, a student of Xu Guangqi, was a native of Gaoqiao in Pudong. He made important contributions to the introduction of Western studies and military affairs to China. The famous people in modern Pudong include Li Pingshu, Yang Shicheng, Huang Xiexun, Li Wenyu, Zhong Tianwei, Huang Yanpei, Mu Ouchu, Zhang Wentian, Du Yuesheng, Huang Zi, Fu Lei, and so on. They were industrial giants, or political elites, or cultural authorities, or noted public figure. These prominent individuals were born in Pudong and worked actively in Puxi or all over the country, so they were well-known in Pudong, in Shanghai, and all over the nation.

In history, Pudong was under the jurisdiction of many counties, including Kunshan, Baoshan, Shanghai, Nanhui, Chuansha, and so on. Only not long ago was it merged into the large Pudong New Area. Pudong was not an independent administration in history, so there is no local chronicle covering Pudong and no one has ever written such a detailed history of local development concerning Pudong. In preparing this book, one major difficulty was the extremely dispersed information and another was the scarcely achieved results in the early stage. In this sense, as a result of enduring hardships in this pioneering work, the book *The Legend of China: The History of Pudong Development* becomes a relatively comprehensive and informative book on the history about the development of Great Pudong, which is of great academic value. With 12 chapters in total, this books begins with the explanation of the place names in Pudong, and in turn it narrates the transferring of coastline and the history of Pudong land forming, the development of the salt industry and the prosperity of towns like Xinchang, the development of intensive farming agriculture, the effort and difficulty of Pudong people marching toward the sea, the formation of the gap between Pudong and Puxi, the development of Pudong with the reliance on Puxi, the pioneering work done by the Pudong gentle businessmen as natives of Pudong in the modern times, the transportation links of the two banks of the Huangpu River, the formation of the strategy of developing and opening Pudong, the pilot measures taken in Pudong, and the great achievements in many other aspects.

Xie Guoping has been working in Pudong for a long time. He once served as Deputy Editor-in-Chief of *Pudong Times* and Editor-in-Chief of *Pudong Development* magazine. He loves Pudong and knows Pudong quite well. He has published a variety of works related to Pudong, such as *The Experiment with Wealth Growth: Pudong as an Example* and *The Story of Pudong: A Dream Come True* and other books about Pudong. *The Legend of China: The History of Pudong Development* was based on many previous works and on his accumulated data for many years. The book is strongly appealing with full and accurate information, citation of various authorities, clear context, and elegant language. It is expected that after the book is published, it will be appreciated by readers concerned about the history of Pudong, and will also leave a deep impression on the study of Pudong history.

Xiong Yuezhi
January 27, 2017

Contents

Foreword 1 v
Foreword 2 ix

Chapter 1 From Water to Land: Where Pudong Comes from and Where Pudong Goes to 1

1.1 A Fuzzy Concept 1
1.2 The Piece of Land Frequently and Randomly Divided 3
1.3 Restrictions by "River" and "Sea" 14
1.4 Development Scheme: From West to East 16
1.5 The Constantly Updated Coastline 20
1.6 Endogenous Impetus for Eastward Development 28

Chapter 2 The Development Initiative: Civil and Government Efforts 31

2.1 Not Going Out to Sea in the Real Sense 31
2.2 An Object of Contention for the Colonists 37
2.3 The Modern Industrialized and Urbanized Area Along the Yangtze River 41
2.4 Hometown Construction of Pudong People 47
2.5 The Pioneers of Early Pudong Development 54
2.6 Construction of Pudong Road Only 62

Chapter 3 The Widening Gap: The Outbreak of Shanghai's "Urban Disease" 67

3.1 Investment Without Development 67
3.2 Crossing Surges in Small Boat 73
3.3 The Difficulty in Implementing the Cross-river Project 78
3.4 Sighs from the East and West Banks of the Huangpu River 85
3.5 The Problems Faced by the New Mayor 89
3.6 The Outbreak of "Urban Disease" in Shanghai 94
3.7 Historical Causes for the Huge Gap Between the Two Places 102

Chapter 4 The Mission to Assume: A Trump Card to the World Played by the Chief Designer 107

4.1 Where Shanghai will Advance 107
4.2 The First Voice from Folks 111
4.3 The Formation of Four Alternatives 116
4.4 The Construction of a "New Shanghai" 125
4.5 The Design by Chinese-American Architects 130
4.6 The Trump Card Anticipated by the General Designer 138
4.7 Dramatic Change of Pudong's Fate 143

Chapter 5 Seizing Every Minute: Big Experiment in Specific Areas 151

5.1 A Gorgeous Chapter Written About the History of Pudong 151
5.2 Why People Thought of Pudong 10 Years Later 156
5.3 The Change in the Orientation of Pudong 159
5.4 An Elevation from Local Aspiration to National Strategy 164
5.5 The "Growth Pole" in the 1990s 166
5.6 "New Area" Instead of "Special Zone" 171
5.7 Signal: China's Door Not Closed Yet 176
5.8 A Big Regret Admitted by Deng Xiaoping 180
5.9 "Preference of Witnessing Today's Development to Reading Books for a Hundred Years" 184
5.10 Why Chinese Leaders were so Concerned About Pudong 185

Chapter 6 Little Experience and Much Thinking: Meditation on the Development of Pudong by Standing beside a Globe **189**

6.1 Borrowing "Brain" from the World 189
6.2 Selection of Development Mode 201
6.3 Constructing a Functional Development Area 203
6.4 Form Construction in Service of Functional Development 206
6.5 Orderly and Normalized Development 209
6.6 Wisdom in Legislation 213
6.7 Tertiary Industry Taking the Lead in Breakthrough 215
6.8 Integration of Chinese and Western Cultures like All Rivers Running into the Sea 222
6.9 The Absorption of "Nutrition from the World" and the Opening of Economic Dialogue 227

Chapter 7 The Uphill Battle: Pudong Wearing a Helmet to Withstand **231**

7.1 Idling of Financial Funds and Running of Land Leasing 231
7.2 "Small Government, Big Society" 236
7.3 Reopening of the Stock Exchange 245
7.4 Shanghai's Response to the Chief Designer's Request with Great Action 253
7.5 Doubts from Foreign Scholars 261
7.6 Why Pudong Can Attract so much Foreign Capital 266
7.7 The Past of Shanghai Represented by thc Bund and the Future of Shanghai Represented by Pudong 269

Chapter 8 Big Experiment: Holding High the Banner of Pioneering **277**

8.1 Pre-World Trade Organization (WTO) Previews 277
8.2 Pioneering under the Functional Policies 281
8.3 Great Experiment in the New Century 286
8.4 Dancing in Fetters 296
8.5 The Birth of a Community Service Organization 300
8.6 Giving Full Play to Society 304

Chapter 9 Economic Transformation: Big Airplane and Disney **311**

9.1 The End of the "Crane Economy" Because of the Financial Crisis 311
9.2 The Difficulty of Economic Growth due to Land Insufficiency 315
9.3 The Difficulty in Transformation and Upgrading 318
9.4 The Coming of Big Plane 321
9.5 The Following-up of Chip Manufacture Giants 325
9.6 Why it Took More than 10 Years for Disney to Settle in Shanghai 329

Chapter 10 New Pudong: "Two Centers" and the Merging of Two Districts **339**

10.1 The Priority of Finance 339
10.2 Meanings of Gifts 343
10.3 The Objective of Establishing "Two Centers" 347
10.4 The Development of Shipping and the Economic Significance of Proximity to the River 350
10.5 New Pudong with the Merging of Two Districts 356
10.6 Building the Global "Pricing Center" 360

Chapter 11 Prying up the Fulcrum: Pilot Reform Zone (Version 3.0) **363**

11.1 Small Fulcrum with Great Effect 363
11.2 The Debate over the Translation of the Name into English 368
11.3 The First Case in China and the Pioneer in the World 373
11.4 Institutional Experiment in Specific Zones 382
11.5 Offering Convenience Instead of Preferential Tax 387
11.6 Investment Blacklist 390
11.7 Surprise for Investors 393
11.8 All Efforts for Making the Market More Efficient 397
11.9 Exporting Experience 400
11.10 The Expansion of the Free Trade Zone 405

Chapter 12 Fulfillment of a Dream: 500 Meters up and down, 100 Years to and fro 411

12.1 The Great Story of Our Age 411
12.2 From "Ghost City" to Hot Land 415
12.3 Dreams Fulfilled 416
12.4 Trial and Error: Rebounding and Advancing Step by Step 420
12.5 Whether the Golden Age can be Extended 424

Afterword 431

Chapter 1

From Water to Land: Where Pudong Comes from and Where Pudong Goes to

1.1 A Fuzzy Concept

In the first month of the fourth year of Emperor Yongzheng's reign (1726 A.D.) in the Qing Dynasty, at the Yangtze River Estuary, on the beach of the East China Sea, Qinlian, as a successful candidate in the highest imperial examinations, took up the new post of county magistrate in Nanhui County and felt pleased about establishing a county government in Huinan County, as named today.

This was a new county government set up by the court before the new year. To the east of the Huangpu River in Shanghai, from the third year of Emperor Yongzheng's reign (1725 A.D.) in the Qing Dynasty, the history of the independent organizational system began. The new gate of county government told people that this was the first county-level administrative establishment in Pudong area, which housed the most powerful chief executive in Pudong with the highest reputation.

Before this, in the area called Pudong by the folks, there was no independent, unified administrative center. A closer look at the history of Pudong shows that there had long been no unified administrative division or a strong administrative center in the area of thousands of square kilometers to the east of the Huangpu River, that is to say, on the administrative map from ancient to contemporary China, an administrative division named Pudong could not be found.

After the reign of Emperor Yongle in the Ming Dynasty, the Wusong River, the present Suzhou River, was severely silted. In the second year of Emperor Yongle's reign (1404 A.D.), a minister named Xia Yuanji organized local people to widen the river course and excavate a larger river as a new sea-going waterway and channel in Taihu Lake area. Till this time in Shanghai, there was a broad river going straight into the East China Sea. And because of this river, known as the Huangpu River and the most important geographical landmark in Shanghai, the name of Pudong, as a separate geographical concept, began to appear in all kinds of literature.

As *Shanghai County Annals* written in Jiajing's reign of the Ming Dynasty goes, "From the gate down the port, the waters of Pudong consist of Yantie Tang, Shenzhuang Tang, Zhou Pu, Sanlin Tang, Yangzi Port and Huangzi Lou, while the waters of Puxi are made up of Ludao Bang, Tangzi Jing, Nanyu Tang, Beiyu Tang, Che Gou, Wudian Tang, Hua Jing, Wuni Jing, Longhua Gang, Richi Bang, Xuejia Bang, Zhaojia Bang, Fang Bang, South Houjia Bang, North Houjia Bang and Yang Jing."

In addition, there were the wordings like "Jiangdong" and "Puzuo".

Today, the word "Pudong" spreads widely throughout China and the world, but in history, it was such a common name and ordinary place that no central government paid any attention to it. Its geographical scope was not very precisely divided, that is, there was no formation of a unified and complete administrative division. Strictly speaking, not until 1992 was there a complete and unified administrative organization in Pudong.

Therefore, in different historical periods, the meanings of "Pudong" are diverse. Even in the same historical period, there are different meanings in a broad sense and narrow sense. By the beginning of the 21st century, Pudong in the broad sense refers to the whole area of Pudong New Area and the east to the Huangpu River in Minhang and Fengxian districts. Pudong in the narrow sense refers to Pudong New Area along the east bank of the Huangpu River with an area of 1429.67 square kilometers.

In other words, since the ancient times the word "Pudong" has been named only in the sense of orientation, and relatively vague.

It is very regretful. From the Chinese landscape map, frankly speaking, Pudong is a good place with a wide expanse of flat land. In the entire territory of China it belongs to the Yangtze River Delta Plain. "The fertile delta avoids drought in the north with shortage of rain and the loss of lime from the soil due to excessive rainfall in the south."

Pudong is surrounded by water on three sides, close to the year-round unfrozen Huangpu River. It is an area of north Asia subtropical monsoon climate, with the annual average temperature about 16 degrees celsius and the annual frost-free period about 230 days. As a typical plain in the south of the Yangtze River, it is mild and humid, with distinct four seasons, adequate sunshine, and developed water system.

Unfortunately, for such a good piece of land there was no relatively stable and unified administrative center as well as administrative division. It was divided so unreasonably, disorderly, frequently, and randomly that there was little cultural accumulation and cultural heritage.

Most people took it for granted that the status quo in Pudong was attributed to the river, the Huangpu River.

In fact, it is not so simple.

1.2 The Piece of Land Frequently and Randomly Divided

If we first take a look at the history of Pudong, we can understand the origin of Pudong — the vague concept.

In ancient times, Pudong was a vast ocean.

Thanks to the power of nature, the sand was brought down from the upper reaches of the Yangtze River. At the intersection of the Yangtze River and the sea, the sedimentation was accelerated by the clashing waves and the deposited sand formed a tidal-flat area, which extended to the southeast and naturally formed a sand bank, standing on the seashore. It formed a natural barrier to the sea water and played a role in protecting the lives and property of coastal residents. The ancients called it "Gangshen", which can be regarded as the earliest coastline of Shanghai.

Along with the tidal flat extended to the east, the coastline moved to the east. In the Wei Dynasty, Jin Dynasty, and Northern and Southern Dynasties, the coastline reached today's Shenzhuang, Fengxian-Zhelin of Shanghai. At this time, Pudong was still below the sea level.

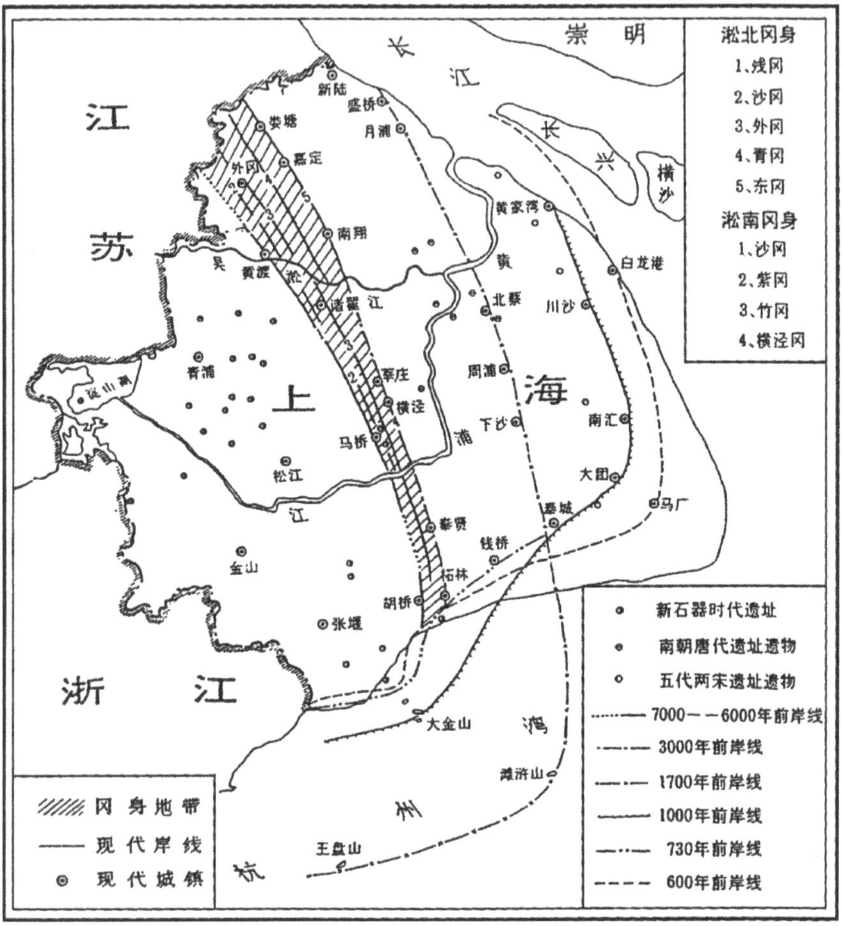

The coastline of Shanghai extended to the east

In the Sui and Tang Dynasties, the western part of Pudong began to surface. Once it became land, there would be people, life, society, and the corresponding political system. Archaeologists have confirmed this too.

On November 25, 1975, a number of artifacts for daily life in the Tang and Song Dynasties were found at the ruins of Yan Qiao, the ruins of the Tang Dynasty located in the south of Zhengjiawan Village, Yanqiao Township, Pudong. This was the first time the relics of the Tang and Song Dynasties were discovered in Pudong. Archaeologists believe that since the Tang Dynasty, Yan Qiao had been a long-term residential village, so it can be said that they were the earliest Pudong residents.

On December 12, 1979, an abandoned wooden ship was unearthed during the excavation of the Beicaixiang section of the Chuanyang River. In the cabin, two cobblestones, a coin and a remnant corner of Kaiyuan currency in the Tang Dynasty, and a piece of burnt clay were left.

In 1975, some artifacts from the Tang Dynasty were unearthed at the site of Yan Qiao Ruins, a Tang Dynasty site in the south of Zhengjiawan Village, Yanqiao Township, Pudong. The left picture is a porcelain basin in the Tang Dynasty, and the right one is a glazed pottery pot.

The shape of the ancient boat from the Tang dynasty is similar to the boat in the Sui Dynasty unearthed in Leizhou Bay, Shandong in 1975. With reference to the unearthed Kaiyuan currency in Tang Dynasty, archaeologists believed that the ancient boat was built in the Sui Dynasty and was still in use until the Wude period of the Tang Dynasty.

The analysis of stratigraphic soil samples made by the micro-chamber of the Marine Geology Department of Tongji University shows, "Here, the oceanity was the strongest, and the foraminifera indicates that at that time, the water depth and salinity were relatively high. The wooden boat seemed to be sunk on the beach, not in the small river that had already become land."

The ancient ships in the Chuanyang River allow people to imagine the life of the ancients in Pudong. At that time, however, most parts of Pudong were a vast expanse of white mud flat, sparsely populated, with reed swaying and seabirds flying. Although at this time in Chinese history it was the most powerful dynasty, poets recited poems in Chang'an, and

The boat in the Tang Dynasty unearthed in Beicai in January 1979 (Source: Pudong Archives)

envoys, merchants, scholars, artists, and monks from many countries continued to arrive in Chang'an, visiting, studying, and doing business.

In the recorded history of the district division of Pudong, the most cited is the 10th year of Tianbao's reign in the Tang Dynasty (751 A.D.). "Zhao Juzhen, the chief of Wu Prefecture cut part of the three counties Kunshan, Jiaxing and Haiyan to set up Huating County with the approval of the throne." Pudong was part of Huating County. Gaoqiao area today in the northeast of Pudong belonged to Kunshan County.

It can be said that in Chinese history, this is an ordinary year, but for Shanghai and for Pudong today, it is of epoch-making significance. Since then, Pudong began to have a relatively independent administrative division within the territory of Shanghai, and laid the foundation for the development and change of the administrative pattern in Shanghai.

An ancient boat in the Tang Dynasty stored in Chongming Museum

In *Yunjian Annals*, published in the Southern Song Dynasty, the names of various townships in Huating County were recorded, but Pudong could not be found as a name of an area. Only in the eastern part of Huating County the names that belonged to Pudong area like Sanlin were found.

In the Song Dynasty there were 13 townships and 44 villages in Huating County. Up to the Tang Dynasty and Song Dynasty, political districts in Huating County did not change significantly. After the Yuan, Ming, and Qing Dynasty, the division of the relevant counties all derived from these townships in Huating County.

By the 10th year of Jiading's reign in the Southern Song Dynasty (1217 A.D.), with eastern Kunshan separated as Jiading County, Pudong area were also divided into two counties, Huating and Jiading.

From the beginning of the Yuan Dynasty to the 29th year of Yuan (1292 A.D.), Huating area was developed in agriculture, prosperous in economy with accelerated growth in population. The town of Shanghai, in particular, was an important distribution center of commodity. The royal court gave an approval to the suggestion made by the Songjiang Magistrate, and five north-east townships in Huating were put into the administration of Shanghai County. Thus Pudong area except Gaoqiao belonged to Shanghai County.

In the third year of Yongzheng's reign in the Qing Dynasty (1725), the southeast Shanghai County was divided into Nanhui County, and the eastern part of Jiading County was divided into Baoshan County. At this time, Pudong area was under the jurisdiction of three counties, Shanghai, Nanhui, and Baoshan. So finally, Pudong area had an independent establishment as a county — Nanhui County.

In the 15th year of Jiaqing's reign in the Qing Dynasty (1810), a new administrative district was separated from Shanghai County and Nanhui County, named Chuansha Fumin Office. Although the administration was nominally independent, the daily management was handled by Shanghai County. It was only after the Revolution of 1911 that it was officially established as a county subordinate to Jiangsu Province. At that time, Chuansha County was only 189 square kilometers, the smallest county in Jiangsu Province.

In the first year of the Republic of China (1912), Pudong was under the jurisdiction of the three counties of Shanghai, Nanhui, and Baoshan and Chuansha County changed from Chuansha Fumin Office. All these county-level governments were subordinate to Jiangsu Province.

After the establishment of the Nanjing National Government, the urbanization of the whole of Shanghai was accelerated. In 1928, the National Government made a large-scale adjustment to the administrative division in Shanghai. Shanghai took over the jurisdiction of 17 cities and towns. In Pudong area, Yangjing and Luhang were merged into Yangjing District, Tangqiao and Yangsi were merged into Yangsi District, and Gaoqiao and Gaohang were merged into Gaoqiao District. Namely, the area along the Huangpu River from Yangsi in the north to Gaoqiao in the south was incorporated into the special city of Shanghai. The other three counties of Shanghai, Chuansha, and Nanhui were subordinate to Jiangsu Province.

On December 15, 1937, the Japanese invaders established the "Shanghai Dadao Government" in Pudong, and changed Shanghai into the "Special City" in the following year. In 1943, the Wang puppet regime integrated Chuansha, Nanhui, Baoshan, and five other counties into "Shanghai Special City", which was divided into three parts: urban area, suburb, and county area. Pudong had two suburbs — Pudong south district and Pudong northeastern district, and three county districts — Chuansha, Nanhui, and Fengxian.

By 1950, there was another big change in administrative division for Pudong. The land that amounted to 167 square kilometers, including Zhangjiang, Huamu, Beicai, Jiangzhen, Shiwan, Liutuan, Huanglou which belonged to Nan Hui and the western part of Sunqiao, and Tangzhen, which were formerly under the administration of Nanhui County, was assigned to Chuansha County, so the area under the jurisdiction of Chuansha doubled ever since.

In 1958, Nanhui and Chuansha were separated from Jiangsu Province and put under the jurisdiction of Shanghai. In August of that year, there was finally the county named after Pudong, which was also the first administrative region officially named after Pudong in history and was written into the administrative map of China. But Pudong County was withdrawn only two years later. As a result, its rural areas were assigned to Chuansha County and the area along the Huangpu River was assigned to the urban area.

In 1958, as to the Shanghai political district, Chuansha, Nanhui and other counties were transferred to Shanghai from Jiangsu Province (recorded in *Historical Atlas of Shanghai*).

Pan Jianlong, a scholar in Pudong, made some comments on the withdrawal of Pudong County more than two years after it was founded: "The withdrawal of Pudong County resulted from the fact that it did not have a root. As a county, from the perspective of Chinese history, there was always a defensive wall, a broad geographical space and a deeper cultural heritage, but Pudong County was too small to have them. Both its establishment and cancellation were carried out in a hurry, so it was easy to establish and quick to withdraw."

By 1984, the Shanghai government put Lujiazui and Yangjing areas along the Huangpu River under the administration of Huangpu District, and Zhoujiadu to Yangsi and other riverside areas under the administration of the Southern Urban District. By this time, Pudong area was governed dividedly by three counties and three districts, taking the pattern of "three countries representing four parties". That is to say, Pudong New Area today was, at that time, under the administration of three districts like Nanshi, Huangpu, and Yangpu and three counties like Chuansha, Nanhui. and Shanghai, so that the urban and rural areas were interlaced, the peasants and the residents were mixed, and the rural production teams were located alongside residential areas. Therefore, there was a local joke: "To Shanghai one needs to take a ferryboat, to the countryside one needs to take only a step".

This is a unique phenomenon in the history of Pudong, that is, there has been an absence of unified administrative division and administrative center, so it developed slowly in a disorderly, multi-governmental, constantly divided state. Of course, the shortage of historical burden and rich dignified cultural heritage draws the foreshadowing of achieving leaping development for Pudong in the days to come. This is a bit similar to Shenzhen, the southern frontier far from the political center and facing the sea, which is far away from the emperor and free from the accumulation of Chinese traditional culture, especially the unified autocracy culture.

From the perspective of economic development history, for an area without the function of trade and transport hub, there are no logistics, capital flow, and people flow, so that there is no function of economic radiation and the region might be divided at will.

According to the statistics made by Professor Lin Tuo, during the 44 years from the founding of New China to the establishment of Pudong New Area, the administrative division of Pudong had been undergoing frequent changes, with more than 20 changes in the administrative area, administrative system, and the name of the political district, with an average of once every two years. As for the villages and towns, the changes of administrative division took place about seven times in each town or village. The most typical is the division of Chuansha County in 1958. At that time, the 13 villages and one town in Chuansha County were divided into 11 communes in September. After more than two months, it was further

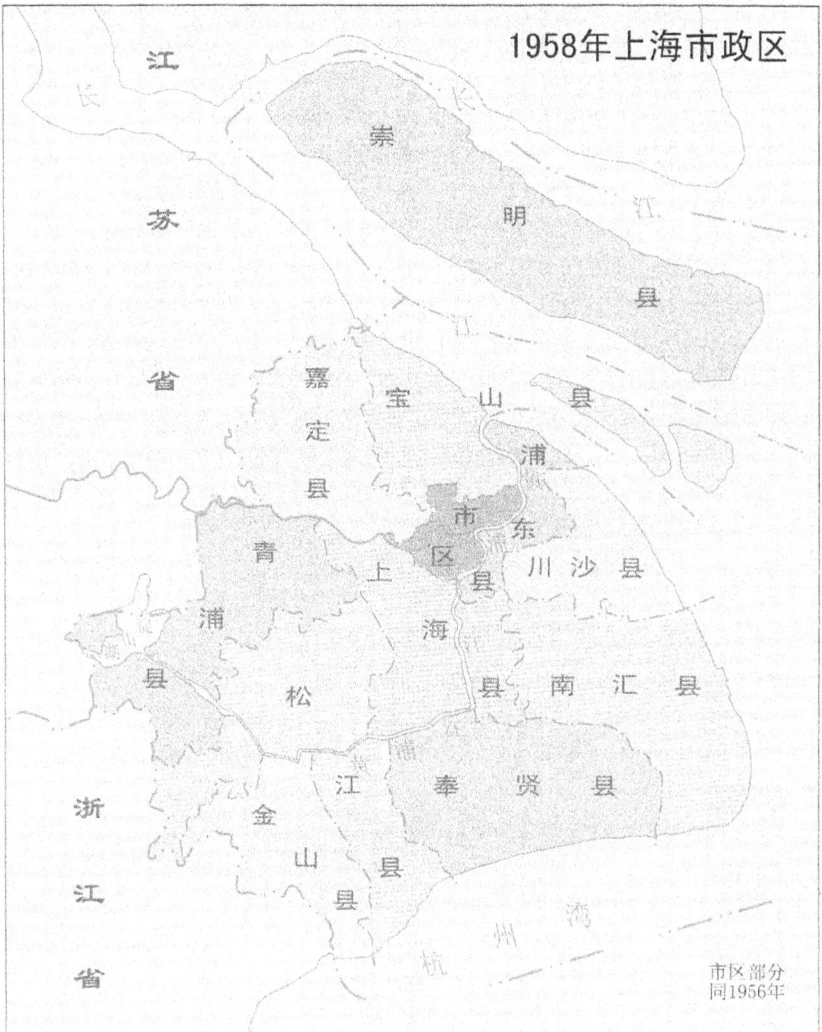

Shanghai administrative district in 1958, with Chuansha and Nanhui counties of Jiangsu province put under the jurisdiction of Shanghai (Recorded in *Historical Atlas of Shanghai*)

reduced to five communes. In the following year, it was forced to change again to 14 communes.

It can be said that this is one of the reasons for restricting the economic and social development of Pudong, and to some extent it is both the cause and the result.

Some people with insight were aware of this problem. As early as in February 1925, Huang Yanpei, a pioneer of vocational education in China and a native of Pudong, once made a proposal in the name of Pudong Association to the ruling government to change Pudong into a special area. Of course, it was only a dream at that time.

This state came to an end in 1990.

In 1990, the Communist Party of China (CPC) Central Committee and State Council decided to develop Pudong. In April of that year, at the third session of the Ninth People's Congress of Shanghai, Huang Ju, the executive deputy mayor, made a special report on Pudong development. He told all the representatives that the Pudong area planned for development referred to the east to the Huangpu River, the north to the Chuanyang River, and the triangular area immediately adjacent to the downtown, most of which was within a radius of 15 kilometers from the city center with a total of about 350 square kilometers.

But two years later, Pudong began to expand. In October 1992, the administrative system and the division of Pudong New Area was formally established. The administrative area of Pudong New Area included the former Chuansha County, Sanlin Town of Shanghai County, and parts of Huangpu District, Nanshi District, and Yangpu District that were located in the east of Huangpu River. The total area was 522.7 square kilometers.

The expansion also resulted from administrative divisions. According to the recollection of Wang Hongquan, former secretary of Chuansha County Party Committee and assistant director of the Pudong New Area Administrative Committee, the idea of Pudong development was put forward as early as in 1986. At that time, the planned boundary was north to the Chuanyuyang River, thus dividing the original Chuansha County into two parts. Jiangzhen, Shiwan, Liutuan, Huanglou, and some other towns would also be divided into two. So this would cause a lot of inconvenience to management. On April 18, 1990, in Shanghai, Premier Li Peng announced the decision of the CPC Central Committee and State Council on the development and opening-up of Pudong. The government of Chuansha County Committee issued a report to the city government, requesting Chuansha County to be incorporated into Pudong New Area, which gained support from city leaders. Thus the current Pudong New Area of 522 square kilometers was shaped.

In 1996, the city government approved that Qingcaosha, the newly rising beach in the south of Hengsha Island at the Yangtze River Estuary, would be put under the jurisdiction of Pudong New Area. In 1999, because the land acquisition by Pudong International Airport covered the 6.8 square kilometers of land originally under the jurisdiction of Donghai and Zhuqiao towns in Nanhui County, this piece of land was administratively assigned to the Pudong New Area. In 2000, the People's Government of Pudong New Area was officially established.

In 2009, a new piece of land was incorporated into Pudong. On April 24, the State Council issued "The Reply on Approving the Adjustment of Some Administrative Divisions of Shanghai", which agreed to withdraw Nanhui District of Shanghai and incorporate it into Pudong New Area of Shanghai's administrative division.

Location of Pudong New Area (Source: *Pudong Yearbook in 2010*)

This adjustment of regional division is mainly attributed to the perspective of economic development. Xu Lin, the former Party Secretary of Pudong New Area, recalled, "The core functional areas and the main battlefields of the 'two centers' are Pudong and Nanhui. In the past, the wording of 'Golden Triangle' in larger Pudong mainly referred to Lujiazui, Waigaoqiao, Yangshangang and other areas, but this 'Golden Triangle' belonged to two different administrative bodies of Nanhui, Pudong. At the same time, a series of major projects also run across two areas, the most typical of which were Disneyland and Pudong Airport. The incorporation of Nanhui into Pudong can solve the problems like independent development as a result of the multi-administrative subjects caused by the administrative divisions. And it is beneficial to integrate the resources of many strategic elements that were originally separated in the two districts. Thus with this strong support, the construction of 'Four Centers' in Shanghai took shape."

As a result, the area of Pudong New Area increased to 1429.67 square kilometers, including the former Nanhui area of 860.1 square kilometers, the former Pudong New Area of 569.57 square kilometers. The governmental administrative center of Pudong New Area was still located in No. 2001, Century Avenue.

Actually, as to the regional division, the history of Pudong New Area is very short. Therefore, Zhao Qizheng, the first Director of the Pudong New Area Administrative Committee, called Pudong a "beautiful teenager" in a poem.

1.3 Restrictions by "River" and "Sea"

The frequent change of Pudong administrative division is related to the development of Pudong itself. Namely, the development of Pudong area and its evolution in political district were potentially restricted by the process of land formation and the pattern of water system in Pudong.

It was very late for Pudong's formation, so it was late for its development. This area had long been in the peripheral zone of the affiliated government or county. In addition, there were frequent natural disasters. The tide disasters can be taken as an example. According to statistics, the tide disasters in Chuansha County from 1135 to 1949 reached more than 50 times. Such a frequency was rarely seen in adjacent areas. It is indeed difficult for such a disaster-prone region to become the center of local administration.

From the history of Shanghai, people wonder why there was no county establishment in Shanghai before the Tang Dynasty. Tan Qixiang, a famous historical geographer in China, once noticed that "in the more than 970 years from the Qin Dynasty to the 10th year of Tianbao in the Tang Dynasty, on the mainland of Shanghai only Haiyan County was set up during the 220 years of Qin and Western Han Dynasty. In the latter 80 years of the Southern Dynasty, Qianjing and Xupu counties were set up successively. In addition, during about 660 years from the Eastern Han Dynasty to the early days of the Nan Dynasty and from Sui to Tianbao period in the Tang Dynasty, no county was even set up, but instead under long-term administration of Jiaxing, Haiyan, Kunshan counties currently located in Zhejiang and Jiangsu."

It is certain that Shanghai was so backward at that time that it belonged to the "wilderness beside the sea". "As late as more than a thousand years ago, it was not well developed," Tan Qixiang concluded. "This is mainly due to the fact that the seawall was not built at that time and the land was often flooded with salty tides."

In addition to the attack by tides, the estuary of Yangtze River was constantly silted, with the tidal flat in the coastal area of Pudong also growing and spreading. And the area of Pudong continued to expand in the process of land formation, thus causing Pudong to be divided into different county-level administrative districts for a long time.

The development of Pudong was also greatly restricted by the "river" and "sea". The sea to the east and the Huangpu River to the west, like a natural moat, cut off the economic and cultural exchanges between the two sides. After Shanghai opened its port in 1843, the western part of the Huangpu River underwent dramatic changes. The superior geographical position and powerful commercial and trade functions soon made Shanghai become the national economic center, radiating to the whole country and even the Far East. Unfortunately, as to the east of the Huangpu River, despite the vast land, the logistics, capital flows, and people flows from all directions came to a stop at the Huangpu River.

Zheng Zu'an, a scholar from the Institute of History of the Shanghai Social Sciences Academy, analyzed the reasons why Pudong could not fully develop from the perspective of geography. The east of Pudong was close to the sea, and the result of long-term sediment deposition caused the coastal seabed to be full of "iron sands", so that the ships could not anchor there and it was very dangerous. "When the tide rose, it was water all over, and when the tide fell, it was hard sand all about, known as copper sand. Sea ships would be broken when they got onto it by mistake." There were virtually no ports on the Pudong coast for decades, as the sea blocked people's advance.

Administrative division is a kind of embodiment of state management, so, generally speaking, the boundary of administrative division is not easily changed once it is determined. To a certain extent, the changes of administrative division and the frequency of changes often reflect the historical process of regional economic and social development.

From the history of economic development, the Pudong economy started up from the salt industry. If the salt industry in Pudong had continued to develop, the corresponding regionalization might have been maintained or even expanded. But by the end of the Ming Dynasty, the salt industry in Pudong declined, leaving the related market towns short of economic pillars, and even less likely to have an administrative center.

Therefore, Professor Lin Tuo believed, "After Tianbao's reign in the Tang Dynasty, this area had been in the state of divided administration for a long time. After the formation of the salt industry as the main industrial structure, the corresponding settlement distribution and town pattern took shape. The management of the salt industry in the Song and Yuan Dynasties laid a foundation for the early administrative pattern of Pudong. Along with the transformation of industrial structure to cotton planting industry, the unreasonableness of administrative division was fully exposed."

1.4 Development Scheme: From West to East

The change of the Pudong administrative area is also related to the overall idea of Shanghai development.

Looking at the map of Shanghai and recalling the history of Shanghai's opening as a port, we can find that the development of Shanghai was westward, starting from the west to the Huangpu River. Then there were the public concessions, the Bund, Nanjing Road, and the international hotels as the origin of the city center. In the 1930s, there was the plan to build a new Grand Shanghai Center in northern Jiangwan.

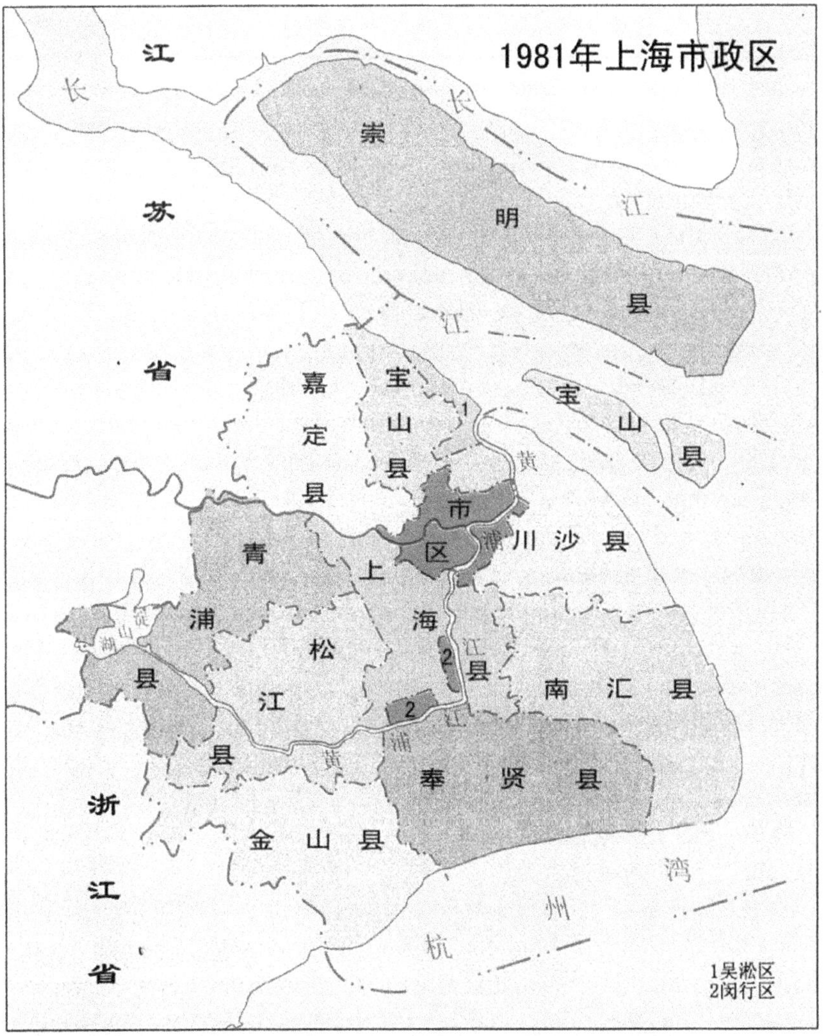

From the administrative division of Shanghai in 1981, Shanghai downtown was very small, and the vast Pudong area left unlimited imagination for people

Because Shanghai development was westward, by 1980s, Pudong and Puxi became totally incomparable.

Before the development of Pudong in 1990, in the west of Pudong along the river from south to north, the main port area of Shanghai was formed. The harbor area, the factory area, and the commercial and living area were crowded together, which is the earliest urbanization area of Pudong. Unfortunately, however, the common prosperity across the rivers was not developed like in the cities of New York, London, and Paris. The municipal construction in Pudong was backward, with narrow roads, poor living conditions, insufficient cultural facilities, and inconvenient land and water transportation.

At that time, Dongchang Road was one of the most prosperous commercial streets in Pudong. It was nicknamed Nanjing Road in Pudong. At the T-intersection with it was Lannidu Road, which means "muddy", about four or five meters wide. When it rained, the water ran all over the muddy road. There was a coal wharf near Lannidu. Most of the dockers came from the rural areas of northern Jiangsu, fleeing to Pudong. There were only simple sheds set up as a shelter against wind and rain. There is a local saying: "If you want to experience bitter life, you just come to Yangshupu, and even more bitter life, come to Lannidu." We can see the basic urban state of Pudong at that time.

History and nature are the roots of regret. Especially after the opening of the port, the gap with Puxi became bigger and bigger, so Pudong became a name of backwardness in Shanghai people's heart. Even in the 1980s, people in Pudong used to call Puxi "Shanghai", since Pudong was not taken as part of Shanghai, but a rural area, even if the other side of the Huangpu River can be reached by only taking a 400-meter ferry.

From the 1980s, scholars began to reflect, seeking new ideas for Shanghai's development.

In the spring of 1986, 10 organizations, such as the Shanghai Urban Economics Association and the Shanghai Economic Research Center, jointly sponsored the "Shanghai Urban Development Strategy Seminar". At the meeting, there was a consensus. In view of the serious swelling disease in Shanghai's old urban area, in order to revitalize Shanghai, they had to think outside of the box, and explore new ways to relieve the overpopulation of the old urban areas and create conditions for the old urban renewal. Since then, four options emerged.

They are: "Westward Advance Plan" — expanding to the West of Hongqiao Airport; "Northward Advance Plan" — development of Baosteel and Wusong Area along the South Wing of the Yangtze River; "Southward Advance Plan" — developing Jinshan District along the North Wing of Hangzhou Bay; and "Eastward Advance Plan" — developing Pudong across the Huangpu River and revitalizing Shanghai.

After repeated discussions and disputes, the unanimous opinion was "Eastward Advance Plan".

The idea of "Eastward Advance" was finally affirmed by the chief designer of China's reform and opening.

During the Spring Festival in 1990, the leaders of Shanghai reported the idea of Pudong development and opening-up to Deng Xiaoping. He said cheerfully that this was a good thing, since it had been long overdue, and unfortunately, it was five years late.

On the evening of February 13, Deng Xiaoping began to return to Beijing and he had a talk with Zhu Rongji, the Communist Party Secretary and Mayor of Shanghai, on his way to the train station. When talking about the development of Pudong, Deng said that they were late, but that things could move faster, and Shanghai, with better condition than Guangdong, might have a higher starting point. From the 1980s to 1990s, he began to encourage reform and opening-up, so there was nothing to be afraid of. As to the preferential policies for Pudong development, he expressed his agreement and suggested to report more to Comrade Jiang Zemin.

After the return to Beijing, on February 17, in the Great Hall of the People in Beijing, Deng Xiaoping solemnly entrusted Jiang Zemin and other newly appointed leaders of the Central Government, "I have retired, but one thing I still need to say is the development of Pudong and you should care more."

He also said to Li Peng, "You are the Premier and you should take charge of the development of Pudong."

In 1990, under Deng Xiaoping's strong push, the discussions concerning Pudong development advanced from paperwork to a substantive start, and the speed was greatly accelerated. As a result, Pudong's fate was changed radically.

At this time, Pudong development was leveled up by the general designer from the desire and vision of Shanghai's local reform and opening-up to the national strategy. At that time, the east bank of the Huangpu River aroused the infinite imagination of Sun Yat-sen, that is, the construction of the Oriental Port. 70 years later, Pudong also aroused a beautiful imagination in Deng Xiaoping's mind. Retrieving *Chronicle of Deng Xiaoping* (1975–1997), we can find that in the 1990s, 26 references were made to Pudong. A place of extreme backwardness in the eyes of the Puxi people in Shanghai, after being drawn a circle by an old man as the focus of development, underwent drastic changes.

History often repeats itself. In 1979, when Deng Xiaoping drew a circle near the South China Sea as the new focus of development, the poor and backward town of Shenzhen, separated by a river from Hong Kong, soon became a modern city.

After 1990, high-level officials from Beijing put their deep hope on Pudong. The development of Pudong was positioned as "the focus of China's development and opening-up in the coming 10 years", "the leader of driving the economic take-off for the Yangtze River reaches", "the symbol of China's reform and opening-up", and so on. Pudong development had become the embodiment of national will and the vehicle of national strategy.

Heading eastward means heading for the sea. Because of this idea, there emerged new Pudong with great changes. Pudong's powerful economic function made it become an important pivot of China's economy, and it naturally became an administrative region.

However, among the folks, Pudong still had a strong orientation color. With the Huangpu river as the dividing line, in the administrative significance people still regarded Pudong New Area, Fengxian District, Jinshan District, and so on as Pudong, and some people called it "Big Pudong" for the sake of distinction.

1.5 The Constantly Updated Coastline

Looking over the historical territory of Shanghai, one can find that Pudong was an expanding land, and our historical and geographical knowledge informed us that until today, Pudong is still "expanding".

Going onto the dike in Pudong near the sea, in the distance one can see vast tidal flats, birds flying in the air, reed swaying and rustling. These tidal flats are the forerunner of Pudong and the predecessor of Shanghai, and the so-called "Shanghai Beach" derives from this.

In ancient times, Pudong at our foot today was actually boundless ocean. Endless sediment was brought down from the upstream of the Yangtze River and accumulated in the ancient Yangtze River estuary. This is the so-called "turbid tidewater, which comes turbulent and unresistant and goes slower with mud settling down". With a long time passing, the surface of Pudong gradually emerged, a coastline gradually formed and tidal flats continued to extend outward.

It has been estimated by some scholars that the sediment carried by the Yangtze River from the upper reaches can form deposits of one square feet and 400 feet high each year. Thus, it can be inferred that the stretching speed of the land on the Yangtze River Delta is about one mile in 60 years (that is, one kilometer extended forward in 37 years).

This estimation is controversial in academic history. However, Pudong is indeed continually "rising". According to *Shanghai Water Resources Chronicle*, the huge amount of sediment brought by the Yangtze River (with an annual sediment discharge of 470 million tons) was the material foundation for Shanghai's territory. 22% of Shanghai's territory resulted from the sediment deposits from the Yangtze River in the last 2000 years.

Due to sediment accumulation, Pudong became a coastal plain. From this point of view, the Yangtze River is the mother river of Pudong. It can be said that because of water, the thrust of water, Pudong emerged. So we can say poetically that the name of Pudong is made of water.

However, with water pushing the sediment to become a plain, this is a process much longer than waterdrops outwearing rocks.

Archaeologists have confirmed that in the western part of central Shanghai, from the line of Taicang in Jiangsu Province, Jiading, Minhang, and Fengxian in Shanghai, within a range of about 130 kilometers in length and 2 to 8 kilometers in width, several silt embankments were running from northwest to southeast arranged in parallel. The ancients called it "Gangshen". Namely, the thrust of water kept piling up the sand and the remains of the crustaceans on the outer edge of the sandpit, and over time, a sand bank gradually built up, which rose up like a natural barrier from the sea.

Annals of Yunjian compiled by the people of the Southern Song Dynasty recorded that "Gangshen is 70 miles east of the county (referring to Huating), extending 50 kilometers in three spots, which belongs to the sea in the south and reaches Songjiang (referring to Wusong River) in the north. It goes deeper into the earth, full of clam shells, which are said to be the remains of turbulent waves. The elevated part of the land is suitable for growing wheat."

Qin Rongguang, a scholar of Pudong in the late Qing Dynasty, in his Zhuzhi poem also described "Gangshen": "There is the old Ganghshen in three places, named Zigang, Zhugang, and Shagang. Several feet deep into the soil there are clam shells, which resulted from the constant turbulent waves."

In 1960 and 1966, Shanghai archaeologists excavated the Maqiao site and found as many as 32 meters thick of shell deposits, the white powder of which was once used by local farmers to paint walls.

"Gangshen" is the most primitive natural seawall in Shanghai, and also the earliest coastline in Shanghai, called Taicang and Fengxian ancient coastline about 6000 years ago.

On March 12, 1961, Professor Tan Qixiang, Chairman of the History Department of Fudan University, published a paper entitled "Re-discussion of the Land Formation in Shanghai: A Reply to Mr. Qiu Zuming." He believed that the whole city of Shanghai should be divided into two parts, the west and east side of Gangshen. The west became land as far as thousands of years ago, while the east gradually went out of water hundreds of years ago.

Namely, the west side of Gangshen was already land, while the east side was sea. When the tide came, it was water. When the tide went, it was mud flat. Therefore, Songze, Fuquan Mountain, Maqiao, Guangfulin, and other cultural sites were discovered in the places which Gangshen passed by, that is, Qingpu, Songjiang, Minhang, Jiading, and Jinshan today.

In addition to the natural seawalls, the ancestors along the coast-built seawalls one after another on the beach in order to resist sea disasters, and began the process of contending for land against the sea again and again. In this process, Pudong gradually became land. Therefore, the change of seawalls was the yardstick of Pudong's "expansion".

Seawall is the customary saying by Shanghai people, that is, the dikes along the sea, the Yangtze River and Qiantang River were called seawalls, and the dikes on both banks of the Huangpu River and its branches were called river levees.

The earliest artificial seawall in Shanghai is recorded in *New Book of Tang — Geographical Records*. In Yanguan Town, there was a defending seawall with a length of 62 kilometers, and was rebuilt again in the first year of Kaiyuan Period. The so-called "rebuilding" indicates that there had been a seawall before, and during the Kaiyuan Period, the seawall was built again on the basis of the previous project. The later generations named it ancient defending seawall.

This record is too simple. It says that the seawall extended "62 kilometers". So it only shows the actual mileage of the seawall, but it does not indicate its origin or destination. Then, *Annals of Songjiang County* in the Zhengde Period of the Ming Dynasty also simply put that "in the first year of the Kaiyuan Period of the Tang Dynasty, a seawall was built, extending 75 kilometers from Yanguan Town of Hangzhou to the Wusong River."

Because there is too little literature, there is still a lot of controversy about this ancient defending seawall.

According to Tan Qixiang, there was also a Xiasha seawall in Pudong, "another seawall to the east of the old one, which was built around the time of Qian Kingdom in the Wu-yue Era of Five Dynasties in the early 10th century". Namely, there were two seawalls in the early period of the land formation of Pudong: the defending seawall the Kaiyuan Period of the Tang Dynasty and Xiasha defending seawall in the Wu-yue Era of Five Dynasties.

Through geological investigation, modern archaeologists found that there was an intermittent sand belt, about 30 kilometers to the west of Gangshen and parallel to it, starting from Hangtou of Pudong in the southwest through Xiasha, Zhoupu, Beicai, and Jiangwan and Yuepu in Baoshan to Shengqiao. This sand belt took a kind of physiognomy form which was pushed by the silt rushing on the tide and accumulated in the over-tidal belt for a long time, and many artifacts of the Tang Dynasty had been unearthed in the west side of the sand belt.

Some scholars suspected that what was known as Xiasha Sandbelt might be the remains of the defending seawall built during Kaiyuan

Period of Tang dynasty. Some other scholars believed that Xiasha Sandbelt was the defending seawall of Xiasha recorded in *Shanghai Chronicles* written in the Hongzhi Period of the Ming Dynasty.

One thing is certain, however, in the scholars' arguments, that since the land came up out of water, the ancestors began to live and multiply here. As the population and the demand for food increased, more and more land was cultivated, which gradually developed from the inside of Gangshen to the outside. Therefore, the constant construction of seawalls became necessary.

As a result, Pudong kept "expanding" eastward. The ancestors built seawalls, then sand silted, and they built seawalls again, so the coastline continued to advance eastward.

By the beginning of the Song Dynasty, most of Shanghai's urban district today had basically become land. At this time, the salt industry in Huating area, including Pudong, was developed and became a great source of wealth in the imperial court. However, the area was invaded by the sea tide for many times. In order to protect the salt fields in Xiasha, a large dike for sea protection was built, which was named as ancient defending seawall, and also named as inner seawall, inner defending seawall, and grand defending seawall.

With the construction of the ancient defending seawall, the coastline was located in the former Laoboshan, Chuansha, and Nanhui county, and then gradually turned southwest to the line of Datuan, Fengcheng, Zhelin, and Jinshanwei. The coastline formed by this seawall shows the basic formation of the territory of Shanghai. For example, the main sites of salt fields in Yuanpu, Qingcun Xiasha, and so on, which flourished in the Song Dynasty, were all scattered in the ancient defending seawalls.

In December 1978, an ancient ship was unearthed in Qinjian Village, Huanglu Township of Pudong, one kilometer east of the ancient defending seawall. According to the textual research, it was a junk in the Song Dynasty. Therefore, it is known that there were people living inside the defending seawall. According to Zhang Minghua, an archaeologist in Shanghai, all the following cultural relics fully confirmed the land formation of Pudong before the Northern Song Dynasty, such as the yellow glazed ewers from Five Dynasties (907–960 A.D.) unearthed in Chenqiao, the porcelain from Five Dynasties in Xuanqiao, the porcelain pieces from Five Dynasties in

Shuizha of Datuan, and more than 800 well-bundled clayware bowls from the Song Dynasty in Santuangang of Fengxian, the grate-lined porcelain bowl from the Song Dynasty in Huinan of Pudong, Sixi-shaped pottery bottles and iron anchors from the Song Dynasty in Sanzao, and the iron cattles and other relic remains from the Song Dynasty in Laobaoshan. All these proved that here the land had been formed before the Song Dynasty.

The porcelain bowls from the Song Dynasty unearthed in the Dazhi River of Huanglu Commune in the original Nanhui County (Exhibited in Nahui Museum)

Because of this seawall, some towns and villages became prosperous, with increased population and enriched natural resources, which promoted the flourishing of ancient towns like Gaoqiao, Chuanhsa, Xinzhen, and others.

In the Ming Dynasty, Japanese pirates invaded again and again, so the old defending seawall served another function, that is, the defense fortifications. Exterior trenches were dug and sentry posts were set up. On the suspension bridge above the trenches, there were guards and officers. Usually, people entered and exited freely. If enemies came to invade, the suspension bridge would be removed and the seawall can be used as a guarding post, resisting with spears and fighting with arrows and cannons from afar.

By the 12th year of the Wanli Period in the Ming Dynasty (1584), outside the ancient defending seawall, the new defending seawall was built, also named the exterior seawall, commonly known as the new defending seawall. In the 11th year of the Yongzheng Period in the Qing Dynasty (1733), Qingong Seawall was built on the foundation of the exterior defending seawall, which restrained the retreat of the land and restored the silting. The ancient defending seawall accomplished the historically great mission and retreated to the back line.

In the 10th year of the Guangxu Period in the Qing Dynasty (1884), Wang Chunyin, the Magistrate of Nanhui County, proposed to build a new seawall and make the people cultivate the land when he saw a wide expanse of silting outside the seawall. Finally a low seawall with a height of six feet was built. The seawall extended 42 kilometers, generally parallel to the Qingong Seawall. People called this Wanggong Seawall. It was also called Penggong Seawall, because it was built with the donation sponsored by the village gentry Peng Yifan. This seawall marked the coastline of Pudong in the late Qing Dynasty.

From the end of Guanxu in the Qing Dynasty to the 36th year of the Republic of China, many sections of Qingong Seawall and Wanggong Seawall were destroyed by the sea tides. Li Chaocong, magistrate in Nanhui County of the Qing Dynasty, and Yuan Xiluo, magistrate of Nangui County of the Republic of China and others, built Ligong Seawall

Shiji Seawall was completed in 2000 (Photo by Wu Huiquan)

and Yuangong Seawall outside Wanggong Seawall successively. However, the distance between these seawalls and Wanggong Seawall was not more than one kilometer, so the coastline did not change much.

In July 1949, Renmin Seawall was built on the basis of Ligong Seawall and Yuangong Seawall. Renmin Seawall became the coastal line of Shanghai in the early period of New China.

Later, a large area of beach land was formed with constant silting. So Shengli Seawall, Qijiu Seawall, Bawu Seawall, Sanpai Seawall, Jiusi Seawall, Shiji Seawall, and Lingang Xincheng Seawall were built one after another.

Most historical geographers believed that Shanghai's sea-to-land history was hard to calculate with a fixed formula and could only take the outward advancing of building the seawalls as the process of coastline change.

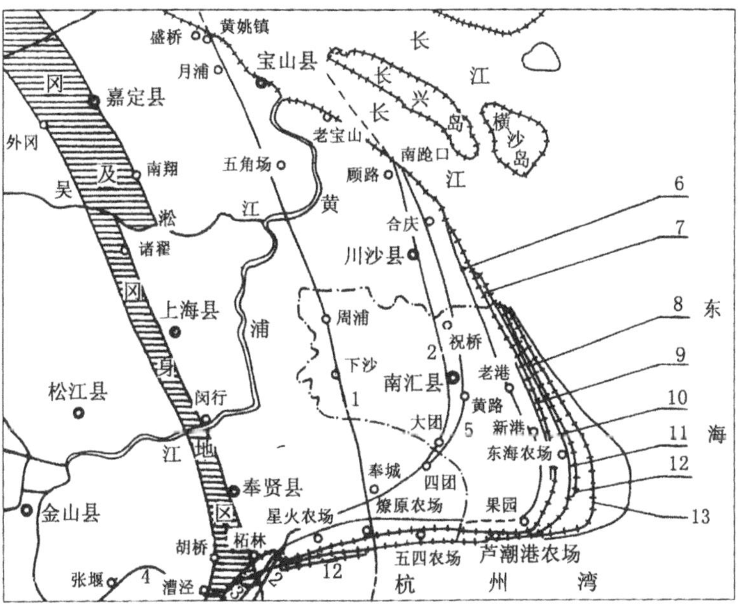

As Pudong stretched eastward, a series of seawalls were built. 1. Ancient Defending Seawall in the Tang Dynasty 2. Laohu Seawall in the Song Dynasty 3. Dade Seawall in the Yuan Dynasty 4. Chenghua Defending Seawall — Shiba Defending Seawall in the Ming Dynasty 5. QinGong Seawall in the Wanli Period of the Ming Dynasty 6. Penggong Seawall in the Qing Dynasty 7. Ligong Seawall in the Qing Dynasty 8. Yuangong Seawall in the Republic of China 9. Yubei Seawall in the Republic of China 10. Renmin Seawall 11. Tuanjie Shengli Seawall 12. Qijiu Seawall 13. Bawu Seawall

1.6 Endogenous Impetus for Eastward Development

Pudong continued to "expand", changing from sea to land, with the gradual eastward extension of its coastline, so Pudong's development followed the eastward expansion of land in Shanghai.

From the map, with the extension of the coastline, Pudong's territory was becoming larger with a greater speed. Wang Zuojiu, Deputy Editor-in-Chief of *Annals of Nanhui County*, calculated this process.

It took 459 years to extend 16 kilometers from the site of the ancient defending seawall rebuilt in the first year of the Kaiyuan Period of the Tang Dynasty (713 A.D.) to the site of Lihu Seawall reinforced in the eighth year of the Qiandao Period of the Southern Song Dynasty (1172 A.D.). At an average, it extended one kilometer every 29 years.

It took 208 years to extend 3.5 kilometers from the site of Lihu Seawall built in the eighth year of the Qiandao Period of the Southern Song Dynasty (1172 A.D.) to the site of Qingong Seawall built in the 13th year of the Hongwu Period of the Ming Dynasty (1380 A.D.). On average, it extended one kilometer every 60 years.

It took 525 years to extend 8.5 kilometers from the site of Penggong Seawall built in the 13th year of the Hongwu Period of the Ming Dynasty (1380 A.D.) to the site of Penggong Seawall built in the 31st year of the Guangxu Period of the Qing Dynasty (1905 A.D.). On average, it extended one kilometer every 62 years.

Since then, Pudong's "extension" speed accelerated.

From 1905 to 1935, the distance between the sites of the north and south Yuangong Seawall was 0.75 kilometers, with an average of one-kilometer extension every 40 years. From 1935 to 1958, the distance between them was 1.25 kilometers, with an average of one-kilometer extension every 20 years. From 1958 to 1985, the distance between them was 0.75 kilometers, with an average of one-kilometer extension every 36 years.

A large area of beach land constantly silted and extended, and the seawalls were also built one by one. As the ground near the seawall was relatively high and habitable, villages and market towns appeared on the edge of each seawall, and the population gradually flourished.

For example, near the ancient defending seawall there were Gulu, Gonglu, Cailu, Chuansha County, Liutuan, Zhuqiao, Yancang, Nanhui

County, Datuan, Situan, Tangwai, Qianqiao, etc.; near Qingong Seawall in the Ming and Qing Dynasty there were Jiangzhen, Shiwan, Huanglu, etc.; and near Penggong Seawall there were Laogang, Xingang, Guoyuan, etc.

In modern times, the functions of the constantly built seawalls also changed. For example, because of the use of Wanggong Seawall, Qingong Seawall gradually lost its sea-defending function and was used as a road for pedestrians, and then the seawall served the function of tourism and viewing.

In 1977, with the excavation of the Pudong Canal, the only traces left of the thousand-year-old defending seawall finally disappeared, with only a few names left reminding future generations from time to time that the old man of history turned sea into land in a long period of time.

Tan Qixiang believed, "After the ancient defending seawall, Xiasha Defending Seawall built in the Wu-Yue Era and Lihu Seawall built in the Southern Song Dynasty also played a great role in promoting the development of Shanghai. With the extension of the land, the seawalls were built outward one by one, and the area of the cropland was enlarged day by day. Finally, at the beginning of the 19th century, nine counties were established on the mainland of Shanghai in 1050 years after the establishment of Huating County in the 10th year of Tianbao Period."

By 1990, the land seawall in Shanghai reached as long as 170.8 kilometers. From the founding of New China to the development and opening of Pudong in 1990, in Shanghai there was 1.01 million mu (about 673 square kilometers) of land. Seawalls protected the land for peace and promoted the development of coastal land. The extension of the coastline has become a symbol of economic development and social progress in Pudong.

The Pudong scholar Chai Zhiguang thought, in this historical course, "Pudong was a growing area. Its coastline continuously extended, a large number of tidal flats became good fields, the population increased, the natural resources were abundant, and taxes were heavy. All these reflect the development of this area."

It is also the endogenous driving force for the development and opening of Pudong in the future. Understanding the change of Pudong coastline, we can answer such questions: Where does Pudong come from? Where will Pudong go?

Chapter 2

The Development Initiative: Civil and Government Efforts

2.1 Not Going Out to Sea in the Real Sense

Pudong is in close proximity to the sea, and in history, Pudong people also made the history of Chinese navigation, going out to the sea. In the Yuan Dynasty, Zhang Xuan, a Chuansha and Gaoqiao native, wrote a gorgeous page on the history of Chinese shipping.

Zhang Xuan (1245–1303), born in Badu, Jiading County, Jiangsu Province (now Gaoqiao Town, Pudong), originally trafficked salt at sea, robbed merchant ships by killing people and grabbing goods, and was later recruited by the Southern Song Dynasty as a coastal defense soldier. When the Yuan army went down south, this armed force at sea was summoned to surrender, and Zhang Xuan became an official of the imperial court.

The man was illiterate, cruel, and insolent, but in his rudeness there was also a brilliant shrewdness. In the early days of the Yuan Dynasty, due to the frequent silting of the Beijing-Hangzhou Canal and the difficulty of grain transportation, Zhang proposed ocean shipping to the Emperor Kublai. The court ordered him and Luo Bihui, the then Chief of Shanghai, and a pirate named Zhu Qing, who was in charge of sea transportation, to set up a sea transport office in Shanghai. Zhang Xuan led the fleet starting at Liujia Port in Taicang, with 60 flat-bottomed ships, carrying grains more than 46,000 shi (1 shi = 59.2 kilogram). It was the first large-scale shipping in Chinese history.

Because of the shallow sand along the way, they built flat-bottomed sea boats with large hull, strong structure and shallow draft, which were not easily damaged or capsized when it ran aground on the beach. Flat-bottomed boats ran between sand and water, later known as the "sand boat".

Sea transportation was much cheaper than river transportation and it took less time. Downwind they could arrive in a few days. "When boats travelled with wind, from the west of Zhejiang to the capital it took no more than 10 days." Therefore, sea transportation grew with a high rate. In the 21st year of the Yuan Dynasty (1284), 29,500 shi of grain was shipped and 275,610 shi arrived in the capital. In the second year of Tianli

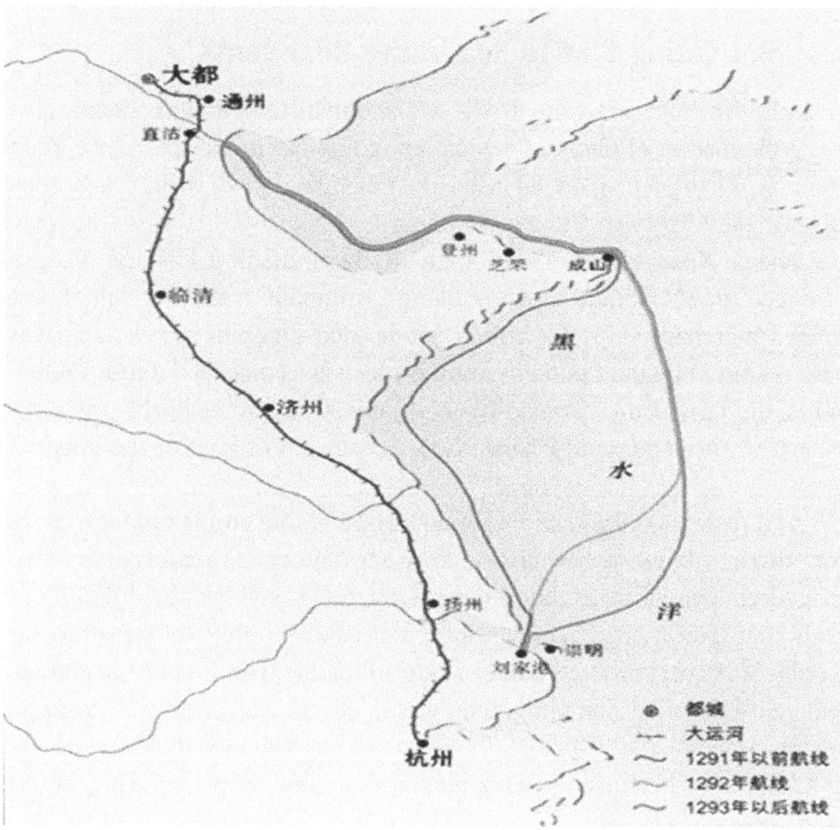

Canal transportation and sea transportation in the Yuan Dynasty

(1329), the transport volume increased to 3,522,163 shi, with the arrival of 3,340,360 shi.

As the pioneers of transportation with sand boats on Beiyang route, Zhang Xuan and Zhu Qing succeeded in starting the sea transportation, which provided the north-south transportation with a new passage on the basis of land transportation and river transportation. This contributed greatly to transportation in the Yuan Dynasty and was also an epoch-making event in the history of water transportation in China. As a result, the political status of Shanghai obviously rose. So Zhang Xuan was repeatedly awarded with titles by the court, up to Junior of Jiangnan Province, who enjoyed great honor, wealth, and rank. He even enjoyed the privilege of issuing paper money. All of a sudden, he became infinitely rich, as both an official and businessman.

Before Zhang Xuan opened the sea transportation, his hometown, Gaoqiao, gradually became a town of sandboats, and many local people were also engaged in the sea transportation. After Zhang's death, Gaoqiao in Pudong commemorated his achievements in pioneering sea transportation. In his birthplace, now the village of Tunliangxiang in Gaoqiao, King Xining Temple was built in which he was sealed as the god and enjoyed the incense as human tribute forever.

Because of the sea passage, sand boats were widely used. Before the port opened in Shanghai, Shanghai became the most important transit hub of the river and sea transportation in China. The total number of sand boats was about 3,600 and more than 100,000 sailors were employed on board. Shanghai enjoyed the reputation of "reaching out to both river and sea, the Capital of southeast China."

The fame and fortune of Zhu Qing and Zhang Xuan reflects the easing sea policy in the Song and Yuan Dynasties. During this period, although there were several prohibitions, most of them were short-lived. In the Southern Song Dynasty, there was financial tension, so maritime tax was heavily counted on. After the Yuan Dynasty, the society mostly "relied on the sea trade by imposing taxes". As a result of shipping, ports of Shanghai were developed, and cotton textiles could be sold everywhere. Cotton planting, textile, trading, and shipping as a whole developed as an industrial chain, which exerted immeasurable influence on the local social, economic, and cultural progress.

In the 10th year of the Yongle Period in the Ming Dynasty (1412), Chen Xuan, as the Chief Officer, took charge of the grain shipping by sea and he wrote a report to the court. "In Jiading, which is near the sea and where sea meets with river, the ships berth here, without high hills as guide. It is requested that in Qingpu (now Gaoqiao Town in Pudong) earth hill be built, 100 zhang (1 zhang = 3 1/3 meters) in length and 30 zhang in height, to be used as watchtower."

So, in Waigaoqiao of Shanghai, near the exit of the Yangtze River, a 30-zhang-high "earth hill" was built, that is, Baoshan Watchtower. "Smoke during the daylight and fire during the night" were used to guide ships, which provided a sign for Zheng He's fleet to enter and exit the Yangtze River estuary. Emperor Yongle gave the name Baoshan, and wrote a 391-word inscription to commemorate it, that is, "Yongle Imperial Stele of Watchtower". The name "Baoshan County" of Shanghai derives from this.

"Baoshan Watchtower" is the earliest and only official navigation identifier in China. It plays an important role of navigation for the safety of Zheng He's voyage to the India Ocean and the Yangtze River estuary at that time, and is of milestone significance in the history of Chinese shipping. The "Yongle Imperial Stele of Watchtower" is also known as China's first imperial stele, which is now located in Gaoqiao Middle School in Pudong.

In the 10th year of the Xianfeng Period of the Qing Dynasty (1860), Zhu Qiang and Zhu Qihao, the Pudong native brothers, under the instruction of Li Hongzhang, set up the Ship Business Soliciting Bureau to be engaged in shipping. The sea ships travelled as far as to Japan, Philippines, Singapore, and so on.

Pudong is near the sea, so it is supposed to develop overseas trade rapidly like the European Mediterranean countries. However, due to the geographical constraints of the natural environment, along Pudong coast there was hardly any harbor dock for a large number of ships to anchor. As recorded in *Annals of Fenjian Nanhui County*, "Along the coast there is only shallow water, so the ship cannot berth. Huangpu and Wusong's entrance to the sea belongs to Shanghai, so although it is close to the sea, trading and exchanging is impossible. As the old annals put, the produce is less than one-hundredth of that in Fujian and Zhejiang, nicknamed as poor sea, with only salt as profitable business."

Yongle imperial stele in the Ming Dynasty (Source: Pudong New Area Archives)

Yongle imperial stele is now kept in Gaoqiao Middle School

In addition to the difficulty for sea ships to berth there, "when sea ships ran onto it by mistake, they got damaged in most cases. The coastal residents grabbed goods in the name of lifesaving, which is called fishing for foreign goods." In this way, the trading among merchants naturally became impossible.

Zheng Ruozeng, a famous military strategist of humble origin during the Ming and Qing Dynasties, believed that sea defense in Songjiang was different from that in Suzhou. In Songjiang there was a seawall, but no seaport, and its facilities were mainly built for land force, while in Suzhou there was a seaport, but no seawall, and its facilities were mainly built for sailors. What does it mean for a seawall without seaport? Along the seawater near Songjiang, which began at Dushan and ended at Xiaotangwa, as long as 124 kilometers, there was the seawall as separation, as tall and thick as a city wall, and there was no branching stream to the sea.

More importantly, all the efforts by Pudong people to go out to the sea failed because of the closed-door policy in the Ming and Qing dynasties. Pudong people facing the sea could only boil the salt off water on the beach or fish at sea day by day. Finally, the phenomenon appeared, as recorded in *Chronicle of Shanghai County* written in the Jiajing Period of the Ming Dynasty: "The people of the state made great effort in teaching their children to study, while the townships relied on fishing and salt-boiling as their business. As to working, they did not go out of their village, and as to trading, they did not go out of the nearby areas. With a clear division of labor, the males were engaged in ploughing and the females in sewing. Sometimes in the villages the women may help in farming, while in towns the men may know sewing."

Every day, as the sun rose from the vast sea, the people of Pudong began a day of labor, having nothing to do with what was beyond the sun despite the great changes that had taken place there. Even though agriculture and handicrafts developed in Pudong later on and Pudong became a land of fish and rice, and even though people in Pudong endeavored to explore the sea and created the history of shipping in China, the deep-rooted yellow-land culture ruthlessly wiped away their yearning and efforts.

On November 17, 1843, after the official opening of Shanghai as a port, foreign merchant ships arrived successively. Soon, Shanghai became the largest port in China, overtaking Guangzhou and becoming the first of the "five ports".

2.2 An Object of Contention for the Colonists

On November 29, 1845, the British opened the first Chinese concession in Shanghai. Then the great powers successively opened concessions in Shanghai, and extended the scope of the concessions by means of building roads across borders.

The original concessions were mudflats, farmlands, and cemeteries, wild and desolate. But the westerners offered this particular region a new entrepreneurial environment, which gave people around the world the opportunity to dream of making money, and attracted ambitious and dreaming people all over China. For a time, a large number of adventurers wandered around the concessions in Shanghai. The old feudal autocracy and traditional culture was helpless to the most advanced western system in the concessions. The institutional change made Shanghai the largest and most important business center in China.

At the end of the 19th century, Pudong was also an object of contention between British and French colonists. In order to expand the border in Pudong, in addition to diplomatic rhetoric between Britain and France, on December 21, 1898, Britain sent five warships of Far East Fleet to Nanjing, pressing on the Governor of the two rivers Liu Kunyi and also displaying its strength against France. Two days later, officers in charge of foreign affairs in the Qing Dynasty met with British ministers to discuss how to reject the French request to expand its border in Pudong, and asked if there were a conflict, whether Britain would provide substantial assistance. The Qing government also instructed Luo Fenglu, the ambassador in Britain, to ask for direct consultation between Britain and France on whether to agree to the expansion of French border in Pudong. Finally, after a series of diplomatic mediation, the big powers continued to expand their spheres of power in the concessions. But fortunately, Pudong was not involved.

Pudong did not become a concession, but the power of foreign capital already entered the riverside zone of Pudong. According to *Annals of China-Japan Business Ports* written in 1867, "For many years Pudong was just a piece of wild land, with several old-style Chinese shipyards and several narrow paths for boat trackers. But in recent years foreigners bought lots of land along the river and built spacious warehouses, docks, and ports."

Pudong, located along the river, had a geographical advantage. It was not a concession, and there was no treaty allowing foreigners to buy land to build warehouses on the dock. However, due to the weakness and ineptitude of the Qing government, the foreign businessmen forced the Daotai of Shanghai to issue the lease according to the land transfer law of the concession, and the Daotai even granted land lease on the grounds that these areas were adjacent to the concessions.

As a result, since the 1860s, foreign businessmen began to lease land in Pudong to build wharves, storehouses, and oil depots in succession. So Pudong's economic structure underwent major changes.

The first foreign terminal in Pudong was built in the third year of the Xianfeng period of the Qing Dynasty (1850), located in the area of Tangqiao today. By the 1920s, there had been 37 main wharves along the river, the layout of which was so dense that there was almost no interval. From the speed and scale of the construction, Pudong greatly exceeded Puxi in the same period. According to the figures provided by *Complete Volume of Shanghai Ports*, in the 9th year of the Republic of China (1920), the Pudong foreign business wharves stretched 3,811 meters, 2,205 meters longer than those of Puxi. The total length of wharves in Pudong was 13,384 meters, while the length of those in Puxi was 5,827 meters.

In Pudong, the British merchants held 60.6% of foreign terminals and 66.7% of the total warehouse capacity. Merchants of the United States held 14% of foreign business wharves and 9% of the warehouses. Japanese businessmen owned 25.4% of foreign business ports and 23% of the warehouses. English merchants were the largest foreign investors in Pudong wharves, followed by Japanese merchants. Compared with Puxi, foreign businessmen preferred to invest in Pudong wharves.

At that time, two British firms, Yihe Company and Taigu Steamship Company, and one Japanese firm, Japan Liner Commune, were the three major groups in the wharf industry.

The western powers conquered the coast of Pudong to build wharves and warehouses, and at the time took Pudong as the main area for ship building and repairing.

In 1856, a foreign ship-repairing yard appeared on the east bank of the Huangpu River. In 1859, a Scottish named Mohyde also set up Pudong Steamship Plant in Pudong with its leading technology and equipment in the industry. As written in the English-language newspaper published in Shanghai, Zilinxi Newspaper, this plant was "the most striking of the few things that foreigners were able to show themselves in Shanghai".

In 1865, Mohyde built Dongjiadu Shipyard, called "the best shipyard in the Far East" at that time, running shipbuilding, ironworks, steelmaking, machinery engineering, and some other businesses.

Shipyards, on the one hand, could cope with the rapid increase in repair, maintenance, and other businesses, and on the other hand, aimed to monopolize the shipbuilding industry, so as to further grasp the lifeblood of maritime transportation. In the five years from 1860 to 1864, of the nine newly built foreign shipyards in Shanghai, five of them were in Pudong.

Some other important industrial projects were also developed along the river in Pudong. British and American oil companies such as Mobil, Asia, and Texaco, which occupied a long coastline in Pudong, built wharves for oil deposit.

The wharves along the river in Pudong was almost only for foreign businessmen. One Chinese was very indomitable. Since 1918, he started to operate the wharf stack business, and purchased the land of Yihe Company and Asia Oil Company at a high price, and under the name of China, established China North Stack, South Stack, and West Stack, that is, Yitaixing,

Dongjiadu, and Zhoujiadu docks. He is the famous industrialist Liu Hongsheng. He felt so proud to say, "Around the whole city the dock companies run by foreign merchants are scattered everywhere, but what can compete fiercely with the foreigners are only the docks run by Hongsheng."

In the second half of the 19th century, the construction of wharves, warehouses, and stacks reached its climax, with the stacks and shipyards densely lined along the river. By 1949, the area along the river from

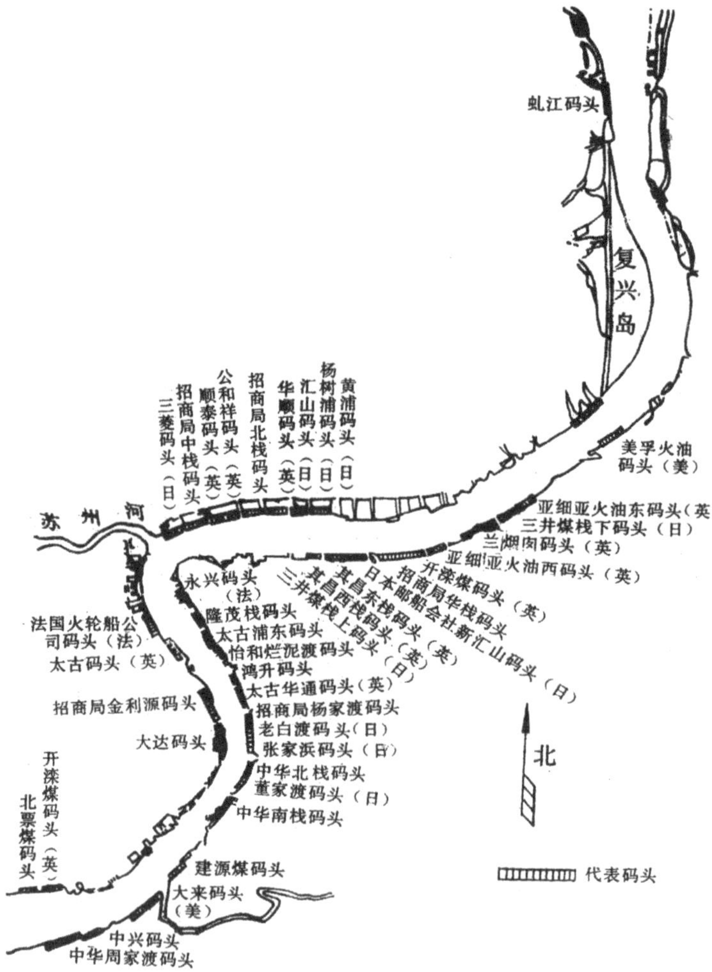

The Layout of the Huangpu River Wharves in 1937 (Recorded in *Shanghai Port History*)

Gaoqiao to Zhoujiadu was almost entirely occupied by the wharves, stacks, warehouses, and factories. There was hardly any surplus land along the river in Pudong. There was such a description in *Midnight*, the famous writer Mao Dun's novel:

> The evening tides from Huangpu rise imperceptibly, and now the assortment of boats along both sides of the Suzhou River rise high, with their decks some six inches above the dock. The Bund music flows here with wind, but only the copper drums sound like stir-fried beans is the most distinct, and the most exciting. Looking from the bridge to the east, you can see the ocean stack in Pudong, like a huge monster, squatting in the darkness, with lights flashing like thousand small eyes. Looking to the west, what is surprising is the huge neon-tube advertisement high on the roof of a foreign house, shooting out a blaze of red light and green phosphorus-like flame: Light, Heat, Power!

The dock economy became a big landscape of Pudong. However, most of the cargo loaded and unloaded at Pudong wharves was transferred to the West Bank, but not consumed or reprocessed in Pudong. The reason why there were a large number of docks in Pudong was analyzed in *The Urban Plan of Grand Shanghai* (*Second Draft*) compiled by the Shanghai Government in 1947: "At first, this kind of wharves were built along the Bund of the Huangpu River, but then developed on the other side of the river, that is, Pudong. The reason for this was that the land price in Pudong was very low and the labor cost in Shanghai was very low in general."

If we compare it with the port of Rotterdam in the Netherlands, we can feel this regret even more strongly. Although in the long past there was already a dock, port, and waterway in Pudong, it did not develop as rapidly as Rotterdam. Rotterdam was originally a fishing village, but because of port construction and the development of overseas trade, it became Europe's largest seaport, and even the world's largest seaport.

2.3 The Modern Industrialized and Urbanized Area Along the Yangtze River

Shanghai developed from the ports, and Pudong is no exception. In modern times, the factories in Pudong were concentrated in a narrow strip north to Yangsi Port, west to Shangnan Qiche Road, east to the Huangpu River, and north to Pudong Avenue, accounting for about 7% of the total factories in Shanghai.

In addition to the shipbuilding industry in Pudong, there were also industries like cigarette, textile, steel, match, paper, and so on.

There was a big cigarette industry in Pudong. British and American tobacco companies and Nanyang Brothers Tobacco, the two foreign capital giants, and some Chinese capital giants were set up in Pudong.

In 1892, the American-invested Maosheng Company opened the Maosheng Cigarette Factory in Lujiazui, which became the forerunner of the foreign-invested cigarette industry in Shanghai. In 1897, American businessmen set up American cigarette companies and cigarette factories in Lujiazui, Pudong. And Japanese Muraka Brothers Chamber of Commerce opened Muraka Cigarette Factory in Pudong. In 1902, British-American Tobacco Co., Ltd. was established and in the same year, it purchased a cigarette factory in Lujiazui and opened the British-American Cigarette Factory (i.e., No. 1 British-American Tobacco Factory). Then it successively purchased the early-established cigarette factories, and expanded its capital and production capacity. In 1914, a new factory was established in Pudong (No. 2 British-American Tobacco Factory), and in 1916, the printing factory of No. 2 British-American Tobacco Factory was under construction in Pudong.

When British-American Tobacco Co. was established in Pudong, there were only a few hundred employees. By 1937, the total number of employees had reached 25,000, with an increase of 140 times more than when it started.

In 1925, Nanyang Brothers Tobacco Company, a giant of the Chinese national cigarette industry, opened a branch factory in Pudong, and started 18 branches and more than 10 business agencies in Hankou, Yingkou, Qingdao, Tianjin, Nanjing, Wuhu, Hangzhou, Ningbo, and so on.

The Pudong textile factory was also owned by foreign companies, mainly of Japanese and British capital. As early as 1888, businessmen from five countries, namely Britain, America, France, Germany, and Japan, set up a joint venture in Pudong: Shanghai Machine Embossing Bureau. In 1897, American-invested Maosheng Company set up Hongyuan Gauze Factory in Lujiazui. In 1918, Rihua Textile Co., Ltd. purchased

American-invested Hongyuan Textile Factory in Lujiazui, Pudong and established No. 1 Rihua Textile Factory, and No. 2 Textile Factory was set up in Lujiazui in the same year. In 1931, British-invested Longchang Textile Dyeing and Printing Co., Ltd. invested 6.95 million silver to purchase more than 80 mu (about 53,333 square meters) of land in Lujiazui, Pudong to build Longchang Textile Factory.

According to statistics, from 1900 to 1930, there were six national cotton textile factories and two knitting factories in Pudong. The larger one is Zhanghua Woolen Mill, the first woolen mill in China founded by Liu Hongsheng in Zhoujiadu, Pudong in 1929. Another one was Hengda Textile Factory, which was jointly run by Mu Xiangyao, agentry in Pudong, and others. It produced cotton yarn of "Airplane" brand, marketed at home and abroad.

By 1937, there were 202 modern towel factories in Chuansha, with 5371 machines and 869 workers, with an annual output of 2.6 million dozen towels. The products were sold well in China and entered the markets of Singapore, Philippines, and other Southeast Asian countries and regions. The products had been able to compete with Japan's "Iron Anchor" towel brand.

In the steel industry, what was worthy of pride was Shanghai's first private steel plant that was born in Pudong.

In 1913, Lu Bohong, a national capitalist, was commissioned by the Shanghai General Chamber of Commerce to pay visits to the steel factories in the United States, Britain, France, and other countries. After returning to China, with the donation under his influence in industry and finance, he set up the first private steel plant in Zhoujiadu, Pudong — Hexinghua Iron Plant. It was built and put into operation on August 18, 1918. The profit for the first three months of its start was equivalent to the original invested capital, but it was encroached by the Japanese Army during the Anti-Japanese War. After the victory of the Anti-Japanese War, it was taken over by the National Government and renamed as No. 3 Steel Plant of Shanghai Iron and Steel Co., Ltd., the well-known No. 3 Shanghai Steel Plant, the large-scale national enterprise.

In the match industry, the earliest match company established in Pudong was Yingchang Match Company. In June 1911, Ningbo businessman Shao Erkang set up Shanghai Yingchang Match Co., Ltd. in Lannidu,

Pudong. Liu Hongsheng was determined to make the enterprise big and strong, so he put forward the proposal of industry amalgamation to collect more funds and collaborate for survival. He persuaded Yingchang Match Company and China Match Company in Zhoupu into merging and established Shanghai Grand China Match Co., Ltd. in July 1930. Its total capital increased to 1.91 million yuan. Liu Hongsheng was appointed General Manager.

After the establishment of Grand China Match Company, the production scale expanded day by day. Liu Hongsheng also built a flatten stem plant in Donggou, Pudong, with new machines used. Grand China Match Company became the largest national match enterprise in the country at that time, and Liu also enjoyed the reputation of "Match King" in China.

In the paper industry, Huachang Paper Mill is the second one set up in Shanghai. In 1899, it was started by four foreign businesses, British-invested Yesong Company, Russian-invested Daosheng Bank, French-invested Lixing Company, and American-invested Maosheng Company. According to *History of China's Modern Paper Industry*, "The machine paper mill invested by foreigners that first appeared in China was Huazhang Paper Mill, located in Lujiazui, Pudong, Shanghai. The construction and installation were designed by Japanese technician Hiraburo Okawa, and after three years of construction, in 1901 it began to produce paper."

Later, Huazhang Paper Mill was resold to Japanese Mitsubishi Co., Ltd., and its name was changed to Nippon Paper Mill, whose production and operation improved greatly. In 1904, the Japanese opened another paper mill near Lannidu in Lujiazui, specializing in the production of packaging paper.

By virtue of the superior geographical location of the Huangpu River, Pudong became one of the two shipbuilding and ship repairing centers in Shanghai. Along with it, the wharf warehouse and stack industry grew, and meanwhile, the cigarette, textile, steel, match, and paper industries also developed. At the same time, modern brewing, food processing, and construction industries came into being and were developed, and the use of machines gradually changed the economic structure of Pudong which had been dominated by handicrafts previously. This also meant that Pudong's single self-sufficient economic structure began to change and the modern economy began to sprout.

However, most of these new industries were located on the east bank of the Pujiang River. Because of the traffic inconvenience, few enterprises entered the hinterland of Pudong, and the enterprises in the hinterland of Pudong were relatively small in scale with obsolete equipment, so the industrial clusters and the industrial chain did not develop.

The development of the coastal dock economy in Pudong also disrupted the former rural landscape of village houses in the riverside area, and the riverside area of Pudong started to become urbanized. The original separate settlements along Pudong coast, from west to east, disappeared in batches, and factories and residential areas appeared instead. Residential neighborhoods can be broadly divided into three types: shanty areas, old-style mansions, and urban towns.

The evolution of urbanization in the area along the river in Pudong started in a rather harsh environment. A large number of people immigrated to the area along the river, living in accommodations with poor conditions, which were mostly shabby "sheds on water", "low-ceiling sheds", and reed sheds. Gradually a shantytown was formed.

A hundred years ago, a visitor described the scene along the river in Pudong:

> Looking out at the beach with reeds all over, everywhere one can see the boat wrecks and floating cargo, as well as piles and puddles. In summer, when the sun sets down in the west, on the river beach the heat is unbearable. In winter, the northwest wind is wild and howling. People lingering here may get some bit of benefit, but it is hard to admit that this is an ideal living place for residents with growing families.

Along the bank of Pudong, due to the increase in population, the real estate industry flourished gradually, which promoted the formation of old-style lanes and alleys in the early period of Pudong. In the late period of the Guangxu Period (around 1900), in the current Dongchang Road, the old-style alley appeared — Renjili, the first one built in Pudong. There were more than 20 old-style lanes and alleys in total in the South District of Pudong, according to *Annals of Geographical Names in Nanshi District*. In the Huangpu District of Pudong, there were also more than 100 of such lanes and alleys. These old-style lanes and alleys were all built from the beginning of the 20th century to the period before the Anti-Japanese

War. According to *Annals of Geographical Names in Huangpu District*, in the early 20th century, 120 old-style lanes and alleys were built along the river in Lujiazui today.

Along with the increase of settlements along the river, some market towns appeared like Bailianjing, Zhoujiadu, Nanmatou, Lujiazui, Lannidu, Yangjiadu, Laobaidu, Qingningsi, Qichangzhan, Jujiaqiao, Shengli, etc. This area became the early urbanized area.

Some of these market towns developed because they were located on vital traffic routes, and some others developed because the factories and trestle houses were concentrated there. The increase of residents and employers also attracted firms to open shops and do business in Pudong. So the city became increasingly prosperous, and in the area along the river commercial streets began to take shape. For example, Qingningsi was originally a settlement for villagers, but in the second year of the Xuantong Period of the Qing Dynasty (1910), the Pudong Seawall Bureau opened the first water route from Donggou through Qingningsi to the Bund of Nanjing East Road. In 1925, Shangchuan Railway set up a station at Qingningsi. Together with the ferry transport, it became the main passage for people in the east region of Pudong to go to Puxi. In Qingningsi there was a rapid increase in the flow of people and it became a thriving market town in Pudong.

After the 1920s, electricity came into use along the river in Pudong. In the 8th year of the Republic of China (1919), geographers Tong Shiheng, Huang Yanpei, and Mu Ouchu raised funds to establish Pudong Electric Co., Ltd. in Zhangjiabang and it became the earliest power supply institution in Pudong. "Since the new machines generated electricity, the power was sufficient. The lights were bright, and users gave praise for the convenience. There were continuous requests for installing electric lights." After the 1930s, it expanded from the coastal area to the southeast.

However, there was no planning for the urbanization of Pudong along the river. For a long period of time, Pudong's urbanization evolved naturally in a disorderly and low-level state.

By about 1930, the National Government built Pudong South Road, Pudong Avenue, and Dongtang Road, as named today. The road extended from north Gaoqiao to south Zhoujiadu. When the road was completed, it became the demarcation line between the urban and rural Pudong. To the east, the roads were still muddy, with village houses scattered. To the west, it was the industrial and commercial residential area. Except the old Yangjing Town, Qingningsi, and other market towns, it was still rural to the east of the road until 1949.

Generally speaking, in Pudong, the urbanized area along the river, shaped in modern times, was backward in municipal construction, with narrow roads, poor living conditions, insufficient cultural and entertainment facilities, and extremely inconvenient and slowly-developed land and water transportation. The saying by people in Shanghai that "it is better to have a bed in Puxi than a house in Pudong" is a true reflection of the long-lasting backward state of the municipal construction in Pudong.

The Huangpu River, Shanghai's mother river, is really a bit partial. She made a bend on its way to the sea, offering prosperity to Puxi, leaving backwardness to Pudong. By the 1950s and 1960s, Pudong could not yet be compared with Puxi at all.

2.4 Hometown Construction of Pudong People

After Shanghai was opened as a commercial port, the gap between Pudong and Puxi in economic and social development began to widen rapidly. In particular, since 1907, the Huangpu River began to be dredged as the waterway, and the broad river surface, became the golden passage of ten-thousand-ton ships. This also made it more difficult to bridge the Huangpu River, because the bridge deck must be several tens of meters above the river so as to not affect navigation. And a very long approach bridge must be built to make it easy for cars to cross. To build a bridge can only be a dream and the difficulty of crossing the river came into being.

The Huangpu River became a natural cut, the biggest obstacle to the people, material, and capital flows on both banks.

The Huangpu River was not only a natural barrier, but also a psychological one. Residents living in Puxi called people from the east of the Huangpu River as "Pudong people" and the tone contained more or less the meaning of "rural people". And as "Pudong people" went to Puxi, they named it as "to Shanghai".

There was an extreme imbalance between the economic and cultural development in Pudong and Puxi, showing Pudong people "a difference in the way of life, a gap in the process of civilization transformation, a huge impact of a western-style urban culture on the life of traditional Chinese agriculture, industry, and commerce".

Pudong people of insight saw this, especially Pudong people who were working and thriving in Puxi. In the 31st year of Guangxu in the Qing Dynasty (1905), the Pudong Fellowship Association was established under the initiation by Li Pingshu, Huang Yanpei, Ye Huijun, Zhang Zhihe, Yang Sisheng, Gu Lanzhou, and other people, organized by the fellows living in Shanghai who came from the areas like Baoshan, Shanghai, Chuansha, Nanhui, Fengxian, Jinshan, and Huating (now Songjiang).

The famous gentry Li Pingshu was elected as chairman of the Pudong Fellowship Association. Later, *Pudong Newspaper* was founded.

In 1911, when Shanghai recovered after the Xinhai Revolution, Li Pingshu served as the chief of civil affairs in the military government of Shanghai. After Yuan Shikai usurped power, Li was forced to exile in Japan, having no time to deal with the affairs in the Pudong Fellowship Association. During this period, Huang Yanpei, Zhang Zhihe, etc. presided over the association.

In his later years, Li Pingshu was sick and frail. In 1924, the association moved from Wangjia wharf to Wangping Street, and Huang Yanpei, the vocational educator, was elected as Chairman of the board.

From July 1928 to January 1932, the Pudong Fellowship Association was renamed to Puzuo Fellowship Association, Association of Pudong People in Shanghai, Pudong Hometown Association, and so on. The scope of Pudong's "fellows" expanded from the five counties Fengxian, Nanhui, Chuansha, Baoshan, and Shanghai when it was originally established to the seven counties of Pudong area, Baoshan, Shanghai, Chuansha, Nanhui, Fengxian, Jinshan, and Songjiang.

Shanghai Green Gang tycoon Du Yuesheng, born in Gaoqiao of Pudong, was also enthusiastic about taking part in the activities of the association and was elected president of the Executive Council of the association. The association took advantage of Du Yuesheng's prestige to improve the social status of the hometown association.

After the founding of the Pudong Hometown Association, it began to focus on the development and construction of Pudong.

Pudong Hometown Association in Pudong mansion

After the commercial port was opened in Shanghai, the transportation modernization of Puxi developed rapidly, but in Pudong it was almost blank. Soon after the establishment of the association, it spared no effort in developing the construction of Pudong's transport and other public utilities.

On October 8, 1925, a train set out from Qingningsi Station along the river in Pudong, heading for Chuansha. The train was smaller than the usual train and its tracks were narrower. The seats in the car, like those in the current subway car, were two rows of long seats on both sides. The car doors, like those in the subway now, were pulled opened on both sides. It was said to facilitate the farmers along the line getting their load on and off. When the little train was running, a loud whistle would be heard a few miles away.

This 13.9-kilometer-long railway was contributed by the Pudong Hometown Association.

As early as the first year of the Xuantong Period in the Qing Dynasty (1909), Li Pingshu appealed for the construction of Hu-Jin Railway to the gentlemen of the other five counties and one office: Shanghai, Chuansha, Nanhui, Fengxian, Huating (now Songjiang), and Jinshan. But the project was not carried out because of the insufficient capital. In January 1921, Huang Yanpei, Zhang Bochu, and others called on the fellows to establish Shangchuan Transportation Co., Ltd. It was supported by the fellows, and they actively subscribed and very quickly sufficient shares were raised. In the next year, the construction started, and the tracks were laid. In 1925, the section from Qingningsi to Chuansha in Pudong was fully opened to traffic. Later it extended to Zhuqiao, Nanhui County, with a total length of 33.35 kilometers. At the same time, local gentry Mu Xiangyao and others made preparation for building Shangnan Railway from Pudong Zhoujiadu to Zhoupu Town of Nanhui. It was completed in 1925.

Public transport was undertaken by the people, which was also a major feature of the early development of Pudong. Although the people and organizations in Pudong made limited contribution to the development and construction of Pudong, the grassroot power from the people was very valuable.

At present, on the west side of Chuansha Martyr Cemetery located in Huaxia East Road, an old-style small locomotive is quietly parked. As a witness of history, it silently tells visitors the history of the construction of Shangchuan Railway by the hometown association.

Pudong, which is near the sea, was frequently damaged by tides. Building seawalls and dredging rivers had always been two major projects in Pudong. Initiated by the Pudong Hometown Association in 1929, the branches near Huangpu such as Lannidu and Chengtanggang were dredged. After the Anti-Japanese War, Majiabang and Dutaipu (namely Cao Jiagou) were also dredged.

Coastal seawalls, due to the lack of a dedicated institution for governance, suffered from long-term disrepair, with serious hidden dangers. In April 1931, a special tidal disaster occurred along the coast, causing great damage. In September of the same year, more than 20 people from the Pudong Hometown Association, such as Du Yusheng, Huang Yanpei, and Mu Ouchu, held a meeting. After deliberation, they decided that Du Yuesheng, Mu Ouchu, and Yang Qingyuan would go to Baoshan, Taicang to meet the Seawall Affairs Bureau for a negotiation about unified establishment of a seawall committee. In addition, three people went to Baoshan, Taicang, Liuhe, Gaoqiao, Jinshanzui, and other places for field investigation of the potential danger. The day-to-day regular management of seawall relevant matters was run by Mu Ouchu.

On April 3, 1937, all the directors and supervisors of the association decided that the four executive directors Mu Ouchu, Huang Peiyan, Shen Menglian, and Lv Yuequan would sign their names on *Letter to Chairman Du Yuesheng*, requesting Du to agree to turn over the gifts for his 50th birthday to build Pudong seawalls.

Du Yuesheng replied with full approval on May 27 of the same year.

Of course, the construction of seawalls was a huge and expensive project. It was far from enough to rely on the birthday money alone. The Pudong Hometown Association called the municipal government to request funds for constructing seawalls as soon as possible. Unfortunately, in a few days the full-scale war broke out, and the building of the seawalls was put on hold. But the actions taken by the Pudong Hometown Association in building its hometown are admirable.

The lack of public wharfs along the river in Pudong is not conducive to the economic development of Pudong due to the inconvenience of ships going in and out of Pudong. So the Pudong Hometown Association initiated the "Preparatory Committee for Local Public Management of Municipal Ferry" and issued an appeal to the municipal authorities to build public wharves along the river in Pudong in order to take the advantages and eliminate disadvantages, and achieve the purpose of revitalizing Pudong economy.

In January 1934, the Pudong Hometown Association made a request to the Mayor of Shanghai, Wu Tiecheng: "Today all traffic wharves along Huangpu are owned by the city, and ordinary citizens are not allowed to use them freely. From now on, beside the road wharves that the city ferry occupies, a public terminal must be built to facilitate the public in case the ferry operators manipulate and monopolize the traffic."

At that time, the city ferry business income was an important source of fiscal revenue in Pudong, but since the ferry was turned over to the government, there were a lot of abuses. Therefore, in the same month of the same year, the Pudong Hometown Association also put forward the proposal that the city ferry which managed to be officially transferred to local public management: "Because the ferries were turned over to the municipal public utility for operation, the frequent rise in ticket prices became a great burden for villagers." So they requested that "this association initiate a preparatory committee for the local public management of municipal ferry to handle Pujiang Ferry".

For the association, the realization of regional autonomy was also a major task.

In the late Qing Dynasty, many events promoted the widespread "local autonomy" all over China such as the artillery of the Eight-Power Allied Forces in 1900, the victory of Japan in the Russo-Japanese War in 1904 and the agreement of Empress Dowager in the inaccessible palace to constitutionalism in 1905. Local elites became the main players of autonomy, such as the Pudong people Li Pingshu, Huang Yanpei and so on, who spared no effort to defend the rights of the township.

In the early 20th century, when China's political situation was in turmoil, there were revolution, coup d'etat, scuffle, and separatism, and the central government alternated like a revolving door, with the flags constantly changing on the top of the city wall. It is easy to imagine the administrative ability of local government. Therefore, the demand for civil autonomy became more and more intense.

In Shanghai, the demand for autonomy was stronger and the actions were greater. In the half century after the opening of the port, three regions were formed: the Chinese quarter under the jurisdiction of the Qing government, the public concession governed by the great powers, and the French concession. In the concessions, the foreigners built houses, and ensured water, electricity, coal, and other public utilities. The concessions were clean and tidy, but the Chinese quarter was dilapidated, with the supply of water, electricity, and coal dependent on the attitudes of foreigners. The sharp contrast stimulated the gentries in Shanghai. In particular, from 1905 to 1911 in Shanghai, the local autonomy movement was carried out, such as the establishment of General Engineering Bureau, Autonomy Office, and so on. In this period, the thought of local autonomy was deeply rooted in the hearts of the people. The squires naturally became the protagonists of the autonomy movement and actively participated in social activities.

The Pudong Hometown Association can be regarded as an active advocate, taking the implementation of local autonomy as a matter of urgency in developing local undertakings as local autonomy was an important part of revitalizing industry.

On April 22, 1932, the lawyer Li Chengzhi drafted the thousand-word *Proposition of Trial Autonomy in the Six Counties — The Old Subjects to Songjiang* for the Pudong Hometown Association, requesting the realization of local autonomy in Pudong. The proposition suggested to open a special industrial zone along the Huangpu River to attract foreign capital, allowing foreign investors to enjoy living freely together.

The proposition also pointed out, "To revitalize industry, it is necessary to open up a section along the two sides of Huangpu as an industrial area, and to employ experts as designers. The funds needed can be raised from countries abroad, and foreigners are allowed to invest in this area. The foreigners who wish to obey the laws of our country may also be allowed to live together with the natives and run business freely."

On July 20, 1937, Du Yuesheng and others sent a letter to Shanghai Mayor Yu Hongjun, requesting Pudong autonomy. The letter put it, "We believe local autonomy is not only the most important system of a democratic country, but also the fundamental politics in the founding plan written by Prime Minister Sun Yat-sen. … In view of the present state in Shanghai, it is necessary to adopt the principle of cooperation between the government and the people and lay down the foundation for local autonomy. With Pudong people as the starting, this association would like this plan to be put into practice in Pudong, Shanghai."

Therefore, four practical propositions were put forward such as "selecting local talents frequently to serve the local areas", "delimiting the funds for enterprises", "defining the steps of autonomy", and "setting up administrative agencies."

In the chronicle of events of the Pudong Hometown Association, relief and charity were also important work.

In those days, natural disasters and man-made disasters occurred from time to time. On September 2 and 18, 1933, two strong typhoons did great damage to coastal areas, so the Pudong Hometown Association and other regional non-governmental organizations raised 366,563 silver yuan, plus the materials equivalent to more than 18,000 yuan, and distributed them to the disaster areas.

2.5 The Pioneers of Early Pudong Development

After Shanghai opened its port, a number of Pudong people with lofty ideals changed their ideas and began to pursue the development of Pudong. For example, Shen Yuqing, who was well-read and well-versed in stone tablets and golden tablets, even "abandoned reading and went into business", setting up a towel factory in his home as a pioneer of the modern Chinese towel industry. Li Ping, a gentry, devoted himself to the reforms of municipal administration and local autonomy. Huang Yanpei, the well-known educator, insisted, "To save China, the only solution is to run schools everywhere," pushing vocational education by training students to use both the hand and mind. The industrialist Mu Ouchu introduced the scientific management system of the United States to "save the nation by industry".

What is more commendable is that they were open-minded towards local development and construction.

Shanghai historian Xiong Yuzhi pointed out in the preface of *100-year Pudong Hometown Association* that there were "Pudong consciousness" and "Pudong complex" in some Pudong natives who led the urban trend. He stated, "In the advanced Puxi, a number of Pudong natives were actively leading the urban trend, such as Li Pingshu, Mu Ouchu, Yang Sisheng, Huang Yanpei, Du Yuesheng, and so on. Looking at Puxi, they were homesick and naturally developed the 'Pudong consciousness', which was the consciousness of urbanization and modernization, the consciousness of emulating the better with the reluctance to lag behind."

This kind of consciousness is in essence a kind of open-mindedness.

In addition to the peoples' concern about the early development of Pudong, Pudong also attracted the attention of a great figure.

Sun Yat-sen came to Shanghai on June 26, 1918, when he was in pain and even in despair.

At first Sun Yat-sen temporarily lived in No. 63, Huanlong Road (now Nanchang Road), Shanghai. The house was cramped and underlit, and the light had to be switched on during the day. Sun Yat-sen had been in exile abroad since his revolution for decades, without his own housing in China. Such a large China could not accommodate a revolutionary leader like him. Four overseas Chinese felt so sympathetic that they donated a two-story house to him.

This was a western-style garden villa at No. 7, Xiangshan Road, Shanghai, located in the French concession.

In this house, Sun Yat-sen meditated daily, sitting indoors, determined to make new explorations in both the theory and practice.

Eight years after the 1911 Revolution, the whole country was still in a scuffle under the rule of the warlords of the North and the South. "The situation of the country is getting worse day by day, and the poor conditions make people unable to live." Sun Yat-sen felt uncertain and "helpless" about the future and he acknowledged that he had "no concrete solution to the current situation", so he could only "hide his capacities and enjoyed himself by writing". Almost completely in despair, he only wanted to concentrate on writing books to "enlighten the nation".

During the more than one year from 1918 to 1919, Sun Yat-sen lived in seclusion, writing *The Theory of Sun Yat-sen* and *Industrial Plan*. These 2 books and *Preliminary Civil Rights* written in 1917 made up *The Strategy of State Founding*. This is the most important and most concentrated period in which Sun Yat-sen was engaged in writing.

The Theory of Sun Yat-sen was written on December 30, 1918 and published on May 20, 1919. The book argued for the truth that "it is easier to do a thing than to know the why", taking as examples the ten things of dieting, money-spending, writing, house-building, shipbuilding, city-building, river-opening, electricity, chemistry, and evolution. The book gave a systematic summary of the lessons learned since the 1911 Revolution.

The Industrial Plan was written in English and was originally known as *The International Development of China*, published in *Far East Times* in June 1919. Later, it was edited as *The Second Strategy of Founding China: Material Construction*, which consisted of 6 plans in 33 sections. In *Industrial Plan*, Sun Yat-sen advocated that foreign investment should be used to make profits, such as opening-up markets, building factories, building railways, building canals, and developing minerals, to lay out a grand blueprint for China's construction. Perhaps this is one of the reasons why Sun Yat-sen wrote this book in English.

It is in *Industrial Plan* that Sun Yat-sen put forward the idea of building the Grand Oriental Port.

Sun Yat-sen had been educated in western countries since he was a teenager, and later he frequently visited the British Museum and studied there when he was exiled for revolutionary activities. Therefore, Sun Yat-sen had a broader vision and advanced consciousness. Building a world-famous port and adapting to global economic integration were deeply hidden in Sun Yat-sen's conceptions, even though China was very backward at that time. In his books, he proposed to build 100,000 miles of railways and one million miles of roads. Sun Yat-sen cherished a more ambitious goal to construct a world-class port "like New York Harbor" along the northern, central, and southern coasts of China.

Regarding the construction of the "Grand Oriental Port", Sun Yat-sen designed two construction plans: to build a planned port and to take Shanghai as the big oriental port.

As to the first plan, Sun Yat-sen planned to build a deep-water port in Zhapu, Zhejiang Province, south of Shanghai, so it was called a "planned port", which was new, planned, and designed. Zhapu, located on the north bank of Hangzhou Bay, had been a commercial port since the Southern Song Dynasty. Since ancient times, it had been known as "the Gateway of Zhejiang and Suzhou" and "a Strategic Town at Seaport" and was listed, together with Shanghai Port, as the two largest ports of South-Yangzte area in the early Qing Dynasty. Sun Yat-sen believed that the biggest advantage of the "planned port" was that the water surface was open, the water was relatively deep, and there was no silt blockage. Moreover, the land price was cheap and there was little need for demolition. By means of the state's control of land, when the harbor was completed, land price would rise and the government would gain huge benefits. "Because of preeminence of this planned port, there are various possibilities for the port to rival New York."

The first plan is Sun Yat-sen's ideal one. One of the main reasons why he chose Zhapu to build the "planned port" as the first plan was the silting of Shanghai port. "The sand and mud from Yangtze River choked the passage in Shanghai every year at an abnormal speed, which was the demon for preventing Shanghai from becoming a world business harbor in the future." Sun Yat-sen repeatedly consulted foreign dredging experts for investigation, but he could not find a countermeasure.

But the most realistic problem in building a new port is that it was hard to raise huge sums of money, and it might take too long time. So Sun Yat-sen proposed a second plan, that is, "taking Shanghai as Grand Oriental Port".

Since its establishment, as a result of its superior geographical conditions, Shanghai Port had attracted the flows of material, people, and capital from the Yangtze River Delta, Yangtze River Valley, and even the whole country. After long-term development, Shanghai had become a hub of domestic and foreign economic exchanges and an international metropolis. Direct transformation of Shanghai port had the advantage of low investment, great speed, good continuous operation, much economic benefit, and so on, and the investment environment can be further improved and more foreign capital can be attracted more quickly. Therefore, Sun Yat-sen thought that "Shanghai enjoys a special status, from which we can obtain a remedy for Shanghai".

In his book *The Strategy of State Founding*, Sun Yat-sen elaborated his plan, drew a map, and made a detailed analysis:

> According to my plan, when the waterway opened by Dredging Agency is extended and expanded to the bend on the right bank of the Huangpu River, a new river will be opened at the confluence of the Gaoqiao River, running straight through Pudong, and at the second curve of the upper reaches at Longhua Rail connection it meets with the Huangpu River. So from this point to the place diagonally opposite to Yangshupu, the river runs straight like a rope, and thus reaches Wusong with a gentle curve.

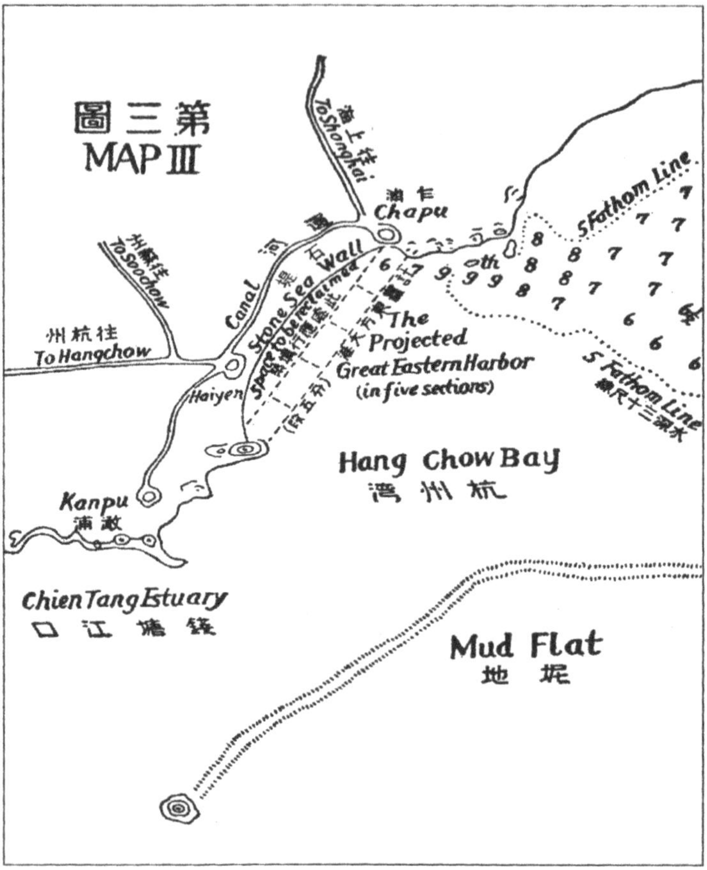

The third picture of Grand Oriental Port (From *The Strategy of State Founding*)

Sun Yat-sen envisioned that an arc canal should be excavated at the intersection of the Gaoqiao River and Huangpu River in the northeast of Pudong, Shanghai, so that ships entering Shanghai from the Yangtze River or the East China Sea would be allowed to go straight up to the middle of the the Huangpu River through this canal in Pudong, and the lower reaches of the Huangpu River which were curved and heavily silted would be landfilled.

As for the land from the Huangpu River to be filled and leveled up to the newly excavated river, according to Sun Yat-sen's conception, "The land around the new river about 30 miles will be enclosed as the city center

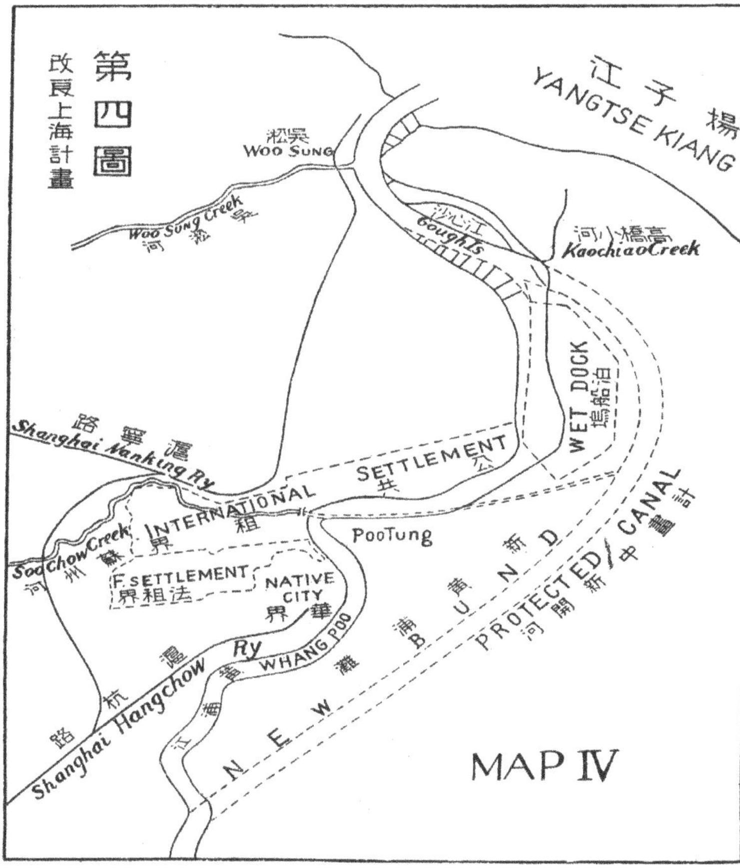

The fourth picture of Grand Oriental Port (From *The Strategy of State Founding*)

and as a new Huangpu beach. Now, the part of the Huangpu River which twines and winds in front of Shanghai will be filled and used as roads and shops. It goes without saying that the land formed by filling, of course, is state-owned. And the vicinity from this line to the middle of the new river should also be nationalized and operated by the state and administrated at the disposal of the agencies for international development. In this way, Shanghai can catch up with the aforementioned planned port, and the construction aimed at economic development can introduce foreign capital."

Obviously, Sun Yat-sen's design takes into account the concessions in Shanghai. The western powers only cared about interests of the concessions and were not interested in the construction of Pudong. Therefore, the Chinese government would open a new river course by itself, it could be used to build a city residence center, and the income from the rising land prices in these new busy areas could be taken as a source of funding for the transformation of the Shanghai port. In this way, Puxi and Pudong could become an integral whole, and the land belonged to the Chinese government, then the western powers, which occupied concessions in the western Huangpu River, had no alternative.

Sun Yat-sen thought that in his plan, making profit would be taken as the first principle, so all plans should be strictly adhered to. Therefore, it is necessary to create a city residence center in Pudong and build a new Huangpu beach along the left bank of the newly opened river in order to increase the value of the new land enclosed into Shanghai. Only in this way can Shanghai be worthy of being built as a deep-water port. But for this dying port, only when the new land of great value could be opened, could Shanghai compete with the planned port.

As a leading statesman, Sun Yat-sen also took "making profit" into account and hoped to attract foreign investment. "The construction, which is aimed at economic development, can introduce foreign capital." But in that age, there was incessant fighting among warlords, people lived in dire poverty, and western powers were dividing up the spheres of power influence in China, so it was not easy to introduce a huge amount of foreign capital. Without the support of funds, the conception of making use of land appreciation, selling land at high prices, or "the disposal of international development agencies" was only building castles in the air.

In Shanghai, Sun Yat-sen devoted himself to writing *The Strategy of State Founding*, almost to the degree of ecstasy. A foreign journalist named Dana put it like this:

> Sun Yat-sen brought a six square foot atlas, and as he unfolded it on the floor, I saw one of the most convincing evidence. He was not only a crazy man, but a completely mad man. Undaunted by the obstacles on the map, he held his brush and filled the provinces and territories (including Mongolia) with railway lines on the map as much as he could. I say that he was mad, not because he had drawn lines on the map, but because he had naively thought that by drawing these lines, foreign

capitalists would invest enough money to build them all in five to 10 years.

Later, Chiang Kai-shek said at the inaugural meeting of Shanghai Special City on July 7, 1927, "Shanghai should not only become a model city in China, but also the plans in the Prime Minister's *The Strategy of State Founding* will be completed one by one accordingly." From the spring of 1929, the Construction Committee of the State Government established later actually sent over some people to Zhapu and Haiyan of Zhejiang Province for exploration to collect hydrological and geological data. However, history has shown that neither the planned port nor the back-up plan "is an easy solution or even an operational solution" for the State Government.

In April 2006, Lien Chan, then Honorary Chairman of Kuomintang, said excitedly during his visit to the deep water port in Yangshan of Shanghai, "It was hard for me to imagine that the experimental plan, written by Sun Yat-sen 90 years ago, has become a reality today. I really appreciate that."

It is worth pondering why at that time Sun Yat-sen's ideal could not be realized.

History cannot be assumed, but some historical phenomena can often arouse people's reverie. Had Sun Yat-sen been able to realize his grand idea at that time, Pudong would never have lagged behind so far from Puxi.

Of course, Sun Yat-sen's ambitious plans left more room for imagination for the subsequent governments in the urban planning of Shanghai. Since the late 1920s, many urban construction experts in Shanghai had been drawing on Sun Yat-sen's grand ideas and planning to develop Pudong.

Yang Jianwen, former Director of the Institute of Sector Economics, Shanghai Academy of Social Sciences, recalled that in the 1980s, Chen Minzhi, then Deputy Director, presided over the national "Sixth Five-Year Plan" project, *Strategy Research on Shanghai Economic Development*, and "he led us to refer mainly to *The Strategy of State Founding* on the construction of Shanghai Grand Oriental Port and the plans for the development of Pudong".

At the moment, when in the library Yang Jianwen first saw *The Strategy of State Founding*, he was surprised. "The global thinking of this book has a great impact on us, with a great field of vision and bearing. What is discussed is the problem of the whole country. In accordance to this train of thought we should consider the problem of Shanghai, consider the development of Shanghai from national, global perspective, otherwise only short-term concrete problems can be solved."

It can be said that by the 1990s, Shanghai finally made the decision to develop Pudong, *The Strategy of State Founding* playing an important role as reference.

2.6 Construction of Pudong Road Only

In the early 1920s, Shanghai had become the largest commercial port and international trading port in China. Shanghai was formerly under the jurisdiction of Jiangsu. Chiang Kai-shek, who made his fortune in Shanghai, knew that the stability of Shanghai played an important role in the regime that had just been established. Shanghai's industrial and commercial circles were his main source of wealth, as well as the interests of the great powers in the concessions, so the Nanjing government gave special privilege to Shanghai. On May 27, 1927, the Political Conference of the Central Committee of Kuomintang passed *The Provisional Regulations on Shanghai as a Special City*, which stipulated Shanghai as the special administrative area of the Republic of China named as the Special Shanghai City, directly subordinate to the Nanjing Central Government, legally divorced from the jurisdiction of Jiangsu.

It was also in this year that Shanghai ended the 700-year-long county-level administration, and became a city, with the first mayor, and its area expanded. Rising from an ordinary county to a city, as a central municipality directly under the Central Government, Shanghai achieved an astonishing advancement in history.

After that, Shanghai Special City included the 17 cities and townships of Shanghai and Baoshan County, which were renamed as districts, with the jurisdiction sphere of 527.53 square kilometers. Among them, the 6 districts Gaoqiao, Gaoxing, Luxing, Yangjing, Tangqiao, Yangsi in Pudong area were under the jurisdiction of Shanghai Special City.

In 1920s, Shanghai underwent abnormal development. The urban heartland had already been occupied by concessions, and the bustling downtown was concentrated in the privileged concessions. Within the boundary of old Chinatown, the urban area was aging and densely populated. In the layout of the city, the concessions lay across the city center, forming a divided pattern of the British Concession, the French Concession, the American Concession, and then the Anglo-American Public Concession and the jurisdiction area of the National Government. The municipal facilities were segmented, the road traffic was not smooth, and the transport of goods was inconvenient. The port throughput increased sharply, so the wharves were not enough for use. In the deformed development of Shanghai, there was an urgent need for an overall development plan.

Similar to the situation in which the Shanghai city government planned to develop Pudong to solve the varied urban problems in Shanghai 70 years later, Shanghai was just as old and densely populated, and there was an urgent need to open up a new urban area. But the concessions, like a rope, strangled the development of Shanghai as a whole.

So at that time, the State Government turned its attention to Jiangwan in the northeast of Shanghai, where it planned to build a new Shanghai, gradually shifting the center of Shanghai.

In November 1927, the city government set up the Municipal Construction Committee. In August 1929, the Shanghai Downtown Construction Committee was established. In January 1930, the drafting of *The Outline of Shanghai Urban Central-region Plan* was completed. In December of the same year, Shanghai city government formally put forward *The Plan for the Construction of Shanghai Urban Centre Area*, which mainly decided to develop the area to the north of the concession, with Jiangwan as the center. In order to establish the status and the foundation of the development of Shanghai under the direct jurisdiction of the State Government, a new urban area was opened between Wusong and Jiangwan, which was the most downstream of the Huangpu River and adjacent to Wusong.

This is what people later called "Big Construction Plan", or "New Shanghai Construction Plan". The plan drew on Sun Yat-sen's vision of "constructing a world port in Shanghai".

Subsequently, the committee successively proposed the regionalization plan and the road plan of the city center, the construction plan of Qiujiang wharf at the Huangpu River, and the Shanghai regionalization and transportation plan, which were collectively referred to as the "Grand Shanghai Plan".

Then why did Pudong not become a new urban area for development? After all, there were no concessions in Pudong.

In *The Plan for the Construction of Shanghai Urban Centre*, the site selection and development for the new urban center had been comprehensively explored and compared. "The current commerce of this city is concentrated in the southeast part of the public concessions. The French Concession and the west Shanghai area are mostly residential areas." Because it was necessary to keep away from the most prosperous and densely populated part of the city, that is, the concession area, and there was no room for development in the old city, so there were only two new urban areas, Pudong and the north of Shanghai.

According to the analysis in the plan, "In Pudong, at present, there are only a few wharves along the river, and most of the rest are farmland. It is located only a river gap away from the concessions, but there was great disparity in land prices. In regards to future transportation, if there is a satisfactory solution, it will count on the future development of Pudong, unlimited and promising."

However, even if the transportation problem were solved and the development of Pudong were achieved, because it was too close to the concession, "its status will not be independent from the concessions, and it cannot escape from their control, so that the future city center will eventually fail".

As a result, a large area of the undeveloped land between Wusong and Jiangwan was chosen as the new city center of Shanghai.

In this plan, although Pudong was not the focus, it was included in the scope of development. According to the "Grand Shanghai Plan", the area along the river from the south of Wusong Town to the north of Yinhang Town would be a business port, and the shoreline in Pudong was intended to be the extended zone of the business port area. In view of the situation that in Pudong the near-shore factories and stacks were adjacent to each other and it was densely populated, but the traffic was backward, the planned route to take was the area north to Shangnan Road in Yangsi District, south to Dongdu Road of Luhangji, east to the Huangpu River, and west to Pudong Road. And it was planned to widen the road built by Qiantang Construction Bureau, or open a new road, so as to expedite the water and land traffic.

In these plans, the cross-river traffic planning appeared for the first time, which planned the two projects respectively, that is, the projects of crossing the Huangpu River by both railway and highway.

As to the railway, it was planned to extend the Shanghai-Hangzhou line to the east and build the Huangpu River Bridge to reach Gaoqiao directly to the north, so that the goods on the Shanghai-Hangzhou line could arrive directly in Pudong to link up with water transport. There were two locations for crossing the river by railway. As the first alternative, in the south of Shanghai (now the northern end of Longhua Airport), a bridge would be built to run across the Huangpu River. The second alternative referred to the area near Malu Bridge in Pudong. The former planned to build a bridge, while for the latter it was not decided whether to build a bridge or tunnel. But it is the first time to envisage building a cross-river tunnel under the Huangpu River.

As to the highway, it was planned to build a north-south main road, starting from the town of Baoshan, through Wenzaobang, through Jiangwan Town, through the north of Sichuan Road, and then through the concession area, through Laochengxiang in the south, South Station, through the South Road after running across the river, then directly to the town of Zhagang.

Before that, the government of the Republic of China had considered the construction of roads in Pudong. In 1929, the Works Bureau to the municipal government submitted a report: "In the area along the river in Pudong, the foreign trade factory warehouses cover a large area and there is no wide road for passage, so that the traffic running among Tangqiao, Yangjing, and Gaoqiao must bypass Puxi. It is so inconvenient. So it is planned to build a highway starting from Dongjiadu of Tangqiao, running northward along Pujiang and across Zhangjiabang and Yangjing harbors … and then going northward to cross the Xigou, Donggou, and ending at Gaoqiao port. A line will be drawn and it will be built part by part in turn. When the road is completed, the branch roads will be built to pass through all the towns in the future. So hopefully, municipal construction between the sections in Pudong should be able to develop step by step."

Due to limited financial resources and the outbreak of the Anti-Japanese War, to a larger extent, the "Grand Shanghai Plan" was not put into practice. But of course, some of the planned projects were implemented. On December 2, 1930, the 160th Municipal Council of Shanghai Municipal Government decided to open Pudong Road, in the south starting from Shangnan Road, running northward through Bailianjing, Tangqiao, Zhangjiabang, Yangjiadu, Dongchang Road, Lujiazui Road today, to North Hutang Road (this section is Pudongnan Road today); and then from Lujiazui Road today, running northeast through Qichangzhan, Yuanshen Road, Minsheng Road, Yangjing Town, Qingningsi, to Donggou (this section is named Pudong Avenue today). The road, parallel to the Huangpu River, extended 17 kilometers in length, and also it was the widest road in Pudong, only 10 meters.

In October 1935, the road was completed and put to operation, linking with the Shangchuan Railway, from which the traffic extended to the hinterland of Pudong. So this road played a role in promoting the economic and social development of Pudong.

Chapter 3

The Widening Gap: The Outbreak of Shanghai's "Urban Disease"

3.1 Investment Without Development

In the 1950s and 1960s, the modern economy of Pudong was further developed, especially when the state began to invest heavily in the riparian area of Pudong, building a group of backbone enterprises mainly engaged in heavy industry, and made the large-scale transformation of some original enterprises, which shaped four pillar industries such as petrochemical, iron and steel, textile, and the manufacturing of transportation equipment. Overall, hundreds of large-scale or medium-scale enterprises were built in the 1950s to 1960s, such as Shanghai Refinery, Gaoqiao Chemical Plant, Hudong Shipyard, Shanghai Shipyard, Jiangnan Branch of China Shipyard, No. 3 Shanghai Steel Plant, Shanghai Yaohua Glass Works, No. 10 Shangmian Textile, No. 27 Shangmian Texile, No. 28 Shangmian Texile, etc.

At that time, that is, before 1990, heavy industry in Pudong accounted for a very high proportion. According to statistics, in 1990, the output value of heavy industry in the Pudong New Area was 10.06 billion yuan, accounting for 62.9% of the region's total industrial output value, much higher than the proportion of Shanghai's heavy industry, which accounted for 48.15% of the industrial output value in that year.

The industry in Pudong was very "heavy", mainly "heavy" in raw material industry. In the heavy industry, the raw material industry accounted for 58.2%, and the processing industry for 41.8%. The output value of large-scale enterprises accounted for a large proportion. In

Pudong New Area there were 29 large-scale enterprises, accounting for 2.3% of the number of industrial enterprises in the area, but their industrial output value accounted for as high as 53.6% of the industrial output value of the whole region.

Although the government carried out considerable industrial construction in Pudong and invested in constructing a number of large backbone enterprises, until the early 1980s, these large factories were still quite dispersed and there were only a number of "industrial spots" in Pudong without the upstream and downstream industrial chain. There were only two enterprises in some industries. More importantly, these enterprises did not promote the large-scale urbanization in the Pudong area.

The local investment in Pudong was mainly concentrated in the towel, clothing, embroidery, construction, dairy, and flower planting industries, each of which developed its own traditional characteristics and advantages. In particular, Chuansha County was known as the town of architecture, milk, towel, and flower.

Thanks to these investments, the township enterprises in Pudong grew rapidly, especially in the 1980s. Chuansha County can be taken as an example. In 1978, there were 531 township enterprises in the county, with an annual industrial output value of 191 million yuan. By 1985, it had grown to 1136 enterprises, with an annual gross industrial output of 1,294 billion yuan. By 1989, there had been more than 3,850 township enterprises, with an industrial output value of 2.9 billion yuan. The economic development attributed to township enterprises made Chuansha County one of the top 10 of the top 100 counties of comprehensive strength in China.

It was indeed worthy of pride to become one of the top 10 of the top 100 counties in the country, but in terms of economic structure, industrial level, environment, and institutional system, it had yet to get onto the track of modernization. And no matter whether it was the investment made by the state and the Shanghai municipal government or the local investment of Pudong, the development and construction in the real sense had not been realized, so the urbanization process of Pudong was quite slow.

Away from the riverbank and deep into the hinterland of Pudong, the larger area was still mainly agriculture. This also continued the thinking of the experts in the Shanghai Urban Planning Committee in 1946, namely, considering the development of Pudong from the perspective of Puxi. Therefore, naturally, the vast countryside in Pudong became one of the important bases for the supply of non-staple food in Shanghai. By 1990, various kinds of non-staple food bases, vegetable bases, dairy farms, and pig farms had been scattered all over Pudong, providing 191,000 tons of vegetables, 0.7 million tons of milk, 17,000 pigs, 282,000 fowls, and 3,283 tons of eggs.

On the map of Pudong, the development of Pudong started in 1990, with the new area (estimated at 522.7 square kilometers) of 479.2 square kilometers of rural area (including 20.3 square kilometers of rural market towns) accounting for 91.7% of the total of the new area. Except some factories and business and residential areas along the river, two kilometers away was a field of vegetable land. Therefore, since the development and opening of Pudong, quite a large number of reporters often described Pudong as a vast field.

A reporter who had covered Pudong for many years wrote, "For decades, the three garbage dumps of this oriental urban city — Shanghai, that is, Laogang, Jiangzhen, and Sanlintang, are all located in Pudong. Such a 'design' is a very clear proof for the previous positioning of Pudong."

Before the development of Pudong in 1990, in the west of Pudong along the river from south to north, the main port area of Shanghai had been shaped. The harbor, the factory, and the commercial and residential areas were crowded together, which was the earliest urbanized area of Pudong. Unfortunately, however, there was no common prosperity on both banks like New York, London, and Paris.

The municipal construction in Pudong was backward and the roads were narrow. For example, the roads in Pudong were mostly designed according to the county standard, with the narrow road surface, lower grade, and without overpass. Yanggao Road, which at present is an 8-fast-lane and 2-slow-lane road running east-west to the northeast of Pudong, was dubbed "lamb road" in the 1950s as it was only a 3.5-meter-wide road paved with gravels and slacks. The public transport in Pudong New Area

Yanggao Road was originally a 3.5-meter-wide road paved with gravels and slacks

was even weaker. By the end of 1990, there had been 48 bus lines and only 35 taxis in Pudong New Area.

The living conditions of residents were very poor. Before 1987, for example, none of the residents in Pudong used pipeline gas. The details in history can show more of the reality. On the afternoon of January 4, 1996, Zhao Qizheng, vice mayor of Shanghai and director of the Pudong New Area Administrative Committee, arrived in Zhangjiabang, the most concentrated shanty place in Pudong New Area. Zhao looked up to see the doorplate "Donglajitang" (which means east garbage pond) and asked, "Why do you take this as the road name?" The cadres of the streets replied, "Before the founding of New China, no human lived here, and only garbage piled up. Later, some outsiders arrived only to find nowhere to settle down and then put up shelters on the rubbish dump. Now this area covered 24.6 hectares, with thousands of households living in shelters."

After hearing the reply, Zhao Qizheng didn't feel good, and asked the photographer to take a picture of road plate and doorplate called "Lajitang" (garbage pond). "It is a testimony to the vicissitudes of history."

Before the development of Lujiazui, residents washed clothes in front of public faucets (From *Dream Realized in Lujiazui*)

Pudong had few cultural facilities. Lu Xingsheng, a reporter in Shanghai, recalled that in the 1980s he went to Pudong for an "in-depth interview", just because in Pudong there was no public Xinhua bookstore and the students in Pudong who wanted to buy review materials had to go to Puxi, so a young man surnamed Zhang in Tangqiao of Pudong put up a one-and-a-half-story houselet, selling books at the shop facade and sleeping in the attic which was too low for him to stand straight up.

Crossing the river was even more difficult. Before the development and opening of Pudong, for the people who lived in Pudong and worked in Puxi, or those who lived in Puxi and worked in Pudong, the most difficult thing was the "difficulty to cross the river". By the end of 1990, there had been 16 passenger ferry lines along the Huangpu River, with an annual number of 346 million people crossing the river. However, it was more difficult for the Pudong or Puxi enterprises to cross the river than the ordinary residents. The number of vehicles crossing the river was 3.99 million times a year. During the rush hour it was very crowded. The daily traffic flow waiting to cross was long. Sometimes, for crossing the river, people had to wait in lines for about 10 hours. Once it was foggy, the situation became even more serious.

Not until June 10, 1971 in Shanghai was there the first highway tunnel running across the bottom of the Huangpu River. Its construction and operation accelerated the process of urban population moving to Pudong. By the mid-1980s, the population living in Pudong had exceeded the population in Puxi. But it made the transport problem — "the difficulty of crossing the river" — more serious, so there was the Shanghai people's saying that "it is better to have a bed in Puxi than a house in Pudong".

In fact, the statistics show that the reality was worse than what was described in the folk proverb. At that time, among the more than one million people over 15 years old in Pudong, the average education period was only 8 years, which is 0.4 years lower than the average of the whole city of Shanghai. According to the school building standards of primary and secondary schools issued in Shanghai in 1990, among the more than 300 primary and secondary schools in Pudong, only seven of them met the standard in terms of lot size and floorage. As for the medical condition, there were only 3.14 beds per thousand people in Pudong, compared with the average of 4.98 beds in the whole city, and there was no third-class medical institution in Pudong.

According to the recollection of Li Jianeng, former Assistant Director of Pudong Development Office who participated in Pudong Development Program, "Pudong's social and economic base is mostly rural, and a small part is semi-urban." Although there had been four major industries in Pudong, oil, shipbuilding, textile, and steel-making, a serious problem was brought about, that is, pollution. In 1988, World Bank appointed eight experts to Shanghai to carry out the project "Shanghai Urban Development Program". The four major industries and their pollution were also one of the reasons why the experts did not approve of the development of Pudong.

From the port-opening in Shanghai to 1949 and the 40 years since 1949, the focus of Shanghai's urban development had always been on Puxi. Because of the western-oriented development thinking in Shanghai, and because of the relatively sluggish urban construction in Pudong, the further development of the Pudong economy had been hindered. By the end of the 1980s, Pudong could not be compared with Puxi at all.

3.2 Crossing Surges in Small Boat

The most obvious manifestation of backward urbanization was the difficulty in crossing the river and the various "difficulties" caused by the difficulty of crossing the river. This began in the early years of the Ming Dynasty.

In the early Ming Dynasty, the drainage channel of Tai Lake was not smooth, and the local officials were ineffective in governance. The area of Suzhou and Wusong suffered from frequent floods. The disastrous floods made the people destitute and homeless. Zhu Di, Yongle Emperor in the Ming Dynasty, dispatched the minister Xia Yuanji to regulate rivers and watercourses.

In August of the first year of the Yongle period of the Ming Dynasty (1403), after Xia Yuanji arrived in Shanghai and Zhejiang Province, he inspected the damage and explored the river courses, and found that the lower reaches of the Tai Lake Basin were so flat, curved, and narrow that they often got silted. In the lower reaches of the Wusong River, "reeds and water caltrops grew in clusters and flat land had been formed". He accepted what a local scholar Ye Zonghang suggested, "To dredge the Wusong River, regulating Huangpu should be done first." It was necessary to dredge Huangpu and widen Fanjiabang, a small river north of Lujiazui, that is, the section from Baiduqiao of Jinwai to the east of Fuxing Island, so that Huangpu, which originally flowed northward into the Wusong River near Baiduqiao of Jinwai, could flow northeastward into the sea.

The Yongle Emperor in the Ming Dynasty approved of his plan, and Xia Yuanji led more than 100,000 civilian workers to work and live at the construction site, implementing the water-control project of "the confluence of Wusong and Huangpu". In two years, a new river was dug up in Shanghai, running from Tai Lake down to the sea, which completely changed the direction of the water system and the pattern of shipping and logistics in the area of Suzhou and Wusong.

This river is the famous Huangpu River, also known as the mother river of Shanghai.

The water control measures taken by Xia Yuanji established the status of Shanghai as a good port along the southeast coast of China, and created favorable conditions for the development of Shanghai Port, following the port of Qinglong Town. Then, the opening of Shanghai Port brought to full play the natural advantages of Shanghai as a city connecting with both "river and sea". "The huge ships can run directly to Guo (Shanghai County)." The seaboats, fully loaded with Wuzhong silk, Songjiang fine cloth, and even Jingdezhen ceramics and rice of Dongting Lake, continuously ran from the Huangpu River into the sea, to Ryukyu, to Malacca, towards the Persian Gulf. So Shanghai Port made a leap by replacing Liujia Port as a maritime key post, and opened a new page in the ancient development history of Shanghai.

Later, the Huangpu River became wider and deeper, and as a result of the river control by the famous official Hai Rui in the Qing Dynasty, the Wusong river became a tributary of Huangpu, named as Suzhou River, while Huangpu was upgraded to Huangpu Jiang (big river), with vast and mighty waves, flying seagulls, and thousands of ships running forward.

When Huangpu became the "main stream", Shanghai began to take the present pattern. Due to the separation by Huangpu, the city was divided into two parts, Pudong and Puxi, which became more and more distinct from each other. However, the term "Huangpu River" only appeared in the late Qing Dynasty. In the previous literature, it was recorded as Huangpu Pond, Huangpu, and Big Huangpu.

The Huangpu River gradually evolved from a trickle to a mighty river on the Yangtze River Delta, finally into the embrace of the sea. The river also brought about some difficulties for cross-river exchanges, and also created social, economic, and cultural differences between Pudong and Puxi.

First of all, it was difficult to cross the river.

In the Ming Dynasty, when the Huangpu River was widened from Fanjiabang to Big Huangpu, the river was full of water and its surface was wide and vast.

At that time, there was no capacity to build bridges, so all the cross-river exchanges relied on the ship transport. In the second year of the Jiajing period in the Ming Dynasty (1523), Zheng Luoshu, the Magistrate of Shanghai County, allocated 13 wooden ships with long hull, and opened six "official ports" in Gaochang, Nanchang (now the South Dock), Beicang (now Dongjiadu), Yangjing, Songjiagang, and Chegou.

It is very interesting that in the Ming Dynasty, the ferry of the Huangpu River was named the official ferry, managed by the government, but in the Qing Dynasty, it was changed to "folk ferry", managed by the Folk Ferry Bureau, that is to say, the construction of wharves, the purchase of ships, workers' wages, and other expenses were obtained by voluntary fund-raising. It was a change from state-run to privately-owned ferry, which, of course, was approved by the government.

For example, in the late Qing Dynasty, the largest and most representative charity organization in Shanghai — Fuyuantang of Tongren — opened a dock along the river, set up a ferry system, and assigned some specialists to manage and operate it. In the Tongzhi period, there were 10 ports from Longhua to the lower reaches of the Huangpu River: Caoandu, Zhoujiadu, Gaochangdu, Nancangdu, Beicangdu, Yongjidu, Zhangjiabangdu, Lao Baidu, Yangjiadu, and Guanqiaodu.

According to the historical record, there were 35 ports, which were formed naturally in the Huangpu River and Wusong River, and more than 200 people were engaged in ferries. In addition, there were privately owned ferries that were not approved by the government.

After the Opium War, factories and docks on both sides of the Huangpu River increased, and the fixed ferry terminals on both sides of the Huangpu River also grew, such as Dongchanglu Dock, Fenshan Dock, Chunjiang Dock, Nanyang Dock, Longmaozhan Dock, and Yulonglu Dock. Lanlu Port (now Lanzhou Road), Qichangzhan Port, Weisai Dock, Yangjinggang Port, Yangjia Dock, Shenjiatan Dock, Yangshupu Dock, Zhoujiazui Port, Damatou Port, Tangqiao Port, Dongjia Port, Jiangbianmatou Port, Nanmatou Port, etc.

At the end of the Qing Dynasty, all ferries were wooden small boats, mainly canoes and sampans. The larger one could carry 30 to 50 people.

From the second year of the Xuantong period in the Qing Dynasty (1910), this situation began to change. At first, in order to facilitate handling official business, the Pudong Seawall Rehabilitation Bureau rented a small ferry to facilitate commuting from the east and west bank of the Huangpu River. Sometimes the ferry carried some passengers, who were charged a small fee. But there was a growing demand for crossing the river. In September of that year, the Pudong Seawall Rehabilitation Bureau, "after reporting to the agencies of the county waterways for registration and got approval", "rented a ferry to carry passengers by charging a ferry fee", which "is the start of the official ferry". On December 5 of the same year, it was officially open to set sail, with the initial route from the current Tongren Port on the Bund of Beijing Road straight to Donggou. In the sixth year of the Republic of China (1917), the

At that time, the ferry boats were powered by bamboo poles and wooden oars

In the early 20th century, the ferry boats were uniformly numbered

access to Xidu (now Xiepu Road) was opened, and in the eighth year, the access to Xigou (now Qingningsi) was opened. At that time, all the boats were leased.

The cross-river ferry began to change from free to commercial, which stimulated the development of the Huangpu River ferry industry. By the 1930s, the shipping system gradually changed to being government-run as the main body and the civilian-run commercial ferry as the complementary part.

In the 17th year of the Republic of China (1928), the Public Utilities Bureau of Shanghai Special City took over the Pudong Seawall Rehabilitation Bureau, and successively opened several new routes for crossing the river. Before the full outbreak of the Anti-Japanese War in 1937, six routes were opened in total: Qingding, Qiwei, Donglu, Chunbei, Tangdong, and so on. In addition, a number of private ship-owners also opened several cross-river routes in succession.

Motor vessels were only used for carrying passengers on the routes operated by the ferry companies and limited private ferries, and on other ferry routes sampans and small boats were still used to carry passengers, so accidents occurred frequently due to the poor equipment. Even for the small motor vessels, due to overloading, accidents occurred now and then. In the eyes of the Shanghai people, the Huangpu River was like a natural cut, so with the vast water, for the small boats, once there were strong winds and violent surges, tragic deaths resulted from boat turnover. This is the so-called saying that "Huangpu wind is raging, and the small boats are struggling among surges".

In 1937, the full-blown Anti-Japanese War broke out. The Japanese troops occupied the wharves, bombed the ferries, and banned the river-crossing, so the ferry industry in Shanghai was severely damaged. After the victory of the Anti-Japanese War, the ferry routes along the Huangpu River gradually resumed business.

After the liberation of Shanghai in 1949, the municipal government took over Shanghai Ferry Co., Ltd., and established Shanghai Ferry Company. In October 1954, the private ferry companies and individual ferries were invested in the socialist transformation, and the wharves and boats and other ferry equipment started to be improved. By means of adjustment, river-crossing routes for men and vehicles increased from 6 to 14.

Lannidu Road in Pudong, after Pudong development, became the financial and trade center. Zhao Qizheng said with regret, "Perhaps the road should not have been renamed like this one."

In the 1980s, with the emergence of new residential communities in Pudong, the number of people who had to cross the river increased year by year, and the passenger flow increased at a rate of 10% per year. Between 1983 and 1985, more than 920,000 passengers crossed the river per day, with a total of 928 million passengers transported in 3 years.

The difficulty in crossing the river naturally promoted the construction of the cross-river project. Before 1949, the government of the Republic of China did have plans, but they stayed on paper. It is a very sad story.

3.3 The Difficulty in Implementing the Cross-river Project

After the Shanghai Special City was founded in 1927, the problem of the difficulty in crossing the river began to be put on the conference table of the municipal government. The municipal government first affiliated the ferry run by the Pudong Seawall Rehabitation Bureau to the official management, and made large-scale investment for expansion. With six routes, the official municipal ferry became the main force of the city's ferry industry.

In 1930, Shanghai Government issued *Plan for the Construction of the Urban Center of Shanghai*, which formally incorporated the cross-river project into municipal planning.

As for the funds, it was estimated in the plan that the Huangpu River Bridge would cost five million yuan.

At that time, the finance of the Shanghai municipal government was always in a tight state. From 1927 to 1935, although the income of the Shanghai municipal government increased from 3.4 million yuan to 12 million yuan, it still could not make ends meet. In 1936, the budget deficit reached six million yuan. The reason is simple. According to Wu Guozhen, the former mayor of Shanghai, 50% of the revenue of the Nanjing government came from Shanghai. So five million yuan for the Shanghai municipal government was a huge expenditure.

Without money, there was definitely no bridge.

After the victory of the Anti-Japanese War, mainland enterprises moved to the east and Shanghai became the national economic center again. In order to meet the needs of Shanghai's economic development, the Shanghai government put the cross-river construction project on the agenda again.

On May 10, 1946, the 30th Municipal Conference of the municipal government discussed and adopted *Methods for Preparing for the Transportation Project of Cross-river*, and decided to set up the Shanghai Cross-river Engineering Committee, which was fully responsible for the scheme selection, survey site selection, and the follow-up work. In order to save funds, the design office entrusted the China Bridge Company to do the work, and verified that the design drilling cost was 200 million yuan, and the time limit for the project was one year. Mao Yisheng was appointed Director of the Cross-river Project Design Division of the Committee.

At 4 in the afternoon on May 13, the first meeting of the Shanghai Cross-river Project Committee was held in the conference hall of the Shanghai Government on Hankou Road. Mayor Qian Dajun, Pan Gongzhan, the Shanghai Council speaker, and other city officials, as well as Du Yuesheng, Wang Xiaolai, and other prominent individuals gathered at the meeting. At the meeting, Zhao Zukang, Director of the Municipal Works Bureau; Mao Yisheng, General Manager of the China Bridge Company; and Zhao Zengyu, Director of the Municipal Public Utilities Bureau, respectively reported the construction objective and preliminary design of the cross-river project, so that the long-awaited project was announced to start.

Sun Yat-sen's wishes echoed in the conference hall, and the Shanghai people's years-long dream of the cross-river project finally began to take a shape.

But on the next day, Mayor Qian Dajun left office, and many other city officials resigned. Wu Guozhen, the American doctor, took over as mayor.

Although the beginning was not smooth, Wu Guozhen was very confident. He also served as Chairman of Cross-river Project Committee and hired Mao Yisheng to design the scheme of crossing the Huangpu River.

The Cross-river Project Committee also set up the Technical Advisory Sub-committee to assist in the argumentation and study of the construction scheme. This advisory team was made up of "a group of talents", including architect Lu Qianshou, the designer of the Bank of China building on the Bund; Lin Tongyan, engineer in charge of former Chengdu-Chongqing and Yunnan-Myanmar railway bridge; Zhu Guoxi, expert in bridge structure; Zhuang Jun and Hu Huiquan, the famous architects, etc. After its establishment, the committee completed *Research Report on Shanghai Cross-river Project* with high efficiency, and put forward four schemes for the cross-river project.

On January 6, 1947, Shanghai *Shenbao* (a widely read newspaper) detailed this project: "China Bridge Company was allocated the design funds in August of last year, and started the first phase of work. Based on the research, four schemes of the cross-river project were worked out: to build a tunnel to run through the bottom of the Huangpu River; to build an elevated fixed bridge so that high-mast ships can pass under the bridge; to build a low movable bridge so that it can be opened for ships to pass by and closed at specified time; and to build fixed bridges at the upstream of the Huangpu River to allow only medium-sized vessels to pass, and high-mast ships would be berthed at the downstream of the bridge site."

After repeated comparison and argumentation, Zhao Zukang, Municipal Secretary of the Municipal Works Bureau, held a seminar with the Second Technical Group Advisory Committee of the Cross-river Project, and they believed that the tunnel and the low movable bridge were more suitable and economical for construction. The construction of a tunnel was taken as the first choice.

On January 5 of the same year, Zhu Guoxi, Director of the Engineering Structure Division of the Municipal Works Bureau, said at an interview, "Although the construction of the tunnel is very expensive, it is beneficial to the traffic above, so it is a project once and for all. The adjustment of traffic must depend on the tunnel. After the construction of a movable bridge, the passage of vehicles and ships is subject to time constraints, while a tunnel can save time and is not limited by resistance from slopes."

According to some analysis, firstly, national security was taken into consideration. The tunnel could avoid the destruction from air attacks, and even in case of destruction, the waterway would not be blocked. Secondly, the construction of an elevated bridge necessitated too long of a bridge approach and bridge piers in great numbers would also hinder the water traffic. Also the geological situation of the Huangpu River may also cause the pier foundation to suffer from chronic subsidence. As for the movable bridge, due to the limited height, it is necessary to open the navigation at the middle section from time to time, which would inevitably affect the traffic volume.

As for the site selection of the cross-river project, after on-site investigation, the experts decided the specific location of the above-mentioned three cross-river sites, selected from the four sites of the Bund on Zhongzheng East Road (now Yanan East Road), Shiliupu, Dongjiadu, and Rihui Port. Finally, after preliminary discussions made by the Technical Advisory Subcommittee, "the following preliminary decision was made: to keep the Bund on Zhengzheng East Road (now Yan'an East Road) as the site for building the tunnel; and to choose Shiliupu as the site for building the movable bridge."

This option, according to the report by *Shenbao*, was made by taking a variety of factors into account. For example, it should not be too far from the urban area lest the road detours waste most passengers' time and expense; during construction and after completion, the obstacles to water traffic above must be minimal; and the outlet of the tunnel should not be affected by the reverse irrigation of river water at high tide.

According to the budget of the China Bridge Company, "About 76 billion is needed for building the tunnels and 42 billion for the bridge." Where can such a large sum of money come from?

It was suggested that the municipal government issue bonds. It was also proposed that Executive Yuan allocate funds to the construction from the national construction fund.

The industry and business sectors proposed to organize the Cross-river Transport Company to raise funds by issuing shares or bonds, and to levy passage fees and land appreciation fees after the project was completed. In addition, because of the land appreciation potential in the future in Pudong that cannot be underestimated, recouping the project investment would not be a problem.

On May 9 of the same year, Zhao Zukang announced, "Americans may invest in building an elevated bridge, and if so, we can request the United States to allocate part of the US$500 million loan to Shanghai, then we can start."

As early as on January 6, 1947, on *Shenbao*, a reporter wrote optimistically about the river-crossing project: "About the funding of the cross-river project, we are going to adopt the land appreciation." As soon as the cross-river project was completed, the price of the one-kilometer-long land along the two banks of the river would be increased. Therefore, "if the original landlords hand in the value-added, or the lands are bought by the state and the value-added would be resold, the value-added can be estimated 10 times, so that the cost of the project will be out of question. And once the cross-river project is decided, the Bank of China and other institutions may be willing to invest, so there would be no problem with the budget."

Unfortunately, none of these proposals and ideas could be realized, and the funding was absolutely problematic.

It resulted from the outbreak of the civil war between Kuomintang and Communist Party, which began in the second half of 1946. As soon as the guns were fired, tons of gold were needed. Chiang Kai-shek wished to spend all the money in the treasury for military purposes, but it was unrealistic and almost impossible to draw out such a large sum of money from the Nanjing government. Zhao Zukang's wish to "request to allocate part of the $500 million United States loan to Shanghai" was nothing but an illusion. Chiang Kai-shek was waiting for the money to fight the civil war. How could he allocate money to Shanghai for building bridge and tunnel?

The civil war led to the financial insufficiency for the national government, so they had to print more legal tender in an unreasonable amount. As a result, prices became out of control, and at last, currency had to be reformed. A golden coupon was issued, but it made the economic crisis even more severe. With the devaluation of currency, who was willing to invest in stocks and bonds? Not to mention the land appreciation. At that time, it was most important to hold on tight to the gold bars and silver coins in hand.

At the beginning of the establishment of the Cross-river Project Committee, it promised to pay the China Bridge Corporation 200 million yuan for designing and drilling, but the municipal government failed to keep the promise. As a result of repeated pressing by Mao Yisheng and others, they got 100 million yuan at last. At the end of 1946, with this 100 million legal tender, 1000 pieces of fine cloth could be bought, but in 1948, when Mao Yisheng got the money, only more than 10 pieces of fine cloth could be exchanged. It was hard to imagine the high speed at which prices were rising. When Shanghai people went to a restaurant to eat a bowl of noodles, the price when they left their home became different from that when they entered the restaurant, because prices had gone up. People even used the 100-yuan note as wallpaper, and even beggars did not want a bill of 1000 yuan or less.

In September 1948, the Fifth Meeting of the Cross-river Project Committee decided to abandon the tunnel scheme due to the shortage of funds and replace it with a new scheme for erecting a movable elevated floating bridge. The construction cost of the movable elevated floating bridge was lower, only a quarter of the tunnel, and there was no need to build piers, which could save time and cost, and the fixed clearance could be kept and the position could be moved at will.

However, even such a greatly simplified plan ended up on the paper. After the fifth meeting, the technical consultants never got together again. With the collapse of the Kuomintang government, the cross-river project, as well as that generation's dream of crossing the Huangpu River, ended up in soap bubbles, and all the drawings and memos of the meetings were kept in archives.

Many years later, Wu Guozhen, who settled in the United States, recalled with regret: "As for public projects, it is impossible to do more in this case. But at first I held great hopes and even tried to seek for foreign capital to build a tunnel across the Huangpu River ... Some British American companies were interested in this project, and the British companies had even come up with plans. By 1948, the political situation had deteriorated to such an extent that we could not proceed with it."

There is also an important reason for the failure of the cross-river project.

On August 17, 1947, Mao Yisheng made an address on radio. Mao presided over the construction of the first large modern bridge designed and built by the Chinese themselves — the Qiantang River Bridge. As an academician of three academies — the Chinese Academy of Sciences, American Academy of Engineering, and Academia Sinica, he devoted all his life to studying bridges, building bridges, and writing about bridges.

Mao Yisheng said there were three types of cross-river engineering — bridge in the air, floating bridge in the water, and tunnel underground. The cross-river project was the lifeline of Pudong, just as the Huangpu river was the lifeline of Shanghai. But the two lifelines should not clash with each other. The aim of the project was to run across the Huangpu river, but the large and small ships on the Huangpu River hustled day and night, so the tunnel plan must be the most ideal.

Mao Yisheng also talked about raising funds: "Project funds could be raised from two sources: passage fee and land appreciation fee." But he believed, "Pudong was not yet developed. The biggest problem was the domestic economic maladjustment. When would people come to Pudong for construction? If Pudong did not develop, can the cross-river transport be boosted?"

He was not optimistic about the practice of issuing government bonds for the cross-river project: "How about Shanghai people's confidence in the project? Can it be compared with other international cities? How many people would like to invest in such bonds rather than buy gold and dollars?"

Mao Yisheng, as an academician of the three academies, not only talked about engineering technology, but also pointed out an important reason why the cross-river project had not been realized for many years. "The cross-river project is part of 'Big Shanghai Urban Plan', which required that other related plans must be carried out to the same extent so that they could cooperate with each other. Otherwise, without the simultaneous development of Pudong, even if the cross-river project was completed one day, would it be a gain instead of a great loss?"

That is to say, one of the prerequisites for the construction of the bridge and tunnel on the Huangpu River is the development of Pudong.

In fact, after the Anti-Japanese War, Shanghai's economy rapidly declined, and the ferry business on the two banks of the Huangpu River gradually withered. Even after the victory of the Anti-Japanese War, the ferry on the two banks had not yet recovered.

3.4 Sighs from the East and West Banks of the Huangpu River

In September, 1953, Mu Xin, the Soviet Union urban planning expert, was invited to Shanghai to guide the compilation of *Schematic Diagram of Shanghai General Plan*. On this basis, in 1954, in *Brief Specification of Schematic Diagram of Shanghai City Planning* compiled by the Shanghai Municipal Construction Committee, it was pointed out that at Gongping Road and Longhua Road, a river-cross tunnel should be designed for connecting the urban inner-ring lines. This was the first time that the Shanghai Municipal People's Government formally proposed a cross-river project.

In 1956, the fourth session of the first Shanghai People's Congress formally proposed the construction of the Huangpu River river-crossing project. In August 1958, the Shanghai Planning and Designing Institute complied *Report on Planning Shanghai Cross-river Project*, which made an analytic demonstration of the eight alternative sites for the cross-river project: Ningguo Road, Jiangpu Road, Gongping Road, Yan'an Road, Fuxing Road, Dongjiadu, Jiangbian Road, and Jinji Road (now Wanping South Road). After the analysis and demonstration, it was suggested that before 1962, a two-lane tunnel should be built at Ningguo Road and Dongjiadu Road, with that at Ningguo Road as the first one.

In 1958, the State Council approved that the 10 counties of Jiangsu Province, Jiading, Nanhui, Chuansha, Songjiang and so on, were incorporated into Shanghai, so the area of the Shanghai urban district was expanded from 606.18 square kilometers to 6185 square kilometers. Therefore, in 1959, the Shanghai People's Commission invited the Planning Workgroup of the Construction Engineering Department to complete *The Preliminary Suggestions on Shanghai General Urban Plan*, which proposed the urban construction and development policy, that is, to "gradually transform the old urban areas, strictly control the development scale of the industrial area in the suburbs, and plan to build satellite cities". *The Preliminary Suggestions on Shanghai General Urban Plan* also pointed out that, according to the survey in 1958, there were no convenient facilities to cross the Huangpu River, resulting in 92% of Shanghai's urban residents and 95% of industry concentrated on the west bank of the Huangpu River, compared with only 8% of the residents and 5% of industry on the east bank of the Huangpu River. On the other hand, because in Pudong there were more and better deep-water shorelines, most of Shanghai's wharves, warehouses, and stockyards were concentrated in Pudong, which increased the freight transfer cost.

In order to open up Pudong and solve the problems of industrial and residential land shortage and cargo transfer in Shanghai, the Infrastructure Construction Committee of Shanghai Government organized the departments concerned with argumentation and demonstration. They believed that among the three types of projects like the large-scale ferry, bridge, and tunnel, the tunnel was the most appropriate. It had advantages such as non-hinderance to the Huangpu River shipping, short access, and convenient transportation, as well as safer national defense.

As for the location of the cross-river tunnel, *The Preliminary Suggestions on Shanghai General Urban Plan* proposed to build four tunnels to cross the Huangpu River, namely, Ningguo Road, Yan'an East Road, Dongjiadu Road, and Jinji Road.

In 1964, the plan of building cross-river tunnels was put on the agenda again. The Tunnel Division of the Municipal Construction Bureau, in *Periodic Report on Site Selection of the Shanghai Huangpu River Tunnel*, argued that the quantity of cargo transfer in the south of the Suzhou River is larger than that in the north of the Suzhou River, so the first tunnel should be built in the south of the Suzhou River. Among the seven alternative sites for building tunnel in the south of Suzhou River, including Jinji Road, South Wharf, Fuxing East Road, Jiangbian Road, Dongjiadu Road, Dapu Road, and Yan'an Road, since the riverbed of Dapu Road was shallow, more attractive for passenger transport, and the stacks on the two banks made it low in removal and favorable for construction, it could be used as the best site of the first test-stage of the cross-river tunnel in Shanghai.

In early 1965, Shanghai municipal leaders personally surveyed the seven alternative tunnel sites and decided to formally submit to the Central Government a report on the construction of a tunnel on Dapu Road. The project encoded "651" was carried out as a confidential work. After six years of construction, the Dapu Road Tunnel, the first cross-river project on the Huangpu River, was finally completed in June 1971. With a total length of 2736 meters and a height of 4.4 meters, the tunnel had a maximum two-way traffic capacity of 1000 motor vehicles per hour.

The Dapu Road Tunnel took the lead in ending the long-standing impassability between the two banks of the Huangpu River and fulfilled Shanghai people's hundred-year-old dream of turning a deep chasm into a thoroughfare, which is also a prelude to the development of Pudong.

However, in the 1960s, China's relation with the Soviet Union deteriorated, and the great tension on the border made war-preparation become a national strategy. Therefore, the construction of the cross-river tunnel stood more on national defense. Until the 1980s, as part of tunnel defense and war preparedness, the Dapu Road Tunnel was still only open to licensed vehicles, that is, normal vehicles must have a letter of introduction to access the tunnel, and vehicles with foreign license plates were not allowed to enter at all.

In 1978, a deputy to the National People's Congress proposed to build a second tunnel. In the following year, Shanghai decided to build a two-lane cross-river tunnel on Yanan Road. In November, 1980, it was approved by the State Planning Commission. After the news came out, it attracted wide attention. Some people put forward that drilling underground was no better than borrowing part of heaven, and Shanghai's *Wen Wei Po* also published a proposal that on Yan'an East Road an "Electric Vertical Lift Bridge" be built. After experts' argumentation, it was considered that the operation of the "Electric Vertical Lift Bridge" was intermittent, with low flow rate, easy to cause traffic jams, and the piers in the Huangpu River may influence the channel capacity. In addition, people had no experience in manufacturing large electric vertical lifts at home and abroad. So it was better to build a tunnel. In April 1982, the State Administration of Urban Construction sent specialists to Shanghai for investigation, who finally believed that the plan and documents of preliminary design on Yan'an East Road Tunnel approved by the State were correct. In September of the same year, the cross-river tunnel was finally started, completed, and opened to traffic in May 1989.

During this period, with the rapid increase in the population in Pudong, the problem of "difficulty in crossing the river" became more and more serious. The daily cross-river traffic mainly depended on ferry. Although the ferry lines continued to increase, it still could not meet people's needs of crossing the river. By the late 1980s, the transport capacity on Lujiazui ferry line alone was 200,000 passengers a day. In case of fog, the ferry service was suspended and there were 20 or 30 thousand passengers waiting at the dock. As a result, the city ferry company was greatly worried about the growing pressure on the ferry.

At last, at the end of 1987, the Lujiazui ferry tragedy took place.

On the early morning of December 10, 1987, due to the heavy fog, all ships on the Huangpu River were stopped, and tens of thousands of people were crowded at the Lujiazui ferry station of the Huangpu River anxiously waiting to cross the river in order to go to work. When the fog cleared and the ferry service resumed, a large number of people rushed onto the ships and it was out of order, and the crowd was mixed with all kinds of bicycles. When people squeezed with each other, it was hard to push their way through the crowd, and even harder for bicycles to go through. Suddenly, a middle-aged man, along with his bicycle, was crushed down by a heavy crowd, and then one after another were pushed down, and the fallen men struggled to get up, but the crowd was pushed forward by a great force, frantically stepping forward on those who had fallen down to the ground. At this time, the ferry gate in front was closed, but the people behind were still rushing forward. This is how the tragedy took place.

16 people were trampled to death, 30 were seriously injured, and nearly 100 were crushed. The tragedy of the Lujiazui ferry line shocked both China and foreign countries.

At that time, the Shanghai Municipal Government building was facing the Huangpu River, just opposite the Lujiazui Ferry Station where the tragedy occurred. The sad news was spread in the building with the humid and cold wind on the river. The coldness of winter in Shanghai was the special humid coldness in south China, the kind of chill to the bone, and the sad news was even more chilling to the heart.

"It was difficult to cross the river", and it was more difficult for the cross-river project, which became the pain in the hearts of people on both sides of the river. On the two banks of the river, sighs echoed east and west.

3.5 The Problems Faced by the New Mayor

Soon after the tragedy at the Lujiazui Ferry Station, at the beginning of the following year, a sudden wide-spreading epidemic disease took Shanghai into an emergency period.

As soon as the calendar of 1988 was opened, hepatitis, an epidemic, prevailed in Shanghai. At the beginning, about 100 people caught the disease per day, and then it increased to about 1,000 people a day. By the end of January, about 10,000 people became ill per day, and by February 1, the peak came with 19,000 people on that day. In the end, nearly 300,000 people were infected all over the city. According to the law of medicine, the number of people who carried the hepatitis virus, but did not go to the clinic, was four times more. This means 1.5 million people in Shanghai carried the hepatitis virus. At that time, Shanghai population reached 12 million.

Natural and man-made disasters put great pressure on Zhu Rongji, who just presided as mayor of Shanghai. From April to June 1988, 60-year-old Zhu Rongji spent most of his nights in his office. On television people seldom saw a smile on the thin face of Zhu Rongji.

Shanghai people who had gone through that time knew that the city was beset with difficulties. The common people had a saying that "Shanghai can never do well". And the intellectuals said that Shanghai Bund (pronounced as tan in Chinese) really fell into paralysis (pronounced as tan in Chinese).

At that time it was really not an easy job to be the mayor of Shanghai. Zhu Rongji was confronted with a string of embarrassing figures. After

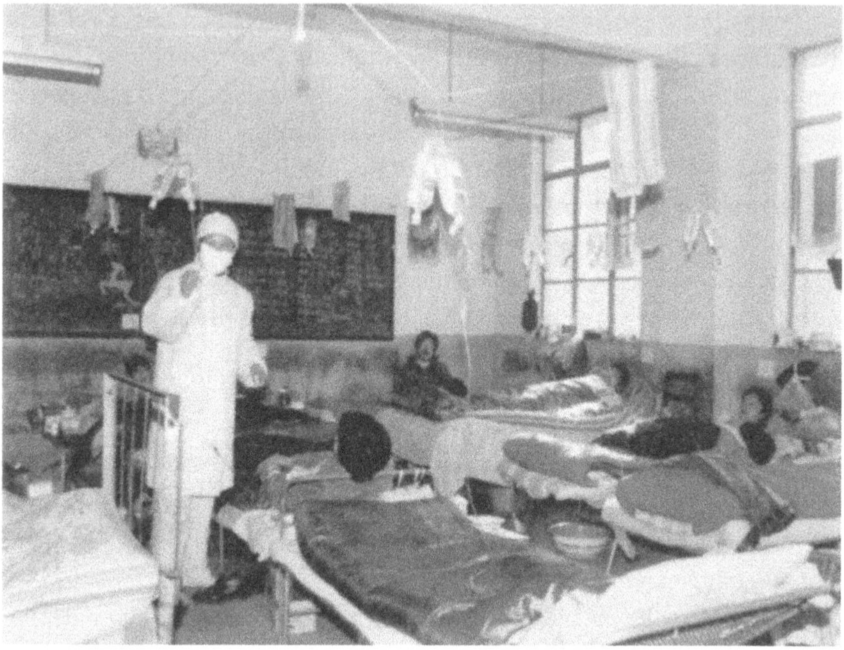

In 1988, the epidemic of hepatitis prevailed in Shanghai. Wards were not enough, so some school classrooms and factory warehouses were used as temporary wards for treating patients with hepatitis. (Recorded in *Reform and Innovation* (*1978–1992*))

the founding of New China, Shanghai, under planned economy, had an average annual price rise of only 1.3% in the 30 years from 1949 to 1979. In the late 1980s, after the implementation of the dual-track system, the prices of a large amount of raw materials rose, but the production, sales, and pricing of Shanghai products were still firmly controlled by the hands of the planned economy. With planned pricing, the profit of a cotton sweater was only two cents, so how can the enterprises survive?

That was the year when Chinese leaders tried to push through price reform. On May 29, 1988, when Deng Xiaoping met with foreign guests, he said that only by rationalizing prices could reform speed up. Price reform must be carried out, despite risks and difficulties.

Deng Xiaoping said, "In China, we have a story about Mr. Guan (named Guan Gong in Chinese) who won a glory in battle by 'passing five checkpoints by force and slaying six captains', and maybe we have to pass more 'checkpoints' and slay more 'captains' than Mr. Guan, so it is not easy but very risky to overcome the difficulties in the way."

On May 8, 1988, the People's Bank of China announced that it would issue RMB 100 yuan and 50 yuan notes.

Then, on August 17, at the Beidaihe Conference, the Central Committee of the Communist Party decided to liberalize the prices of the vast majority of commodities, changing long-term pain into short-term pain by forcing the implementation of price reform. At that time, prices soared, so the rush of purchase ran across the river north and south all over China. People bought whatever they saw: matches, soaps, towels, leather jackets, sheep blankets, washing machines, tape recorders, and even gold jewelry. In that year, prices rose by 18.5% compared with the previous year.

Shanghai was China's largest industrial and commercial city, well-known for its well-developed circulation and stable market supply, but at that time when the planning as a tool of control was about to break down, it became so abnormal that people felt destabilized and anxious.

Jiefang Daily, the official newspaper of the Communist Party Committee of Shanghai, published an article frankly stating that in Shanghai, the price of thousands of commodities had risen on the one hand, and the local revenue had declined for many years on the other hand.

More disappointing for Shanghai people, throughout the 20th century, the comprehensive economic strength of Shanghai had been taking the lead all over China, and especially in the 30 years since the founding of New China, Shanghai had always been the pillar of China's industry and finance, ranking as the eldest son of the economy of the Republic. However, in the 1980s, economic development of Shanghai began to get into trouble. For example, from 1978 to 1988, the proportion in the whole country declined year by year. The gross national product of Shanghai dropped from 7.9% to 4.7%, the national income from 8.2% to 4.9%, and the total industrial output value from 13% to 6%. The total export volume (port) fell from 29.7% to 9.7%, and the local fiscal revenue from 14.9% to 5.9%.

During this period, Shanghai was still dominated by planned economy and its industrial structure was dominated by state-owned enterprises. The wave of rural reform, which began in 1979 from Xiaogang village in Fengyang, Anhui Province and swept across China, did not directly benefit Shanghai. And as for urban reform, Shanghai was five years later than other cities in China. Reforms in the contracting, leasing, and employment systems had taken shape in Chongqing, Wuhan, Shenyang, and Guangdong, but Shanghai did not embark at all.

As written by foreign scholars in their analysis of overseas investment in China, in short, Shanghai was an area that Japanese companies wanted to evade, largely because it was "the most bureaucratic and frustrating city in China".

Experts in RAND Corporation, a prominent consulting think tank in the United States, said that China's economic centers had moved southward and Guangdong would replace Shanghai.

But as the "eldest son", the "obedient eldest son", Shanghai still remained "responsible for mainland economy", still supplying blood to the whole country. Before 1985, the Central Government's financing for Shanghai was basically "monopolized revenue and expenditure". In the words of Wang Daohan, a former Mayor of Shanghai, "For Shanghai it is the central finance." Shanghai's revenue from profits and taxes was turned over to the central government, and Shanghai should apply to the central government for expenditure. After all, Shanghai was an important source of revenue for the central government. From the founding of New China to the end of the 20th century, Shanghai turned over nearly 400 billion

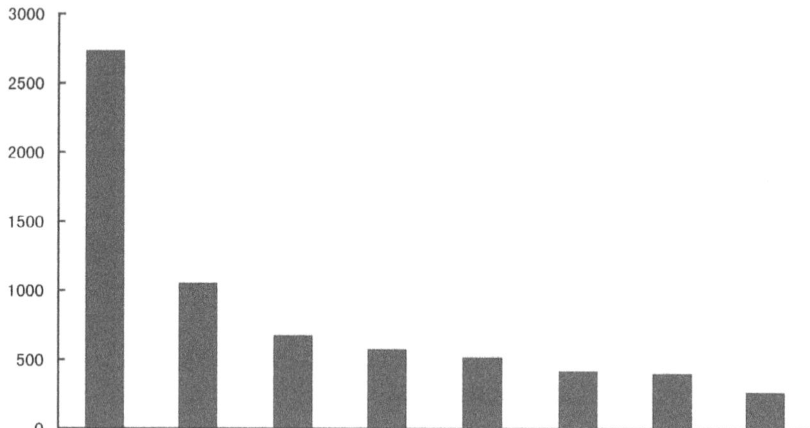

	上海	辽宁	江苏	天津	北京	山东	浙江	广东
53-92年	2732. 89	1049. 76	673. 31	577. 36	518. 71	418. 96	403. 75	270. 22

单位：亿元

After the founding of New China, the top eight regions to turn over to the Central Treasury were Shanghai, Liaoning, Jiangsu, Tianjin, Beijing, Shandong, Zhejiang, and Guangdong

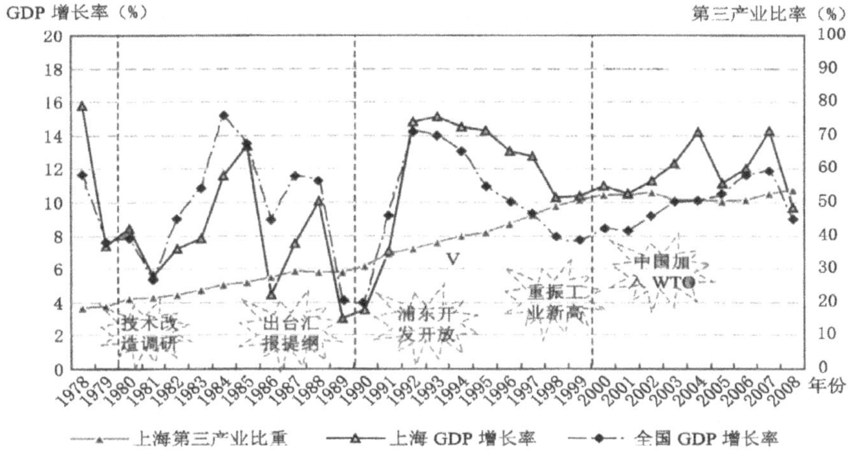

In the late 1980s, Shanghai's economy fell into a low ebb (Recorded in *Shanghai Evolution and Prospects*)

yuan in total, accounting for one-sixth of the country's total revenue. At this time, the land area of Shanghai was only 1/1500 of the country, and the population was only one-hundredth.

Shanghai was once called the stronghold of China's planned economy. By the late 1980s, China had a dual-track system of planning and free market, and the game between planning and free market was constantly played, which caused many strange phenomena. For a period of time, the "path dependence" resulting from the long-term planning system forced Shanghai to endure even greater difficulties.

Zhu Rongji came to Shanghai from the State Economic Commission. When he took office, he found that he had no money or anything in his hands. At this time, Shanghai had become an industry-based single-function city. In 1952, the tertiary industry in Shanghai accounted for 50% of the total industrial output value. By 1978, the proportion had dropped to 18.6%.

Shanghai had no mineral resources, and the raw materials needed for production were allocated by the state's unified planned transfer, but after the dual-track system, Shanghai had to trade Santana, color television, and refrigerators for raw materials with other provinces and cities, and even for pork. At city hall meetings, pork stocks had to be notified.

Yao Xitang, an Economist and Vice President of the Shanghai Academy of Social Sciences, recalled that Mayor Wang Daohan often called a meeting of ministries and commissions, talking about the same topic every time: "What about the insufficiency of raw materials this year?"

Yao Xitang explained the reason. In Shanghai there were technologies, talents, tradition, and experience, but no raw materials. In the past, the state was relied on to safeguard Shanghai. In 1978, with the reform and open policy, the economy of the southern cities represented by Guangdong grew rapidly, the coastal areas of Jiangsu and Zhejiang also burst into strong vitality, and the economy of various regions developed quickly. When a larger amount of raw materials was needed in these places, Shanghai was clearly in even shorter supply of raw materials.

It is not an overstatement to call Zhu Rongji an economic expert. He also served as Dean of School of Economics and Management of Tsinghua University when he was appointed Assistant Director of the State Economy Commission. The title of Zhu Rongji, Doctoral Supervisor at Tsinghua University, was not a fake one. He supervised four PhD students in technological economics. But the poor economic situation in Shanghai also gave him, the Doctoral Supervisor in Tsinghua University, a challenge.

3.6 The Outbreak of "Urban Disease" in Shanghai

On October 3, 1980, *Jiefang Daily* published an article on the front-page headlines, "What do Ten Firsts and Five Lasts Mean? — Discussion on Shanghai's Development Direction". The author was Shen Junpo, a Researcher at the Institute of Sector Economics, Shanghai Academy of Social Sciences. The article took up half the page, and a long editorial note was also added in the newspaper.

Shen Junpo is an Economist. He began that article with at least 10 "firsts" of Shanghai in regard to the national economy:

> First, the total industrial output value accounted for one eighth of the country, with the output value ranking first among the provinces and cities all over the country.
>
> Second, the total value of exports accounted for more than a quarter of the country, of which the local products accounted for 60%, with the capability of earning foreign exchange ranking first in the country.

Third, fiscal revenue accounted for one-sixth of the country's total income, and the taxes turned over to the state finance accounted for one-third of the central financial expenditure, with the amount turned over to the state ranking first in the country.

Fourth, the labor productivity of all industrial workers was 30013 yuan in 1979, more than 1.5 times higher than the average of other provinces and cities, ranking first in the country.

Fifth, as to the profits realized per 100 yuan of fixed assets in industry, in 1979, the city averaged 63.73 yuan, four times higher than the national average, ranking first in the country.

Sixth, the turnover rate of industrial funds was 69.5 days, with the speed of turnover ranking first in the big cities of the country.

Seventh, according to the average population, the annual gross national product (GNP) per person was US $1,590 in 1979, with the level of production ranking first in the country.

Eighth, in 1979, the effective utilization rate of energy was 33%, higher than the national average of 28%, ranking first in the country.

Ninth, the amount of commodities allocated by the commercial departments of Shanghai accounted for 45% of the total amount of daily industrial products allocated by the whole country, ranking first in the country.

Tenth, as to the transfer of technical forces, since liberation, in Shanghai more than 300 factories moved to inland, and through various other ways, more than one million technicians and skilled workers have been supplied, ranking first in the country.

The article also enumerates Shanghai's five "lasts" in the country:

First, the urban area was an average of 41,000 people per square kilometer, with the urban population density ranking "top" in the country.

Second, the density of buildings was as high as 56%. According to the average population, each person had only 1.57 square meters of roads and only 0.47 square meters of green area (that is, as large as a *Jiefang Daily*), with the density of buildings, crowdedness of workshops, narrowness of roads, and limited green land ranking "top" in the country.

Third, according to the average population of Shanghai, the living floor space of each person was only 4.3 square meters (including shanties, simple houses, and attics). More than 918,000 households suffered from house shortage, less than 4 square meters (including 69,000 households in hardship, married households, extremely poor households, and houseless households who transferred to Shanghai), which accounted for about 60% of the total number of households in the whole city, with the proportion of households suffering from shortage of houses ranking "top" among the big cities in the whole country.

Fourth, the average death toll per vehicle in Shanghai is 42.5 per year, and the vehicle accidents were the "most" among the major cities in the country.

Fifth, due to the serious pollution of three wastes, the incidence rate of cancer in Shanghai was the "highest" of the cities in China.

The article challenged how to explain the coexistence of Shanghai's 10 "firsts" countrywide and 5 "lasts" countrywide. This showed that while Shanghai was making significant progress and important contributions, there were many contradictions, mainly because the comprehensive balance was broken, with quite obvious imbalance in proportion.

When this article came out, it reverberated strongly. The article poked the pain in Shanghai. The newspaper received more than 300 contributions and *Jiefang Daily* was out of stock that day.

Many reasons resulted in the abnormal development of this kind of city, such as the unrestricted city development and all-around disorderly city sprawling. Over time, the layout of the city was seriously unreasonable and the operation of the city was seriously uneconomical. Shanghai in the 1980s can be taken as a classic example of this performance.

Wang Daohan, who served as Mayor of Shanghai from 1981 to 1985, said with regret, "During my time as Mayor of Shanghai, I acted worthily of the 'court' (referring to the central government). Every year, what Shanghai turned over to the state finance accounted for one-sixth of the total state financial revenue, but I'm unworthy of the common people (referring to the people of Shanghai). Every morning I see so many coal-fired stoves on the road, smoke everywhere, and many toilets were brushed on the road. I really feel heartache that Shanghai government really does not have extra funds to improve and develop the life of the city citizens."

His successor, Jiang Zemin, the Mayor of Shanghai since 1985, also wrote, "When we see the overcrowded crowd in the train carriages at the station, when we see children having class in the rough and even dangerous classrooms, when it is difficult for tens of thousands of young children to enroll in the kindergartens, which make young parents quite worried, when we learn that some pregnant women have miscarried due to squeezing themselves into the crowded bus to go to work, and 20,000 workers in the city spend more than four hours on their commute to work, and when we see a heavy rain flooding the homes of 110,000 residents, we feel deeply disturbed."

Hu Wei, a former Head of the Pudong New Area, recalled, "At the beginning of the 1980s, I was the Director of the Real Estate Bureau of Huangpu District. At that time, the living environment of Shanghai people was very poor. At that time, the welfare-oriented public housing distribution system was adopted, so only the households in hardships could enjoy welfare housing and the requirements was as little as 2 square meters per person. I visited a household of three generations of seven people, who lived in an 11-square-meter space. How did they live in such a narrow space? In the house there was a bunk bed, in which four people slept on the bed, one slept on the floor, one on the table, and another slept on a board on a box." If you want to use toilet, others have to go out to make room for you. And if you want to have a summer bath, others have to go out to evade, which makes Shanghai's alleys always so boisterous.

Because of the guilt and deep unease, since the early 1980s, Wang Daohan began to plan the opening up of a new Shanghai district in order to solve Shanghai's difficulties in urban development. This kind of guilt and uneasiness was deeply buried in the hearts of many leading cadres in Shanghai and would become a strong motivation for developing and opening up Pudong in the future.

To put it in an analogy, a dysfunctional Shanghai looked like a giant "standing on the ground" and was actually an "unhealthy" patient. Shanghai caught a kind of urban disease, quite out of breath.

The work that residents did when they got up every early morning: setting fire to coal stoves (Published in *Lens of Old Pudong*)

There were several metaphors in the press circles at that time.

First, the city of Shanghai looked like a "big pancake" with onions in it. Decades of urban construction with pancake-like sprawling resulted in the disorderly clustering of dwellings, factories, businesses, schools, and others. "Conducting a religious rite in the snail shell" became the most vivid saying about Shanghai people's housing at that time. The narrow space also squeezed the vision and heart of Shanghai people. "Haggling over every ounce" became an adjective used by outsiders to laugh at Shanghai people.

Second, the city of Shanghai looked like a workshop of a "big family". Energy and raw materials from all over the country were transported to Shanghai for all-night processing and production. While large quantities of industrial products were being shipped to all parts of the country, waste

The stinkpots commonly seen on roadsides (Published in *Lens of Old Pudong*)

water, gas, and residue remained in Shanghai. A former international metropolis had become a large workshop, which was both a workshop and a residential place, and the living environment of citizens was deteriorating day by day. When Zhu Rongji became the Mayor of Shanghai in 1988, he lamented, "Now every day we receive more than 100 letters from the people, all of which are about overflowing excrement, piled-up rubbish, heavy traffic, and housing shortage. Such a state is stretched almost to the breaking point."

Third, Shanghai city functioned like an "old man" with heart and lung failure. Disorderly expansion and unrestricted use of infrastructure made Shanghai's transport and electricity infrastructure like a man with heart and lung failure. Shanghai, like an old cow, was constantly whipped to go forward, so its productive capacity was irretrievably extracted, let alone the environmental preservation.

Shanghai was once a city with concessions, and the western powers operated only for themselves in each of the concessions. For example, the pipeline operation, telephone interface, and others varied from concession to concession, which, later on, caused great difficulties for people to carry out maintenance and renovation of the old city. It was even more expensive than building a new area. This is also an important reason for the backwardness of Shanghai's urban reconstruction.

In the late 1980s, Shanghai suffered from serious "urban disease", with crowded roads, serious air pollution, the lowest greening space per capita in the country, 800,000 coal-fired stoves, and 800,000 stinkpots. Shao Yudong, the former propaganda Minister in the Pudong New Area, recalled that later Shanghai leaders made it a pledge to eliminate the city's

In Pudong, along the river, the modern economy developed, but the urbanization process was still slow

800,000 stinkpots, 800,000 coal-fired stoves, and solve the difficulties in housing by the year 2000.

In 1970s, with the thaw in Sino-United States relations, our country door opened slightly, and a small number of foreign friendly people were able to enter Shanghai, which had once been an international metropolis.

In 1972, then United States President Richard Nixon visited China and American writer Reston accompanied him to Shanghai, where he had been living for many years. Except for the magnificent architecture of the semi-colonial era, the municipal construction of Shanghai left no impression in his mind.

In 1974, Lowndes, a French sociologist, visited Shanghai. He wrote a note on the results of his investigation. He wrote that he saw a small cottage set up by a stagnant river, the roof draped with skewed woolen felt, on which dozens of bottles and cans pressed against it. The glass of the window was all broken, showing the shape of sharp teeth. In as little as 10 square meters of space, a household of 5 people lived. From time to time the smell of rotten vegetables rippled around the cottage. That scene reminded him of Mumbai, Calcutta, New Mexico City...

After the end of the Cultural Revolution, overseas Chinese who returned to visit their relatives and friends could find their old homes from decades ago almost unchanged in most parts of Shanghai. What changed was that there was more rust and rotten wood than ever before. Shanghai was called a "rusty city" by American President Ford at that time. Even more, the Italian film artist Antonioni, who was China to collect folk songs, called it "the living fossils of western architectural art before World War II".

Shanghai is like a black-and-white photograph, stagnant in the 1950s, so lifeless.

The past events were found unbearable to recall. For Shanghai people who did not experience that era and even those foreigners who just arrived in Shanghai in that age, it was difficult to understand why China's largest industrial and commercial city, which used to be named "Paris in the East", fell into such a poor state.

Because of this difficulty, later in Shanghai there was the strong impulse to develop Pudong — to build a "new Shanghai" and to ease the pressure of "old Shanghai".

3.7 Historical Causes for the Huge Gap Between the Two Places

How about the urban construction in Pudong at that time? The older generation in Pudong knew that Dongchang Road was one of the most prosperous commercial streets in the Pudong area, nicknamed Nanjing Road in Pudong. What formed a T-shaped intersection with it was named Lannidu Road (which means muddy road). Lannidu Road was about four or five meters wide and whenever it rained, the water spread all over the muddy road.

Since the 1950s and 1960s, the world cities developed from "mother-child cities" to "sister-sister cities". However, Puxi of Shanghai was still adopting the development mode of "spreading large pancakes", which finally led to the concentrated outbreak of "urban disease" in 1988.

Many cities in the world are run through by a river, such as New York, London, Paris and Budapest, and these cities have achieved common prosperity on both sides.

For example, the Hungarian capital Budapest, known as the "Pearl of the Danube", was once a sister city across the Danube — Buda and Pest, which were formally merged in 1873. Buda, located on the west bank of the Danube River, became a city in the first century A.D., and became the capital in 1361, where Hungary's imperial dynasties founded their capital. It was built on a hill. The villas were dotted on the hillside, and scientific research institutions, hospitals, and recuperation centers were built and clustered there. Pest was founded in the beginning of the third century, located on the east bank of the Danube River. It was a flat terrain, where the administrative agencies, industrial and commercial enterprises, and cultural institutions were concentrated. Budapest had been badly damaged in the two world wars, and all the bridges on the Danube were rebuilt after the wars. Since the 1970s, Budapest began planning and building in accordance to its new layout, with residential and industrial areas separated and government agencies moved to the suburbs, so that its urban industrial distribution was more balanced, and the city became more prosperous and orderly than in the past.

The calm Danube River meanders from northwest to southeast across the city center. Eight distinctive iron bridges and a subway tunnel link the sister cities tightly into a thriving one.

But why was the gap between Pudong and Puxi so great in Shanghai, the famous oriental city?

In fact, before the port-opening of Shanghai, there had been little difference between the east and the west. After the port-opening, modern economy started very early in Pudong, such as the earliest shipping and shipbuilding industry which was almost in line with Pudong. From the 1920s to 1930s, the shipping, shipbuilding, tobacco, and textile industries along the river in Pudong developed vigorously, and there were also railways and highways. From the 1950s to 1960s, modern economy developed further, especially after the state invested in building a number of key enterprises mainly in the heavy chemical industry. Furthermore, Chuansha County, the large agricultural county in Pudong, once ranked among the top 10 of the top 100 counties with comprehensive strength in China.

But with the passage of time, Puxi's urbanization proceeded rapidly. In the late 1940s, Shanghai became the world's fifth largest city. The gap between Pudong and Puxi widened, with 92% of Shanghai's urban residents and 95% of industry concentrated on the west bank of the Huangpu River, compared with only 8% of residents and 5% of industry on the east bank of the Huangpu River, according to a survey in 1958.

On the surface, it resulted from the separation by a great river and the lack of convenient facilities for crossing the river. But the root cause did not lie in the Huangpu River. Wang Daohan, the wise Mayor of Shanghai, said several times that in each of the big cities all over the world, there was a famous river running through it.

But only in view of the cross-river construction of the Huangpu River, the reasons for the non-synchronous prosperity of Pudong and Puxi can be found out.

First of all, the concessions caused a huge difference between the east and the west. In spite of the interest of western businessmen in Pudong along the river after the port opening, the wish of the concession authorities to expand across the river did not succeed, so the concession authorities were not interested in the development and construction of Pudong. The British and American Concession and French Concession were located in the main parts of Puxi along the river, while the east bank was under the jurisdiction of the Chinese government. On the two sides, the sovereignty was different, with different governmental authorities. So to build a cross-river facility, either a bridge or a tunnel, the interests of both parties must be involved.

In the 1940s, when the concessions were withdrawn, and after the victory of the Anti-Japanese War, the Republic of China did not think about developing Pudong on a large scale. Pudong was only used as an agricultural area to supply subsidiary agricultural products to the urban area and as a residential area to solve the problem of congestion in the urban area. At most, the river-side advantage could be taken to develop water transport and the related industries along the river. In the late 1940s, the government of the Republic of China did want to start a cross-river project, but it had no money, due to the huge cost in dealing with the war.

During this period, quite a lot of people really saw the huge difference of land price caused by the separation between Pudong and Puxi, and some investors thought that as long as there was the traffic for crossing the river, it would attract investments and land price would rise and, as a result, the profits earned would be used for the development and construction of Pudong. Therefore, civil society called on people to raise funds for construction, but in the long-term turbulent society, all of this was only an armchair strategy.

After 1949, China introduced a planned economy, in which all investments were planned by the state, and land was owned by the state under the Constitution, allocated for free use according to construction needs, and even land owned by rural collectives was not allowed to be bought and sold. Therefore, there was no land market, not to mention the land price gap between Pudong and Puxi. Because a cross-river facility was expensive and dependent on just government investment, Shanghai, in spite of being a relatively wealthy region, was still unable to afford it.

When conceiving the facility for crossing the river, both the government of the Republic of China in the 1940s and the people's government after the 1950s took into account the factor of war, which Sun Yat-sen had not thought about when he sketched the Big Oriental Port. On November 7, 1946, at the second meeting of the Shanghai Municipal Urban Planning Commission, someone said that an atomic bomb could destroy it completely. Zhao Zengyu, Director of the Shanghai Public Utilities Bureau, answered angrily, "If the destructive power of the atomic bomb is always taken into account, the planning would be totally meaningless."

However, the war-awareness did influence municipal construction all the time. Especially after 1960s, when the national strategy of preparing for war and famine was implemented, until the early 1970s, Shanghai did not have a cross-river tunnel. The tunnel was used only for national defense, and only licensed vehicles for war-preparation were allowed to pass, rather than for the development and construction of Pudong.

It is with great regret that before the development of Pudong in 1990, only the area along the river in Pudong was urbanized, where the ports, factories, and the commercial and living districts were crowded together. Shanghai as a whole did not achieve the common prosperity on the two banks like New York, London, Paris, and other cities. This situation did not change until the opening-up of Pudong in the 1990s.

Chapter 4

The Mission to Assume: A Trump Card to the World Played by the Chief Designer

4.1 Where Shanghai will Advance

Since China carried out its reform and opening-up in 1978, the southern region rose rapidly, especially Shenzhen and five other special economic zones in the lead. With the economic and social development at a tremendous speed, new ideas and new thinking constantly impacted the people of Shanghai.

The Shanghai people's sense of loss was stronger than ever as the fiery southern wind violently blew the water of the Huangpu River. The Shanghai people were thinking hard: What was the crux of Shanghai? What was the way out for Shanghai? If the economy of Shanghai would continue to develop greatly, the functions of Shanghai as a big city be fully exerted, and Shanghai would again become the hub and center of China's exchanges with the world, then how to overcome the current poor situation? After all, six decades ago, Shanghai had been the most prosperous city in the Far East.

It was in the process of thinking about these urgent issues that a consensus was taking shape among the Shanghai people. Shanghai must take a big move and open a new space for development in order to reshape the image of the Far East Metropolis.

It happened that people turned their eyes to the piece of land to the east of the Huangpu River.

Sha Lin, the former Deputy Director of the Development Office in Pudong New Area, recalled, "I remember that at that time, our old leader, Comrade Chen Guodong, asked clearly at a meeting whether Shanghai was going to sink. This is a very alarming warning and a cry. It is also a reflection. In particular, where is the new development space in Shanghai? What is the new growth point in Shanghai? By the mid-1980s, the trend of reform and opening-up throughout the country had reached an irresistibly high degree, and in such a background, the research on Pudong development was pushed further, advancing from the shallower to the deeper."

On March 13, 1980, Wei Ming, Assistant Director of the Municipal Planning Commission, came to Shanghai Political Consultative Congress (SPCC) to present the *Report on the Perspective Long-term Planning of Shanghai* to the SPCC members. The SPCC members listened and discussed the report very carefully, and on March 20 and April 4, an expanded session was held by the Economic Research Committee of the SPCC to discuss the long-term planning of Shanghai's economic development.

At the seminar, most members advocated for the construction and development of Pudong. Pudong was the virgin land, with the city center across the river, easy for development according to the requirements of modern cities. In order to develop foreign trade, Shanghai needed to build port facilities, so it was the most favorable and reasonable choice to develop Pudong. In view of the general premise of municipal construction along the river in Pudong and the conditions for development, it could also be built into a special economic zone, which would be attractive to foreign businessmen. Tunnels and bridges could be built between Pudong and Puxi. The urban district could be properly expanded to solve the overcrowding problem. Satellite cities and towns should be built into an independent social unit, not a single industry. Overall considerations should be taken into, such as evacuating population, supporting policies, adjusting industrial structure, and so on.

What the commission members recommended was based on the consensus that the population in urban centers should be evacuated and the old urban district should be reformed. Later, many suggestions made by them were incorporated into *The Outline of the Urban Overall Plan of Shanghai*. However, at that time, the understanding of Pudong development was still limited to the solution of Shanghai's urban plight and the development space.

From 1981 to 1982, the whole city of Shanghai set off a discussion upsurge of "where to go and what kind of Shanghai to build".

During a visit to Shanghai in August 1983, Hu Yaobang, the General Secretary of the Communist Party of China (CPC) Central Committee, proposed that Shanghai should give full play to its role as a port and a central city, play its function as an economic, scientific, technological, and cultural base, and serve as a pioneer in the development of the Four Modernizations of the country.

In August 1984, after listening to the report of Shanghai, the Central Finance and Economics Leading Group decided that the State Planning Commission should take the lead to propose a strategic plan for transforming and revitalizing Shanghai after conducting investigation and research together with Shanghai. In September, the State Council Reform and Revitalization Research Group conducted a half-month investigation and research, under the leadership of Song Ping, State Councilor and Director of the State Planning committee; Ma Hong; and other leaders appointed by the Central Government. They listened to the reports made by 19 committees, offices, and bureaus of the Shanghai Municipal Government and carried out a survey on 6 topics.

On this basis, Shanghai Mayor Wang Daohan immediately organized a group of experts and scholars, together with the State Council Research Group, to invite experts and scholars from the Central Government and all over the country, and held a conference with nearly 100 participants in Hengshan Hotel entitled "Seminar on Strategic Campaign for Economic Development in Shanghai". This high-profile seminar, known as the "Hengshan Conference", made a far-reaching impact on the future development of Shanghai.

According to the recollection of Zhu Jinhai, who worked in the Department of Economics Research Institute of the Shanghai Academy of Social Sciences, and who was in charge of recording the conference, despite its high standard and numerous attendees, did not pay much attention to the display of splendor and form. "There were not even seat cards, and attendees were not arranged in the order of seniority. They just took a seat and began to listen." The meeting lasted for two or three days and at a discussion, Ma Hong said, "Comrade Song Ping, would you please give a talk?" At this time, the young Zhu Jinhai found that it was Song Ping who happened to be sitting next to him and had been listening quietly for a few days.

In December, the Shanghai People's Government submitted *The Outline Report on Shanghai's Economic Development Strategy* to the State Council.

In the history of Shanghai's urban development, this is a very remarkable report. Although it was still a rough one, it was indeed the first operational outline of Shanghai after New China, focusing on the strategy of Shanghai's economic modernization. It was on this basis that the successively appointed leaders of Shanghai promoted the modernization of Shanghai.

According to the outline, Shanghai should be a pioneer in the development of the Four Modernizations in the country, giving full play to its role of opening to the outside world as a multi-functional central city, and striving to become an open, multi-functional, highly civilized socialist modern city with reasonable industrial structure and advanced science and technology by the end of the 20th century.

On February 8, 1985, the State Council approved and forwarded the report. *The Notice of the State Council's Approving and Forwarding of the Outline Report on Shanghai's Economic Development Strategy* clearly pointed out, "Under the new historical conditions, Shanghai's development should take the path of transformation and rejuvenation, and give full play to the multi-functional role of a central city, so as to make Shanghai become the pioneer in the construction of the Four Modernizations of China. By the end of this century, Shanghai would strive to be an open, multi-functional, and highly civilized socialist modern city with reasonable industrial structure and advanced science and technology."

The outline report referred to the development of Pudong and pointed out, "It is necessary to create conditions for the development of Pudong and plan the construction of the new urban area. In the future, new industrial enterprises will be put in the new area, and some of the old enterprises in the old urban area will gradually move to the new area to carry out technological transformation." It also proposed that during the "Seventh Five-year Plan" and "Eighth Five-year Plan", Shanghai should plan and carry out a number of large-scale backbone projects, including the cross-river tunnels and bridges connecting both sides of the Huangpu River.

Obviously, the main purpose of Pudong development at that time was to implement the policy of combining the gradual transformation of the old urban area with the active construction of the new urban area and, in fact, it aimed to solve the problem of transferring industry in the city center to the outside.

4.2 The First Voice from Folks

It can be said that since 1984, Pudong development was formally put on the table of local governments for discussion, and its research was incorporated into the conception of the Shanghai development strategy, and the call for developing Pudong became increasingly louder.

The first voice from folks is worth writing about.

In February 1980, Chen Kunlong's proposal on the construction of a new urban area in Pudong was published in the Shanghai Construction Committee's briefing of *Capital Construction Situation*. In October of the same year, Shanghai Academy of Social Sciences' *Social Sciences* monthly magazine published Chen Kunlong's article, "Development towards the Vast Area of Pudong". Chen put forward the new point of view of "building Pudong area into a new town in Shanghai".

Chen Kunlong, an engineer in the Shanghai Municipal Planning Bureau, wrote, "What is the way out to fundamentally change the 'messy, crowded, and dirty' situation in Shanghai? In my opinion, it is ideal to extend the development to the vast area of Pudong. It has many favorable conditions. Pudong has a good location, that is, the current urban area across the river, east to the East China Sea, the Huangpu River in the back. In addition, there is more land, fewer factories, and lighter pollution. It is adjacent to Baosteel Industrial Zone in the north and Jinshan, Minhang, and Wujing in the south. There is Sancha Port at the Wusong estuary, Bailong Port in the east, and Luchao Port in the south. The transportation of both the inland river and the ocean is very convenient."

In view of the urban disease of Shanghai's pie-style development, Chen Kunlong proposed a similar development pattern of many foreign cities. According to the plan, Pudong New Area would be Shanghai's political and cultural center, and its architectural form and layout should be different from that of the old one. Now the urban area and satellite towns were gradually expanded as a result of bulk-type radiating to the four sides. The new town adopted the form of a "belt-type" city, with living areas of the urban area located on both sides of a highway, which gradually developed to the outside on both sides.

In order to write this article, Chen Kunlong took his son on a bicycle to explore the vast area of Pudong. To verify the data and make a complete argument, he cycled across the river again and again, making deep and on-the-spot investigation.

In the same year, Yi Xin, a member of the Shanghai Society of Urban Economics, published an article entitled "Building a New City Center along the River in Pudong: Making Full Use of the Land of 6,100 Square Kilometers" in the sixth issue of *Social Sciences*. Yi Xin thought, Pudong area has very good construction condition, such as facing the current urban center across the river, vast land, fewer factories, sparse population, and lighter pollution. For construction, it is still a virgin land, with big development space. As the beach rises along the coast area, the land in Pudong can be increased by adding mud to the enclosed beach. The modern urban political city center, which would be completely built 20 years later, would look east at the harbor center near the sea, west across the Huangpu River at the commercial and business center, south at Jinshan petrochemical and textile center, and north at Baoshan Iron and Steel Center.

These two articles, one after the other, aroused reactions and were echoed all around.

In 1981, at the Fifth Plenary Session of the China People's Political Consultative Conference (CPPCC), Yin Tiyang, a CPPCC member, a city construction expert, and a professor at Tongji University, submitted "A Proposal on Establishing an Organization for the Construction and Planning of Pudong Development". Lu Zifen and Yu Yingsheng, CPPCC members, put forward a proposal entitled "Preparing Actively for Establishing Pudong New Area and Making it a New Model of International Cities". In addition, Li Lixia, Jiang Qingxiang, and others, members of the CPPCC, submitted the proposal entitled "Developing Shanghai Economy by Introducing Foreign Capital to Build Pudong".

Lu Zifen and Yu Yingsheng were both professors of the Shanghai Maritime Institute located in Pudong, so they knew very clearly about the status of Pudong. In that proposal, the two CPPCC members wrote as what follows:

> In the past few years, the municipal government built a large number of houses and relocated large numbers of residents in Pudong in order to reduce the urban residential density and traffic congestion. But due to the absence of scientific planning, the residential layout was not reasonable, the roads were not networked, and the water and land terminals were not properly expanded. There was no definite plan to repair the existing Pudong Avenue, so the traffic was often blocked. At commuting time, on Pudong Avenue and Pudong South Road, there was a very heavy burden of traffic, and the ferry piers were overcrowded.
>
> In addition, although the commercial network was equipped, the quantity was insufficient and the varieties of commodity were few, with a great shortage of medium- and high-grade goods. Pudong Central Hospital was mainly relied on for medical and healthcare. Because of the relatively dense population, the out-patient department was the most crowded of the district, so that patients often failed to get chance for proper treatment.
>
> As to vehicles, except for buses, there were only five aging tricycles that were about to be scrapped, which was very inconvenient for passengers with luggage. There were fewer entertainment places and restaurants, and a far poorer supply at vegetable markets than that in the west of Shanghai. In addition, in the vicinity of Chuansha County, there were road damages, which the city and county shirked from the repair.

The three proposals included the excavation of tunnels, the construction of bridges, the expansion of water and land terminals, the building of trunk roads, the opening of commercial outlets, and increasing the number of cultural, education, and sanitary facilities. As to the introduction of foreign capital, the principle of investment proposed was to operate mainly by foreign capital without damaging China's sovereignty, and can also operate jointly if necessary and, at the same time, it was proposed that the operation term be stipulated and payoff be done upon expiration. As to the planning and institution of Pudong New Area, it was proposed to make an overall plan in Pudong area, with setting up Pudong New Area as the first step and merging parts of the suburb as the second step to uniformly use and manage the land in Pudong area with the users paying the land use fee or land premium, and establishing the Pudong Development Corporation. Among them, Lu Zifen and Yu Yingsheng put forward 12 very specific proposals on the construction of Yan'an Road Tunnel, the construction of a bridge, and so on.

In 1983, "Research on Shanghai Economic Development Strategy" led by Chen Minzhi, Deputy Director of the Institute of Sector Economics of Shanghai Academy of Social Sciences, was listed in the key programs of the "Sixth Five-Year Plan" of National Philosophy and Social Sciences. This program proposed that Shanghai should be put on the agenda of the urban development strategy, and should occupy an important position. The concrete tentative plan was that "it should be considered to build Pudong into a political center in Shanghai, supported as a cultural center, an education center, a science and technology center, and an information center".

This bold and far-sighted plan transcended the traditional view of Pudong as a supplementary extension of the urban area in the past, which was an important change in thinking about Shanghai's urban development.

In the 1980s, scholars and experts wrote a large number of research articles on Pudong development.

During this period, scholars of governmental policy research departments, institutions of higher education, scientific research institutions, and democratic parties published a large number of articles, such as "Building a New City Center along the River in Pudong" (March 1981), "Excavating Pudong Canal: Comprehensive Solution to the Problems about Urban Reconstruction in Shanghai" (February 1982), "Some Views on Developing Pudong" (June 1983), "Discussion on the Direction of Shanghai Urban Development" (November 1983), "Where is the Manhattan District in Shanghai?" (October 1984), "A New Shanghai Expected to Take Shape in Pudong" (June 1985), "In Shanghai a Special Foreign Exchange-earning Economic Zone Supposed to be Built in Waigaiqiao" (October 1985), "Comprehensive Development of Pudong: Construction of Shanghai New Town" (March 1986), "Speeding up the Pace of Developing Pudong with the Convenience for the Masses as the Key" (September 1986), and so on.

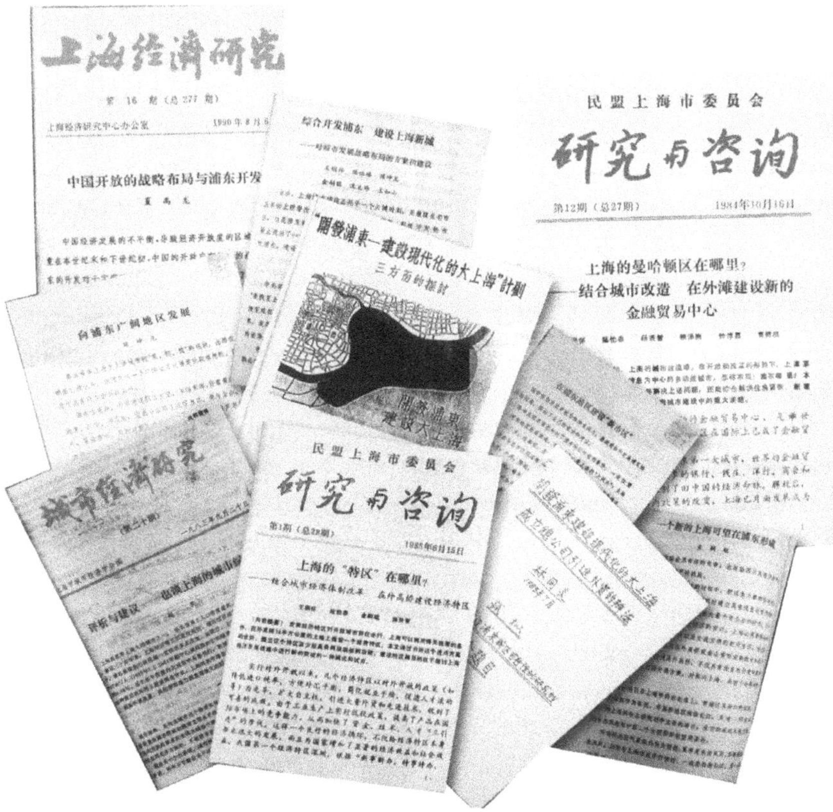

In the 1980s, scholars and experts wrote a large number of research articles on Pudong development

Even Shanghai Free Trade Zone, which was established more than 20 years later, can also be traced back to relevant research in that year. In June 1985, Wang Ganghuai, member of the Jiu San Society, wrote an article entitled "Where is the Shanghai Special Zone: Building a Special Economic Zone in Waigaoqiao in combination with Shanghai Reform". And in September 1986, at the First Seminar of the National Open Cities Research Society, Yu Pinhao of Shanghai Economic Research Center submitted his paper "Exploration of Establishing a Free Port Zone in Shanghai".

The former proposed to build a special economic zone in Waigaoqiao of Pudong to play the role of "two springboards", namely, from the interior to the coast, from home to abroad, from abroad to home, from the coast to the interior. The latter was bolder to propose to build a free port zone in Shanghai, whose function should not be single, but comprehensive. The free port zone should be a tariff-free warehouse zone, export processing zone, free trade zone, and science park.

These articles were published one after another and in the first five years of the 1980s, which led to the emergence of the public call for establishing a new development zone in Pudong, which aroused the attention of all sectors of society.

The proposals and explorations on developing Pudong New Area made by the experts and scholars were attached great importance by the Central Government and the relevant government departments in Shanghai. In the last five years of the 1980s, the government's attitude towards Pudong development became more and more definite.

It was during this period that in April 1984, the Central Government decided to further open up the 14 coastal port cities. Shanghai was also on the list. The news was a great surprise to the scholars who had been looking for a way out for Shanghai. How would Shanghai be further opened?

4.3 The Formation of Four Alternatives

In the spring of 1986, with the support of the municipal government, 10 organizations, such as the Shanghai Municipal Economic Association, Shanghai Economic Research Center, and so on, jointly sponsored "The Seminar on Shanghai Urban Development Strategy". The participants expressed their own views freely and fully, with heated debates and a warm atmosphere.

At the meeting, a consensus was reached, that is, in view of the serious swelling disease in the old urban area of Shanghai, in order to revitalize Shanghai, it was imperative to go beyond the convention and find new ways to relieve the population of the old urban area and create conditions for the transformation of the old urban area. After the meeting, Shanghai Economic Research Center first entrusted the Shanghai Municipal

Committee of the Jiu San Society to carry out "The Pre-feasibility Study of Shanghai New Urban District Construction".

After that, different research departments put forward four options for the development of Shanghai, namely, "westward expansion", "northward expansion", "southward expansion", and "eastward expansion".

The "westward expansion" referred to the expansion to the west of the central city, to the west of Hongqiao Airport, and the gradual expansion of the urbanized area. But this idea, like "spreading large pancake", was quickly rejected because more human, material, and financial resources were to be invested in the reconstruction of the old area than in the construction of a new area. And there were few successful examples in the history of the transformation of the old cities in the world, so it was rejected first.

The "northward expansion" referred to the development of Baoshan and Wusong areas in the north along the south flank of the Yangtze River with Jiangwan Airport as the center and was to be linked with Baosteel in construction. Obviously, the idea of "northward expansion" used the "Big Shanghai Plan" in the early 1930s for reference.

The "southward expansion" referred to the development of Wujing, Minhang, Jinshan and so on, which were adjacent to Jiangsu and Zhejiang provinces, all the way to Hangzhou Bay. Yu Guangyuan, a famous Economist, despite his old age and frailty, took part in the discussion. He proposed the "southward expansion" plan, that is, the development of Jinshan, located to the south of Shanghai and 70 kilometers from the city center. Moreover, the environment of Jinshan was very good. Although Shanghai Petrochemical moved to Jinshan after the mid-1970s, the environment of Jinshan was not much polluted since all the equipment used were imported. It can be said that the "southward expansion" was the mostly accepted plan at that time.

"Eastward expansion" was the development of Pudong across the Huangpu River. But the biggest difficulty in eastward advance was how to cross the Huangpu River. Yang Di, former Vice Mayor of Shanghai and director of the Municipal Capital Construction Committee, recalled, "At that time, it was very difficult for us to carry out such a cross-river project in terms of technical equipment, level, and conditions. Therefore, more people tended to prefer northward and southward development, focusing

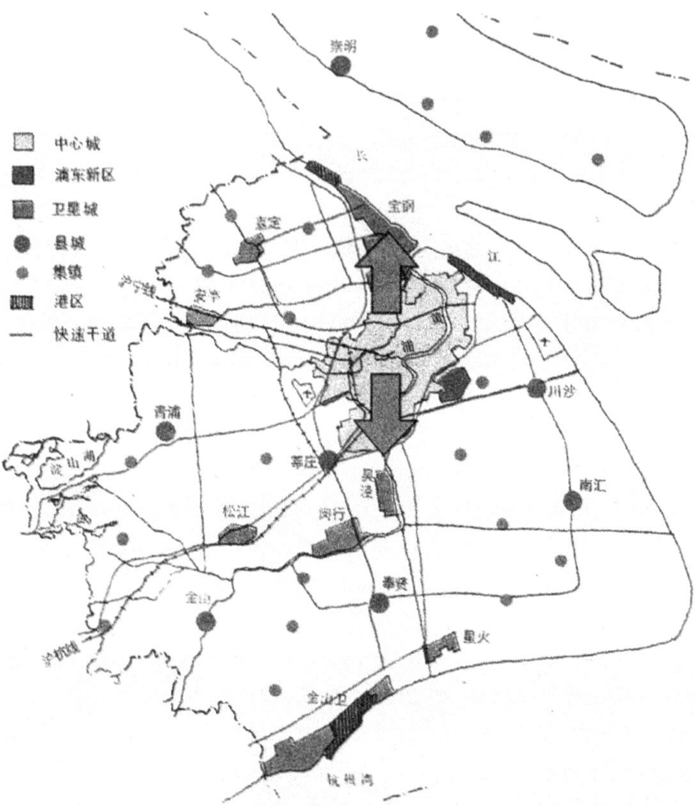

The "southward expansion" and "northward expansion" plans

on the construction of a central urban area, and then gradually on the development of the two wings."

The foreign experts sent by the United Nations to cooperate with Shanghai to carry out the research of Shanghai Urban Development Program disapproved of Pudong development, since Pudong was at the end of the continent, facing the Pacific Ocean. They proposed to expand the city along the Shanghai-Nanjing railway and the Shanghai-Hangzhou railway.

For a time, the idea of eastward advance into Pudong and northward and southward development became the mainstream.

That, too, was reflected in official documents. In 1984, the municipal government and the Research Group of the State Council jointly submitted to

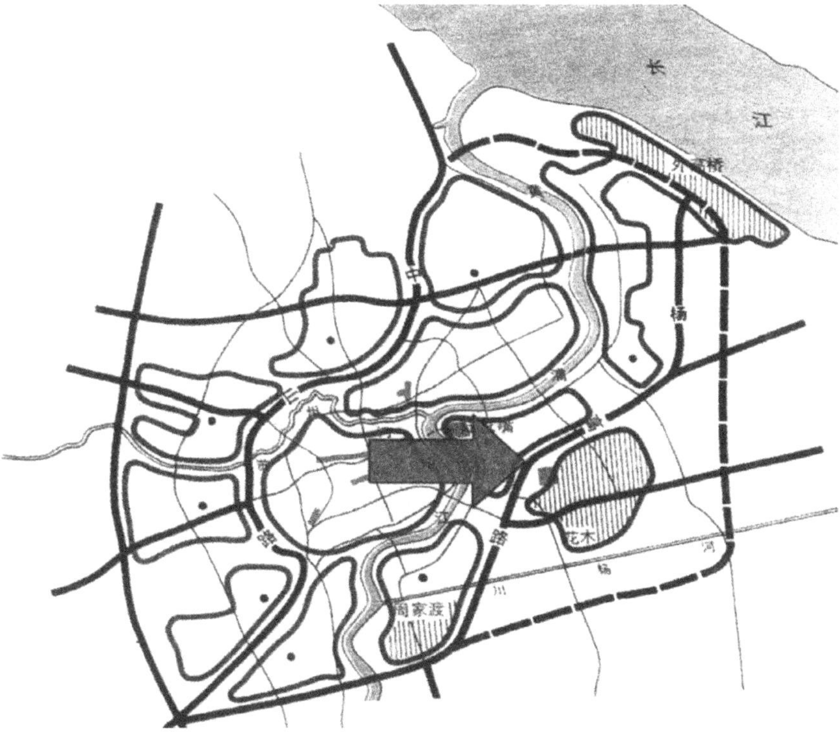

The "eastward expansion": Pudong development across the Huangpu River

the State Council *The Outline of the Strategic Report on Economic Development of Shanghai*, which specified that the urban and industrial layout of Shanghai should "focus on the north and south flanks of Hangzhou Bay and the southern bank of the Yangtze estuary. Conditions should be created for the development of Pudong to plan for the construction of the new urban area."

On October 13, 1986, the official reply of "Shanghai Urban Master Plan" by the State Council pointed out, "It is necessary to focus on the development of the north and south wings of Jinshanwei and Wusong and accelerate the construction of some new areas. At present, special attention should be paid to the planning of the construction and transformation of Pudong area. We should build bridges and tunnels along the Huangpu River as soon as possible, and develop finance, trade, science and technology, culture, education, and commercial service facilities in Pudong, build new residential areas, and make Pudong area a modern new district."

After repeated discussion and argumentation, at last, the "eastward expansion" scheme gained everyone's approval.

According to Li Jianeng's recollection, "Economist Yu Guangyuan was more inclined to Jinshan Development. He was not necessarily wrong, because Jinshan was far from Shanghai and had the conditions for being built into a relatively unique big city. However, if we wish to solve the insufficiency of the functions of the tertiary industry such as Shanghai finances by merely adopting the 'southward expansion' plan, Jinshan plan seemed not enough. Pudong, precisely with the Huangpu River as the boundary, was the most suitable. 'Eastward expansion' was also in line with the law of the development of the international metropolis, that is, the development along the two banks of river, from upstream to downstream, from the river estuary to seaport. Shanghai has actually verified this. You see, across the Huangpu River and then to Luchao Port, this is the development law of Shanghai's international metropolis. In particular, Lujiazui can solve the original insufficiency of some functions in finance, trade, and other economic aspects on the Bund."

Jin Oubu, the fifth Vice President of the Chinese Association of Architecture and the first president of the East China Architecture Design Institute, insisted on "eastward expansion". In May 1984, at the seminar of urban planning in Shanghai, Jin Oubu put forward, "Pudong development is the most economical and convenient shortcut to relieve the overstaffing of Shanghai central city." He suggested to revise the original plan of developing Shanghai to the two wings like spreading pancake and discussed about the 10 benefits of developing Pudong.

In his opinion, "Shanghai urban area extended to the west, the south, and the north, and is now overspreading. The greater the spreading, the more contradictions there would be. So this is not the best policy. Some people suggested to develop Pudong, but failed to achieve this because they felt powerless and frustrated before the seemingly insurmountable Huangpu River. In fact, the Huangpu River was only 350 to 500 meters wide. It was not difficult to build a bridge, open a tunnel, or even a subway with modern technology... It would take at least two or three years and cost two or three hundred million yuan to build bridges and tunnels on the Huangpu River to reach Pudong."

It was just then that Jin Oubu returned from Istanbul and Hong Kong, and he had witnessed the undersea tunnel built in Hong Kong that drove the development of Kowloon, and the bridge built over the strait in Istanbul connecting Europe and Asia. Before he returned to Shanghai, he thought when people in another country had crossed the straits, Shanghai could not even cross the golden waterway of the Huangpu River, and it was a pity to make only half a large pancake.

He also went to meet Chen Guodong, the then Party Secretary, and Wang Daohan, the Mayor, to elaborate on the necessity to develop Pudong.

As a result of these proposals, Jin Oubu was later regarded as one of the proposers of Pudong development.

In this decision, the old Mayor, Wang Daohan, played a big part. He said, "The principle is to revitalize a city by depending on the ports, so the development of Shanghai as the big city of the national economic center must rely on the ports. With the ports of Shanghai located in the east, to develop Shanghai, it is imperative to develop Pudong." He added, "All the famous big cities in the world developed across the river. So did Shanghai. The earliest development area was the south to the Suzhou River, then across the Suzhou River to the north to the Suzhou River. For further development today, we must cross the Huangpu River and develop eastward."

At the same time with the heated discussion, under the leadership and organization of the Shanghai Government, the Shanghai Urban Planning and Design Institute worked out and completed *Shanghai Overall Planning*. On October 13, 1986, the good news came that the State Council formally approved the plan, which was the first urban master plan approved by the state in the history of Shanghai's urban development.

This plan offered a more specific concept for Pudong development. "Construction and transformation of Pudong area should be planned. Certain areas will be allocated for the development of financial, technological, cultural and educational, information and commercial service facilities. A new financial and trade center will be formed near Lujiazui as a continuation of the center of Shanghai. Therefore, it is necessary to construct Huangpu River Bridge and tunnel as soon as possible to solve the problem of cross-river traffic. In Pudong area, it is also planned to have Waigaoqiao port area as a standby site, a rear service base for offshore oil drilling in the South Yellow Sea and the East China Sea, and the second international airport, which will form a new modern transportation hub... The Pudong area has the advantage of being close to the river, and will become a beautiful and modern socialist new area in Shanghai, attractive and beautiful, by means of reform and opening to the outside world through careful planning."

The Central Government approved of the plan made by Shanghai and in the *Official Reply* clearly pointed out, "At present, special effort should be made to plan the construction and transformation of Pudong area well."

This is the first time that the Central Government mentioned the construction of Pudong in an official document. As Hu Wei, former leader of Pudong New Area, said, "This is a great leap in the thinking of planning Pudong." Before 1986, Pudong was one of the industrial and residential evacuation areas in Shanghai. In order to alleviate the growing expansion of Shanghai, Pudong accommodated the factories and residents who had moved out from the old downtown of Puxi.

As for Pudong development, since the founding of the People's Republic of China, the urban planning department of the Shanghai Government had made three plans in 1953, 1959, and 1983. The strategic status planned at that time was to move the center of Shanghai to the east, build the central urban area of Shanghai on both banks of the Huangpu River, and then on this basis expand further to Pudong, so as to evacuate the industry and population in Shanghai, gradually relieve the pressure of the old urban area of Puxi, then transform the old urban area and build a large Shanghai across the Huangpu River.

This strategic orientation was only the extension of the old industrial area and residential area of Puxi. After *Shanghai Overall Planning* in 1986, it was changed to developing Shanghai's function as the economic center and pivot. The strategic orientation of Pudong development changed from a single-function industrial base to a metropolis with many functions such as industry, commerce, finance, and service.

After that, as to the "eastward expansion", consensus was gradually reached from all walks of life. The departments concerned begun to carry out more specific studies and argumentation about its feasibility.

In February 1987, the research report of the Shanghai Municipal Committee of the Jiu San Society, entitled "Pre-feasibility Study of Shanghai New Urban District Construction: Construction Strategy of

Pudong New Area", was passed after experts' evaluation. The report, with Wang Ganghuai in charge, who was a member of the Jiu San Society, made a detailed design and elaboration about the guiding ideology, planning ideas, overall layout, recent arrangements, funds and policies, legislation, and system concerning developing Pudong New Area.

In addition to the Shanghai Municipal Committee of the Jiu San Society, the Shanghai Economic Research Center, Municipal Planning Commission and Municipal Science and Technology Commission, Tongji University, Shanghai Urban Planning, and Design Institute also submitted two significant research reports entitled "Comprehensive Report on the Development Pattern of Modern Pudong Area" and "Outline of the Economic, Scientific, Social, and Cultural Development in Pudong New Area".

Scholars also gradually reached a consensus that Pudong development was no longer a coordinated plan subordinate to the urban transformation of Puxi, but a core content of the strategic conception for the reconstruction of Big Shanghai, namely, the coordination of Pudong development and the transformation of Puxi, with Pudong development to drive the transformation of Puxi and making full use of the solid foundation of Puxi to support Pudong development.

In this research process, the old Mayor Wang Daohan played a great role as a hands-on leader.

According to the recollection of Li Kaiya, former Deputy Secretary-General of Shanghai Government, "In the early 1980s, he (referring to Wang Daohan) took the lead in proposing the strategic goal of developing Pudong. Although few people responded to his suggestion and even though there was some resistance, he still persisted with deep research and discussions with a lot of experts and scholars, such as the Chinese American Lin Tongyan, and put forward a series of forward-looking suggestions on the strategic target, construction policy, function orientation, and planning concerning the development and opening of Pudong... These recommendations were mostly adopted later on. Therefore, later, as Mayor Zhu Rongji said, 'Comrade Daohan was the major activist in putting forward the plan of developing Pudong.'"

On February 11, 1987, a program review was held in an auditorium of the Shanghai Municipal Committee of the Jiu San Society on No. 186,

Shanxi North Road, and Wang Daohan attended the whole meeting. He said, "I have always been interested in developing Pudong in Shanghai. It has a bright future. The experience of Singapore, Hong Kong, and so on (Asia's Four Little Dragons) in this field is worth studying. The development of Pudong New Area should depend on the old urban district, and the development of the new urban areas will drive the construction of the old urban areas. To develop Pudong, we must have a guiding ideology, a national concept, and an enterprising spirit, so that developing Pudong makes great sense."

Many years later, Wang Ganghuai, who was in charge of the program "Pudong New Area Construction Strategy", recalled, "The participants and insiders at that time all highly praised the grand old mayor, who took pains to attend the program review undertaken by the democratic party. It was quite rarely seen."

From September to October of the same year, the coupled issue of *Urban Economic Research* published these reports. Wang Daohan wrote with pleasure, "We should develop Pudong and build a modern new urban area, so as to promote the transformation of the old urban area and promote the economic revitalization of Shanghai. It is the common wish of many people of insight in Shanghai to make Shanghai become one of the largest economic and trade centers on the west coast of the Pacific as early as possible. Over the years, they have written a lot of articles on how to develop Pudong and put forward many good suggestions. In particular, under the organization of the Economic Research Center and Municipal Science and Technology Commission, several commissions such as the Planning Commission and the Economic Commission, and many researchers and staff members of the Jiu San Society, Academy of Social Sciences, Urban Planning and Design Institute, Tongji University, and so on carried out some research and put forward many insightful views, which provided the basis for the further study of the pre-feasibility report of Pudong development."

Wang Ganghuai believed that by February 1987, Pudong development had gradually transitioned from a "semi-official" state to an "all-official" state and the "folk" researches had gradually completed the mission.

However, from the historical point of view, before the launch of Pudong development, its theoretical research had already taken a step ahead and laid a solid foundation, which was also one of the important reasons for the future development of Pudong at a high starting point, high level, and great speed. This is a phenomenon never seen in other special zones. But this phenomenon that both the folk and the government focused on the economic and social development of an area and took the initiative to carry on a large body of research no longer emerged after the early stage of Pudong development.

At that time, however, it was mostly on the medium and micro level that Pudong development focused only on the construction of Shanghai itself and the development of a new urban area in step with reducing the pressure of the old urban area. The development of Shanghai was not evaluated from the perspective of national strategy, and from the structure of the world.

But soon, the focus on Pudong's development began to shift.

4.4 The Construction of a "New Shanghai"

The official attention to the development of Pudong also reached an unprecedented level.

First, as early as July 1986, Lin Tongyan, the Chinese-American architect, wrote a 10,000-word article to Jiang Zemin, the then Mayor of Shanghai, proposing the development of Pudong, and suggesting to take a foothold in Pudong and have the whole world in horizon. Jiang Zemin attached great importance to this and asked the old Mayor of Shanghai, Wang Daohan, to promote it with all his strength.

In July 1987, the Shanghai Municipal Government established a joint-development and research team for Pudong. Vice Mayor Ni Tianzeng was appointed head of the Chinese team, Lin Tongyan the leader of the foreign team leader, and Wang Daohan the general consultant. By this time, Wang Daohan had withdrawn from the frontline and served as Director of the Shanghai Economic Planning Office of the State Council. The group consisted of experts in the fields of planning, design, law, finance, land, and so on.

According to the four aspects of strategic research, policy research, legal regulation research, and fund-raising research, the Chinese team of the research advisory group divided the research into 15 programs, and conducted research for about one year. The completed documents included "Pre-feasibility Study Report for Pudong Development (Outline)", "Report on Several Major Issues about Pudong Development", and so on. The foreign team, represented by Lin Tongyan and Chen Naidong, completed the research on "Pudong Development: Construction of Modern Shanghai".

According to Zhou Hanmin's recollection, the former Deputy Head of Pudong New Area, who was a member of the Joint Advisory Research Group for Pudong Development, became a member of the group with his expertise in international economic law and all the members were in the group on a part-time basis. On the ground floor of the building of the Shanghai Government at No. 12, Zhongshan East First Road, a row of iron sheds was put up, one of which was loaned to us as our office."

70-year-old Wang Daohan worked day and night. In his own words, "Before I leave the world, I must work out a good way for the economic development of Shanghai, solve more practical difficulties for the people of Shanghai, so that with my dedication I will not feel guilty when I see Marx in heaven later on."

The second research was focused on the planning of Pudong New Area. In August 1987, the Municipal Planning Bureau compiled and completed "The Outline of Pudong New Area Planning (draft)" and the corresponding preliminary plan.

This outline defined the three key issues in Pudong New Area. First, Pudong New Area was the extension of the central city, and one of the ways to relieve the pressure of the central city. Second, with the development focused on the tertiary industry, some sectors of the area should be specified mainly for the development of finance, trade, science and technology, culture, education, and commercial service facilities. Third, the potential functional role of Pudong should be explored. In developing the tertiary industry, some industrial zones could be arranged and the Waigaoqiao port area might be appropriately developed.

It can be seen that at that time, the consensus reached by the official and the folk was still on the development of Pudong as the solution to the difficulties in Shanghai's urban transformation.

At this point, however, Beijing's high-level leadership was seeking greater openness. As Zhou Hanmin recalled, "The year of 1987 was a very critical year. The Party Central Committee resolutely began to advance an important work, that is, China proposed to restore the seats in The World General Agreement on Tariffs and Trade."

The General Agreement on Tariffs and Trade (GATT) is the predecessor of the World Trade Organization (WTO). Undoubtedly, Beijing's top leaders were also seeking to promote China's greater openness and deeper reform by entering the world trade family.

By April 24, 1988, when Zhu Rongji delivered a speech as a candidate for mayor at the Meeting of the Ninth National People's Congress of Shanghai, he formally referred to the phrase "Pudong development".

In his speech, he first introduced his curriculum vitae, political achievements, and policy agenda. He told the participants that he was an orphan whose parents had died early, and that in the 1950s he had been labeled right-wing, expelled from the Communist Party, sent to the countryside for rural labor, farming, herding cattle, raising pigs, cooking, and so on. He said, "My creed is to think independently. Whatever I think about, I should speak out accordingly."

Zhu said frankly, "In the three months after arriving in Shanghai, my white hair grew more than ever." But he said with confidence, "If I were elected as mayor, I am determined to make the next municipal government an efficient and clean government to serve the people wholeheartedly."

He said loudly, "The current difficulties in Shanghai have not yet reached the bottom of the valley, so we should have a sense of crisis, from which the spirit of stamina and diligence should be stimulated. An oppressed army fighting with desperate courage is sure to win."

As for overcoming the plight of Shanghai, Zhu Rongji mentioned "Pudong development". He said, "At present, our hope is to develop Pudong. Above the Huangpu River, a few more bridges can be built to move the factories and people to Pudong, so that the old urban areas can be easily transformed. This matter is of great importance. Pudong is the hope of Shanghai in the future. In Pudong, a 'new Shanghai' will be constructed to relieve the burden of the 'old Shanghai'. Therefore, Comrade Jiang Zemin, who attaches great importance to the development of Pudong, recently presided over the discussion on this issue. This construction is a grand plan, so it cannot be realized in the short term. But we should always work in a down-to-earth manner, hoping for the good times to come after bitter experience."

In fact, in the earlier time, Shanghai leaders had turned their attention to Pudong, aiming to develop Pudong to revitalize Shanghai. Therefore, Zhu Rongji solemnly told the delegates at the People's Congress that Pudong was the hope of Shanghai's future and that a "new Shanghai" would be built there.

Zhu Rongji's frank and confident speech touched the delegates like a fire that ignited the confidence of the delegates present at the meeting in revitalizing Shanghai, and there were bursts of applause.

Seeing it was time to end his speech, Zhu Rongji turned around and asked, "Host, can you give me some more time?" Before the host answered, applauses resounded in the meeting hall, and some people were so excited that they had tears in their eyes, because Shanghai, in its urgent plight, needed such a loud outcry.

According to counting of a careful journalist, a total of more than 30 rounds of applause sounded at the venue. No doubt, the delegates had put their hopes of revitalizing Shanghai on this new mayor.

Zhu Rongji's frank and open-minded language style was rarely seen in the officialdom, but was highly praised by the common people. In the afternoon, Wu Bangguo, Executive Chairman of the General Assembly, announced the results of the election, and Zhu Rongji was officially elected as the seventh Mayor of Shanghai.

That night, Shanghai residents saw on television the new mayor's face, thin but with a bit of sternness. In Shanghai dialect, the pronunciation of "Rongji" in the name of Zhu Rongji is the same as the pronunciation of "rooster". At that time, the Shanghai people placed their sincere hope on the new mayor and hoped that the new mayor would "sing aloud and the world would hear the rooster".

On May 1, 1988, a sunny day, the International Symposium on the Development of Pudong New Area was held in Xijiao Hotel, located at No. 1921, Hongqiao Road, Shanghai. The meeting lasted for three days. More than 140 Chinese and foreign experts from the World Bank, Asian Development Bank, Hong Kong, China, the United States, Brazil, Canada, Singapore, and other places attended the meeting, which was a milestone in the history of Pudong development. For the first time, it spread the message of developing Pudong to the whole world.

Prior to that, the 13th Congress of the CPC had been held. The meeting called for greater opening-up to the outside world in both breadth and depth, especially in coastal open cities. People should endeavor to develop the export-oriented economy and accelerate the development of foreign economic and technological exchanges and cooperation.

Jiang Zemin, the then Party Secretary of Shanghai, and Zhu Rongji, the Mayor of Shanghai, delivered ebullient speeches at the meeting. Jiang Zemin put forward the policy of building a modern new area in accordance with the transformation of the old urban area, and stressed the need to recreate "the function as the economic center and the function as the internal and external hub". When Jiang Zemin pointed out that Shanghai had "weakened in its function as the economic center external and internal hubs" in the past 30 years, he shouted, "Of course, this situation cannot continue any longer."

At the meeting, Jiang Zemin made a speech:

> As a world-famous city, Shanghai has become the largest international trade center and financial center in Asia since the 1930s. However, despite the economic prosperity on the surface, there are still many contradictions that are hard to overcome. In the more than 30 years since liberation, we have attached great importance to economic development, especially industrial development. Due to various historical reasons, we failed to carry out the corresponding urban transformation and construction in time, which thus weakened its function as the economic trade center and the external and internal hub. Of course, this situation is not allowed to continue. We have adopted a variety of ways to transform the old urban area, but the cost is huge and there are many difficulties, so we put forward the policy of the combination of transforming the old urban area by building a large new modern urban area. In my opinion, it is necessary to think about and study problems in this way. Obviously, it is necessary for Shanghai to accelerate the development of an export-oriented economy so as to build the largest economic and trade center on the west bank of the Pacific Ocean in the socialist era. Without the development of Pudong, we cannot achieve the goal by merely transforming the old urban area.

In fact, the idea of developing Pudong had been in Jiang Zemin's mind for a long time. According to *He Changed China: Biography of*

Jiang Zemin written by the American writer Kuhn, in 1985, Jiang Zemin made every effort to promote the development of Pudong after he became mayor of Shanghai: "The biggest plan of the new mayor is to lay the foundation for the development of Pudong New Area in the future. This is an important attempt for regional development that will affect the whole country."

In the early 1980s, Jiang Zemin served as Assistant Director and General Secretary of the China Import and Export Commission and the Foreign Investment Management Committee, and was in charge of the implementation of special policies, flexible measures, and pilot running of special economic zones in Guangdong and Fujian. According to Qin Wenjun, former Secretary of the Shenzhen Municipal Party Committee, Jiang Zemin visited the Shenzhen Special Economic Zone so often that he could not remember clearly how many visits he had made. In the first few years when the Shenzhen Special Economic Zone started up, Jiang Zemin poured in a lot of effort. Gu Mu, Head of the State Council, and himself visited the newly-established Shenzhen Special Economic Zone, and in windy and rainy weather, their boots were filled with mud and sewage.

On the morning of August 26, 1980, at the meeting of the Standing Committee of National People's Congress, Jiang Zemin also made a statement on behalf of the State Council on the establishment of the Special Economic Zone and the formulation of *Regulations on the Special Economic Zone*, which was finally passed. Therefore, Kuhn believed that Jiang Zemin's ambitious plan had much to do with his previous experience of establishing the special economic zone.

By this time, in May 1988, Pudong development had become an opportunity to unite the forces from all walks of life in Shanghai.

At this time, Shanghai's two main leaders reached a consensus: without the development of Pudong, it would be hard to achieve the goal by only relying on the old urban transformation.

4.5 The Design by Chinese-American Architects

Another man, Lin Tongyan, who was hailed as the first person to propose Pudong development overseas, should also be dwelt on. He also made a speech at the International Symposium on the Development of Pudong New Area held on May 1, 1988.

The Chinese-American architect Lin Tongyan was identified as one of the greatest structural engineers of his time. He founded the theory of "pre-stressed concrete" and created a new milestone in the world of architecture engineering, enjoying the reputation of "Mr. Pre-stressed Concrete". As a master of bridge construction, the bridges and buildings he designed are found all over the world. He told the journalist of Associated Press, "If millions of dollars are spent on building powerful bombs and other weapons, they will fall behind in less than a decade, and you have to abandon and even destroy them. Let's build bridges, because they are eternal."

The eldest brother of Lin Tongyan is Lin Tongji, a famous Professor at Fudan University, and an expert in Shakespeare research. At his brother's call, in 1979, Lin Tongyan returned to China for the first time. He strolled on the Shanghai Bund, and the flood of the Huangpu River sparked his desire to build a bridge over the river. In 1946, the National Government had a plan to bridge the Huangpu River, and Lin Tongyan, as an expert, also participated in the bridge-building argumentation, but at last it came to nothing.

He knew clearly that Shanghai, located at the mouth of the Yangtze River, was a commercial, financial, and industrial center in China. If there were a bridge, it could connect Pudong and Puxi more closely. More important, Pudong, with a lot of usable land, can solve the problem of the densely populated Puxi.

When Lin Tongyan returned to the United States, he got off the plane and drove to the company to call a meeting of his men. The first sentence he said was, "A mission comes from motherland." Then he put forward the idea of designing the Huangpu River Bridge. Soon he drew up "A Plan for the Huangpu River Bridge" in no time, which was sent to the Shanghai Government in 1980.

Different from other designers, Lin Tongyan paid more attention to the development of Pudong in designing the construction of the bridge. In October 1985, in San Francisco, he recommended himself to Wang Daohan, the recently retired Mayor of Shanghai, and proposed to develop Pudong. Lin Tongyan said, "I am willing to help the motherland to make great contributions to the benefit of its people." He put it in detail,

"Shanghai can first open up a piece of land in Pudong to build bridges and roads. After the land price rises, it can be leased or sold out. In this way, the state can build a modern Pudong without spending a penny and the size of Shanghai can also be multiplied." Lin Tongyan also presided over the "Lin Tongyan China Company" which designed and argued for land lease of Pudong and promised to help to raise funds.

Wang Daohan was very interested in this and said gratefully to Lin Tongyan that the country would not forget him. In 1986, Lin Tongyan put forward the report entitled "Developing Pudong: Building Modern Big Shanghai", which aroused the high attention of the Shanghai Municipal Party Committee and Municipal Government.

As Lin Tongyan wrote in the introduction to the report "Developing Pudong: Building the Modern Big Shanghai":

> Shanghai is the cradle of industrial and commercial talents, as well as the hub of railway, highway, riverway, and port, and is actually the center of industrial and commercial cultural exchange. It is a pity that its area is limited and it is unable to exert its function and realize its potential. Fortunately, on the other side of the Huangpu River, there is a large piece of good land in Pudong, which has not yet been developed. Only because of the separation of the river, Pudong and Puxi as neighbors become far apart from each other. So we must connect Pudong with the center of Shanghai to build a modern big Shanghai.
>
> At present, there are only one or two narrow tunnels between Shanghai and Pudong, which are insufficient for use, so building a bridge to connect the two sides is the top priority. If the infrastructure in Pudong is further developed, its land value will inevitably rise, so we can receive high-priced use fees, so that Pudong becomes an important place for industry, business, and finance. The government can succeed in building the most modern city, meeting world-class standards, including the true spirit of socialism, and taking the advantages of Chinese tradition. This pivot of Chinese and Western cultural exchanges can earn a sufficient amount of wealth and tax revenue for the country.

Lin Tongyan's report also made specific suggestions on planning and designing, financial investment, infrastructure construction, and so on, and made a comparison between building big Shanghai by means of developing Pudong and the construction of Singapore and Hong Kong. He wrote:

Just look at Hong Kong and Singapore. They are so small, but why are they thriving? It is mainly because they built them as the centers of development in the Far East. Much of the centers' productivity depended on the coordination of bankers, light industry, management, technology, commerce, finance, and import and exports. Because of such centers, all parts of the world invested in it. Because of the convenience in transportation, living, and so on, people felt at home, so that everyone settled down and ran their businesses to promote the prosperity of this place.

And just look at these two places. How did their governments make their fortune? The British government made their fortune by selling land. The price of the land was extremely high and was sold to the Chinese people in Hong Kong to build high-rise buildings. Where did the money go? The United Kingdom took it, so that Britain made a fortune and thus Hong Kong thrived.

In Singapore, the state also put out a lot of land and opened sealed tenders for lease and purchase, so the government made a lot of money. However, they mostly targeted the local rich or overseas Chinese, Chinese, and some foreigners. But China's target in Pudong is different, that is, most of the land should be leased to foreigners to earn foreign currency. However, the principle is the same. Of course, we cannot copy Hong Kong or Singapore completely, but we can draw on their achievements and experiences, learning from their strong points to offset their weakness.

Hong Kong and Singapore are small, but Shanghai, with a background of 100 million people, with the products and technologies for at least 30 million people passing through it. In addition, the industry in Shanghai is relatively advanced, so the importance of this region is incomparable. However, we must ensure that the state policy is indeed open to the outside, constantly introducing technology and management, improving quality and reducing costs, increasing efficiency and production, and supplying import and export goods. This opportunity, unrivalled in the world, can not only create great modern Shanghai, but also makes limitless contributions to the whole country.

Lin Tongyan devoted great efforts to the development of Pudong. He wrote 12 reports altogether.

At the age of 14, Lin Tongyan, with top results, was admitted to the Department of Civil Engineering, Tangshan College of Jiaotong University, the most prestigious college of higher education in engineering. He, who scored the highest in every test, was the favorite pupil of President Mao Yisheng and Professor Sun Baoqi. He accepted the advice of his respected teacher Mao Yisheng and changed the last character of his original name, which is pronounced the same way but with a different meaning, believing that "it is easier to understand and refers to himself as a Chinese descendant".

Someone asked him, "Are overseas Chinese are more patriotic?"

He replied, "Because they live overseas, they take their motherland as more lovely, and they want their motherland to be more lovely."

At the International Symposium on the Development of Pudong New Area, Lin Tongyan made the following speech:

> It is obviously an unprecedented opportunity to develop Pudong area and build a modern Shanghai. This is an opportunity in hundreds or even thousands of years in the world, because we have such a treasure land next to the city center of Shanghai. Although there are still many problems and it requires wise leadership and the masses' efforts, we will certainly be successful at the end. We have seen that the government's goal is to attract foreign capital and build world-class cities by innovation. And we have already had a planned area of 350 square kilometers, which is a far-sighted policy. We hope to get formal approval from the Central Government soon.
>
> After the discussions by the joint consultation group of the Municipal Government, the principle of developing Pudong has been correctly formulated. The questions raised two years ago have already been obviously answered. Someone may ask questions: Will a concession be made? Can't we Chinese do it? Why can't we develop northward and westward? These questions were carefully considered in great detail by the research group. Now, it has been decided to develop Pudong area. However, many of the approaches and steps are still under study. This is just the purpose of our meeting today. Within 20 years, we will build an area equal to that of the Shanghai center into a modern financial, industrial, commercial, and science and technology hub, which, of course, is not a 'simple' move. However, considering that Singapore, Hong Kong, and the original Shanghai were built within only 20 or 30 years, we must make use mainly of modern human resources, material resources, and financial resources, avoiding the old feudal and bureaucratic habits. We also know that the overall backwardness in the country is the biggest

obstacle, but this is also the best opportunity, because the lower the starting point, the faster the progress will take place. We can start from a very low place, but the future must be very bright. Pudong, not yet developed, is promising for development. On the other hand, China's determination is very important. In view of the current situation, both the government and the people are determined. As long as they have made up their mind, it is hard for you to imagine the great achievements China will make.

I am very optimistic about Pudong. No other place in the world can be comparable to the status of Pudong New Area. With only a river away from the center of Shanghai, bridges and tunnels are under construction. As soon as they are completed, the importance of this place will be greatly enhanced. So the land must be developed as much as possible to achieve the desired goal. If we are unable to make the best use of this treasure land, we are sorry not only for ourselves, but also for our descendants. Therefore, the meeting today is very important. Of course, the development of the new area is a very complicated job, but, in a nutshell, there are at least a few important questions like how to make full use of land lease to open our doors, how to run a company to coordinate the Sino-foreign cooperation such as the discussion of laws and regulations and the decision of privileges.

Cultural exchanges are important, because we are building neither a purely westernized city, nor an ancient city. We should depend on the exchanges of Chinese and Western cultures, adopt high technology, and so on. Planning is a big problem. Over the years, no country has ever planned such a large plot of land. For example, in Brazil and Australia, the capitals they designed were not built on such a good site as Shanghai. Also, Zhao Zukang had already suggested to build bridges long before. So this condition is incomparable. But there are still some problems. In spite of the opportunity, the people of our country have no experience in it. However, our people are very smart and will surely succeed as long as they are well trained. These problems have been analyzed by the municipal advisory group, so all of them are likely to be resolved. I hope the presiding officer will explore how to adopt appropriate methods to raise funds and set up the system.

In short, the developing Pudong and modernizing big Shanghai, after two years of promotion, has become a national policy. Now, as to how to attract foreign capital to build a first-class city, you are welcome to contribute your opinions. I would like to take this opportunity to thank the host and the organizers of the conference, and all the foreign advisers who have traveled all the way to Shanghai, especially Jacob. He came from Europe ... At the end, let me wish the meeting a success. Thank you all!

At the same meeting, the members of the Joint Research Group on the Development of Pudong respectively made presentations on special topics such as Zhang Shaoliang's "Development of Pudong to Construct a World-class New Urban District" and Yu Pinhao's "Two Important Conditions of Pudong Development: Further Opening-up and the Establishment of a New System", and Li Jianeng's "General Planning Concept of Shanghai Pudong New Area", Yu Hanqing's "Conception of Land Policy", and Chen Zehao's "The Fund-raising and Operation for Developing Pudong New Area", etc. These reports made deep research and argumentation on the development of Pudong.

This international conference was a great success. As the old Mayor Wang Daohan said at the meeting, for the development of Pudong, the weather was good (referring to the international and domestic situation), the geographical condition was in their favor (referring to the old urban area as support and the links with the Yangtze river delta and the whole nation), and the people were harmonious (referring to the support and help from all sides at home and abroad). The opportunity to build a first-class new urban district was maturing.

Since then, the preparation for the development of Pudong increasingly accelerated.

On September 30, 1988, Jiang Zemin, Zhu Rongji, and Wang Daohan briefed the leaders of the Central Government in Beijing on the preparations for Pudong development in Shanghai. The leaders stressed that the main principle of developing Pudong was to make use of foreign capital and agreed to establish a preparatory organization for the development of Pudong.

In November of the same year, after the general agreement of the Central Government to develop Pudong, the Shanghai People's Government announced the establishment of the Pudong Development Leading Group, which was headed by Gu Chuanxun and Ni Tianzeng, the two Vice Mayors, as the Director and Vice Director, respectively, and Wang Daohan was appointed as a consultant. The office of the group was headed by Ye

Longfei, the Vice Director of the Foreign Investment Committee. Zhu Rongji held many on-the-spot meetings in Pudong and conducted on-the-spot investigations.

On October 9, 1989, at a meeting with the representative of the Shanghai Mayor's International Entrepreneurs Advisory Conference, Zhu Rongji reiterated his intention to accelerate the development of Pudong and make it play a strategic role in building a new Shanghai and expressed his wish for foreign investors to invest in Pudong.

In order to hold this meeting, Zhu Rongji invited 18 world-renowned entrepreneurs from 10 countries, including the United States, Britain, Japan, France, Canada, Germany, Italy, etc. In particular, Morris Greenberg, Chairman of the American International Group Corporation, was invited to chair the meeting. The leaders of Shanghai once again listened with an open mind to the world's talents about developing Pudong and revitalizing Shanghai.

By this time, the development of Pudong had become a matter of time.

In October of the same year, "The Preliminary Plan for the General Planning of Pudong New Area" was completed, and the planned land was expanded from 63 square kilometers planned in "The General Urban Planning of Shanghai" in 1986 to 150 square kilometers, and the population also increased from 0.9 million to 1.5 million.

In fact, while making theoretical discussions and argumentation, Shanghai leaders began to implement Pudong development from paper to concrete actions. On December 5, 1988, under the command of Jiang Zemin and Zhu Rongji, the first pile foundation was laid for Nanpu Bridge across the Huangpu River, which means the river-crossing project started in Shanghai. It is said that according to the design budget at that time, the funds of a cable-stayed bridge could be used to build three cross-river tunnels. However, Zhu Rongji, despite some people's opposition, made a resolute decision to build bridges.

This was indeed a wise move. For Pudong development, multiple bridges must be built. In history, the cross-river project was basically designed without considering the precondition of Pudong development. In short, if Pudong had not been planned to develop, it would have been unnecessary to build bridges. This was also proven by the history that followed.

Li Jianeng recalled, "It was a debriefing held in May 1989 about Pudong development. As soon as Comrade Zhu Rongji returned from his visit to Beijing and Tianjin, he immediately went to Pudong for a debriefing about the study of Pudong development. The venue was decided at a workshop of The Fifth Public Transportation Plant beside Yanggao Road. After hearing the reports, Mayor Zhu immediately said he would like to learn from Beijing and Tianjin and strengthen the effort for the development of Pudong in Shanghai. Later, unfortunately, due to the influence of political turmoil, the Pudong development agenda was delayed."

4.6 The Trump Card Anticipated by the General Designer

During the Spring Festival in 1990, it snowed, which was not common in the south of China. The snowflakes were a little surprising, but Shanghai residents were celebrating their holiday as usual, visiting relatives and friends, gathering at home, and chatting over melon seeds.

In a greenery-shaded hotel in the western outskirt of Shanghai, Deng Xiaoping, the out-of-office Chinese leader, was celebrating his third Spring Festival in Shanghai.

Since 1988, Deng Xiaoping had spent the Spring Festival in Shanghai for seven consecutive years. Deng Xiaoping's stay in Shanghai drew the attention of some political observers. At this time, the general plan of China's reform and opening-up was initially settled, and the special economic zones in the south developed rapidly. As a strategic layout, Deng Xiaoping began to think about the next breakthrough of the reform and opening-up.

Outside the window, from time to time, people heard the sound of firecrackers, saw the burst of fireworks flashing in the sky in celebration of the Spring Festival, and the atmosphere was peaceful and full of warmth. But Deng Xiaoping, at the age of 86, did not take a rest. He was thinking, smoking one cigarette after another. Although he appeared calm, a major strategic decision was taking shape in his mind.

During his stay in Shanghai, he spoke candidly to Zhu Rongji and other Shanghai leaders, asking the comrades in Shanghai to think about the major actions they could take to put up the banner of further reform and opening-up in the world.

Among China's leaders, Deng Xiaoping spoke briefly and in a straightforward manner. Without ambiguous theories, his humble words meant a lot. The listeners also understood the weight of Deng Xiaoping's remarks. Then, what kind of actions could be taken?

Since the end of the 1980s, the international situation had undergone great turbulence.

On November 9, 1989, Egon Krenz, the General Secretary of the Socialist Unification Party of Germany, suddenly ordered to pull down the Berlin Wall and to open the dividing line between East and West Berlin, and East and West Germany. For a long time, the Berlin Wall, a symbol of the East-West confrontation, was pulled down, and the East German people rushed to West Germany like a tidal wave.

The fall of the Berlin Wall was like a domino, and the eight socialist countries of Eastern Europe and the Soviet Union were greatly transformed.

On November 17 of the same year, more than 100,000 people held a demonstration in Prague, the capital of then Czechoslovakia. After that, a large number of people went to the streets for demonstrations every day, demanding an end to the Communist rule of the Czech Republic. The Czech government held its first multi-party election to complete the peaceful transfer of power, which is known as the Velvet Revolution.

On December 19 of the same year, the People's Republic of Poland was renamed the Republic of Poland, and the white eagle with the crown on the red grounding became the national emblem of Poland. Poland formally embarked on the development path of Western-style parliamentary democracy in politics and privatization of its economy.

Romania's upheaval was one of the most turbulent in Eastern Europe. On December 16, 1989, the residents in Timishwara, a city in western Romania, clashed with the military police, leading to a nationwide crisis. On December 22, the demonstrators occupied radio and television stations. Then there was a fierce clash between the army and the security forces. President Ceausescu and his wife, who had fled the country, were arrested and sentenced to death by military courts for corruption and massacres, and were immediately executed.

There was an avalanche of change in global politics, like a magic trick that stunned audiences all over the world.

In this summer, the Japanese-American scholar Francis Fukuyama published "The End of History" in the American Journal *The National Interest*. This article held that the liberal democratic system practiced by western countries may be the "end of the development of human ideology" and "the last form of human domination". This theory shocked the ideological field.

On New Year's Day of 1990, British Prime Minister Margaret Thatcher sent a New Year message to Soviet leader Mikhail Gorbachev, saying in the tone of the Iron Lady that socialism must be doomed.

On February 2, the news came, which made communists all over the world upset, that the plenary session of the Central Committee of the Soviet Communist Party agreed to amend the Constitution, to end up the Communist Party's monopoly on power, and implement a multi-party system. The Communist Party developed an unprecedented sense of crisis, and the divisions within the party were widened.

At the time, China's economy was not preferred by overseas investors.

In 1988, China's overheated economy and the government's high-profile price reforms led to a rush to buy goods, especially in big cities, where people were all terrified by rumors into buying everything. In order to prevent the economy from running out of control, the Chinese government had to make a decision to "rearrange and rectify" the national economy.

The economic rectification movement resulted in a slowdown in economic growth. In 1989 and 1990, China's economy was the lowest since the reform and opening-up in 1978. Shanghai's gross domestic product (GDP) growth did not exceed 4%. And the austerity policy tightened cash liquidity. Some local governments could only give IOU notes instead of cash to the farmers when purchasing their grain, named "the blank bill", which caused the farmers' widespread dissatisfaction.

After the political turmoil in 1989, Europe, the United States, and other countries launched "sanctions" against China. The United States, which took the lead, announced sanctions against China twice, followed by more than 20 developed countries. Some international organizations affected by the United States also took corresponding actions. The World

Bank stopped its US$780 million loan to China, and the WTO announced the indefinite suspension of discussions about China's application for membership. China's external environment was seriously deteriorating. Overseas investors were held back with hesitation. Most western companies in China had stopped operating, and they could only wait and see what would happen. China's access to medium- and long-term loans in the world market had been closed, and foreign investment in China reduced by 75%. Officials in China's foreign trade sector were also complaining that foreign investment was falling and it was hard to do business.

Like a dark cloud in heaven, China encountered serious difficulties in many aspects like reform and opening-up, economic construction, domestic stability, and international relations. This situation of the "meeting of three hardships" had been rarely seen since the founding of New China.

The western public also looked suspiciously at China's economic reform. In March 1989, the British newspaper *The Guardian* published a headline article entitled "The Downfall of Beijing Reform into a Standstill", and in June, the American magazine *Newsweek* published an article entitled "The Great Reversal of Deng Xiaoping", and in September, the British newspaper *The Economist* published "Why the Giant Dragon is Stuck in Stagflation". And the domestic leftists in China used propaganda as a tool to raise opposition to market-oriented reforms.

All these made the whole of China extremely uneasy by the early 1990s.

After observing the general situation of the world, Deng Xiaoping came out to make a remark. On Junc 16, 1989, just after the political turmoil in Beijing subsided, Deng Xiaoping, in his talks with several Chinese leaders such as Jiang Zemin, suggested that they should further launch the opening-up and do more things conducive to reform and opening-up. Obviously, he was eager to show the world, "Our policy of reform and opening-up remains unchanged, and further reform and opening-up will be carried out."

As to the sanctions and blockades imposed by the western countries, the great man Mao Zedong was confident and adopted the strategy of self-reliance, stamina, and diligence. He wrote in his well-known commentary *Farewell, Stuart*, "We are not afraid of the few difficulties.

Lock our door up. Lock it up for 10 or 8 years, and all of China's problems will be solved." In contrast, Deng Xiaoping, also a great man, insisted on the opening to the outside world, and opening the country door wider.

In subsequent conversations, Deng Xiaoping emphasized China's openness to the outside world:

> Now that the international community is worried that we will close our door, we will have to do a few things to show that our policy of reform and opening-up remains unchanged and that further reform and opening-up will be executed.
>
> I used to say that we should rebuild several more "Hong Kongs", which means that we should be open, not closed, and more open than in the past. Without opening-up, there would be no development.

In 1979, Deng Xiaoping made the final decision, approving that local officials in southern China establish special economic zones in the border city of Shenzhen, which adopted a special economic policy to attract foreign investors. Prior to this, in the Mao era, foreign investment was not welcome. In order to avoid the troubles that might be caused by the introduction of foreign capital, Deng cautiously and pragmatically chose a small town far from Beijing, the political center, and opened a window to the world. Deng's move was proved correct. After 10 years of development, Shenzhen had been transformed from a small border town into a modern city, creating a miracle of the special economic zone at its dazzling annual economic growth rate of 26.9%.

An American press delegation once paid a visit to China and during their stay, they went to Shenzhen. A dialogue was recorded in a note written by a member of the delegation:

> Unexpectedly, there are so many tall buildings in this city (Shenzhen) that ordinary Americans have never heard of. Compared with it, I feel our city is just like a small fishing village.
>
> I think I've been fooled by my peers over the years, and they're always talking about how poor China is.

10 years later, Deng Xiaoping was clearly not satisfied with the opening-up of the special economic zones of Shenzhen and Zhuhai. He

wanted to find stronger supporting points to move China's reform and opening-up to speed up development at a higher starting point. As a result, he said, several more "Hong Kongs" should be rebuilt.

Where should new "Hong Kongs" be built?

After Deng Xiaoping resigned as Chairman of the Central Military Commission, his mind was still working fast for China's reform and opening-up.

At this time, the word "development" became a key word in this old man's mind. Deng Xiaoping stressed, "In order to achieve an appropriate speed of development, we should not only get stuck in immediate affairs, but should analyze problems from a macro-strategic perspective and take concrete measures. We should seize the opportunities, make timely decisions, and study where the conditions are better so that more extensive resources will be obtained."

Deng Xiaoping's eyes turned to Shanghai, where he had boarded a ship from the Huangpu River to start his work-study in France when he was young. Deng, fond of playing bridge, made an analogy, "Developing Shanghai is a big move. Shanghai is our trump card, so it is a shortcut to develop Shanghai."

4.7 Dramatic Change of Pudong's Fate

As the Chief Designer of China's reform and opening-up, the development of Pudong, in Deng Xiaoping's eyes, was by no means merely for Shanghai. He saw clearly the advantages of Shanghai opening to the outside world, such as geographical location, transportation conditions, human resources, natural resources and historical accumulation, experiences in international exchanges, etc.

Deng Xiaoping, who is quite fond of playing bridge, regarded the development and opening of Pudong of Shanghai as a trump card in his hand. He believed that the development of Pudong was not only a matter for Pudong but also an issue related to the development of Shanghai. It was an issue of taking Shanghai as a base to develop the Yangtze River Delta and the Yangtze River Valley.

This means that in the 1990s, China's opening-up to the outside world began to shift from the south to the north. This was a strategic shift in the history of China's reform and opening-up.

Since 1990s, China's reform and opening-up, economic development, and urbanization had all reached a critical and historic turning point of a new stage. At this key "crossroad", it was urgent to find a new breakthrough in overall thinking. As for regional development, it was necessary to choose a city or an area which had a strong driving force, vast hinterland, and great leading effect at home and abroad to carry out further opening-up experiments and thus help to deepen China's opening-up to the outside world.

The chief designer, Deng Xiaoping, saw through history and the future across layers of fog. A brand new way of thinking was formed in his mind that Pudong development and opening-up was to become a cross-century national strategy.

Later, almost all economists and historians used the expression that the development of Pudong was known as the "T-shaped development strategy" or "bird-shaped economic development strategy". The names derived from the geographical location of Shanghai. Shanghai lies in the middle of the coastline (bow-shape), and Pudong is like the head of an arrow with a full bow. Relying on the two wings and the provinces of Jiangsu, Zhejiang, Hunan, and Sichuan along the Yangtze River, Pudong is the junction of the economy of the Yangtze River Valley and the coastal areas.

As Yu Qiuyu, a well-known Chinese cultural historian, said, "Anyone who has a little geographical vision of the modern world would take a fancy to Shanghai. Beijing is a typical Chinese capital, leaning against the Great Wall, facing south, sitting there solemn and stable. Shanghai, on the contrary, faces east, the vast Pacific Ocean, and behind it is the thousand-mile Yangtze River running across China. For a self-sufficient China, Shanghai is located at a corner, with no great significance at home. But for the open contemporary world, it overlooks a vast sea, with huge cargo handling capacity and unusual potential."

Deng Xiaoping played a trump card of reform in the extraordinary period after the political disturbance, so the decision of Pudong's development and openness was naturally elevated to the national strategy. Deng Xiaoping, who had lived through the war years and commanded thousands of troops, knew well that the good chance was fleeting, and deep in his heart he felt that Shanghai's reform started late. So Deng Xiaoping was more anxious than Shanghai's leaders. With a full bow, the chief designer expected Pudong to be the most powerful arrow in China in the 1990s.

For Pudong, this was really an unusual Spring Festival. The sunshine of early spring lightened up the future of Pudong development, illuminated the future of Shanghai, and brightened the hearts of Shanghai people. The wishes of several generations were finally put into practice since this Spring Festival. A great experiment in wealth growth began in the Spring Festival of this year.

After the Spring Festival, on the evening of February 13, 1990, Deng Xiaoping left Shanghai on a special train to return to Beijing and spoke with Zhu Rongji on the way to the railway station. When talking about the proposal to develop Pudong, Deng Xiaoping said with a slight regret, "You are late. But now things are moving faster, since Shanghai is better than Guangdong. It has a little higher starting point. From the 1980s to 1990s, I was encouraging the reform and opening-up. Be bold, be afraid of nothing." When it came to the preferential policies for Pudong development, he said that 'I agree. You should report more to Comrade Jiang Zemin.' "

On February 17, Deng Xiaoping met with all the members of the Hong Kong Basic Law Drafting Committee in Beijing. He solemnly entrusted the central leadership present before the meeting, saying, "I have retired, but still I would like to say a few things. One of them is the Pudong development in Shanghai. You should pay more attention to it." Deng Xiaoping specifically requested Li Peng, then Prime Minister, to take charge of the development of Pudong and the development of Shanghai. He said, "You are the Premier. You should take charge of the development of Pudong."

He Chunlin, then Deputy Secretary-General of the State Council and director of the Special Zone Office of State Council, recalled, "Comrade Li Peng asked me to meet him at noon on that day to learn about the development plan of Pudong and asked me to speed up the drafting of documents on the large pieces of land developed by the foreign investors in the development zone. Comrade Li Peng put forward three principles for the document: no loss of sovereignty; the management of public utilities in the hands of the government; and no permission of 'horse-running to occupy land', no speculation of land and insistence on project-driven development."

In the afternoon, He Chunlin made a call directly to Zhu Rongji. Zhu admitted that the report on Pudong development had been discussed for two or three months and he was not yet satisfied, but he promised to work overtime that night and send it to the Central Government immediately.

Under the strong impetus of China's top leaders, Pudong development entered into a substantive start out of the discussions on paper, and the speed greatly accelerated.

On February 18, the second day after Deng Xiaoping's entrustment, Zou Jiahua, a State Councilor and Director of the State Planning Commission, and his team visited Pudong, Shanghai for investigation. Accompanied by Zhu Rongji, the group also sailed to Waigaoqiao Newport. Zhu told Zou Jiahua, "At present, the general planning and the planning for the step-by-step implementation of Pudong development has worked out preliminarily. The construction of cross-river traffic has made great progress, and there are good prospects for hydropower, gas, communications, and so on. The conditions for starting Pudong development are becoming mature." After listening, Zou Jiahua agreed, "Good, good! We should start with the infrastructure framework, the construction of roads, energy, communications, and water supply."

On February 26, the Shanghai Municipal Party Committee and the Municipal Government formally submitted to the Central Government the report "Request for Instructions for the Development of Pudong", in which the basic conception of Pudong development and opening-up was put forward.

On the same day, Zhu Rongji reported to Qiao Shi, the leader of the Central Government who visited Shanghai, and said earnestly, "We now hope to strengthen the determination of the Central Government to approve this report. We pledge to devote ourselves to it and contribute to the overall development, so that Shanghai can truly make its due contribution in a national chess game, and we have this determination."

On March 3, Deng Xiaoping once again met Jiang Zemin, Li Peng, and other leaders of the Central Government, and mentioned Shanghai in his talk: "We should analyze problems from the macro-strategic perspective and put forward concrete measures. Opportunities should be seized and decisions made in time. Developing Shanghai, for example, can be taken as a major measure. Shanghai is our trump card, a shortcut to the development of Shanghai."

Obviously, promoting the development of Pudong in Shanghai had become a trump card in the minds of the general designer, and a shortcut was to achieve a greater degree of openness on the land of the east side of the Huangpu River in Shanghai. Deng Xiaoping was going to tell the western world with the big move of Shanghai that China would not its doors, but instead would open it even wider.

From March 28 to April 8, Beijing sent a higher-level delegation to Shanghai, headed by Yao Yilin, Vice Premier of the State Council, made up of the leaders of the Special Economic Zone Office of the State Council, the State Planning Commission, the Ministry of Finance, the People's Bank of China, the Ministry of Economic and Trade, the Ministry of Commerce, and so on, to carry out special research and demonstration on the development of Pudong. After listening to the report made by Shanghai on the basic ideas and overall planning of Pudong development, they conducted an on-the-spot investigation on Waigaoqiao of Pudong.

Zhu Rongji made reports to Yao Yilin on the development of Pudong on March 29, April 2, and April 7.

At the report meeting on March 29, Yao Yilin said, "When Comrade Rongji, Guodong, Lijiao, and Daohan went to attend the Sixth Plenary Session of the Central Committee in Beijing, they told me where Shanghai was going. I reported this to Comrade Jiang Zemin and Li Peng. Comrade Jiang Zemin would like me to come to Shanghai for a visit. At that time Comrade Li Peng was also ready to come to Shanghai. I discussed it with Li Peng. I would like to come here first to prepare for his visit. Comrade Li Peng gave me a salute... So this time, we, as an advance party, would like to exchange views with all of you, study the steps and methods of Pudong development and opening-up, and when we go back, we will report to the Central Government."

Yao Yilin's visit to Shanghai also conveyed the strategy of the Central Government for Pudong development. Wang Liping, the then deputy secretary of the Shanghai Municipal Party Committee, recalled, "This time, he (Yao Yilin) clearly said that Comrade Xiaoping would like not only to develop Pudong, but also open it. Comrade Xiaoping added the Pudong opening-up, which was not included in what we had talked about before, which only included the development of Pudong."

Starting from the afternoon of March 29, the party of Shanghai was divided into six theme groups, namely, special zone, investment, public financing, foreign trade, commerce, and finance. They made detailed reports to the relevant departments of the State Council.

At the meeting on April 2, Zhu Rongji expressed his idea:

> The last question is the announcement of the timing of further opening of Shanghai. Comrade Yilin raised this question that day. I think it's a very good question. It's an important issue. Personally, I think it is better to announce this after Comrade Li Peng pays a visit to Shanghai. This is a political trump card and will be beneficial to the transformation of the international situation. Foreigners are now looking at us, how stable we can be in April, May, and June. Some people want us to collapse, but others want us to be stable and thus they can benefit from it. If, at this time, Shanghai is declared to be more open and a number of preferential policies are announced, and in addition, Shanghai is still a good place for investment in the minds of foreigners, I think it may have some advantages in changing the situation. So I hope Comrade Yilin will consider my opinion and I suggest that when Comrade Li Peng comes to Shanghai in mid-April, he can announce this policy. The effect of propaganda will be very good.

At this time, Zhu Rongji had fully grasped Deng Xiaoping's intention. The development of Pudong was not a regional issue, but related to China's opening to the outside world. It was a political trump card.

At the briefing, Zhu Rongji also said with strong emotion, "Today, I told Comrade Tianzeng that I am over 60 years old and they are also in their early 50s, so only a few years are left for us to struggle. We still have some important work to do. We can do some good things for the people of Shanghai."

After Yao Yilin and his team made special investigations into Pudong, "The Outline of Several Issues on Pudong Development in Shanghai" was completed in only five days.

On April 7, a small-scale meeting was held again to study the outline. At the meeting, Yao Yilin also fully understood the sense of urgency on the side of Shanghai. He said, "What you talked about, I think, are all very good. First of all, I would like to point out that this outline is not a final decision, but only a preliminary opinion that has been put forward after our study. The matter could have been studied in more details again, but it was too late. Because you would like Comrade Li Peng to come to the announcement on April 18, and today is already April 7. I want to race against time."

On April 10 of the same year, Premier Li Peng presided over the State Council meeting in Beijing, listened to Yao Yilin's special report on the development of Pudong, and made a series of studies on several issues in the process of development and opening-up. Two days later, in the same meeting hall, General Party Secretary Jiang Zemin presided over the meeting of the Political Bureau of the Central Committee and agreed in principle to the plan for Pudong development submitted by the State Council.

At the same time, domestic and foreign experts were also invited to Shanghai to research on the feasibility of Pudong development and opening-up.

On the afternoon of April 15, after listening to the work report of Shanghai and the idea of developing Pudong in Shanghai, Li Peng said that after Comrade Yilin returned to Beijing, he reported to the executive meeting of the State Council. "We held a meeting and later, he also made a report to the Standing Committee of the Political Bureau. We agreed in principle to the wording of 'developing Pudong, opening to the outside world'."

He also told the Shanghai leaders, "Historically, Shanghai has been the largest commercial center, economic center, and industrial center in China. Based on our analysis of the international situation at that time, we should prepare for a big fight, an early fight against a nuclear war, so we did not properly deal with the relations between the inland and the coastal areas. In the 30 years after the founding of New China, Shanghai's development was slow, but in the recent decade, Shanghai developed to some degree."

Li Peng also compared Guangdong with Shanghai. "Shanghai's economic hinterland is much larger than Guangdong's. Guangdong's economic hinterland is basically the Pearl River Delta. Even if there is more radiation after the Hengguang Railway is completed, only parts of Fujian, Guangxi, and Hunan can be added to it. But Shanghai's radiation range is the entire Yangtze River Valley, a comparatively economically developed region in China, and has a golden waterway like the Yangtze River."

He also told the Shanghai leaders in a positive tone, "In the next 10 years, the State Council feels that Shanghai should be taken as the focus of national development and that the advantages of Shanghai should be brought into full play. This is unanimously agreed in the State Government."

On April 18, 1990, a moment of historic significance came. At the fifth anniversary of Shanghai Volkswagen Co., Ltd., Li Peng announced the important decision made by the CPC Central Committee and the State Council on the development and opening of Pudong, Shanghai, that is, approval of Shanghai's request for speeding up the economic development of the Pudong area and the implementation of the policies of economic and technological development zones and some special economic zones in Pudong.

As a result, a city's development strategy grew into a national strategy, and Shanghai changed from a defender to a vanguard in China's reform and opening-up.

Thus, the destiny of Pudong changed completely.

Chapter 5

Seizing Every Minute: Big Experiment in Specific Areas

5.1 A Gorgeous Chapter Written About the History of Pudong

On the morning of April 18, 1990, the local residents of Pudong got up as usual. In the shantytown on Lannidu Road, bleary-eyed people carried wooden toilets out of their homes, and the cleaners dumped their droppings and then washed them clean. There was a constant choking smoke from the sidewalks where people started to set fire to stoves to cook their breakfast and then hurried to work.

But this day was destined to be the beginning of Pudong's great historical change. On that bright and sunny day, Premier Li Peng attended the celebration of the fifth anniversary of the establishment of Shanghai Volkswagen Co., Ltd. When the meeting began at 8.30 in the morning, Li Peng made a speech of congratulations, and then, on behalf of the Central Committee, announced that the Party Central Committee and the State Council had agreed that Shanghai should speed up the development of Pudong. The policies adopted in economic and technological development zones and certain special economic zones would be implemented in Pudong. He also pointed out that this was another major deployment for deepening reform and widening opening-up to the outside world.

The Prime Minister's voice quickly spread through the media at home and abroad. Keen overseas observers found that the development and opening-up of Pudong, Shanghai became a national strategy of the Chinese government in the 1990s.

From this day, the history of Pudong turned into a gorgeous chapter, and China's reform and opening-up also stepped into a new stage.

At that time, a Xinhua News Agency reporter wrote the following news:

> During his visit to Shanghai from April 14 to 18, Premier Li Peng announced that the Communist Party of China (CPC) Central Committee and the State Council had agreed to speed up the development of Pudong and implement the policy of economic development zones and certain special economic zones in Pudong. He urged the comrades in Shanghai to further adhere to the "Four Cardinal Principles" (the socialist road, the people's democratic dictatorship, Marxism-Leninism and Mao Zedong thought, and the leadership of the CPC), persist in reform and opening-up, do a good job in management and rectification, make full use of Shanghai's advantages, make concerted efforts and work hard so as to do a good job in developing Pudong, to further develop the export-oriented economy, and to consolidate and develop political, economic, and social stability.
>
> On April 15, Comrade Li Peng listened to the report of Shanghai and the idea of developing Pudong and made an important speech on the development of Pudong and the current political, economic, and international situation. He said that the CPC Central Committee and the State Council listened to Comrade Yao Yilin's special report on the development of Pudong, and the Central Committee agreed in principle that Pudong should further open to the outside world. In order to develop and open up Pudong, the Central Committee had agreed to give some preferential policies, namely, implementing the policies adopted in the economic development zones and certain special economic zones.
>
> As Li Peng said, to develop Pudong, Shanghai's advantages should be brought to full play. Historically, Shanghai was China's largest economic center. Because of historical reasons, the development in the past 30 years was relatively slow, but in the recent decade the development was relatively fast. The steel, petrochemical, car, shipbuilding, electronics, and textile industries took the lead in the whole country. Shanghai had the Yangtze River Valley with a relatively developed economy as the hinterland, and the Yangtze River as the golden waterway. In short,

> Pudong had advantages for development that other areas did not enjoy. Shanghai could make full use of its comprehensive advantages, absorb more foreign capital to develop Pudong, and develop its modern and export-oriented industry.

On April 30, the Shanghai Government announced 10 preferential policies for Pudong New Area for opening to the outside world. The news quickly spread all over the world, conveying not only an action made by the Chinese government, but also an attitude and confidence of the Chinese government that China's reform and opening-up would never stagnate.

At 3 in the afternoon on May 3, like celebrating festivals, hundreds of Pudong residents, young and old, gathered around No. 141, Pudong Avenue, which was decorated with fresh flowers, waiting for the opening ceremony of the Pudong Development Office and Pudong Development Planning Research and Design Institute. An old man craned his neck and said excitedly, "This is hope for Pudong, hope for Pudong indeed."

When two shingles of the Pudong Development Office of the Shanghai Municipal People's Government and the Pudong Development Planning Research and Design Institute decorated with big red-thread-woven balls were hung on the wall, the crowd which gathered around gave a warm applause. The ordinary people in Pudong greeted the change with great enthusiasm. They were eager for change and eager to become rich. The development of Pudong activated their desire, which, after the development of Pudong, was transformed into great passion and energy. Their passion surged in the countryside, factories, schools, and shantytowns along the Huangpu River, and the docks with rising and falling tides. And their passion was constantly rising. The Communists took advantage of the new situation and made them become an important force to promote the development of Pudong.

Sha Lin, former Assistant Director of the Pudong Development Office, recalled those days and still felt excited. "On that day when the shingle of the Pudong Development Office was hung up, an ordinary man stood at the doorway, waiting for the ceremony. He wanted to donate his two acres of land and a cow. When the news of Pudong development

The shingles with the names of the Pudong Development Office and Pudong Development Planning Research and Design Institute were erected

came, the common people in Pudong seemed to see the light at dawn and they wanted to donate their little property to the government, to the Pudong Development Office."

At 8.30 in the morning on May 3, the first guest of the Pudong Development Office, Yao Weiquan, a businessman, rushed there from Hong Kong. Yao's hometown was Pudong. As soon as he heard the news of Pudong development in Hong Kong, he immediately flew over, planning to invest in opening a plant at his hometown.

On that day, Zhu Rongji also walked into the newly renovated building of the Pudong Development Office. Zhu extended his admiration and gratitude to the dedication of the Pudong Cultural Center in Huangpu District, which handed over the office building in one day and finished the renovation of the Pudong Development Office in three days. Holding the hand of the Director of the Pudong Cultural Center, he said, “For Pudong development, you gave a good service.”

On the ground floor of this two-story building along the road, there were also bathrooms, restrooms, and storerooms which were very messy, piled up with a lot of stuff. After clearing these rooms, in order to “cover the ugliness”, the staff blocked the lower aisle with a door plank. When Zhu Rongji saw the plank, he found it very strange and asked what was inside. The staff member replied that they were sundries with strong mildew, so he had to block them off. Zhu opened the door plank and looked inside, pointing at the dark corridor. “Don’t block the aisle with the plank,” he said. “Let the Development Office have a look and they will know what kind of foundation Pudong development started on.”

In the conference room, Zhu Rongji was obviously a little emotional, with his eyes a little red and moist. He said, he can do a good job in Pudong development, worthy of Shanghai people’s hope.

On that day, nearly 100 investors from Japan, France, Canada, Taiwan, Hong Kong, China, and other places, entered No. 141, Pudong Avenue. By June 1, more than 600 groups of merchants from more than 20 countries and regions had entered the Pudong Development Office. Reception staff received a group of merchants on an average of 20 minutes. They talked so much that their mouths became dry, their tongues became sore, and their lips were full of blisters, and they even did not have time for food. At night, this small building shaded with green trees was still brightly lit, a truly bustling place.

Many Puxi residents also spontaneously rushed to Pudong for inspection, most of whom were entrusted by relatives and friends overseas. A large number of visitors, who crowded into the originally lonely Pudong, brought popularity to it. It is said that what became rich first was a cake business, which was so good that the cakes were sold out very early every day.

On April 18, 1990, Pudong roared off like a locomotive, driving Shanghai, an oversized city, onto a fast lane. And after the spring of 1990, the mental state of Shanghai people also began to change.

5.2 Why People Thought of Pudong 10 Years Later

When the special economic zones like Shenzhen rose in a whirlwind in 1980, and when the rapid growth of wealth first took place in southern China, some scholars and officials wondered why the Chinese government set up special economic zones in the remote villages in the south, and why they did not take Shanghai into account. Why did they think of Pudong, Shanghai 10 years later?

One scholar said in anger, "If economic principles are applicable, then people will ask why similar policies were not adopted in major industrial cities such as Guangzhou, Shanghai, and Tianjin, where the existing industrial foundation and the environment of skilled labor were more attractive for foreign investment. In other words, if the current 'growth pole' strategy were adopted in these cities, the marginal cost of unit investment would be lower."

In history, Shanghai was the most open city in China, and also the city most favored by foreign businessmen. It was called "Adventurers' Paradise". In Shanghai there were more than 100,000 foreigners at most. In this city, "western suits and Chinese long gowns were side by side with each other, and the dialects were mixed with the languages of Europe and America". Chinese and foreign cultures were in harmony, and things were natural and harmonious.

There are two explanations for this. One of them is that in the absence of any experience and case studies, setting up a special economic zone in Shanghai without careful consideration was too risky to be put onto the first agenda. It had to wait.

Shanghai was called the fortress of the planned economy. The "path dependence" under the long-term planning system made the market-oriented reform in Shanghai more difficult than in other regions. Gao Shangquan, a Chinese economist, came to Shanghai in 1956 to investigate an absurd case. In that year, the weather in Shanghai was so hot that companies needed to buy some cooling blowers. But the enterprises did not have the right to buy them by themselves, so they had to write a report to the superior, and the report must pass the examination and approval of seven departments, but when the last official seal was stamped down, the summer had already passed. Gao Shangqun wrote an article entitled "The

Enterprise Must Enjoy Certain Autonomy" about this issue, which was published in *People's Daily*, in which the article was illustrated with a cartoon named "The Necessary Formalities". Because of this article, Gao Shangquan was almost condemned to be right-wing.

From this case it can be imagined that if Shanghai would like to move towards the market economy, it had to bear the pain brought about by "path dependence". After 12 years of reform and opening-up, Li Liangyuan, then Director of the Shanghai Planning Commission, commented that "Shanghai is the 'perfect' city of the planned economic system and the 'mother ship' of China. Shanghai has no experience in reform, so if Shanghai took the lead in reform, it would be too risky."

Gu Mu, Vice Premier of the State Council, who was once responsible for the construction of China's special economic zones and was called "CEO of China's special economic zones" by foreign media, held the same view. "Shanghai accounts for one sixth of the total national economic output value, and the four special zones have not yet risen up, so it is hard to imagine what Shanghai will be like. Reform and opening-up must be done, but as to how to do it, there have been no experience yet."

In 2012, Long Yongtu, chief representative of China's World Trade Organization (WTO) negotiations and former vice minister of the Ministry of Foreign Trade and Economic Cooperation, said at a television interview that the development of Pudong had not been formally proposed until the 1990s, because Shanghai's economy at that time accounted for one-sixth of China's total, so if there were any big fluctuations, Shanghai's economic impact on the national economy would be much greater than it is now. Therefore, at that time, Shenzhen was chosen as a place for the test of opening-up to the outside world, while the first wave of opening-up was not set up in Shanghai.

Zhu Jinhai, a Shanghai scholar who personally experienced this historical process, said, "The development and opening-up of Pudong cannot be carried out earlier, because at that time, Shanghai played the role of a defender for the national reform and opening-up, with Shanghai's financial revenue at that time accounting for one-sixth of the country and a large number of textile products in many places relying on Shanghai's supply. Without Shanghai as a defender, it would be difficult for the coastal 'four special zones' to open up boldly. By the late 1980s and early

1990s, the opening of the ‘four special zones’ had essentially succeeded, and the coastal opening-up had gradually taken shape, so the development and opening-up of Pudong started in time.”

In addition to the saying of “too risky”, there is another saying of “eldest son”.

A participant in Pudong Development recalled that, on one occasion, a certain leader of the Central Government came to Shanghai for investigation and made some sincere remarks. For several decades, China’s system and mechanism were rigid and took a long detour. By means of reform and opening-up, a new road may be taken, but in this process there might be some risks. The risks can be taken by poorer places, but if the risks were taken in Shanghai, the cost would be too high. At the same time, the country was like a big family, a poor family, and Shanghai was the eldest son of the family. In order to take good care of the family, he may have to bear more burdens and marry later than others.

In contrast, Shenzhen was just a small backward county, with a relatively weak planned economy and relatively little resistance to institutional reform. Close to Hong Kong, it was easier to attract foreign capital. The local population was sparse, so immigration was easier. Thus it was easier for foreign businessmen and migrants to become new driving force for reform.

These were the two points that Shanghai did not have in the era of the planned economy.

The timing of the development of Pudong had much to do with China’s experience of “wading across the stream by feeling the way” during the reform and opening-up. In other words, at the beginning of the reform, China did not have a clear strategy and plan. If any, it was partial and controversial, which could be said to be “felt and found out”. People did not know where they were going. The continuous “trial and error” was an important experience for the success of China’s reform.

It is because of this “trial and error” thinking that in the south, with special economic zones set up, people “fought their way out”. If the trial was successful, it would be promoted, but if the trial failed, it would be shut down. This “trial and error” method can minimize the political risk of reform, and people can “learn from the process of doing”, groping their way out slowly.

This practice of "wading across the stream by feeling the way" made the steps of China's reform and opening-up steady and definite and also avoided the economic and social instability seen in Latin America and Russia.

In the 1990s, when Pudong development was launched, the trial operation of special economic zones in the south provided a lot of experiences and lessons, which enabled the development of Pudong to embark on a fast and stable high-speed track and drove the economy of the Yangtze River Valley.

This is also the good luck of Pudong.

5.3 The Change in the Orientation of Pudong

On April 18, 1990, after the launch of the development and opening-up of Pudong, Shanghai began to run fast. The governmental agencies, like a high-speed engine, operated almost day and night.

On April 21, Shanghai Mayor Zhu Rongji made the "Government Work Report" at the Third Session of the Ninth Municipal People's Congress. He said with strong emotion that it was the long-cherished hope of Shanghai people to develop and open up Pudong. After years of effort, the conditions for Pudong development became mature. In accordance with the strategy of "facing the world, facing the 21st century, and facing modernization", people can draw on the successful experience of the economic development of new areas in big cities at home and abroad, consider the planning and construction of both sides of the Huangpu River as a whole, and implement them in a hierarchical and step-by-step manner.

Obviously, at this time, as the leader of Shanghai, Zhu Rongji attempted a conception of Pudong which was already different from that at the People's Congress in 1988.

On the afternoon of April 23, Huang Ju, Executive Vice Mayor, entrusted by the Shanghai Municipal Government, made a special report on the development of Pudong to the National People's Congress (NPC) deputies at the Third Session of the Ninth Municipal People's Congress.

This was the first time that the Shanghai Municipal Government made a report to the people of Shanghai represented by the participants of the meeting on the brewing and decision-making process and the tentative plan for Pudong development.

Huang Ju told the representatives that Shanghai proposed to develop Pudong a long time ago. As early as in 1984, the "Outline of Shanghai Economic Development Strategy Report" formulated by the Municipal Government put forward Pudong development. In reply to the outline, the State Council clearly pointed out that it was necessary to create conditions for the development of Pudong and plan for the construction of a new urban area. Later, when the State Council approved of the "Shanghai Municipal Overall Plan", it again pointed out that Pudong should be built and transformed in a planned way so as to make Pudong a modern new area. In order to implement the instructions of the State Council, Shanghai set up the Joint Consultation Group for Pudong Development, headed by a vice mayor, and a number of overseas celebrities were invited to serve as consultants.

In May 1988, the Municipal Government held the "International Seminar on the Development of the Pudong New Area", at which Comrade Jiang Zemin expounded the necessity of developing Pudong from the perspective of summarizing historical experience, and put forward the transformation of the old urban areas and the policy of building a modern new area. Since then, Shanghai accelerated the preliminary research on the development of Pudong. The Municipal Government specially set up a leading group for the development of Pudong, headed by two vice mayors, to coordinate the development of Pudong.

In 1989, Mayor Zhu Rongji and Vice Mayor Huang Ju and Ni Tianzeng held several on-the-spot meetings in Pudong for on-the-spot investigations. Under the care and support of the older generation of proletarian revolutionaries and leaders of the Party Central Committee, on February 26, 1990, the Municipal Party Committee and the Municipal Government formally reported to the Party Central Committee "The Request for the Development of Pudong", which was highly valued by the Party Central Committee and the State Council. From March 28 to April 8, Vice Premier Yao Yilin, entrusted by the Party Central Committee and the State Council, headed the comrades of the relevant departments of the State Council to Shanghai to carry out a special study and survey on the development of Pudong. During his visit to Shanghai from April 15 to 18, Premier Li Peng inspected the Pudong area and on April 18, he formally announced to both Chinese people and foreign countries that the Party Central Committee and the State Council agreed to accelerate the development and opening of Pudong.

Huang Ju then introduced the preliminary plan to develop Pudong. The planned area of Pudong for development referred to a triangular area to the east to the Huangpu River, north to the Chuanyang River, and close to the urban area. Most of the area was within a radius of 1.5 kilometers from the city center with a total area of about 350 square kilometers. In accordance with the strategy of "facing the world, facing modernization, and facing the 21st century", by drawing on the successful experience of developing new urban areas at home and abroad, it is envisaged that with great efforts, Pudong would be built into a modern and export-oriented industrial base with complete supporting facilities and a new window for Shanghai and even for China to further expanding its opening to the outside world. At this time, the vision for the future of Pudong was oriented to "building Pudong into a well-equipped, modern, and export-oriented industrial base". On April 18, when Li Peng announced the development and opening of Pudong, he also said so.

Historically, the idea of positioning Pudong as an "industrial base", which is based on the secondary industry, quickly changed.

In the report, Huang Ju also talked about the significance of Pudong development and opening-up.

He said, since the beginning of the 1990s, due to the dual challenges brought about by the increasingly fierce competition in the domestic market, Shanghai was faced with two choices: the first was to allow existing comprehensive advantages to continue weakening, with the economy shrinking day by day and its position in the country constantly declining; the other one was to give full play to its comprehensive advantages, take advantage of the favorable environment in which investment was gradually improving, further deepen reform and expand the opening-up, accelerate the development of an export-oriented economy, take a new path of revitalization, and strive to turn Shanghai into an export-oriented, multi-functional, and modern international city. The Municipal Party Committee and the Municipal Government, after making repeated studies, believed that Shanghai, as China's largest economic center and an influential international city on the west coast of the Pacific, had gained new economic impetus after 40 years of development, especially in the past decade.

Shanghai's advantages in industry, science and technology, and talents had ensured that Shanghai should be in the forefront of the country in economic development and reform and opening-up. This was the ardent expectation of the Party Central Committee and the State Council for Shanghai, and it was also Shanghai's duty. In regard to the conditions in Shanghai, it was possible to take greater actions in opening-up to the outside world. In fact, the development of Pudong mattered far beyond Shanghai itself. Leaders of the State Council repeatedly stressed that the development of Pudong should not only influence Shanghai, but also promote the economic development of Jiangsu and Zhejiang, and even the two banks of the Yangtze river. People were greatly inspired and encouraged by the demands of the leaders of the Central Committee to take the development of Pudong as a strategy, and realized that opening-up Pudong was not only a matter of strategic significance for Shanghai but also for the whole country. It was also a further demonstration of China's determination to adhere to opening-up to the outside world.

As a local leader, it is not easy to grasp the gist of the Central Committee like this. According to Deng Xiaoping's conception, Pudong development was "not only a matter of Pudong, but also a matter related to the overall development of Shanghai, and the development of the Yangtze River Delta and the Yangtze River Valley". In other words, the "leading" role of Shanghai should be brought to full play to promote a new leap in the economy of the Yangtze Delta and the entire Yangtze River Valley. As Fei Xiaotong, a famous Chinese sociologist, said, "The Yangtze River is a dragon that can lead the whole Chinese economy to take off, and Shanghai is the head of the dragon."

Huang Ju mentioned in the report, "Shanghai, with its advantages, is likely to take greater actions in opening to the outside world." This was precisely a response to Deng Xiaoping's request to the leaders of Shanghai in 1990, "Ask the comrades in Shanghai to consider what major actions can be taken to set up the flag of more reform and opening-up in the world."

The meeting also announced Huang Ju as the head of the Pudong Development Leading Group, and Gu Chuanxun and Ni Tianzeng, the Deputy Mayors, as the deputy heads.

On April 30, the Shanghai Municipal Government held a press conference on the development of Pudong. Huang Ju told the journalists that

Pudong development was a grand cross-century project. Pudong development and opening would be implemented in three steps. The first step, the "Eighth Five-Year Plan" period (1991–1995), the initial stage of development and opening-up, would focus on formulating plans, improving the environment, and solving transportation problems to actively create conditions for attracting foreign investment. In the second step, during the Ninth Five-Year Plan period (1996–2000), as the key development stage, the key roads and municipal public facilities in the region would continue to be built, and a large pattern of Pudong New Area with relatively complete infrastructure would be preliminarily formed so as to lay the foundation for the great development in the next few years. The third step, two or 30 years or more after 2000, would be the overall construction phase. At that time, through the construction of Pudong and the transformation of Puxi urban area, Shanghai would be built into an important modern industrial base and the center of finance, trade, science and technology, culture, and information with well-developed facilities and an export-oriented economy.

At the meeting, Zhu Rongji announced the establishment of the Pudong Development Leading Group, which consisted of the Pudong Development Office and the Pudong Development Planning Research and Design Institute, and introduced to the journalists Sha Lin as the head of the office, who was then assistant director of the Shanghai Science and Technology Commission and had been professor of electronics at Fudan University.

On September 10 of the same year, the Shanghai Municipal Government held a second press conference for the development of Pudong, at which nine laws and regulations concerning the development and opening of Pudong were issued, together with English and Japanese versions. Chen Yuan, Deputy Governor of the People's Bank of China; Xiang Huaicheng, Deputy Finance Minister; Dai Jie, Director of the General Administration of Customs; and Huang Ju, Executive Deputy Mayor of Shanghai, announced the regulations.

At the meeting, Zhu Rongji replied to questions from journalists, including those of *Time Magazine*.

A British journalist of *The Independent* asked, "Overseas, the development of Pudong is largely linked to your name. Once you leave Shanghai, what will happen in the future?"

Zhu Rongji replied, "I think the development of Pudong is not linked to my name, but the strategic decision of the Party Central Committee and the State Council. No matter who is the leader of Shanghai, this decision must be carried out. As for me, I still have three years left in office."

"At the conference, he talked effusively as he introduced Pudong as if he were charged with electricity, full of power and ambition." 19 years later, Jimmy, the American journalist who was at the press conference at that time, was still deeply impressed.

5.4 An Elevation from Local Aspiration to National Strategy

At that time, Pudong development had been elevated from Shanghai's local aspiration to the national strategy by the chief designer of reform and opening-up, and Pudong development had turned into Pudong development and opening-up.

The heat of Pudong development, which flew to all parts of China, also stimulated governments everywhere to have the strong urge to accelerate their development.

On August 2, 1990, Li Peng, Premier of the State Council, reminded participants at the National Industrial Production Conference, "After the announcement of the opening and development of Pudong, some provinces and cities were unable to sit at ease, but felt eager to absorb more capital from Hong Kong, Taiwan, and foreign countries. Some believed that the existing development zones were not enough, so they wanted to build new development zones. Some others would like to establish their own development zones on the basis of cooperation with Pudong development and opening. I suggest that we should stay clear-minded on this issue." Li Peng stressed that the Party Central Committee had decided to develop and open Pudong, which, as an important strategic plan, was not only related to the development of Shanghai, but also to the economic development of the Yangtze River Valley and the whole country.

In November of the same year, Jiang Zemin, General Secretary of the CPC Central Committee, further explained the significance of Pudong development at the commemoration of the 10th anniversary of the establishment of the Shenzhen Special Economic Zone, "With far-sighted strategic view, the Party Central Committee and the State Council made a decision this year to develop and open Pudong New Area. This will give full play to the economic resources and scientific and technological advantages of Shanghai and the hinterland along the Yangtze River, and bring about a new situation in China's opening-up to the outside world."

We can also see the Central Government's thinking on the development of Pudong from the previous reports of the Communist Party Congress.

In 1992, Jiang Zemin pointed out in the report at the 14th National Congress of the Communist Party of China (CPC), "The development and opening of Pudong can play the leading role in further opening the cities along the Yangtze River, and Shanghai should be built as soon as possible into one of the international economic, financial, and trade center to bring about a new leap forward in the economy of the Yangtze River Delta and the entire Yangtze River Valley."

In 1997, Jiang Zemin pointed out in the report of the 15th National Congress of the CPC that Pudong should "continue to take the lead in institutional innovation, industrial upgrading, and opening-up, and display its influence as a model to the rest of the country".

In 2002, Jiang Zemin said in the report of the 16th National Congress of the CPC, "We should encourage the Special Economic Zones and Shanghai Pudong New Area to take the lead in institutional innovation and opening-up."

In 2007, Hu Jintao pointed out in the report of the 17th National Congress of the CPC, "The Special Economic Zones, Shanghai Pudong New Area, and Tianjin Binhai New Area should play an important role in reform, opening-up, and independent innovation."

History decided that Pudong was bound to shoulder the heavy responsibility of implementing the national strategy. But how to develop and open Pudong? Was it to follow Shenzhen, or take a new road?

First, the strategic thinking decided by the high-level leaders in Beijing for the development and opening-up of Pudong should be taken into account.

On June 2, 1990, the Party Central Committee and the State Council gave a reply to Shanghai's request for instructions on the development and opening of Pudong.

In this reply, the Central Government stressed the importance of using Shanghai's three advantages: talent, location, and external links. It can be said that this reply was relatively macroscopical and principled, and there was no detailed conception of the national strategy of Pudong development.

It took some time for the Central Government and Shanghai Government to understand the development of Pudong.

On February 18, 1990, Zou Jiahua, State Councilor and Director of the State Planning Commission, paid a visit to Pudong. A Xinhua news bulletin used "two benefits": beneficial to alleviating the burden of the industry, transportation, and population in the old urban area; and beneficial to speeding up the adjustment of economic structure and urban layout.

On April 8 of the same year, Yao Yilin, Vice Premier of the State Council, arrived in Shanghai. He said that the development of Pudong had a strong radiation power at home, which can promote the economic development of both sides of the Yangtze River, and was also an important strategic measure for further opening-up to the outside world. Yao, with a higher position, had a broader view of the matter.

In 1992, the Central Government made a clear statement about the development of Pudong. In April of the year, Premier Li Peng mentioned Pudong development and opening in his government work report three times at "two national conferences", and pointed out clearly that the development and opening of Pudong was the focus of China's economic development strategy in the 1990s, which can also promote the economic development of the Yangtze River Delta and the Yangtze River Valley.

In October of that year, Jiang Zemin specified in the report of the 14th National Congress of the CPC, "Taking the development and opening of Pudong as the lead or dragon head, we should further open the cities along the Yangtze River, build Shanghai into one of the centers of international economy, finance, and trade as soon as possible, and promote a new leap in the Yangtze River Delta and the entire Yangtze River Valley."

After that, Shanghai's leaders proudly summed it up as "one head, three centers".

5.5 The "Growth Pole" in the 1990s

In China's reform and opening-up, there was a popular saying "wading across the stream by feeling the way", referring to a trial-and-error attitude in promoting reform. If the test was successful, just go ahead. Without experience, without theory, Chinese people were constantly engaged in theoretical exploration in wading across the stream. In the 1980s, Chinese scholars introduced the economic theory of growth pole from Europe.

This theory, put forward by the famous French economist François Perroux in the 1950s, argued that the country's leading sectors with rapid growth and innovative industries were often clustered in large cities with the functions of aggregation and innovation of talent, capital, commodity, technology, and information, and thus they became the "growth pole" of the surrounding areas. The development of such an economic center with strong attraction, radiation power, and competitiveness would surely promote the economic development of the surrounding areas.

Later, the growth pole theory was further enriched and developed by the French economist Budweil, the American economist Milton Friedman, the Swedish economist Karl Gunnar Myrdal, and the American economist Albert Otto Hirschman. This theory was applied by many countries to regional development planning as an important tool to guide economic development, to eliminate poverty in backward areas, and to promote the coordinated development of the regional economy.

After 1949, the Chinese people were more influenced by production allocation theory proposed by the Soviet Union, and the theoretical circle widely accepted the Marxist classical writers' theory of balanced development in a mechanical and dogmatic way, in addition to some historical reasons and changes in the international political and economic situation, so that the balanced development strategy occupied the dominant position in China's regional economic development, that is, the excessive pursuit of the regional economic system and the scattered distribution of industry. The practice of an egalitarian approach, which departed from the reality of China as a developing country with great regional differences, characterized by the blind pursuit of developing large and inclusive, small and all-embracing industry in all regions, resulted in low macro and microeconomic efficiency.

After China's reform and opening-up, Deng Xiaoping resolutely adopted the strategy of allowing some people and regions to become rich first. The setting up of special economic zones in the 1980s and the developing and opening-up of Pudong proposed in the 1990s allowed these regions to develop first by taking advantage of institutions and special policies. These special regions, as the growth pole of China's economy, changed from backward regions to economically developed regions, and relied on their radiating influence to drive the development of the backward regions and eventually achieve common prosperity.

Scholars argued that the establishment of special economic zones in the country was the application of the non-balanced development theory of regional economics represented by Perroux's "growth pole" theory, which coincided with Deng Xiaoping's theory of earlier prosperity for the few and later prosperity for the most.

In the history of China's reform and opening-up, the theory of "growth pole" was very popular. Undoubtedly, China's leaders also hoped that Pudong would become China's new growth pole in the 1990s and become an economic center with strong attraction, radiation power, and competitiveness to drive the development of the surrounding regions.

Prior to this, a young scholar in Beijing proposed to implement the strategy of "international great circulation" in China in light of China's national conditions.

On November 1, 1987, Wang Jian, an associate researcher of the Economic Research Institute of the State Planning Commission, published an article in *Trends Digest*, the internal publication of Xinhua News Agency, entitled "The Possibility and Requirements for Taking the Economic Development Strategy of International Circulation", which proposed to further expand the opening-up in coastal areas, develop a processing-oriented economy with the features of importing and exporting in large quantities, and participate in the international economic cycle. This article was published in *Economic Daily* on January 5, 1988, with the title "Choosing the Correct Long-term Development Strategy: The Conception of Economic Development Strategy of International Great Circulation".

The key points of the strategy are: to make full use of the advantages of abundant human resources in China to vigorously develop labor-intensive industries in coastal areas and make great efforts in processing with imported materials; for the coastal processing industry to maintain the practice of putting both ends of production and operation (raw materials and sales markets) into the international market so as to solve the contradictions in these two aspects between the coastal areas and the inland areas; to actively introduce foreign capital, especially foreign investment, to vigorously develop foreign-invested enterprises; and to advocate the large circulation with the development sequence from labor-intensive industry to heavy industry to agriculture.

Although before the strategic concept of "international great circulation" was put forward, the gradient theory had been embodied in the measures taken by the state to gradually expand its opening to the outside world, the strategic concept of "international great circulation" proposed by Wang Jian also greatly expanded the way of thinking about the form and connotation of China's participation in the international division of labor. For some time, the response was tremendous.

In comparison with the gradient theory, the strategy of "international great circulation" further put forward the solution to alleviate the contradictions between the coastal areas and the inland areas in the struggle for raw materials and markets, and the way to develop the export-oriented economy with the advantage of China's labor resources with the focus on industrial restructuring at the same time. This strategy was highly valued by the leaders of the Central Government and provided the basis for the formal establishment of the coastal area economic development strategy at the beginning of 1988. This theory also provided theoretical reference for the development and opening of Pudong. As a result, Wang Jian was awarded "1988 China's Top 10 Outstanding Young People".

In the 30 years since the founding of New China, China, drawing on the experience of the Soviet Union, chose to give priority to the development of heavy industry to promote light industry and agriculture, and thereby promote the development of the whole economy and implement the strategy of catching up with developed countries in economic development. At that time, a leader explained the strategy of China's economic development in simple words: "One is grain, the other one is steel. With these two things, everything is easy to do." To ensure the elements needed for the development of heavy industry, interest rates, wages, and, in the end, prices of agricultural products had to be lowered down, which was a practice of tightening one's belt as a result of hunger that surely led to structural imbalances in the overall economy.

This was very painful choice, both realistic and historical. And in theory, there was a support.

After World War II, many development economists argued that poor countries could not achieve economic take-off and national affluence by means of opening-up. They believed that the exports of poor countries were mainly primary commodities such as agricultural produce and minerals, while only the rich countries can produce industrial goods. The prices of primary products such as agricultural produce and minerals tended to become lower and lower in the international market. Thus, the more agricultural produces and minerals the poor countries exported, the less industrial products can be exchanged. On the contrary, if poor countries imitated the economic structure of the rich countries, through national mobilization and allocation of resources, to establish an independent industrial system, produce their own industrial products, and replace the imports of increasingly expensive industrial products in the international market, the poor countries would gradually develop their industries and accumulate wealth. The former colonial and agricultural countries, such as the United States and Germany, developed through protecting their own markets and developing their own industries.

These development economists also argued that the economic structures of developing countries were different from those of the developed countries, and capital accumulation and industrialization were the primary problems of economic development. Given the need for rapid industrialization and the market to be nurtured, and the wide economic disparity between the poor and rich countries, developing countries must pursue economic planning, trade protection, and import substitution.

At that time, China, India, Brazil, and the vast majority of poor countries in Asia, Africa, and Latin America also took the path of import substitution for industrial development.

By the 1980s, China was faced with strategic options: the "export-oriented" road of industrial development and "import substitution" as the road for industrialization development. Because China's Hong Kong, Taiwan, South Korea, and Singapore turned to export-oriented industrialization as the road for development from the 1960s, they ran very quickly on the road of development, once known as the "Four Asian Tigers".

Heaven blessed China, and God blessed Pudong. While economists were still debating on "export-oriented" or "import substitution", the developed countries were experiencing a round of outward industrial shift.

The "Four Asian Tigers" were also under pressure of currency appreciation and were shifting to labor-intensive industries. The "export-oriented" strategy had become a historical and realistic choice in China, especially in the special areas and coastal areas such as Shenzhen and Pudong.

The strategy of "international economic circulation" put forward by young and bold Wang Jian promoted the implementation of the "export-oriented" economic strategy for China and the shift in development strategy from the priority of heavy industry to the full play of industry with comparative advantages. In the regional economic development for the past 30 years since China's reform and opening-up, the development strategy of "international economic circulation" played an important role.

In the 1990s, as a result of industrial shift and "export-orientation", good opportunities embraced Pudong.

5.6 "New Area" Instead of "Special Zone"

At the beginning of Pudong's development and opening-up, there was a question about the naming of this area. What should that piece of land be called? Namely, what were its differences from other Chinese development zones? In China, the name is usually of great significance.

More than a decade ago, Chinese leaders also racked their brains to name a special economic region in the southern frontier, which ended with Deng Xiaoping's final wording "Special Economic Zone". Since then, there had been five special economic zones on the territory of the People's Republic of China: Shenzhen, Zhuhai, Shantou, Xiamen, and Hainan.

Then what about Pudong? Was it a special economic zone? Pudong was not called a special zone, but a new area, for three reasons, from which the positioning of Pudong can also be seen:

The first reason was explained by Shanghai.

In 1987, when Jiang Zemin, then Mayor of Shanghai, returned with his team from Guangdong after visiting the special economic zones, he took the initiative to put forward to the Central Government two unprecedented proposals: Pudong would not be built into a "special zone", but a "new area", and not a "development zone", but a "functional area".

Professor Wang Zhan, who, as the former Director of the Development Research Center of the Shanghai Municipal Government, had participated in the demonstration and introduction of all the major plans and reforms in Shanghai since the 1980s, explained, "Building this new area aims to take advantage of the development of the new area to promote the development of Shanghai at large. Shanghai later reported to the Central Government, in hope of making use of the development of Pudong to 'link east with west, recreate a center'. This was different from the special economic zones in that these zones generally had a powerful function of resource absorption, but a new area needs to release energy."

From the beginning of Pudong development, Shanghai had a strong awareness of its radiating power to the surrounding areas and has been releasing energy. And it would not like to follow the road of Shenzhen.

In 2008, in Commemoration of the 30th Anniversary of China's Reform and Opening-up, an article, published in Shanghai's *Jiefang Daily* entitled "Pudong's Exploration of the Development Mode in Creating a New Area", introduced the background at that time:

> Before and after the Central Government announced the development of Pudong, the focus was on whether to build Pudong into a new industrial base or develop it into a new financial and trade center. After the Shanghai Party Committee and the Municipal Government had repeatedly studied and discussed the main connotation of developing Pudong as a national strategy and a series of important guidelines issued by Comrade Deng Xiaoping, they finally concluded that it was unwise to build a single-functioned Pudong, but instead build Pudong into a multi-functional comprehensive economic center with a developed financial and trade industry and also an advanced manufacture industry.
>
> The Party Committee and the Municipal Government also specially paid visits to Shenzhen, and two opinions were agreed on. Firstly, to build a new area instead of a special zone meant not to make Pudong into a relatively independent economy which would not only fail to solve the problems of remolding urban functions in Puxi, but also Pudong development cannot be successful without relying on the urban functions of Puxi. Secondly, to build a functional development area instead of economic and technological development zone meant industry should not the only aim, but some of the functions more suitable for the development of Pudong in Shanghai's overall economy should be placed in Pudong so as to promote the urban spatial arrangement and industrial restructuring in Shanghai.

In Wang Zhan's words, this was different from Shenzhen, and instead was the "recreation of partial center".

It can be seen that the central consciousness of both Shanghai's citizens and officials were very strong. Because of this central consciousness, Shanghai's ambition to develop Pudong was even greater. Can this be attributed to the historical status and cultural heritage of Shanghai as the Far East Economic and Financial Center after the port opening of Shanghai in the 1930s and 1940s?

In the early 1990s, few local governments publicly proposed the theory of a center, because after the planned economy was gradually replaced by the market economy, the local governments focused on developing the local economy. From this point of view, after the launch of Pudong development and opening-up, building a "center" was taken as a far-reaching goal, a major progress in a sense. Its impact on local governments in China, after the 21st century, was that various centers were proposed by local governments as the strategy for revitalizing the economy.

The second reason was explained by overseas scholars.

Unlike the four special economic zones of Shenzhen, Xiamen, Shantou, and Zhuhai, Pudong was part of the super-large city of Shanghai with a special position and role in China. According to a scholar traveling in the United States, "In Chinese, 'Pudong' means the eastern bank of the Huangpu River. 'Pu' is the Huangpu River, 'Dong' means the eastern side. 'Puxi' is the center of Shanghai, which means the western side of the Huangpu River. Therefore, Pudong, closely linked together with the present Shanghai, is a very important part of Shanghai. For the following two reasons, the area should be called 'Pudong New Development Area' or 'Pudong New Area', instead of 'Special Economic Zone' or 'Economic and Technological Development Zone'. First of all, 'Puxi' is the old area of Shanghai, so Pudong should be called 'new area'. Second, perhaps more important, Pudong enjoys more policy privileges than the rest of China, so Pudong has a more special position than 'special economic zones' and 'economic and technological development zones'. Therefore, as to the naming, 'special economic zone' cannot fully represent the characteristics of Pudong. By comparison, the use of the concept 'new area' is more acceptable."

The third reason was based on the memory of Premier Li Peng, the participant.

According to Li Peng's recollection, on March 3 of that year, "Comrade Xiaoping asked Comrade Jiang Zemin and me to have a meeting at his home. He 'entrusted' the task of developing Pudong to us."

In a five-episode documentary television film, *Deng Xiaoping and Shanghai*, Li Peng was recorded in a conversation:

> On March 3, Comrade Zemin and I were invited to the residence of Comrade Xiaoping to talk about the general international situation and domestic situation at that time. Comrade Xiaoping spent a long time talking about the development and opening-up of Pudong. As to the development of Pudong, he said that Shanghai had its unique advantages as an industrial center with technical advantages, and especially the advantages of talents. If it can be developed well, this would be a shortcut to promote the development of China. I especially remember what he said, that this was a shortcut, a shortcut for the development of China's economy. He also said modestly that he felt very regretful that when the four special economic zones were set up in Shenzhen and Zhuhai, Shanghai was not taken into consideration at that time, so it was 10 years late, and he should be responsible for this. He was very modest. After listening to this, we were deeply moved. When we left, Comrade Zemin had a discussion with me. On the one hand, we should do a good job on this matter. On the other hand, we should take into account the real situation at that time. Many cities throughout the country had demanded for the establishment of the special economic zones. If there were too many special zones, they would no longer be special. Then we agreed that Pudong should not be called a special zone, but instead Pudong New Area. I think our conversation on March 3, 1990 was a key talk about Pudong development.

Later, some scholars explained that the different names signified the different development models for Pudong and Shenzhen. The development and opening-up of Pudong, not as a "special zone", meant that it would not rely on the special policies given by the state, but on a new idea, new way of thinking, and new road of development. More importantly, the development and opening-up of Pudong was not only a matter of Pudong itself, but also related to the development of Shanghai, and even the Yangtze River Valley and the whole country. This was different from the development of the Shenzhen Special Economic Zone, which was irrelevant to others, separated from others by nearly 100 kilometers of barbed wire.

However, at that time, some people were doubtful. Maybe the Central Government had not given Pudong a good open policy, otherwise, why was it not called Pudong Special Zone, but Pudong New Area? For this doubt, Zhu Rongji explained that the new area, instead of the special zone, was more special than the special. His words were quickly spread among officials at all levels in Pudong, and they kept telling groups of foreign investors — "In the New Area, new things will be done in the new way according to new regulations."

Li Jianeng recalled, "About the name 'Pudong New Area', in the overall planning of Shanghai city approved by the State Council in 1986, it was still called 'Pudong Area'. At that time, in the Pudong overall planning we made in the Planning Institute, it was also called 'Pudong Area'. The name 'new area', as a result of research by a later research group, suggested that the purpose of the new area was different from that of the special zone, and also different from the economic development zone. In 1987, in the third draft, the concept of 'new district' was used. What is special about it? According to Comrade Zhu Rongji, nothing special was the special, which made it easier to make use of the policies of the Special Economic Zones and the policies of the Development Zones. And it was an area newly developed in the very city, instead of any other place."

According to the recollection of Huang Qifan, the former Assistant Director of the Pudong Development Office, "We gave the new area a definition, that is, all the 10 policies carried out in the economic and technological development zones were also enjoyed and implemented in Pudong; all the nine major policies set by the five special zones before 1990 were also performed in Pudong; the five policies that were not implemented in all the economic and technological development zones and the special zones were also enjoyed in Pudong. That is why Pudong was not called a Special Economic Zone, but a New Area."

Regardless of the explanations, in the first spring of the 1990s, a super-large industrial city began to embark on the overall transformation process with the opportunity of development and opening-up of Pudong. Shanghai, like a leading wild goose, began to lead the entire Yangtze River Valley to share the experience of China's high-speed economic growth in thc golden age.

This piece of land east to the Huangpu River, which has been given different names, had played different roles in the history of China's reform and opening-up. Originally, it was called Pudong New Area, but because it enjoyed the policies of the special economic zones, it was called "special zone without being named as special zone". After that, there was another name, National Comprehensive Pilot Reform Zone. Then, in Pudong, the Central Government set up the China (Shanghai) Pilot Free Trade Zone. The different names were really confusing, but just like conducting different experiments in a lab, there were naturally different names for different samples and results, because China's reform and opening-up was a big experiment.

5.7 Signal: China's Door Not Closed Yet

With the strong support of the high-level of the Central Government, Pudong development and opening-up entered a period of vigorous construction. Builders from all over the country began to pour into Pudong, devoting themselves to the new age of construction with strong fiery passion, whose wings of both ideal and wisdom soared high in the new world. Pudong, once a neglected name, began to heat up in foreign investment. A Hong Kong business consultant said, "Pudong was a hot topic that people talked about at that time. Customers called me and before I told them where to make the best investment, they said 'Pudong, Pudong, I would like to go to Pudong.' Of course, if you go there now, it is still a construction site."

Zhao Qizheng, Director of the Pudong New Area Administrative Committee, was also full of passion despite his science background. He wrote a poem for the development of Pudong, which was translated into English by famous Shanghai scholar and Professor Lu Gusun of Fudan University, and composed by composers of the American Boston Symphony Orchestra. It was sung at a big concert:

Hello, Pudong
A beautiful teenager in China
Growing on the bank of the Yangtze River
Breathing the breeze of the Pacific

Hello, Pudong
A growing teenager
Having the wisdom of the past and the present
Taking the journey of 21st century
Hello, Pudong
You have the passion for the world
People all over the world love you

It can be seen that at that time, Pudong builders got a surge of enthusiasm. When this state of mind, which stemmed from Deng Xiaoping's reform strategy of selecting specific zones for experimental reforms, came into effect, it would be popularized to the rest of China to reduce political risks and the Central Government's failures.

10 years ago, in the vicinity of Hong Kong in southern China, the Chinese government, which conducted experiments by opening special economic zones to implement preferential policies, established special economic zones such as Shenzhen and Zhuhai to implement a market economy and allow the "invisible hand", proposed by one of the founders of modern economics, Adam Smith, to determine the allocation of resources. What was previously executed was a planned economy, and all resources were allocated by the government.

In response to such an experiment, the Chinese government adopted a pragmatic approach, both cautious and bold. At a meeting with an Algerian guest on June 29, 1985, Deng Xiaoping said, "The Shenzhen Special Economic Zone is an experiment and we should wait and see whether the road taken is right. In short, it is a new thing in socialism, so it is our wish if we succeed and it is our experience if we fail. This is a very big experiment, which cannot be learned from any book."

After that, he said to the Japanese guests, "Our opening-up policy as a whole is also an experiment, and from a world perspective, it is also a big experiment."

The development and opening-up of Pudong was also a continuation of Deng Xiaoping's pragmatic thinking, that is, "crossing the river by feeling the stones", as the Chinese put it. "Crossing the river by feeling the stones", a Chinese proverb, is an analogy of trial and error.

In fact, this was also the difference between China's reform and that of the former Soviet Union and Eastern Europe. This was the wisdom of Chinese leaders.

When China embarked on its reform and opening-up in 1978, the leaders had no blueprint in a strict sense, but only operated in the order from the simple to the complex to promote reform. Therefore, the entire reform and opening-up was an experimental process, a gradual process, and sometimes a stop-and-go progress.

By means of "crossing the river by feeling the stones", China's reform and opening-up were carried out step by step, especially through various institutional tests in specific areas. Pudong was such a specific area where the institutional experiments were carried out, the results of which could be shared by the whole China. Just as Yao Yang, a Chinese economist, said, obviously, this practice would greatly reduce the chance that the Central Government choose an invalid system.

The big experiment by the Chinese government attracted attention from Western journalists.

Soon after the launch of Pudong development, out of professional sensitivity, Nicholas D. Kristof, the journalist of the United States *The New York Times* found out the value of the news. On July 15, 1990, *The New York Times* published a lengthy half-page report "China Tells the World: We are Still on the Show". As a worthy American Pulizer Prize winner, journalist Kristof realized the news value of Pudong development, and he wrote at the beginning of the report, "China is building a financial center in Asia, which shows to the world that it still has not closed its door to the world."

Kristof once worked as the chief journalist in Beijing. In 1990, he and his wife, Sheryl WuDunn, also a journalist of *The New York Times*, co-authored a book entitled *China Awakening*, which won the Pulitzer Prize and they became the first couple to win this prize.

Kristof keenly pointed out that this was a major signal for China to adhere to the road of reform and opening-up, and that China was moving its center of economic development from the Pearl River Delta to the Yangtze River Delta.

At first, Kristof had doubts about the development of Pudong. But after he followed the Pudong official Sha Lin to Pudong for field interviews, his view changed. As Sha Lin recalled, "When Kristof saw the actual situation of our Pudong Development Office, he was deeply moved and wrote a very long report about how Sha Lin, 53 years old, the head of the Shanghai Pudong Development Office, led 63 staff members to work in a down-to-earth manner, without any bureaucracy at all, but with an enterprising spirit."

According to the dispatch published in *Reuters* on September 14, Pudong New Area in Shanghai was larger than the sum of Shenzhen and Xiamen, the two special economic zones, and was given the same conditions for development as the special economic zones in hope of revitalizing Shanghai. In addition, the development of Pudong New Area would also become a touchstone for whether the Chinese government would continue the reform and opening-up. In this sense, the development of Pudong was particularly eye-catching.

The western media were paying close attention to Pudong as well as the leaders of Pudong development. The article "China Tells the World: We are Still on the Show" commented, "If there is anyone who can put this plan (Pudong development) into practice, it is no one else but Zhu Rongji. The technical politicians he appointed did not hesitate to support him."

On September 11 of the same year, a long report about Pudong development entitled "Pouring Vitality for the Depressed Shanghai" was published in the *Los Angeles Times*. The article commented on the relationship between Pudong development and Zhu Rongji, in the way that Zhu Rongji, 61 years old, the then mayor of Shanghai, was unanimously regarded as a rising star in Chinese politics. Pudong's success would be beneficial to his political career.

American magazine *Times* believed that if Zhu Rongji's plan was realized, Pudong, which covered an area of 350 square kilometers, about half the size of Singapore and was made up with farmland, would become a "socialist Hong Kong" with a free port, and a financial, trade, and industrial center with branches of foreign banks and high-tech enterprises.

Pudong, a triangular plain without a name on map at that time, attracted the world's attention. The western world, in particular, opened their eyes wide and tried to figure out what had been ignored in the east to the Huangpu River in Shanghai.

5.8 A Big Regret Admitted by Deng Xiaoping

In the early 1990s, Deng Xiaoping expressed his regret more than once that no special economic zone was set up in Shanghai in the 1980s.

On the evening of February 13, 1990, Deng Xiaoping left Shanghai on a special train to return to Beijing and had a talk with Zhu Rongji on his way to the railway station. When talking about the proposal to develop Pudong, Deng Xiaoping said with a slight regret, "You are late, but now you can carry out the plan faster, as Shanghai has a better condition than Guangdong and its starting point can be higher. From the 1980s to 1990s, I began to encourage reform and opening-up. Be bold, be afraid of nothing."

On the evening of January 28, 1991, Deng Xiaoping went to Shanghai for the Spring Festival as usual. On his way to his residence, he listened to Zhu Rongji's report and said with regret that the development of Pudong was at least five years late, and if Pudong, like the Shenzhen Special Economic Zone, had developed a few years earlier, it would have been much better.

At the same time, Deng Xiaoping added, "The development of Pudong will have a great impact, not only on Pudong itself, but also on the development of Shanghai, and with Shanghai as the base, the Yangtze River Delta and Yangtze River Valley would be developed."

On February 18, 1991, on the fourth morning of the Lunar New Year, when Shanghai residents were still immersed in the festive atmosphere of the Spring Festival, Deng Xiaoping happily ascended to the 41-story revolving restaurant of Xinjinjiang Hotel, which was the highest revolving restaurant in Shanghai at that time. Outside the window it was clear and sunny. While overlooking Shanghai downtown through the spacious and bright glass windows, he said to Zhu Rongji, "We say the development of Shanghai is late. We should work harder!"

The chief design of the reform and opening-up was late, so it should race against time.

Inside the revolving restaurant, two large maps were hung upon the walls: a map of Shanghai and a map of Pudong New Area, next to which there was a model of Pudong development.

Li Jianeng, then Assistant Director of the Pudong New Area Development Office, recalled, "To make a report to Xiaoping, our office had been preparing for several days. On New Year's Eve, I received a notice that we should begin to prepare for it on that afternoon. In order to report the development of Pudong more intuitively, we made the model by ourselves and enlarged the photo at Wang Kai Photo Gallery on Nanjing Road in Puxi."

Li Jianeng recalled, "Zhu Rongji guided Deng Xiaoping to the round table prepared beforehand, and everyone sat around for the report, like a family talk. Deng Xiaoping wore a gray dual-purpose jacket, good-spirited, kind, with a smile."

Zhu Rongji began the report, and Xiaoping began to speak during the report. Li Jianeng recalled, "Xiaoping spoke with a strong Sichuan accent, which sounded very cordial, and with a deliberative tone."

Looking at the maps and the model, Deng said with some regret, "In that year, four special economic zones were determined for development, mainly in terms of geographical conditions. Shenzhen is adjacent to Hong Kong, Zhuhai is close to Macau, Shantou was chosen due to the large number of Chaozhou people from Southeast Asian countries, and Xiamen was chosen due to the fact that many people of the Southern Fujian Province do business abroad. But the advantage of Shanghai's talents was not taken into account. The people of Shanghai were clever and their talent good quality. If a special economic zone had been established in Shanghai at that time, it would not have been the case now. Though Shanghai was one of the 14 coastal cities for opening-up, it was quite ordinary. If Pudong had been developed several years earlier like the Shenzhen Special Economic Zone, it would have been much better."

He also urged, "Take your time for Pudong development. Do not hesitate, just go ahead until the completion."

On March 1 of the same year, Li Peng, then Prime Minister, wrote in his diary, "In the morning, I went to Comrade Xiaoping's office. He talked about the international situation, the development of Pudong, the advisory committee, and other issues. Jiang Zemin, Yang Shangkun, and I were present. In Comrade Xiaoping's remarks, there were several key points. The development of Shanghai was 10 years late, at least 5 years late, and he should be responsible for it. Shanghai has many advantages, mainly of talents. He was glad to hear that we had all agreed to it. I should be in charge of this matter and should be more concerned about it."

In Deng's view, the development of Pudong was 10 years late since the establishment of special economic zones such as Shenzhen in 1980, or at least 5 years late since China opened the 14 coastal cities in 1984.

When Deng Xiaoping came to Shanghai again in 1992 during his "South Tour", he even admitted his mistake again. "In looking back, one of my big mistakes was that Shanghai was not added to the four special economic zones. Otherwise, the present situation of reform and opening-up in the Yangtze River Delta, the entire Yangtze River Valley, and even the whole country would have been quite different."

On the afternoon of February 17, 1992, after listening to the report of Shanghai leaders on the Pudong Development Plan and reviewing the Pudong New Area Graph Plan, Deng Xiaoping expressed his regret but still encouraged that although the development of Pudong was late, they could learn from Guangdong's experience, and develop Pudong to be more advanced and modern with a higher starting point. He expressed his belief that its key was thinking, so the latecomers could surpass the early starters.

He added, "The economic development of our country must strive to rise to a higher level every few years. Of course, it is not to encourage unrealistic high-speed, but down-to-earth, efficient, steady, and coordinated development. Shanghai, for example, is now well-conditioned to move faster. Shanghai has obvious advantages in talent, technology, and management, with strong radiation power."

According to historical data, Deng Xiaoping said many times about the delayed development of Pudong, which is a manifestation of his deep regret. Among China's leaders, it is a rare case for one of them to repeatedly apologize for a local construction and publicly acknowledge his mistake.

A reporter once asked Zhao Qizheng, the first Director of the Pudong New Area Administration Committee, what did Comrade Xiaoping mean by saying that he felt that the development of Pudong was a little late?

Zhao Qizheng gave a long reply: "Before the reform and opening-up, Shanghai was the largest industrial and commercial city in China, which provided one sixth or one seventh of the tax revenue in the country. If Shanghai had been chosen as a pilot and failed, the national economy as a whole would be seriously affected. Furthermore, it was on the basis of the accumulated experience of 10 years in Shenzhen development that the development of Pudong began. It was Shenzhen, not Pudong, that moved forward as a pioneer. When Shenzhen was developing, we had so many backward ideas, for example, the land cannot be leased, the joint-stock system cannot be carried out, the cooperation with foreign merchants may lose advantage to others, and it may not be possible to make some people get rich first. All these problems were solved in Shenzhen. Therefore, after 10 years of reform and opening-up and the general success of Shenzhen's development, the Central Government decided to start the development of Pudong. This, in fact, resulted from Deng Xiaoping's sense of responsibility for China. So it can be said that Pudong development was well timed. Then why did Deng Xiaoping say that the development of Pudong was late? I understand that this is nothing more than Deng Xiaoping's encouragement, encouraging us to push forward from behind."

In the spring of 1993, Deng Xiaoping reminded the leaders of Shanghai once again, "I hope you will not miss this opportunity. For China, there are few opportunities for great development. Unlike other countries in the world, China has its own unique opportunities."

Shanghai's leaders were deeply impressed by the following scene. On February 19, 1994, Deng Xiaoping left Shanghai on a special train. At the station, just before the departure of the train, he asked Shanghai Party Secretary Wu Bangguo and Mayor Huang Ju to enter the train and again exhorted them to seize Shanghai's last opportunity at the end of the 20th century. Shanghai had a special quality, and Shanghai had all the conditions to develop faster.

It can be seen that since China's reform and opening-up in 1978, a sense of urgency had accompanied the chief designer of Chinese reform and opening-up. Deng's sense of urgency also became the pressure for leaders in Shanghai and Pudong.

China's third-generation collective leadership, well aware of this, placed hopes on Pudong, positioning its development as "the focus of China's development and opening-up in the next decade", "the leader that drives the economic takeoff of the Yangtze River Valley", and "the symbol of China's reform and opening-up". Pudong development became the embodiment of the national will.

At that time, the officials of Pudong always reminded the reporters who arrived in Pudong for interviews that the development of Pudong could be written into the Communist Party's 14th Congress Report, which was quite unprecedented.

5.9 "Preference of Witnessing Today's Development to Reading Books for a Hundred Years"

Deng Xiaoping had never written poetry, but in 1993 he recited two lines of a verse in Pudong.

On December 13, 1993, Deng Xiaoping strolled across the Yangpu Bridge. It was a new bridge, just two months old, like a rainbow across the Huangpu River.

On that day, the Siberian cold flew south, it still drizzled from time to time, and Shanghai's temperature suddenly dropped to around zero degree celsius. Accompanied by the leaders of Shanghai, Deng Xiaoping rode a van to cross the Nanpu Bridge and headed for the Pudong section of Shanghai Inner Ring and the two overpasses of Luoshan Road and Longyang Road in Pudong. Along the way, he saw the vibrant construction scene of Pudong. He chanted excitedly, "I am glad to see the scene today, better than reading books for years."

Deng Xiaoping's youngest daughter, Mao Mao, said beside him, "I'm in my forties, and this is the first time I hear you recite a poem." Deng told the Shanghai leaders present, "This is not a poem, but words from my heart."

Deng Xiaoping is different from Mao Zedong; the latter is a romantic poet as well as a statesman and whose poems have been widely read by the Chinese people. Deng Xiaoping had never created poems, and these were the only two poetic lines that Deng Xiaoping recited in his life.

From the two lines, it can be seen that Deng Xiaoping was satisfied with the speed of the development and opening of Pudong, and was deeply impressed by the vibrant construction of Pudong, which was the trump card he played to the world three years ago.

The car pulled onto Yangpu Bridge. The accompanying officials, mindful of Deng Xiaoping's age, advised him not to get off the car, but he was so excited to step out of the car and walk on the broad bridge in the cold wind. As the wind and rain grew, Deng walked to the middle of the bridge and looked out at the far-away Pudong, through the string of cables. Zhu Zhihao, the commander-in-chief of the bridge, told him that the bridge, 62 meters high over the Huangpu River, was the world's longest-span cable-stayed bridge. While listening, Deng Xiaoping smiled with satisfaction.

Perhaps for this reason, the names Nanpu Bridge and Yangpu Bridge were inscribed by Deng Xiaoping. The two bridges, as described by the Asian Development Bank, the lender, reached the highest, almost impeccable level in design, safety, and advancement, becoming part of Shanghai's beautiful landscape and landmarks.

Since the spring of 1990, only three years after Deng Xiaoping's decision on the development and opening of Pudong, Pudong began to develop at a high speed. The economy grew at an annual rate of 21%, from 6 billion yuan in 1990 to 164 billion in 1993. From the beginning of the Pudong development to November 1993, there were 1,522 foreign-invested projects. Nearly 3,000 projects were under construction on this 522 square kilometer piece of land.

It was on the next day that the 350-meter main structure of the Oriental Pearl TV Tower on the east bank of the Huangpu River, Shanghai's landmark, was closed off. The TV tower was designed as 463-meter high, the highest in Asia at that time.

It was clear on that day. Under the ray of sunlight, a reporter took a picture for Jiang Huancheng, the TV Tower chief designer and the academician of Chinese Engineering Academy, with the Oriental Pearl TV Tower as the background, clearly visible. Hailed by *The New York Times* as "a symbol of the rise of new Shanghai", the building embodied his poetic design, that is, the pearls, big and small, falling into jade plates.

5.10 Why Chinese Leaders were so Concerned About Pudong

The Central Government leadership showed unprecedented concern about the development of Pudong. This is also an important reason why the development of Pudong could proceed smoothly at a high starting point and at a high speed.

On February 13, 1990, on the way to the Shanghai Railway Station, Zhu Rongji and Deng Xiaoping talked about the development of Pudong. According to the recollection of an official of the Shanghai Party Committee who was present at the time, Deng Xiaoping, who was sitting in the front row, turned around and said solemnly to Zhu Rongji, "I agree to your proposal about the development of Pudong. You should go have a talk with Comrade Jiang Zemin." Zhu Rongji immediately replied, "It is inconvenient for Comrade Zemin to talk about Shanghai, since he just arrived in Beijing lately."

Deng Xiaoping readily promised, "Well, I'll talk about it!"

From *Chronicle of Deng Xiaoping* and *Li Peng's Economic Diary*, between February 17 and April 20, 1990, Deng Xiaoping met with Jiang Zemin and Li Peng three times and talked about the development of Pudong. His talk on March 3 was compiled into the third volume of *Deng Xiaoping's Selected Works*. And it was in this talk that Deng Xiaoping made the famous assertion of "a trump card".

The talk on April 20 was compiled into *Li Peng's Economic Diary*:

> At 10 in the morning, Comrade Zemin, Comrade Shangkun, and I went to meet Comrade Xiaoping to listen to his views on the international situation, the visit of Chinese Prime Minister to the Soviet Union, and the opening-up of Pudong.
>
> There are two major economic policies: the concentrated support for key areas such as Pudong of Shanghai, and for the key industries such as electricity, making use of the capital investment from overseas and offshore Chinese.

Just two days prior, Li Peng announced the development and opening-up of Pudong in Shanghai.

According to historical data, in only as short as five years from the beginning of 1990 to the beginning of 1995, Deng Xiaoping, Jiang Zemin, Li Peng, and Zhu Rongji visited Pudong and Shanghai more than 10 times, especially Jiang Zemin, as the core of the new generation of central collective leadership.

On May 11, 1993, Jiang Zemin visited Pudong. At that time, due to the macro-adjustment policy in the economic field, some people at home and abroad felt worried about whether China's policy of developing and opening Pudong would change, and the overseas media made many inferences. In the face of this situation, Jiang Zemin solemnly declared that the Central Government's policy of developing and opening-up Pudong was unswerving and would not change: "The Central Government placed great hopes on the future development of Shanghai."

Zhao Qizheng recalled a historical detail: "In April 1996, he (referring to Jiang Zemin) inspected Pudong and carefully reviewed the graph plan of Lujiazui Business Center. He asked whether the planned high-rise buildings could be completed by the time Hong Kong returned. We replied what was under construction at that time would mostly be roofed in the next year and Lujiazui Business Center would take shape. After hearing the reply, he was very pleased to say that in time, there would be a decent city on the mainland that could be comparable to Hong Kong."

It can be seen that the background of Hong Kong's return was also an important reason for the Central Government to place great hopes on Pudong development and pay close attention to the development of Pudong. According to Bergere, a French scholar, "One of the important reasons that Shanghai won the understanding of top leaders was the change of the situation in Hong Kong. Hong Kong residents staged unprecedented marches on Hong Kong Island and the new governor, Chris Patten, ignored Beijing's autocracy. This raised fears among Chinese leaders that the protests would spread to the southern provinces of mainland, so it was prudent to move reform centers from Guangdong and Fujian to closer, politically easier-to-control places such as Shanghai and the lower reaches of the Yangtze River."

On the eve of May 1 Labor Day in 1992, Chen Yun, veteran of the Communist Party of China who had long been in charge of the economy, listened to reports in Shanghai. Chen Yun smiled and said to Huang Ju, "Some news reporters asked you about Chen Yun's attitude to the development and opening-up of Pudong? You answered very well. I am really in favor of developing and opening-up Pudong."

When Chen Yun listened to the proposal made by Wu Bangguo, Shanghai Communist Party secretary, that the "China card" should be played in the development of Pudong, he said, "Yes, this should be the case. Shanghai has a very good foundation, especially the advantage in talents. Shanghai will certainly develop rapidly in the future."

Since the launch of Pudong development, leaders of the Central Government frequently visited Shanghai and Pudong to provide guidance and assistance. This had never happened since the founding of the People's Republic of China. In the five years after the development of Shenzhen and other special economic zones, Deng Xiaoping went to Shenzhen only once, even though Guangdong invited him almost every year.

According to an American scholar, these regular inspections had the following special purposes: to keep the world well informed. China's determination to develop Pudong was firm and unshakable, which thus strengthened the confidence of those investors, especially overseas investors, who were undertaking many projects, and also attracted more new investors; to show to local governments the significance that the Central Government attached to the plan and encourage them to do their best; and to continuously provide solutions to new problems during the implementation of projects, so as to ensure the smooth development of Pudong.

Therefore, compared with the Shenzhen Special Economic Zone, there were fewer disturbances, setbacks, and difficulties in the progress of Pudong development.

Chapter 6

Little Experience and Much Thinking: Meditation on the Development of Pudong by Standing beside a Globe

6.1 Borrowing "Brain" from the World

How on earth should Pudong be developed? The Shanghai people had little experience, but they had ideas.

As early as October 26, 1989, at the Shanghai Special Symposium on Pudong Development, Mayor Zhu Rongji proposed with great foresight, "The development of Shanghai must be oriented towards the Pacific Ocean and towards the future. The layout of various infrastructures must be designed in accordance with this requirement." He quoted Professor Wu Liangyong, a famous Chinese architect, saying "We need to be a little bit romantic."

Zhu Rongji pointed out, "Pudong is Shanghai's window, Shanghai's hope in the future. It will be the most modern city, but no city can be modernized overnight. The old city of Shanghai has a history of 150 years. The Bund was built in the 1920s, and is now more than 60 years old. It may take more than 50 years for Pudong to become a new city."

Zhu Rongji also cited the example of Nagoya in Japan: "Nagoya was the best-planned city in Japan. Originally it was a place with a dense aviation industry. Because it was completely blown up during the Second World War, it was planned again after the war, and was really beautiful and well planned. It is said that the mayor at that time planned to widen the roads a little, but people criticized him for his ambition. However, he insisted on his opinion. Now we can see the roads are too narrow. At the time if he had not insisted, it would have been worse. Professor Wu Liangyong spoke very well, 'we need to be a little bit romantic'. Especially Lujiazui, on the opposite bank of the Bund, must be designed well, because this is the very center of Shanghai. The scenery around the Bund, designed in 1920s, is really great, and will surely be well kept in a hundred years."

One year later, in December 1990, Zhu Rongji presided over "The Review of the Overall Planning of Pudong New Area", and planned to start with building the Lujiazui Financial and Trade Zone on the Huangpu River to create a new landmark in Shanghai that would integrate China with the world, the present with the future. It was also a financial and trade zone approved by the Chinese government.

Zhu Rongji said, "Not only the design of Lujiazui, but the design of the whole area should invite the whole world for bid. This line is opposite the Bund. Everyone knows the Bund. This line you will design should have its own features, at least no worse than the Bund. To invite architectural designers from all over the world for bid may immediately raise the popularity of Shanghai."

In April 1991, Zhu Rongji visited France and was very deeply impressed with the new town of Rudd Fans in Paris. It was originally a secluded unknown highland in the suburb of Paris. Built in the 1950s, it became the first urban complex in the world and the main business center in the metropolitan area of Paris. The Chinese side introduced to the French the only financial and trade zone in China named Lujiazui Financial and Trade Zone. The French side was very interested, and the Equipment Department of the French Government signed an agreement with the Chinese side to provide Pudong 2 million francs for the planning and designing of the Lujiazui central area of 1.7 square kilometers. With this amount of money, Pudong took the lead in bidding to the world.

On November 20, 1992, on the third floor of the Shanghai International Trade Center, five elaborately-crafted planning models for the central part of Lujiazui Financial and Trade Zone were placed in the center, and the world's top planning and designing experts sat around the models and expressed their opinions.

Pudong held two international planning seminars attended by more than 30 experts from more than 10 countries, and designers from Britain, France, Japan, Italy, and China designed their unique models.

The planning model by Japanese designers was very modern. Its shape, just like an integrated circuit board, took the form of a bar code, with the residential, commercial, office buildings, and the leisure and tour belt along the river integrated into a surreal information system.

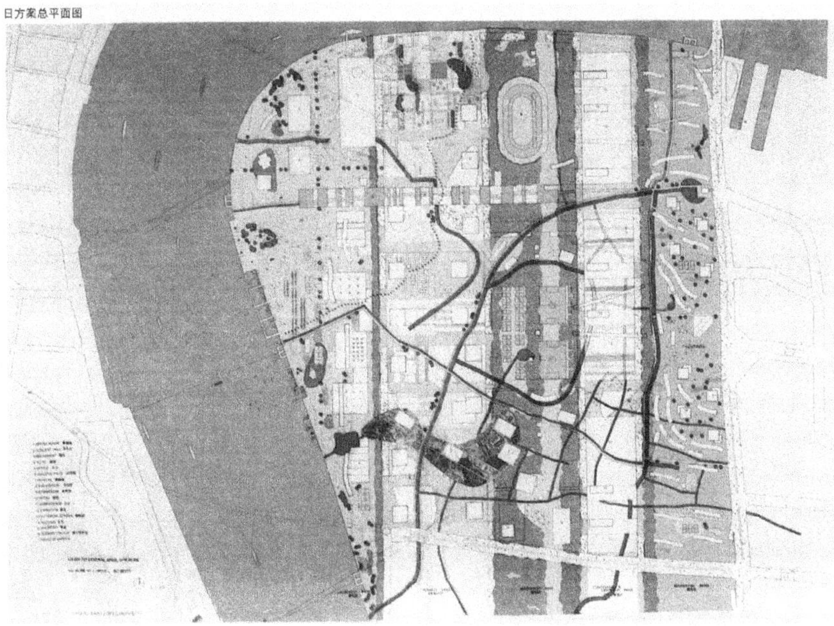

The Japanese Scheme

The designers from Italy, the birthplace of the Renaissance, even played with the oriental culture, and the planning model for the scheme was an oval old castle, with a river in the middle dividing it into two regions of yin and yang, which suggested the idea of yin-yang taiji diagram in ancient China.

The romantic French designers' plan model was very bold, which highlighted the modern, abstract, and simple Lujiazui, in sharp contrast with the Bund's classical exquisiteness.

The rigorous British designers made a model like a gladiatorial arena of ancient Rome, in the middle of which was a large area of green land

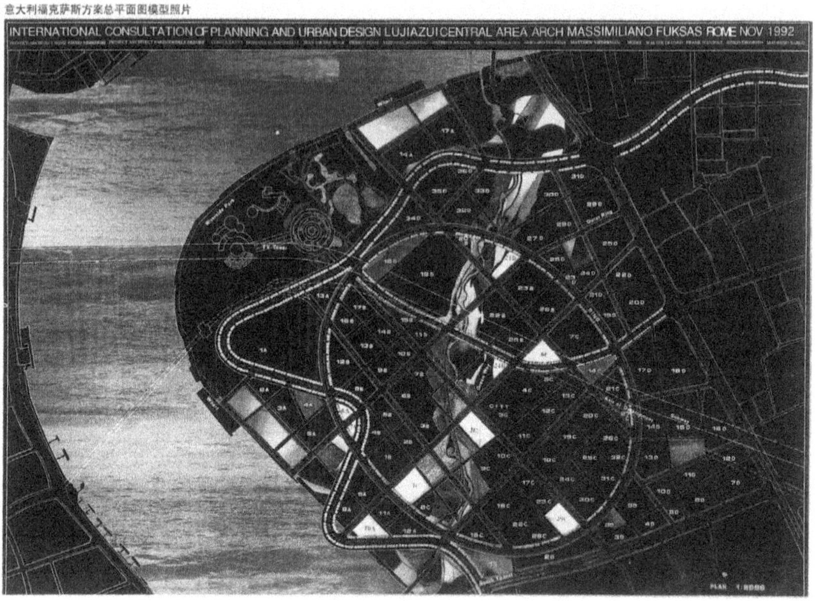

The Italian Scheme

The French Bello Scheme

and pool, rich in classical charm, and fit for the modern life for water, green, and light."

英国罗杰斯方案总平面图

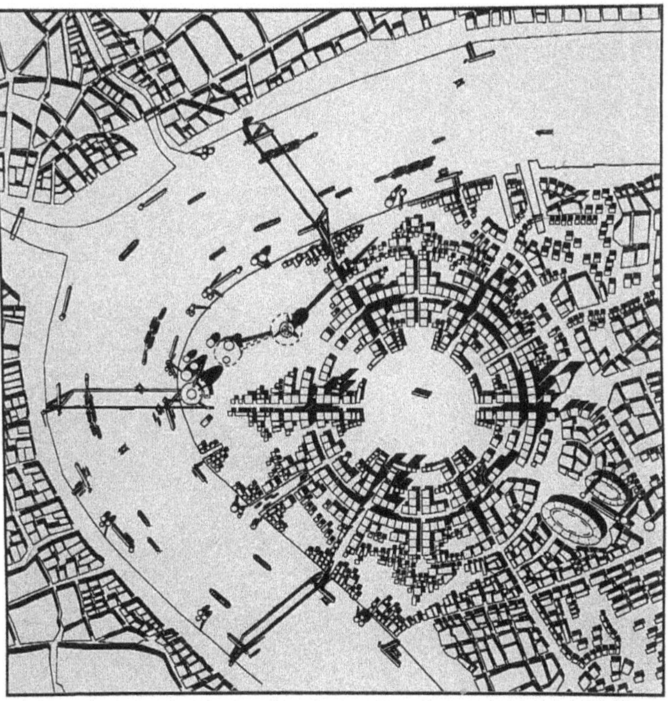

The British Roger Scheme

The Chinese designers' planning model was more practical and reasonable, which emphasized the function of the east-west axis and the development potential.

"The design of each country has its own characteristics. To be honest, all of them are better than our own design," Zhao Qizheng, who attended the meeting, recalled.

After 17 rounds of discussion and revision, it took two years to complete the planning of the Lujiazui central area. This was the first time in the history of China an international consultation on a regional plan was conducted, the first plan to bring together international intelligence.

Rogers G. Richard, a world-famous British designer, remarked, "The brand of a Chinese concept appeared for the first time in the architecture textbook of the 21st century."

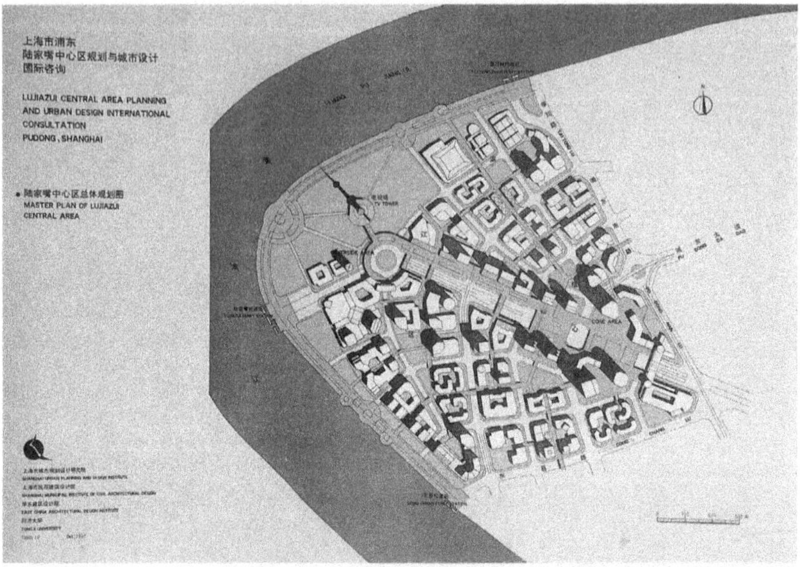

上海方案总平面图

The Shanghai Scheme

The model of the Shanghai Scheme

Interestingly, in the eyes of international designers, Pudong is a "land of excellence". According to the description of an overseas scholar, Pudong comprised of the east bank of the Huangpu River, the southwest bank of the Yangtze River estuary, and the north to the Chuanyang River. This area was an isosceles triangle. The top corner was the junction of the Huangpu River and the Yangtze River, the left bottom corner was formed by the confluence of the Huangpu River and the Chuanyang River, and the right bottom corner was the confluence of the Chuanyang River and the Yangtze River. The vast majority of this region was within 15 kilometers radius from the center of Shanghai, with a population of 1.1 million (in 1989) and an area of 350 square kilometers, as large as the whole urban center of Shanghai at present. In 1992, the area was expanded to 522 square kilometers. The water around the Huangpu River and the Yangtze River estuary was more than 12 meters deep, so ocean transportation could be developed. At the same time, on this piece of land of hundreds of square kilometers, there was also great potential for the development of manufacturing and tertiary industry. Therefore, Pudong was regarded by many world-famous urban planning experts and architects as the last "land of excellence" in the world metropolis in the 20th century.

Because it was a "land of excellence", besides the planning of the Lujiazui central area, the various landmark buildings that would appear on Pudong land also "borrowed brains" from the world and "called on the architectural designers from all over the world for bidding". The Pudong International Airport with wings like a roc and the Oriental Art Center like a blooming Magnolia flower were the masterpieces of Paul Andrews, a famous French designer. The Shanghai New International Expo Center stemmed from the ingenuity of a German. For the Pudong New Area Administrative Office Center, Fujita Company of Japan was invited for the design. The 1.4-square-kilometer Century Park was a fusion of Chinese and Western cultures by British designers.

Because Pudong intended to face the world, many architectural design masters and architectural firms composed of master architects showed up in Pudong such as Leoh Ming Pei, Graves, Heichuan Ji Zhang, Jiqixin, Andrew, Rogers, Nikken Sekkei, Skidmore, Owings & Merrill (SOM), Kohn Pedersen Fox (KPF), and so on.

After visiting Pudong, the former United Nations Secretary-General Boutros Boutros-Ghali heartily exclaimed, "You are playing an international Olympic architectural design contest. It is the pride of Pudong and the glory of the United Nations. I wish you a great success."

Nearby, the Oriental Art Center in the shape of a phalaenopsis was the masterpiece of Paul Andrews, a famous French designer. In the distance, for the design of the Administrative Office Center of the Pudong New Area, Fujita Company of Japan was invited. Far beyond that, the 1.4-square-kilometer Century Park, a fusion of Chinese and Western cultures, was designed by British designers. (Photo by Niu Yixin, Shanghai News Aerial Photography Alliance, China)

By 1994 alone, more than 500 Chinese and foreign architectural design institutions took part in the contest. On the land of Pudong, the design contest of "calling on architectural designers from all over the world to bid" was based on the respect and tolerance for modern civilization and the strong awareness of having dialogues with the world.

Such international tenders are now very common, but it was a breakthrough in China at that time. There were a lot of skeptics. "For the planning of a city, soliciting proposals from all over the world touched a 'red line' at that time," according to Li Jianeng, the former Assistant Director of the Pudong New Area Administrative Committee. In the early 1990s, the city's designing and planning was generally considered "confidential" out of national security considerations, so there were strict requirements for the designers involved, not to mention paying a lot of money to foreigners for designing and planning.

Others thought it was unnecessary, time-consuming, and expensive. In particular, it was quite challenged at the time that for planning Pudong's famous Century Avenue, different design firms from multi-parties were invited to bid and at last, a French firm won the bidding. Was it necessary to invite foreigners to design an avenue at the cost of millions?

But Pudong held on.

Over time, people slowly witnessed the effect of "borrowing brains" from the world.

For example, all the people who went to the Lujiazui Financial and Trade Zone were amazed by the large area of green land, grassland, sunlight, blue sky, lake water, grassland scattered with ginkgo leaves, and birds flying in the air.

The tall phoenix trees on the green land of the Lujiazui Center in Pudong bloomed with red leaves, which added a poetic fairy-tale beauty to Pudong (Photo by Liu Sihong)

It was in the winter of 1992 that the International Consultation Meeting on Regional Planning and Urban Design of the Lujiazui Center was held in Shanghai.

Two experts from the United Kingdom and France made a statement of their ideas: "Lujiazui is surrounded by a complex of buildings, so to build a circular green space in the middle can make people and nature integrated, allowing people to be in the embrace of nature."

Someone asked, "How much land does it take to build a central green space?"

The foreign expert replied, "It would cover an area of 10 hectares."

For a time, people in the meeting hall were shocked. Lujiazui was a piece of treasured land, where the development of real estate would have golden effect. But to construct a central park could not make money, and may even lose money.

Li Jianeng recalled, "Such an idea is not only a breakthrough in design, but also a collision of ideas. The people present cannot sit still anymore."

However, after the international bidding, Pudong builders had reached a consensus in the exchange with foreigners that the financial and trade zone with high-rise buildings should not be a "cement forest" without green land.

A well-known Thailand entrepreneur once said to Zhao Qizheng, the then leader of Pudong New Area, that the land price in the Lujiazui Central Zone was so high that it was a pity to build green land along the river and in the center.

Zhao Qizheng told the entrepreneur, "Considering the function of the city, we are willing to do so." He believed that city needed to breathe, needed "lungs", so it needed green land. This is the need of modern urban functions, the need of the harmonious development of people and nature, and the need for Shanghai to build an international financial center.

The world's most expensive green land, as termed by the media, was like a piece of emerald laid in the high-rise cement forest.

Companies of Pudong and Germany jointly invested in building what was known as the largest exhibition center at the time, but after it was built, some people in the exhibition field said that it was not good-looking, not novel in shape. But since its opening, it has become the most

Lujiazui central green land, 100,000 square meters, was once called the most expensive green land in the world by the media. Embedded in the high-rise concrete forest, it is like an emerald. (Photo by Niu Yixin, Shanghai News Aerial Photography Alliance, China)

popular among visitors and exhibitors, bringing about the most economic profits.

"Why? We adopted the most advanced technology and design concept. For all the passageways and exhibition areas in the Exhibition Center, we chose the design most convenient and comfortable for exhibitors and visitors. All the exhibition halls, built with column-free structures, facilitated the entry and exit of various large-scale equipment. If the exhibition halls were full of staircases and columns, how could the large exhibits be moved in?" Chen Binghui, former Director of the Foreign Affairs Office of the Pudong New Area Administrative Committee, recalled.

The Shanghai New International Expo Center was one of the most successful exhibition centers in China, which attracted about 2 million visitors from home and abroad and more than 20,000 exhibitors from home and abroad every year.

An official of the Pudong government quoted a western proverb: we do not eat beef to become a cow, but to strengthen the body.

At this time, Shanghai people discarded their haughty airs and abandoned their long-standing contempt for outsiders, and showed a more modest attitude and a stronger passion for learning.

In the early spring of 1990, Zhu Rongji, mayor of Shanghai at that time, specially invited the Tianjin Urban Construction Delegation to come to Shanghai to pass on their valuable experiences. Through the exchanges between the two sides, Shanghai attached greater significance to the transportation construction for the development of Pudong New Area, and specified the plan for building the "loop" of two fast-speed main roads at the initial stage of the development of Pudong. First of all, through the two bridges of Nanpu and Yangpu, a circular main road would be built to link Pudong and Puxi. Then a larger circular main road (about 200 kilometers) would be built around the existing Shanghai urban area and Pudong New Area. This was also a valuable experience of urban construction in Tianjin and Beijing in the last 10 years.

On March 14, 1990, Zhu Rongji specially met with Liang Zhenying, Director of Jones Lang LaSalle, Hong Kong, who was later the third Chief Executive of Hong Kong. About the development of Pudong, Zhu asked Liang in detail on how to adopt a new land policy and use differential rent to attract foreign investment.

In the early summer of the same year, Huang Ju, Executive Vice Mayor of Shanghai, led the municipal government leaders to visit Guangdong, Fujian, and Shenzhen and other special economic zones to study and consult in detail the experiences and lessons in regard to the reform and development in the South in the 1980s. This visit to the south offered a lot of important inspirations to Shanghai and improved the policy initiative in Shanghai on the development of Pudong New Area.

In 1990 and 1991, the Shanghai Municipal Government invited experts from the World Bank and other important international financial institutions twice to work with Chinese experts on how to build a financial center in Shanghai and how to raise funds more effectively in the process of Pudong development. These activities, which expanded the horizon and thinking of the Shanghai people, helped them figure out more ways and means of raising funds.

6.2 Selection of Development Mode

As to which kind of development mode Pudong should choose, it was considerably controversial at the beginning.

The first one was the mode of economic and technological development zone. In fact, this type of development zone was an industrial one, and in the 1980s the economic and technological development zones were established everywhere with a high rate of success. But with a single function and small economic scale, they did not have the function of agglomeration and radiation in an urban economy, which was inconsistent with the objective of Pudong development.

The second one was the mode of special economic zone. The special economic zones were relatively large-scaled, but the mode of special economic zone must be premised on the separation between Pudong and Puxi, and the method, like barbed wire, was to be used to split Shanghai into two parts, which cannot meet the target requirements of rebuilding Shanghai as a whole into a national economic center.

The third one was the mode of "recreation of Hong Kong". The Hong Kong mode functioned as an economic center, with the tertiary industry as the focus, but Hong Kong's industrial structure was highly hollowed out, and Hong Kong was a fully free-market economic system. So Pudong can learn from the experience of Hong Kong, but cannot fully transplant the Hong Kong mode.

The fourth mode was the "recreation of Singapore". Singapore adopted a government-controlled economy, and implemented a 5-year plan and a 10-year plan of market economy. The output value of state-owned enterprises accounted for 70% of the domestic economy, while the state-owned enterprises competed equally with foreign-funded enterprises and private enterprises. The government encouraged foreign banks, while domestic banks continued to grow, so it became an international financial center, which transformed the 8-square-kilometer old city into a 298-square-kilometer world-class garden city. Singapore's development mode was worth following, but Pudong was still different from Singapore in institution and industrial structure.

At last, after discussions, the mode of "all-directional, multi-level development of the new area" was determined. For example, the Lujiazui Financial and Trade Zone and the Waigaoqiao Free Trade Zone were to be set up, with a "priority to finance and trade" policy adopted. The Jinqiao Export Processing Zone and the Zhangjiang High-tech Park were to be set up to make full use of Shanghai's industrial and scientific and technological advantages. Pudong should speed up the construction of urban infrastructure, promote the transformation of Shanghai's old city, accelerate the urbanization of Pudong agricultural areas, and so on. Finally, the comprehensive development of all-directions and multi-levels in Pudong can be accomplished. In order to improve the openness of Shanghai as a whole, not only should the linkage between the east and the west be realized, but also a strong radiation effect on the Yangtze River Valley and even the whole country can be achieved.

This option was also related to the development strategy of "developing Pudong, revitalizing Shanghai, serving the whole country, facing the world".

Li Jianeng, Assistant Director of the Pudong New Area Administrative Committee and planning expert, recalled, "The aim to develop Pudong put forward in our research was not to develop Shanghai for the sake of Shanghai itself. Developing Shanghai for the sake of Shanghai was relatively simple, that is, to expand the urban area was easier to accomplish. But from the national perspective, the development of Pudong was not only the expansion of urban area to Pudong. So why did Pudong hold international seminars at that time? After the beginning of the development of Pudong, several national meetings were held. The orientation was that Pudong should be considered from the higher standing-point of Shanghai and the whole country. ...Therefore, such a high strategy guided the development of Pudong, which aimed not only for Shanghai but also for the whole country, and also to serve the whole country and face the world. This guiding ideology ran through the whole process of Pudong development, so that Pudong New Area quickly elevated to a new level."

6.3 Constructing a Functional Development Area

Establishing zones was also a way to promote the rapid development of the regional economy. At the beginning of Pudong development, there had already been four national-level zones. However, the practice in Pudong was different from that in the general economic and technological development zones and special economic zones.

In September 1990, the Development Company of the Waigaoqiao Free Trade Zone, the Development Company of the Lujiazui Finance and Trade Zone, and the Development Company of the Jinqiao Export Processing Zone were established at the same time, and the Development Company of the Zhangjiang High-tech Park was established in July 1992. These were the four famous development parks in Pudong development history. Among them, the Lujiazui Financial and Trade Zone was the only development zone named after finance and trade in China, and the Waigaoqiao Free Trade Zone was the first free trade zone approved by Chinese Central Government.

The economic zone, as an economic phenomenon, first came into being in the Rieghern Free Port Area of Italy in 1574. Since then, free ports, free trade zones, and other forms of economic development zones also emerged all over the world. However, only after the 1950s did the economic zones develop greatly. Silicon Valley of the United States was the model of success. After the 1980s, there was a worldwide upsurge in the establishment of economic zones, with the acceleration of development.

The Chinese people also hoped to achieve rapid growth through the establishment of economic zones, especially local governments at all levels, which had the strong impulse to establish economic zones, and Pudong was no exception. But as to how to run the zones, the brilliant Pudong people placed more emphasis on "recreation of center" and "development of functions".

Professor Wang Zhan, President of the Shanghai Academy of Social Sciences, recalled, "At that time, Pudong proposed not to 'establish economic and technological development zones, but to develop functional development zones'. Since the 1980s, the whole country, especially the eastern coastal areas, had been developing economic and technological development zones. But according to the studies of Pudong, now that a center should be rebuilt, this center must be functional, so it doesn't work if it is to rely solely on the economic and technological development zone and introduce foreign capital to develop the industry. So, what kind of development zone should be set up? What first came to mind was Waigaoqiao, a trade port, so at that time the free trade zone was targeted. With this port, a large number of projects would definitely come in, multinational companies would move in, and an export processing zone would be set up in Jinqiao. Economic activities always need financial support in the end, so further inwards, in Lujiazui, with good regional conditions, a financial trading zone would be established. In the third wave of high-tech development since the mid-1980s, people thought it necessary to develop high-tech, so there was Zhangjiang. At that time, there was also a community called Liuli Modern Residence, which was located roughly in the current Expo Park. It turns out that the idea was quite innovative at that time to establish functional development zones, instead of economic and technological development zones."

What kind of zone was the so-called functional development zone? How on earth did the functional area of Pudong come into being? Sha Lin, former Deputy Mayor of Shanghai and Deputy Director of the Pudong New Area Development Office, recalled, "It was easy to understand and plan Lujiazui as a financial district, since the Bund, which was across the river with Lujiazui, was originally a financial center. So with financial development in Lujiazui, it can be integrated with the old urban area to form a financial and information center. With well-developed finance, the entire city would be activated, and funds would come in. This is one of the most prominent characteristics of the development and construction of Pudong New Area. Moreover, Lujiazui's location advantage was obvious, so we planned to give full play to its differential effect, so that the development efficiency can be maximized."

The Jinqiao Export Processing Zone was the only export processing-oriented development zone in China. Sha Lin said, "In the 1980s, there was an extreme shortage of foreign currency in Shanghai, but many things had to rely on foreign exchange and the cost of foreign exchange was very high, so it was very difficult for export at the beginning. This mainly resulted from the obstacles in the institution, and also our poor product structure, with low added value and mostly raw materials, such as local products, which were exported in boxes. For example, when traditional Chinese herbs were exported, they were low-priced, but once they were processed and sub-packaged in foreign countries, the price became higher a hundred times. Clothing was also exported in large quantities, but little foreign currency was earned. When he was mayor of Shanghai, Comrade Jiang Zemin stressed that Shanghai could develop the most competitive product. Comrade Zhu Rongji demanded Pudong to develop modern, capital-intensive, and technology-intensive industries with a wide labor market, low energy consumption of raw materials, and great ability to earn foreign currency through export."

Thereafter, the Jinqiao Export Processing Zone came into being. But Shanghai proposed to develop products of pillar industry with high added value and deep processing, including aviation equipment, chemical equipment, mechanical equipment, household appliances, and so on. Sha Lin said, "At that time, we felt that to improve the international digestion capacity of our industry, we must first take part in the international exchanges, and then optimize the industrial structure and improve our ability to earn foreign currency through exports. As a result, the automobile industry in the Jinqiao Export Processing Zone became our pillar industry, and the automobile, upgraded immediately, became part of the high-end industrial chain, and participated in the composition of the international industrial chain. ...Thus, in Shanghai, a relatively complete industrial chain in the advanced manufacturing industry was developed, which played an active role in Shanghai's industrial restructuring and product upgrading."

More than 20 years after the development of Pudong, Sha Lin, at an interview, recalled, "The presence of the Waigaoqiao Free Trade Zone meant that after commodities entered this area, they began to enjoy free custom duty at home and abroad. Concerning the establishment of a free trade experiment zone that we talked about today, in fact, at that time, establishing the Waigaiqiao Free Trade Zone was proposed. Comrade Zhu Rongji spoke in English about the establishment of a free trade zone. Later, for various reasons, a free trade zone was set up. The planning of the Zhangjiang High-tech Park mainly took into consideration that the transformation and revitalization of Shanghai should not only depend on traditional industry, but also high-tech industry."

Sha Lin, former Professor of Fudan University, had been engaged in teaching and research in microelectronics. In 1990, he, though in his 50s, was like a young man full of passion and boundless vision for the development of Pudong.

"Recreation of center" and "functional development" was the guiding ideology for constructing the four functional development zones in Pudong.

6.4 Form Construction in Service of Functional Development

The constructors in Pudong attached great importance to functional development, and Zhao Qizheng repeatedly emphasized the functional development after his arrival in Pudong. He said, "Functional design and development should be ahead of form design and development." This mode was proved to be very successful, that is, insistence on function-orientation, form construction in service of functional development, and the introduction of projects subject to function-orientation. This development mode was especially applicable to the areas with weak economic foundation, and areas of direct shift from the agricultural to the urbanized.

In China, it is generally difficult to avoid repetition and blindness in the process of urban development, and so was the history of urban development in Shanghai. Generally, preconceived ideas keep a strong hold. As long as there is a chance for development, the form serves the function and the function serves the project, so that the randomness of urban development may increase, resulting in very serious waste and loss. As a result, foreigners who came to Shanghai in 1980s found an intolerable situation — the mix of factories and dwellings, and even on bustling commercial streets, there were all-size factories along Huaihai Road.

The development of Pudong drew lessons from the blind-expansion urban development of Shanghai in the past, and divided the city into regions based on different functions, locating finance and trade in the Lujiazui area on the east bank of the Huangpu River, across which was the former financial street, the Bund. Export processing was located in the

Jinqiao area, port handling and logistics storage in the Waigaoqiao area at the mouth of the Huangpu River, and high-tech in Zhangjiang of the central Pudong area. It was the first time areas were planned based on their functions in China.

Of course, this was also the result of a long period of research on the functional orientation in Pudong development conducted by Shanghai officials and experts and scholars. Finally it was proposed that Pudong development should reshape the multifunctional role of the Shanghai Economic Center, rather than establish a purely industrial and population evacuation base. Shanghai should build a modern and international new urban area instead of a large-scale economic and technological development zone or an all-inclusive development zone with ambiguous functional orientation.

In April 1991, Zhu Rongji, then Party Secretary and Mayor of Shanghai, headed a friendly delegation to visit the friendship cities in Italy, the Netherlands, Belgium, France, Spain, and Germany to promote Pudong New Area and recommend Pudong New Area to foreign chambers of commerce, employer associations and multinational corporations, and financial giants.

At that time, what the foreigners were most concerned about was how the infrastructure could provide a guarantee. A French banker once bantered, "It takes me an hour and a half to fly from Hong Kong to Shanghai, but it takes me an hour and a half to get to the Bund from Hongqiao Airport, and it takes me 45 more minutes to arrive in Pudong (taking ferry at that time). This is intolerable to us." Therefore, the comrades concerned introduced the Nanpu Bridge and the cross-river tunnel on Yan'an East Road under construction, which aroused an active atmosphere and warm applause at the venue.

Xu Kuangdi, former Mayor of Shanghai, made a recollection: they proposed that the entire Pudong New Area, after the division of regions based on functions, should be equipped with corresponding elements and facilities, such as "seamless" links in the industrial chain of enterprises in export processing zones, namely, factories of components, spare parts, and complete machines should be put in one park as much as possible, and custom, taxation, bank, and logistics should be in "zero distance" service; in high-tech parks, there should be universities, research institutes, "incubators", capital venture firms, and shared testing and computing centers. All of these exerted important influence on the making and revision of the planning of Pudong New Area and even Shanghai as a whole.

These suggestions prompted the developers of Pudong to think further. Xu Kuangdi said, "At that time, we felt that the development and opening of Pudong was by no means enclosing a plot of land, paving several roads, and constructing many high-rise buildings. Instead, it is necessary to draw lessons from the operation and exchange rules of the international mode of market economy, so that we can formulate our development strategies, achieve 'building a nest to attract a phoenix', attract high-level foreign investment projects, and build international first-class development zones."

The reason why functional development was greatly emphasized was related to the recreation of the center in Shanghai, which is why Shanghai can stand higher and look ahead a little further in thinking about the development of Pudong.

According to Zhao Qizheng, "Shanghai is not only an important city in China, but also one of the important cities in the world. What is the most important? It is the function, that is, what it can do, and what role it can play. It is a financial center, a trade center, a logistics and shipping center, and even a communication center. Function should be considered first for the functional design of the city. Functional design and development should be ahead of form design and development. The so-called form refers to buildings, roads, electricity, and factories. At that time there was a very popular metaphor. Why do we want to build a football field? For the World Cup, for the football match. The construction of this football field, laying green land and building spectators stands, is the form construction. Finally, only if the international teams, in accordance with the international rules, come here to play the game, with the international referees as the judge, can the function of the stadium be brought into play. Pudong development is conceived in this way, that is, by constructing buildings, opening factories, building roads, and finally making it operating well up to our expectations, it can become an important part of China's economic city."

At a certain meeting, Zhao Qizheng repeatedly warned the Pudong leaders attending the meeting, "Some people are worried about the extreme emphasis on form development and negligence of functional development in the first five years of Pudong development. This is a warning to the Pudong New Area government, and I think it makes sense, and it's a warning to us."

Also because of the functional development, in Pudong there were three levels of main bodies. Firstly, the country was taken as the main body, the goal of which was to build Shanghai into "four centers". Secondly, Shanghai and the new area were taken as the main body, which can make the market function well. Thirdly, the enterprises were taken as the main body, which aimed to bring the functions of the development zone to full play.

Also because of the functional development, the Central Government and Shanghai gave some of the policies required for the function of the market economy to Pudong as a priority, allowing Pudong to take the test first.

Functional development was also the experience of Pudong development.

6.5 Orderly and Normalized Development

In October 1992, the Shanghai Municipal Government submitted the "General Plan for Shanghai Pudong New Area" to the Standing Committee of the Municipal People's Congress. The general planning objective: in accordance with the strategy of "facing the world, facing the 21st century, and facing modernization" and building a socialist modernized international city, by drawing on the experience of developing new areas at home and abroad, it is envisaged that after several decades of efforts, Pudong New Area will be built into a modern new area with reasonable development layout, advanced comprehensive transportation network, well-developed municipal public facilities, convenient communication system, and good ecological environment. Through the development of the new area, Puxi will be transformed and developed, and the function of Shanghai as the national economic center will be restored and rebuilt, laying foundation for building Shanghai into one of the economic, financial, and trade centers in the Far East.

Such a plan must be well adhered to and carried out. But at that time there was a saying, "planning, planning, drawing on paper, hanging on walls". Many people expressed their doubts about the realization of the plan.

Zhu Xiaoming, former General Manager of the Jinqiao Development Company, had a deep understanding of this. In 1990, when he, former Deputy Director of the Shanghai Textile Bureau, came to Jinqiao, what he saw was the farmland.

"A good start is half the success, and undoubtedly, a good planning for development zones is a good start to us." Therefore, Zhu Xiaoming spent a full three months in doing research and wrote more than 100,000 words for the "Strategy on the Development of the Jinqiao Export Processing Zone", issued to each of the employees.

This research report pointed out, "When the new area started up, there were thousands and thousands of options to be considered. Although much was to be done, we must follow the procedure from formulating the strategy, to making a plan, to implementing the plan. We must give priority to the strategic thinking of development and planning."

Zhu Xiaoming recalled, "Pudong is a development area, facing the 21st century and facing the whole world, and although Jinqiao is oriented as an industrial zone, it must be built according to 'urban planning'."

At that time, many places all over China scrambled to set up development zones, but most of them did not have an overall scientific plan. More often, they made the design in a haste and began the construction in a hurry, so that they achieved half the result with twice the effort, or gave up halfway, or had many regrets left to be repeatedly repaired. According to a Chinese saying, it was "a biscuit turned over and over again".

In order to strictly implement the plan, it took Jinqiao one year to formulate a more detailed and elaborate implementation plan, and the "Planning Atlas of the Jinqiao Export Processing Zone" was printed.

Zhu Xiaoming said, "Attracting investment was a frequent business activity for the development zone. The Jinqiao Development Company usually did not treat guests and accept gifts, but certainly gave investors this planning atlas. This measure was fully affirmed by foreign businessmen."

In compiling the Jinqiao plan, Zhu Xiaoming absorbed the successful experience of foreign export processing zones, with high starting point, accurate positioning, and strict implementation. Many investors came to Jinqiao and found that all things were being orderly implemented in accordance with the precise planning, such as the arrangement of facilities on the ground and underground, the location of each building, or the direction of each pipeline.

In Pudong, a group of high-quality officials adhered to the planning as the initial step, which laid good foundation for the development of Pudong.

Li Jianeng, former Assistant Director of the Pudong New Area Administrative Committee and former Vice President of the Shanghai Municipal Planning Institute, remembered clearly that in the hotel suite, he, as a senior planner, drew a thick stack of charts for Pudong. He said, "At the beginning, the development of Pudong was an orderly and standardized development in accordance with the precedence of the planning, the infrastructure, the finance, and the legal system. This is rarely seen in the world."

The receptionists always guided the visitors who came to interview and inspect the four development zones of Pudong New Area to look at the planning model and told them, "Look, this is our future and we will not deviate from the planning."

On October 25, 1997, when King Harald V of Norway visited Pudong, he felt that Pudong had a very clear plan and concept in its construction. He said, "The development of Pudong is a very unique successful example in the history of urban development in the world. Almost none of the urban development in the world was fully planned in advance, so there was a great randomness in urban construction, and the effect was very poor. But Pudong's construction is carefully planned. It is very valuable."

In September 2002, after a visit to Pudong, Stephenson, the world's leading authority on CBD and the special economic consultant to the mayor of Greater London, told Pudong officials, "Pudong of Shanghai is one of the most successful urban development areas at the turn of the century."

Stephenson, also a planner, once directed and participated in redevelopment projects for the urban core areas of international key economic cities, such as Docklands in London, Brooklyn in New York, La Defense in Paris, Macy in Toronto, the downtown Plaza in Sydney, and so on.

Stephenson explained: the above-mentioned regional development of the international key economic cities was quite excellent, but in terms of the function of the economic engine, Pudong development in Shanghai was the most successful, magnanimous, with a higher starting point. In a short period of more than 10 years, not only was a world-famous international financial and trade center established, but also high-tech industries on a large scale were developed as a result of the encouragement of independent scientific and technological innovation. Not only did the gross domestic product (GDP) achieve an incredible continuous jump, but also the urban and rural areas, cultural prosperity, and the quality of citizens developed at the same pace. When he returned, he advised the mayor of London to pay frequent visits to Pudong.

Of course, plans need to be executed by humans, and in the process of implementation some errors may occur in one way or another.

In April 2013, Wang Ande, former General Manager of the Lujiazui Development Company, was invited to give a speech, and he recalled the past and acknowledged with some regret that there were some shortcomings. This place developed too fast to have sufficient preparations. The first one was too much emphasis on financial functions, and less on life necessities, residential, business, culture, and entertainment. The second one was that the Lujiazui project plot was relatively small, so the buildings rose up like a pencil. The third one was traffic. The fourth one was environmental protection and energy conservation. If we did it again today, we would have a lot of things for introspection and could do better.

In 2015, *A Dream Realized in Lujiazui* was published. In the book, Ni Bing, Deputy Director of the Shanghai Municipal Engineering Administration and planning expert, said regretfully, "Lujiazui was no worse than the financial centers abroad (like La Defense in Paris). But in terms of development efficiency and intensity, we still have a gap with them. Their basic ancillary facilities were developed as a whole and then project construction followed, so the degree of comprehensive development was very high. However, at that time, we were limited in perception, strength, and the requirements for development progress, so we should establish the image as soon as possible, and adopt the rolling development mode in the process. The financial problems, engineering technical problems, and other problems in the implementation of the projects resulted in the failure of some facilities that were not systemized according to the planning (like underground traffic system)."

6.6 Wisdom in Legislation

In early July 1990, the Central Government sent a delegation of Chinese mayors headed by Zhu Rongji to visit the United States. The delegation of mayors, chaired by Wang Daohan, was accompanied by a delegation of five scholars from Shanghai. The five scholars were Ding Xinghao, Director of the American Studies Division of the Institute of International Issues; Hong Wenda, Professor of political economy at Fudan University; Zhou Dunren, Assistant Director of the American Studies Center at Fudan University; Yao Tinggang, Director of the International Economy Institute of Shanghai Academy of Social Sciences; and Zhou Hanmin, Chairman of the Law Department at the Shanghai Institute of Foreign Trade.

The American newspaper *The New York Times* published a long report on the development of Pudong, illustrated with a color map of Pudong. According to the survey, it was found to be the first article published in foreign media using the word "Pudong".

Many years later, a scholar living in the United States made a comment on the development of Pudong: This sent a message to the international community that Shanghai greeted world capitalism, and China needed the world system to develop its economy.

When the delegation held a symposium in New York, an American reporter asked, 10 preferential policies for the development and opening of Pudong were printed in a space as small as a palm in the newspaper, so how can the development and opening of Pudong be promoted on such a basis? Foreign enterprises did not dare to attend the symposium because there was no legal guarantee. Zhu Rongji said resolutely, "We will definitely legislate to protect the development and opening of Pudong and the rights and interests of foreign investors."

In late July, when the delegation returned to Shanghai, the executive meeting of the Municipal Government decided that the development and opening of Pudong must be legislated. When the law was formally promulgated, it was required to be released in Chinese, English, and Japanese to the whole world.

Professor Zhou Hanmin, researcher of international commercial law, recalled, "I was appointed as a member of the legislative panel and later appointed the general reviser of the English version. I remember very clearly that summer, we lived in the rooms of Chunshenjiang Hotel on the upper floors of the Shen Dacheng Building and worked very hard. The main task was proofreading the English version. But the English translation and proofreading of the law was so difficult that I had to seek for help from Gerfander, an American lawyer who worked in the Shanghai Friendship Building. We had known each other in the course of lawyers' business. I explained to him that I was shouldering the heavy responsibility. Because the legislation was required to be accurate, I asked him to help me in 'polishing' the English translation. Whatever I was not sure about in translation, I went to discuss with him. Pudong legislation emphasized how to protect foreign capital and how to promote the improvement of the investment environment. In my opinion, this was an important function of the law."

Two months later, the first batch of laws and regulations for the development and opening of Pudong were released in Chinese, English, and Japanese at the press conference of the Shanghai Municipal People's Government held on September 10. These laws and regulations included "Provisions for Examining and Approving Foreign-invested Enterprises in Pudong New Area of Shanghai", "Interim Provisions for the Administration of Planning and Construction of the Pudong New Area of Shanghai", "The Management Provisions Executed by Custom of the People's Republic of China on the Import and Export Goods, Transportation Vehicles, and Personal Accompanying Article in the Waigaoqiao Free Trade Zone of Shanghai", "Several Regulations on Land Management in Pudong New Area of Shanghai", "Several Regulations of Shanghai on Encouraging Foreign Investment in Pudong New Area of Shanghai", "Guidance on Industry Orientation and Investment in Pudong New Area of Shanghai", "Regulations on the Reduction and Exemption of Enterprise Income Tax and Consolidated Industrial and Commercial Tax for Encouraging Foreign Investment in Pudong New Area", and "Provisions on the Management of the Waigaoqiao Free Trade Zone in Shanghai".

Subsequently, more regulations were formulated and completed, such as "Interim Provisions of Shanghai on Encouraging Non-local Investment in Pudong New Area", "Implementation Regulations for Foreign Currency Management in the Waigaoqiao Free Trade Zone, Pudong, Shanghai", "Interim Provisions on Examining, Approving, and Managing Foreign

Investment Projects in Pudong New Area", "Management Provisions for Foreign Economy and Trade in Pudong New Area of Shanghai", "Regulations on the Waigaoqiao Free Trade Zone of Shanghai", etc. These laws and regulations constituted the legal framework for the development and opening of Pudong.

After the launch of Pudong development, the precedence of legislation laid a solid foundation for the long-term stability and long-term development of Pudong. This was totally different from the delayed legislation when several special economic zones in the south had been developed in the early 1980s, which emphasized its priority. At the beginning of the development of Pudong, Wang Daohan said, "With some wisdom, we do things; with great wisdom, we conduct ourselves; and with far-sighted wisdom, we make legislation," which was the extremely profound thinking.

6.7 Tertiary Industry Taking the Lead in Breakthrough

At 7 in the evening on April 15, 1992, in Bibo Hotel, East Lake, Wuhan, the Shanghai delegation at the Sixth Meeting of the Economic Coordination of the Central Cities along the Yangtze River held a press conference. Huang Qifan, Assistant Director of the Pudong Development Office, told the reporters frankly, "Compared with Shenzhen, the opening of Pudong is highlighted in the policies in the tertiary industry such as finance and commerce. This reflects the shift of China's opening from the secondary industry to the tertiary industry. This is a higher level of openness."

Today, the term "tertiary industry" is well known, but in the 1980s, people were unfamiliar and alienated from it. After the launch of the development and opening of Pudong, it was in the tertiary industry that a major breakthrough was achieved, which was a surprising leap in the process of China's reform and opening-up.

According to Yao Xitang, economist and former President of the Pudong Reform and Development Research Institute, roughly in 1982, the discussions on Shanghai's economic development began to get heated, an important issue of which was whether Shanghai should develop the tertiary industry. By 1984, the heated discussion had reached its climax. With the emancipation of the mind, the new way of thinking became clearer and clearer. The adjustment of Shanghai's economic structure and the development of the tertiary industry became the focus of discussions in this period.

Yao Xitang said, "At that time, many people were unable to understand the need for developing the tertiary industry, because they felt that the tertiary industry did not create wealth. Even the statistical indicators at that time only included the output value of industry and agriculture, and there was no reference to the tertiary industry." At that time, leaders and scholars treated the problem very seriously about whether to develop the tertiary industry.

This is not a joke, but real history.

Such a historical detail can be corroborated. At that time, Shanghai completed the "Outline of Shanghai Economic Development Strategy", which was to be submitted to the Central Government. On the eve of the submission of the report outline, once again Mayor Wang Daohan consulted, with great prudence, two groups of experts who held different views on the development of the tertiary industry in Shanghai, and attached their different opinions to the would-be-submitted report.

Fortunately, the municipal leaders were very open-minded at that time, and for a long time after 1985, expert seminars were held every two weeks in the city. Meetings were comparatively open and casual, and the topics were discussed in depth. Yao Xitang said, "Mayor Jiang often took part in discussions in person, and sometimes argued with others about a particular point of view."

There was a greater background for the open-mindedness of the leaders and scholars, that is, the minds of millions of Chinese people began to break through the traditional cage and ran faster on the road of reform and opening-up.

"For me, the most impressive discussion was on the topic of whether Shanghai should build a stock exchange. This was 'avant-garde' at that time." Wang Xitang recalled that there was a discussion after Wang Zhan returned with his team from visits to the New York Stock Exchange in the United States. The discussion was particularly heated, with the topics ranging from the introduction of international experience to the actual situation in Shanghai. It lasted from 9 in the morning until 12.30 in the afternoon. Finally, Jiang Zemin made a summary, "According to the discussions, I think, to a certain extent, in a country of socialism, a stock exchange can also be established."

This sentence left a profound impression on Yao Xitang. The leader was so emancipated in thinking with such a bold attempt and firmness in reform that Shanghai would have a great breakthrough in the tertiary industry.

It is not easy to develop the tertiary industry in China. In the planned economy era, China's economy, which copied the model of the Soviet Union, was always industry-centered, especially the heavy chemical industry. Even in the 1980s, China's opening to the outside world was dominated by the secondary industry. Despite the rapid development of the market economy, most of the tertiary industries were still closed from the outside world.

Historical opportunity came around. When the development of Pudong started in 1990, Zhu Rongji, Secretary of the Shanghai Communist Party Committee, seized the opportunity to make a proposal, "We should carefully consider the road, the mode, the direction, and the dominant industry for Pudong development and Shanghai's opening-up. It is really worth our thinking and discussion."

In June of the same year, Zhu Rongji visited Hong Kong and Singapore, which prompted his further reflection. When he returned, he asked the participants at the Shanghai Conference of Party Members and Cadres a question: Why did Hong Kong develop so fast in the past decade?

Zhu Rongji once passed by Hong Kong in 1983 and stayed there for three days. But when he visited Hong Kong this time, he found, "Now it is beyond comparison with the past. It is a mode of shop in the front and factory at the back. The front shops were located in Hong Kong and the back factories were located in Guangdong. Tens of millions of people were backing it up, while Hong Kong made most of the money. Why? Because all the valuable things were in Hong Kong, that is, the tertiary industry, including finance."

Therefore, he solemnly proposed, "We should fully understand the role of the tertiary industry in the development of the national economy. The tertiary industry does not only include hotels, but also finance, information, consulting, and other industries that serve the entire economy and industrial production. These industries are so important in that they can make much more money than industrial enterprises."

At this time, as a local leader, Zhu Rongji really had a higher positioning. His thinking on the development of the tertiary industry was not only confined to Shanghai, but to the whole country. He said, "We must develop the tertiary industry to serve the development of the Yangtze River Valley and the Yangtze River Delta. As a window, it may play a much greater role than a few factories alone, and Shanghai depends on this for its own prosperity."

Zhu Rongji was determined to activate the tertiary industry by means of the development of Pudong and pushed Shanghai, a super-large industrial city, onto the road of overall transformation.

In June 1990, the Shanghai Economic Delegation headed by Zhu Rongji and consulted by Wang Daohan visited Hong Kong and Singapore to promote the development of Pudong. Zhu Rongji told the Hong Kong business sector that there were four characteristics for the development and opening of Pudong. Firstly, they aimed to establish a "free port" and a free trade industrial zone that can guarantee tariff exemption for commodities, personnel and merchant ships, and free access. Secondly, they preferred to take introducing the foreign capital bank and enlivening the finance as the leading activity, and to open and develop various kinds of ancillary service industry. Thirdly, they would like to make some experiments on the transfer of land tenure, or land lease, a and the development of the real estate market. Fourthly, they would further improve the approach to attracting foreign direct investment and prepare for a shareholding system, and even absorb private investment in infrastructure construction.

The delegation then visited Singapore to meet with local business leaders and issued invitations to the development of Pudong. Zhu Rongji also revealed a bigger news that Shanghai would set up a stock exchange within the year.

More daring, Zhu Rongji also frankly told foreign businessmen in English that Pudong would also set up a free trade zone. But at that time, in Chinese it can only be called a bonded area. Zhu Rongji clearly knew that foreign businessmen could not understand if he told the foreign businessmen that a bonded zone would be built in Pudong. At this time, soon after the political turmoil in Beijing subsided, "freedom" was still a very sensitive word in China, often associated with capitalism, which was a very serious problem in China at that time. But Zhu Rongji told the world unmistakably that China would also set up a free trade zone, which showed Zhu's courage. But in fact, the free trade zone was established in China 23 years later.

Zhu Rongji also took a helicopter in person and overlooked every corner of Pudong. The higher one stands, the farther he can see. Soon "three firsts" guideline was put forward concerning Pudong development and opening-up, one of which was "finance and trade to be developed first".

Thus, the first free trade zone in China, the Waigaoqiao Free Trade Zone; the first financial and trade development zone, the Lujiazui Financial and Trade Zone; the first Sino-foreign joint venture commercial retail enterprise; the first foreign bank, and so on settled down in Pudong. The development of the tertiary industry ran onto a fast track.

All these resulted from the functional policy that Pudong requested from the Central Government, which was not enjoyed in other special economic zones.

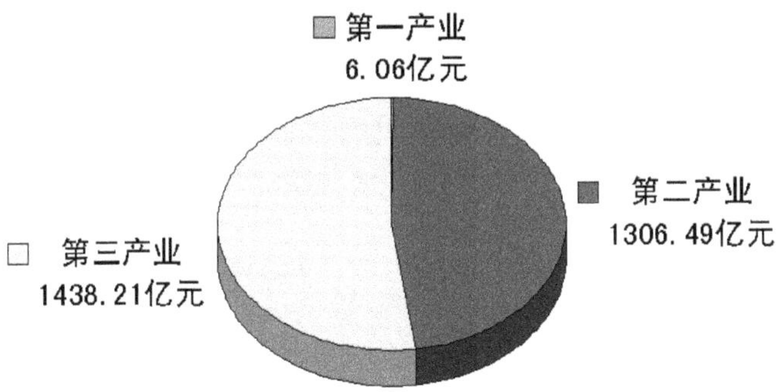

By 2007, the tertiary industry in Pudong had surpassed the secondary industry

On April 15, 1992, during the Sixth Conference of the Economic Coordination of the Central Cities along the Yangtze River, Huang Qifan proudly revealed to reporters that Pudong enjoyed five new policies not accessible in Shenzhen and other special zones.

First, foreign enterprises were allowed to do business in Pudong New Area, and open department stores and supermarkets. Recently, the Sino-Japanese joint venture Shanghai Bachang Co., Ltd. had been approved, which is China's first large-scale Sino-foreign retailer joint venture.

Second, in general, banks, finance companies, insurance companies, and other institutions were only allowed to open in special zones, while for Pudong, foreign finance was allowed to operate in the whole of Shanghai.

Third, like Shenzhen, Shanghai can issue its own shares and bonds within the limits approved by the Central Government, and at the same time allowed shares issued throughout the country to be traded in Shanghai.

Fourth, the most open bonded zone was set up in Waigaoqiao of Pudong, which became the free trade zone.

Fifth, production projects with a total investment of less than 200 million yuan and non-productive infrastructure projects can generally be approved by Shanghai itself.

Some sensitive and experienced reporters noticed that in these five new policies, four of them were about the development of the tertiary industry, two of which were about finance, and the other two were about trade. This was not the same as Shenzhen.

At that time, when the officers in charge of attracting investment in Pudong hosted investors and reporters, they always emphasized, "This is the new policy in the new area."

In the 25 years of development and opening-up in Pudong, two historical moments reflected the "amazing leap" of the development of the tertiary industry.

The first moment was at 11 in the morning on December 19, 1990. In the European-style Pujiang Hotel, Wei Wenyuan, General Manager of the Shanghai Stock Exchange, rang the gong of market-opening, which was heatedly responded in China. Shanghai, once the financial center in the Far East, had the largest stock exchange, and the reopening of the stock exchange that had been wiped out after the political turmoil was a sign of

China's determination to continue to open to the outside world and reshape the financial center.

After the establishment of the Shanghai Stock Exchange, the construction of Shanghai's factor market was in high tide. The Shanghai Futures Exchange, China Financial Futures Exchange, Shanghai Diamond Trading Center, and Shanghai Property Exchange were also established in the Lujiazui Financial and Trade Zone of Pudong. The establishment of these trading platforms preliminarily built a nationwide financial system in Shanghai.

The second moment was on December 20, 1995, when the first Shanghai Bachang Co., Ltd., a joint venture of Japanese Bachang Co., Ltd., Hong Kong Bachang Co., Ltd., and Shanghai First Department Store, opened in Pudong. 1.07 million customers flooded into the mall in the cold wind. That number was recorded in the Guinness Book of World Records.

On December 20, 1995, at the opening ceremony of China's first Bachang Co., Ltd., the first Sino-foreign joint venture, Pudong leader presented gifts (Photo by Li Zili)

Before that, no foreign investors stepped into the business sector in China. For the first time, Shanghai Bachang Co., Ltd. broke the monopoly of Chinese capital management in China's commerce. 20 years later, people could enter Wal-mart and Carrefour at will and stroll into the top famous-brand stores in Lujiazui, Pudong. It was difficult to imagine this in the 1980s.

6.8 Integration of Chinese and Western Cultures like All Rivers Running into the Sea

In the development of Pudong, the builders paid more attention to the integration of Chinese and foreign cultures. As a large number of investors came to Pudong, the construction of buildings became a must. So, what kind of buildings should be built? Pudong investors came from all over the world, with different cultural background, so the integration of Chinese and foreign cultures should be taken into consideration by the builders.

In 1992, the Ministry of Foreign Trade and Economic Cooperation of China intended to find the best place in Pudong to build "China's tallest building" for foreign trade import and export corporations.

The best place was the core area along the river in the Lujiazui Finance and Trade Zone, and the highest building should have as many as 88 floors, and be as high as 420 meters.

The construction of "China's tallest building" in Pudong also attracted the attention of architects from all over the world. In February 1993, Pudong officially launched an international tender for the design of the Jinmao Tower. Many powerful construction firms came to Shanghai. Nine design institutions joined in the competition, including Nikken Sekkei, Portman, and SOM, all of which were the world's top architectural design giants.

SOM was the super-high-rise design authority in the world. It is said that one out of every five super-high-rise skyscrapers in the world was designed by SOM. But Nikken Sekkei, determined to win the bid, spent one million dollars in merely preparing for the plan. On the day of the vote, the 12 judges focused on the two blueprints by Nikken Sekkei and SOM. Kurokawa, who came from Japan, finally gave his vote to SOM. He said, "If Nikken Sekkei wins, I would be ashamed, because the SOM plan is so excellent."

The key to the success of SOM was the integration of the essence of Chinese culture into the building.

After the American designer took over the project's bidding, the first consideration was how to make the modern super-high-rise architecture follow the Chinese historical architecture. They searched for a large number of ancient high-rise buildings in the north and south of China, and finally chose the Big Wild Goose Pagoda in Xi'an as the prototype for the design of the Shanghai Jinmao Tower.

The pagoda, as a memorial building of Buddhism, was introduced into China from India as early as the Eastern Han Dynasty more than 1,800 years ago. After that, it began to spread all over China's cities and villages and became a landscape of Chinese native architecture.

In designing this building, SOM's chief designer, Adrian Smith, a lovely old American man with silver-grey hair, fascinated with Chinese pagodas, had studied more than 2,000 Chinese pagodas. Smith said, "We found that the form of a pagoda was actually an example of the earliest high-rise buildings. The layer upon layer of the tower was seen as moving up into the sky. I found this very interesting, and very suitable for the Jinmao Tower."

Meanwhile, American designers also referred to the plane layout of the Forbidden City in Beijing, another of the most famous ancient buildings in China, and introduced the design elements into the shape design of the Jinmao Tower.

Chinese culture was deeply embedded in the diamond-like exquisite architecture, with as many as 88 stories in an 8-cornered shape. Five years later, the tower was erected in Pudong. Despite many high-rise buildings there, passers-by were attracted by the shape of the Jinmao Tower. This affected people's understanding and evaluation of China's reform and opening-up.

Xing Tonghe, a master architect in China, pointed out that the Jinmao Tower was actually a work of the integration of foreign advanced ideas and advanced technology with Chinese culture.

Smith did not think Jinmao fitted Chicago, just as Woolworth Building did not fit Shanghai. National, regional, cultural, and other factors were taken into consideration for a unique building, only fit for a specific place.

The tower was open to visitors when it was completed. Every day, the elevators in Jinmao Tower flew up from the underground floor at a speed of 9.1 meters per second. After a moment of swelling of the eardrums caused by the sudden high pressure, people reached the sightseeing hall on the 88th floor, which was an excellent experience of the speed of Pudong development.

In the sightseeing hall, people have a 360-degree view overlooking the whole Puxi and Pudong. On the glass curtain wall, the words "in the front, Zhongshan Park: 12 kilometers away; Paris: 9250 kilometers away" were printed. This inadvertently broadened the view of tourists: the world was not detached, but a global village. Hundreds of financial intermediary agencies moved into the building. Its 3rd to 50th floors accommodated more than 10,000 people working at the same time, known as "vertical financial street".

Perhaps because it was known as "the tallest building in China" in the 20th century, all the tour guides in Pudong were willing to recommend the building, which was more symbolic, to tourists.

In 2007, Volume 5 of the *China National Geography* magazine published a picture of two foreigners sitting at a high altitude, one of whom reached out of the platform and turned around with the gesture of two fingers for victory, with the background of the Oriental Pearl TV Tower, the Huangpu River, and high-rise buildings. As the caption put it, it was understandable for foreigners seeking excitement to choose the Shanghai Jinmao Tower as a parachuting platform, which was known as the "tallest building in China". It was meaningful for them to take the western-style adventure over the most modern city in ancient China, which was a connection accomplished between the old and the modern, the eastern and the western.

Interestingly, a Chinese writer named Liu Xinwu thought that the Jinmao Tower in Pudong did not look like an overbearing "sturdy lad", but a cordial, even beautiful girl who gave people a feeling of spring breeze. "It's more like a bamboo shoot," he wrote, "the bamboo in the wild mountains of China, very thick and tall. Its air of skyscrapers was not in the least inferior to the trees like pine, cypress, beech, etc., and at the same time its posture, steadily high and luxuriant with branches and leaves, looked extremely exquisite and elegant. I wondered whether the designers of the Jinmao Tower got inspiration from Chinese moso bamboo."

The Century Park in Pudong was also a work of the blending of different cultures, and the British designers go inspiration from Chinese culture.

At that time, Pudong planned to build a 140-hectare central park. The Pudong leader Zhao Qizheng proposed "the integration of Chinese and western culture" to reflect Shanghai as a city of the merging of multi-cultures.

Pudong invited six design firms from the United States, Japan, Germany, France, the United Kingdom, and China for the design. Finally, the British plan was chosen. According to the recollection of Zhu Chunhong, General Director of the Park Construction Headquarter, "The British designers understood our intentions better, that is, the combination of Chinese traditional garden culture with the western lawn. It turned out that our choice was correct."

It is said that in order to design the park, the British designers rode bicycles around the parks in Shanghai, large and small, to learn about Chinese culture and Chinese life. They saw people playing chess, dancing, singing, drinking tea, practicing Taiji, and so on in the parks.

Different cultures were integrated into the design of the park, later called Century Park. The British designers cleverly achieved "the combination of man and nature and the combination of Chinese and western culture", which made it the largest eco-city park full of natural characteristics in Shanghai. When the people of Shanghai entered the park, they suddenly found that it was completely different from the stereotypical parks built in the previously planned economy era. There were large areas of lawns, forests, lakes, central lake islands, leisure squares, rural fields and international gardens, lawns and other scenic areas, as well as installations such as bird protection, scientific experience, children's amusement park, and others. Visitors were leisurely fishing, flying kites, and even enjoying picnics.

The builders in Pudong repeatedly stressed that for cultural integration, there was an example to follow. The United States is an immigrant country, which combined the cultures of Africa, Americas, and Asia. With the essence of world culture, the advantage of American culture helped the

United States to become the world's leading economic power. Japan also made great efforts to learn from the western culture after the Meiji Restoration, integrating the eastern and western cultures and achieving economic takeoff.

Zhao Qizheng believed that in the development of Pudong, their exchange with the world was not only attracting world capital and technology, but also absorbing the wisdom of the world. Their cross-cultural exchanges and active dialogue with the world, that is, the culture developed during the development of Pudong, played an important role in promoting the rapid development of Pudong.

The integration of Chinese and Western cultures was not only easy for Chinese people to accept, but also easy for foreigners to embrace.

On June 3, 2011, when Zhao Qizheng paid a visit to Yale University, Paul Gweitz, Director of the Chinese Law Center of the Law School, said that he once took his 13-year-old son to China.

"I thought the first impression was very important, so I hoped to take him to a very special place in China for the first visit," Gervais said.

They arrived in Shanghai, went from the airport to the hotel, and after the formalities they went directly to Binjiang Avenue, east to the Huangpu River. At night, bright lights along the Huangpu River and in Lujiazui were quite fascinating. Gervais recollected, "I told my son that I wanted him to stand there and have a 360-degree look around. I hoped he could witness the rapid development of Pudong. He saw the high-rise buildings, the surrounding Huangpu River, and the ships running on the river."

The beautiful scene impressed the 13-year-old boy very deeply.

Gervais told Zhao Qizheng excitedly that his son could speak Chinese very fluently at that time. He was a sophomore and he had been to China six times. He had been living in China for about a year. He felt very pleased with this and would like to show appreciation for Zhao's work in Shanghai because his son had the chance to better understand China, a true story about China.

At listening, Zhao Qizheng felt a sudden rush of emotion. Because many people were present, he tried his best to restrain his excitement. He told Gervais that the Pudong plan was also a worldwide plan, designed by world-class designers from Italy, France, Britain, Japan, China, and so on.

6.9 The Absorption of "Nutrition from the World" and the Opening of Economic Dialogue

According to the recollection of Xie Jinhu and Zhang Chijian, reporters of Xinhua News Agency, who had been reporting the development of Pudong for a long period of time, in those days, the cadres in Shanghai talked mostly about the need for "east-west linkage" to revitalize Shanghai. At the same time, they must play the "Yangtze River card" and "China card" to serve the economy of the Yangtze River Valley and the economic development of the whole country. The starting point for developing Pudong should be higher, facing the world, acting in accordance with international practices, and trying to build Pudong as a link with the world economy.

As a result, a more vivid slogan "thinking about the development of Pudong by standing next to the globe" was hung in the "front-line headquarter" of Pudong development and opening-up, that is, the simple canteen located at No. 141, Pudong Avenue.

The slogan was coined by Zhao Qizheng, then Director of the Pudong New Area Administrative Committee. He once explained that the slogan was to remind all Pudong cadres to have an international vision, thinking, and strategy.

Zhao Qizheng said, "For Pudong development, we should face the world. In terms of its functions, the goal is to build it into an economic city of the world, so it requires the business operators of the world to carry out economic activities here, and needs investment from the world, the experience of the world, and the actions of the world. So we are standing next to the globe to observe Pudong, not to observe Pudong in Shanghai."

Zhao Qizheng made two more vivid metaphors.

The first one was the so-called "world nutrition".

Zhao Qizheng said, the development of Pudong was to serve the whole country, but it had to face the whole world, because it needed experience, knowledge, and capital from all over the world.

He asked a question: If you ate pickled mustard and plain rice in the Yangtze River Valley, could you grow very strong? If you drank water in the Pacific, ate sharks in the Pacific, ate steak, ate half-done beef, you would become very strong. Pudong development was like this. It was a world-class development, so it needed world-class "nutrition".

Of course, this was not an easy job. In the early 1990s, China was in a very difficult period, and many investors, and even some cadres, questioned the need for the development of Pudong to meet such high world standards. Therefore, Zhao Qizheng made another metaphor.

The second one was the "economic dialogue".

Zhao Qizheng gave an explanation. There were two types of dialogue between countries: political dialogue and economic dialogue. A political dialogue is conducted between the capitals, between the country leaders, but an economic dialogue is not a dialogue about territory, which can be conducted mainly among the largest economic cities, such as New York, Chicago, San Francisco, and Tokyo as the interlocutors, instead of Disneyland and Sapporo. China was politically strong, but economically lacked a modern big city that can have dialogues with New York, Frankfurt, London, and Tokyo as an equal counterpart. This type of big city was urgently needed in China.

At that time, he thought, for the time being, Shanghai could not be at the forefront of economic dialogue with the world. Why? Because the economy was not well developed. The purpose of Pudong development was to make Shanghai more qualified for equal dialogue with modern international metropolises. Therefore, Pudong development was to revitalize Shanghai, and the revitalization of Shanghai aimed to promote China's economic development. That is the truth needed for repetitive reflection. The planning of Pudong New Area was supposed to focus on upgrading Shanghai's international level and the economic dialogue between China and the world.

Standing at such a height, Zhao Qizheng explained, "Our planning is different, that is, finance, industry, and trade should be, in line with the world market, an integral part of the world market. In terms of the economy, Pudong's quality and quantity should be enhanced to the international level. Otherwise, it would be difficult to gain a foothold in the world market."

Hu Wei, the former Director of Pudong New Area, also held this view. "From the perspective of the reference-space orientation and function-radius orientation of Pudong development, it was neither Shanghai-oriented nor China-oriented development. If the development was oriented within the system of Shanghai, it was likely to become an evacuation area for some polluting industries or substitute industries in Puxi or a relocation area for residents in old urban areas. If the development was oriented within the system of China, it might focus on becoming the limited channel for attracting foreign investment in neighboring provinces and the distribution center of mainland products. However, neither of these can perform the function of 'three centers'. Only the world-oriented development can meet the logic of Pudong development, which was the very characteristic of the development mode of Pudong."

The leaders of Pudong New Area, at this time, were really thinking about the development of Pudong by standing beside the globe.

Some foreign scholars concluded, "Pudong development must have a high starting point and high standards, which should be based on several factors, including Shanghai's special advantages, Shanghai's important position in China and the world, and the lessons and experiences learned from the establishment of special economic zones in China for more than 10 years."

After the launch of Pudong development, the first popular sentence was, "In the 1980s people should look at Shenzhen, and in the 1990s people should look at Pudong." After that, another popular saying was, "The speed of Shenzhen, the height of Pudong."

Chapter 7

The Uphill Battle: Pudong Wearing a Helmet to Withstand

7.1 Idling of Financial Funds and Running of Land Leasing

The grand experiment of reform in Pudong was, in a sense, forced. After the development and opening of Pudong, more than 3,000 construction sites were opened on more than 500 square kilometers of land at the same time, with cranes towering, construction vehicles shuttling, mixers roaring, mud and dust flying everywhere.

Such a large-scale infrastructure construction required a large amount of funds. Where did the money come from?

On the morning of November 14, 1992, Li Jianeng, Assistant Director of the Pudong New Area Administrative Committee, gave a reply to the visiting delegation of Taiwan's Strait Exchange Foundation: "There were five sources of funds for the development of Pudong: grants and loans from the Central Government; loans from international financial groups like the World Bank; grants and loans from the local government; funds raised by issuance of bonds, stocks, and other securities of Pudong New Area; and the introduction of foreign capital. Each of the above sources of funds constituted one-fifth, 10 billion yuan, with a total of 50 billion yuan." But later, 50 billion yuan was far from enough. According to statistics, Pudong invested 25 billion yuan in the first 10 major infrastructure projects in the first round and nearly 100 billion yuan in the second round.

Zhao Qizheng recalled that on November 21, 1996, Warren Christopher, the then United States Secretary of State, visited Shanghai, and, standing on the west bank of the Huangpu River overlooking the crane-lined Pudong, he asked Zhao Qizheng, "It is said that according to the report by the World Bank, construction cranes in Shanghai accounted for 17% of the whole world, didn't they?" Zhao Qizheng replied, "I also heard about the data, but have not yet seen the report, so I cannot give you an affirmative answer. But I do know that Pudong area uses up 100,000 tons of building materials every day and night."

On May 10, 1997, Kofi Annan, the then United Nations Secretary-General, arrived in Pudong, where he saw tall buildings rising from the ground, with cranes everywhere. So, in his speech that afternoon, he suggested to the host that Shanghai should take the crane as the city bird of Shanghai, because in English, the crane (bird) and the crane (construction vehicle) have the same pronunciation and spelling. So many cranes in Shanghai were operated every day for large-scale constructions, so it would be appropriate to choose the crane as the city bird with the same pronunciation as the crane as used in constructions.

According to the international general experience of similar land development, the investment in infrastructure development per square kilometer was approximately US$100 million. But for Pudong land development, more money was needed due to the original weak foundation in the Pudong area, the high standards in the planning and construction of Pudong New Area development, the role that Pudong was aimed to play in leading the economic development of the Yangtze River Valley, the burden Pudong would take as the future hub of China's opening to the outside world, such that the international airport and international deep-water port must be built to support its functions and status as planned, and cross-river transportation projects such as bridge, subway, tunnel, light rail, and so on, must be put into construction.

Therefore, the capital investment per unit area of Pudong land development was close to or even more than that of the similar development in the Asia-Pacific region. The later data about the actual development input showed that at the initial stage of development, the development cost per square kilometer was 500–700 million yuan, and rose to 600–900 million yuan in 1995 and 1996.

After the launch of Pudong development, the three functional development zones of Lujiazui, Jinqiao, and Waigaoqiao should be started first. How can the start-up capital be raised? Even in 1995, the local government revenue of Pudong New Area was only 2.347 billion yuan, which could only afford the development of a few square kilometers.

At that time, each development company took loans of 2 million yuan from the Industrial and Commercial Bank of China as preliminary costs, but this amount of money for Pudong development was far from enough.

Yang Changji, Director of the Pudong Development Office from 1990 to 1991, recalled the process of raising funds. Mayor Zhu Rongji asked him to prepare for the construction of the three development zones of Lujiazui, Jinqiao, and Waigaoqiao and start to develop more than 10 square kilometers of land as soon as possible. According to the estimation of the development cost of 200 million per square kilometer, 2 billion yuan in development fund was needed. Comrade Rongji said that 300 million yuan would be given to each company, and used by rolling over. A few days later, Comrade Rongji told him that it would not be possible for three companies to get 900 million yuan, because it would also cost some money to revitalize and transform Shanghai. So, each company would be given 100 million yuan to start up. He went back to the development office to make it known immediately.

But a few days later, Zhu Rongji was about to leave Shanghai to work in Beijing. Before leaving, he told Yang Changji, "How much will be needed to start up immediately, at least?"

Yang Changji recalled, "At that time I was too shy to speak out, so I thought about it for a moment and said to Comrade Zhu Rongji, 'I would like to give 30 million yuan for one company.'"

Despite the lack of money, we have land. Can land make money?

Much earlier, Lin Tongyan, a Chinese-American architect, had made a similar proposal.

In October 1985, Lin Tongyan made a proposal in San Francisco to Wang Daohan, the mayor of Shanghai who had just retired from office, that Pudong may adopt the method of land leasing, collecting fees from foreign investors, and by the rolling development, a modern Pudong can be built without a penny, and the scale of Shanghai can be multiplied.

Wang Daohan was very interested in it. In 1986, Lin Tongyan submitted a report entitled "Developing Pudong: Building a Great Modern Shanghai", which suggested that the experience of Singapore and Hong Kong be used as reference. This report drew great attention from Shanghai. As a result, he was hired as a consultant by the Shanghai Municipal Government.

After 1949, China began to implement a planned economy. Land was allocated free of charge by the government according to a plan, so it was not allowed to be cashed at the market. By 1987, the new law made it possible to transfer land tenure. Pudong officials thought of land leasing, so they designed a program that combined land capital with cash capital to achieve a virtuous cycle of the rolling development of land.

Huang Qifan, the young Assistant Director of the Pudong Development Office, volunteered to take the lead in carrying out the project. At first, the Shanghai Finance Bureau issued a check to the three development companies in Lujiazui, Jinqiao, and Waigaoqiao according to the land transfer price as the capital input of the government to the enterprises which should be verified by the Industrial and Commercial Bureau. Then, the development companies endorsed the check, gave it to the Shanghai Land Bureau, and signed a contract for the transfer of land tenure which was verified by the Industrial and Commercial Bureau. After the transfer of land tenure was assigned by the Shanghai Land Bureau, all the endorsed checks obtained from the development companies were turned over to the Finance Bureau, which turned over 0.4% of the land income to the state finance of the Central Government.

In June 1992, the Shanghai Municipal Government decided to transfer 5.51 million square meters of land tenure to the three development companies of Lujiazui, Jinqiao, and Waigaoqiao in Pudong New Area, and the three development companies adopted the operation of transfer acceptance, development, and transfer and re-acceptance of transfer. This was the first land transfer in tracts in Shanghai.

This practice was called by Pudong people as "idling of financial funds, running of land leasing". Yang Changji recalled, "Later, this method was summarized as 'karate' by a vice president of the Communist Party of China (CPC) Central Party School."

When the three development companies gained land, they introduced the overseas financial branches of Chinese commercial banks to establish Sino-foreign joint ventures of land for infrastructure development, and then leased the land piece by piece. In that initial stage of Pudong development with the extreme shortage of funds, this practice played the guiding and demonstrative functions for the government to initiate the investment.

Before the development of Pudong, there had been a big gap in the economy between Pudong and Puxi. In 1946, the official price of land in Puxi of Shanghai was 500 million yuan per mu (1 mu = 0.000667 square kilometers), while in Pudong it was only 5 million yuan, with a difference of 100 times. By the end of the 1980s, there was still a gap of dozens of times. In 1991 and 1993, two bridges were built over the Huangpu River one after another, and then a cross-river tunnel and a subway were completed. The price of land in Pudong rose greatly, and the developers in Pudong got substantial capital from land leasing.

With the land capital, three companies got 1.5 billion yuan of registered capital, and three billion yuan of joint venture capital was obtained through attracting foreign investment, and then six to seven billion yuan was credited on the principle of three loans on one deposit.

By 2001, when the land idling system ended, Pudong had transferred 88.6 square kilometers of land for idling, accounting for about 80% of the total land transfer of the same period. The government leveraged 70 billion yuan by investing 6.1 billion yuan.

Sha Lin, former Assistant Director of the Pudong Development Office, once said, "With a new idea, land can be turned into gold." By means of internal circulation, the land assets were unleashed, and the start-up capital needed for Pudong development shifted from borrowing money from the government to raising money from the market.

Such a large-scale and large-amount land purchase and selling was disputed and criticized at that time. Even some departments concerned asked sternly: What documents was this practice in Pudong based on? Or was there any policy to support this?

This practice in Pudong was different from the first attempt of land leasing in Shanghai in 1988 and also different from the earlier practice in Shenzhen which openly called for bids by listing and inviting companies to construct buildings. The method adopted by Pudong was different from that by Shenzhen in that, similar to the internal transfer, the initiative of land use was still in the hands of the government, so that differential rent could really play its role, and through the cooperation with foreign-funded enterprises, capital problems could be solved and joint development could be achieved.

Later a senior leader of the Central Government stated, "I have observed the pros and cons of the effect and influence for three years. The money earned from land leasing is huge." The top government officials agreed to Pudong's practice.

Huang Qifan later went to Chongqing as mayor, and he recalled this practice. "This mode was also adopted later in building the Zhangjiang High-tech Park. Now I work in Chongqing, and also follow the experience in Pudong. In a number of companies, the mode of idling of financial funds and running of land leasing was implemented."

Huang Qifan also talked about the advantages of this practice. The development was absolutely marketized, but it was absolutely government-oriented as it was a platform for the government, and the government did not borrow money.

7.2 "Small Government, Big Society"

At the same time of economic development, Pudong builders also carried out the government's own experiment of reform — making great endeavor in establishing "small government, big society".

In 1990, when the development of Pudong just started, the government's administrative organization was the Pudong Development Office, which consisted of three departments and two offices, that is, the Comprehensive Planning Department, the Engineering Planning Department, the Information Department, the Policy Research Office, and the General Office. By October 1992, with the approval of the State Council, the districts of Huangpu, Nanshi, Yanggpu, and the Pudong section of Shanghai County were divided from the original administration region, Chuansha County was revoked, and the Administrative Committee of Pudong New Area was set up. The committee was headed by Zhao Qizheng, a member of the Standing Committee of the Shanghai Municipal

Government and vice mayor. At this time, Pudong covered an area of 522 square kilometers, with a population of 1.4 million.

On January 1, 1993, Shanghai CPC's Working Committee of Pudong New Area and the Administrative Committee of Shanghai's Pudong New Area were established. On this day, several thousands of people gathered at No. 141, Pudong Avenue to watch the opening ceremony.

The opening ceremony of the Administrative Committee of Pudong New Area

The Administrative Committee of Pudong New Area, like the previous Development Office, is not a certain level of government, but the dispatched office of the Shanghai Municipal Government at the deputy provincial level. The purpose of establishing the Administrative Committee was to break up the pattern of divided management of the three Pudong districts, two counties, and the Pudong Development Office at that time, and centralize authoritative power to carry out individualized management. No Municipal People's Congress (MPC) or Chinese People's Political Consultative Conference (CPPCC) was set up in the Pudong New Area, but a liaison office assigned by the MPC and CPPCC.

The newly-established Administrative Committee of Pudong New Area made great endeavor in streamlining the government departments. According to the recollection of Hu Wei, former Assistant Director of the Administrative Committee, it took only one day to study the establishment and staffing of the new agencies. This was highly efficient: "After we discussed the plan for the establishment of the agencies in the morning, we went to make a report in the afternoon. After Comrade Qizheng listened to the report, he held a party meeting in the evening, and the next day a report was completed to submit to the Central Government on behalf of the Shanghai Municipal Government."

The establishment of an institution at the sub-provincial level was decided in just one day, and this high efficiency is inconceivable even after a number of years. In the Administrative Committee, the Comprehensive Regulation Bureau was set up to bring together land, planning, construction, and real estate; the Economic and Trade Bureau was set up to bring together domestic capital, foreign capital, commercial, industrial, tourism, and safe production; the Social Welfare Bureau was set up to bring together education, sports, health, and civil administration; an office was set up to bring together the Party Committee Office, the Administrative Office, the United Front Office, and the Propaganda Office.

There were 10 departments in total, with a total staffing of 800 people, of which the staffing for the Party and mass organizations included 100 people, and the staffing for administrative agencies included 700 people (excluding public security authorities). At that time it was called "800 warriors". At that time, it was great for a sub-provincial institution to be composed of only 800 people.

At that time, on average, there were 51 CPC and government agencies and 1,250 civil servants in each district and county in Shanghai, while the number of civil servants in Pudong was only 64% of that in other districts and counties, and the number of agencies reduced by 81%.

There are some basic characteristics for the government management mode of "small government, big society". "Systematic integration" was implemented in the functional management system, and the functions for industry management were merged according to the large-scale system, and comprehensive management departments were set up without the establishment of the bureaus simply in charge of industry. Governmental administration should be separated from enterprises in the economic management system. In administration, a "two-level structure" was implemented, that is, the government of Pudong New Area directly managed the streets and towns without an intermediate level. Zhao Qizheng once said, "Leaders of sub-provincial level directly faced villages and towns. Pudong was the only one in the country."

Practice has proved that such a micro-government is very efficient.

Such an institution was faced with the difficult problem of how to place the personnel from the beginning. According to the recollection of Wang Hongquan, former Party Secretary of Chuansha County, "At that time, the entire Pudong staffing was not much, Vice Mayor Zhao repeatedly referred to 'eight hundred warriors', that is, the 800 staffing. In Chuansha County there were 1,400 civil servants, and only 300 of them can stay on. It means that more than 1,100 people needed to be re-positioned and can no longer work as civil servants."

In China, the placement of government personnel is a very tough business. Pudong New Area was set up with the merger of three districts and two counties. Chen Gaohong, former Propaganda Minister in Pudong New Area, recalled, "In Chuansha County alone there were 1,400 cadres, but the Administrative Committee could only employ 300 cadres, so the difficulty can be imagined in re-positioning the personnel at that time."

But no matter how difficult it was, the Pudong developers adhered to the notion of "small government, big society" firmly.

The administrative mode of "small government, big society" is like a small boat in the vast sea of the traditional administrative system of China, so the conflicts are inevitable.

The conflict first manifested itself in the mismatch between the upper and lower executive branches. In Pudong New Area, there was an organization named the Comprehensive Planning and Land Administration, a multi-functional department, which brought together the Project Planning Bureau, the Real Estate Bureau, the Land Bureau, the Planning Bureau, the Statistics Bureau, the Pricing Bureau, etc., corresponding to the departments of planning, project-planning, national land, construction, and so on in Shanghai. Such an "integrated" organization encountered a lot of troubles in the subsequent operation. A department was likely to constantly interface with several different departments at the higher level.

As a result, Pudong "took some alternatives, and even adopted the method that several official seals are used in one department". Different documents were stamped with different official seals, and according to the different requirements of different higher-level departments, the content, manner, and language style of the report should be adjusted accordingly. Pudong people called this "change of channels".

Jiang Sixian, former Deputy Mayor of Pudong, recalled, "For example, if the director of the municipal Education Bureau held a meeting, the director of the Social Development Bureau of Pudong would have to attend the meeting. If the director of the municipal Health and Care Bureau held a meeting, he would have to attend it. If the director of municipal Sports Bureau held a meeting, he would have to attend it, too. If he did not attend the meetings, the higher authorities would think that Pudong did not attach importance to the work. So it was quite distressing."

So he said, "When I was secretary and chief director of the district, I made a rule that if the heads of the departments were required to attend the meetings presided by the leaders of the district government, including myself, and at the same time they were also required to attend the municipal meetings, then he should attend the municipal meetings, and the deputy directors would attend the district meetings."

In fact, the left and right also did not match either. Until 2009, when the neighbor Nanhui District was merged into Pudong, the problem became more prominent. The Urban Appearance and Environmental Protection Bureau in Pudong corresponded to Nanhui's four bureaus of urban appearance, greening, environmental protection, and water affairs. After four bureaus were merged into one bureau in Pudong, eight chief heads also entered into it at the same time. Xu Lin, a leader of Pudong New Area who once worked in Nanhui, sighed with emotion, as the leaders of the Pudong Environmental Protection Bureau were much fewer before.

Such a practice aroused dissatisfaction, questioning, and even challenge. Hu Wei recalled, "For example, because our organization did not have a propaganda department and united front department, some people challenged our establishment. Was there any governmental establishment without a propaganda department and united front department? In addition, the leaders of some municipal administrative departments said, if

Pudong did not have the institutions corresponding to theirs, they would not allocate funds to Pudong."

Shao Yudong, former Vice Chairman of the CPPCC Pudong New Area recalled, "At that time, when the relevant municipal departments came for inspection, they always noticed the mismatch. Pudong was therefore accused that they did not highly evaluate a certain work, since there was even no organization in charge of the work."

There was the absence of the department, and even if the departments were established, part-time employees were hired because of the insufficient staffing. Shao Yudong also remembered once when he spoke at a Municipal Political Consultative Conference, his name and titles on the screen aroused lot of laughter at the venue. He had a string of titles, such as Director of Propaganda and the United Front Work Department of Pudong New Area, Vice Chairman of the district CPPCC, Deputy Secretary of the Party Committee, Director of the Culture and Broadcast Bureau, Director of the Information Office, Assistant Director of the Spiritual Civilization Bureau, Director of the District Office of Taiwan Affairs, and Director of the Overseas Chinese Office.

But Pudong people felt very proud to call this a small government and big society.

Even Zhao Qizheng himself was given several titles: member of the Standing Committee of the Shanghai Municipal Committee, Deputy Mayor of Shanghai, and Director of the Administrative Committee of Pudong New Area. He once told reporters that after the announcement of Pudong development, in fact, there was no Pudong New Area administration, and no unified planning and unified leadership. Therefore, it was convenient to send to Pudong the cadre who was, at that time, the member of the Standing Committee and vice mayor of the Shanghai Municipal Government. As deputy mayor, he directly attended the office meeting presided by the mayor, and as a member of the Standing Committee, at the discussions of the Standing Committee, he could make reports directly rather than indirectly. In this way, the efficiency could be improved, and especially in terms of planning, there was a lot of convenience.

In institutional innovation, the mismatch between the upper and lower-level management really put the inferiors in awkward situation. It was predicted, "In three months, there will be a repetition of the mistake of 'simplification, expansion, re-simplification, and re-expansion'."

Fortunately, the practice of "small government, big society" in Pudong was supported by senior leaders. The leaders of the State Council firmly pointed out "Pudong must wear steel helmets to resist", "if the municipal departments come to urge you to set up new departments, you just resist and say no!" After all, Shanghai was once described by an American journalist as "a piece of land covered with seals".

Old Mayor Wang Daohan also gave great support to Pudong. He said, "The situation in Pudong New Area is special, different from other urban areas, so it is necessary to give authority to the sub-city level. Some major things need to request for municipal instructions, but other things should be handled by the new area itself. We should carry out bold reforms in the management system of the new area in order to provide experience for the institutional reform throughout Shanghai and play an active role. This is called 'organizational therapy' in institutional reform."

Shanghai municipal leaders also suggested that the institutions should be streamlined as much as possible. The institutional department should not be set up if it was not absolutely necessary to do so, and whatever can be merged in official business should be emerged. At the beginning, the institutions should be fewer and streamlined.

Not only were there fewer organizations and staff members, but there were also small office spaces and very poor conditions.

That year, when people walked into the Development Office of the Pudong New Area and the later Administrative Committee, they were moved by the small number of staff, the small office space, and the poor conditions of the new establishments.

The office building of the Pudong Development Office was transformed from a simple two-story building of the Pudong Culture Museum in the Huangpu District, with 18 almost identical offices, totaling 1200 square meters.

With the arrival of groups of cadres, a "small government" began to operate in a small building of 1200 square meters.

Lou Zulin, who had been in charge of logistics support in the Administrative Committee of Pudong New Area, recalled that he had been prepared for the poor conditions in Pudong when he was transferred from the municipal people's congress to Pudong, but upon his arrival, he was shocked by the poor conditions. Because there was no canteen, every day all the staff had to, with their rice bowl in hands, go to Dongfang Hospital across the street, go through the surgery clinic, and line up for meals in the innermost hospital canteen with the hospital staff. They even treated foreign guests in a very small Shaoxing restaurant next door. Later on, a new Bandao restaurant next door was opened, and only then was there a decent place for treating foreign guests for meals. All four assistant directors were crowded in a 20-square-meter office. The director had no desk of his own, but only a drawer in the middle of the desk, with drawers of both sides for others.

At that time, Zhao Qizheng held the first meeting in a small room less than 10 square meters of the Cultural Center with Mori, the well-known Japanese real estate developer, and the Director and Board Chairman of Mori Building Co. At that time, Zhao Qizheng was worried in private. "Will Mori look down upon us?" Fortunately, Mori, as a visionary entrepreneur with the ability to judge the future of a region, eventually decided to build a 492-meter-high global financial center in Lujiazui.

But just under such conditions, the practice of "small government, big society" achieved very high efficiency and low operating cost in the early stage of Pudong development.

Xia Keqiang, Director of the Pudong Development Office, recalled, "At that time, a large number of domestic and foreign enterprises and merchants poured into Pudong, and for half a day, we had to talk about the leasing of 4 to 5 pieces of land. The relevant municipal departments were very supportive. The City Planning Bureau approved it and stamped the seal in 15–20 minutes. We worked under stress, but with high efficiency. On the ground floor of the Pudong Development office building there was a small notice board, on which, from morning till night, reception tasks were fully lined up. The pace of our work was so fast that we cannot slacken at all."

At night, the light of the building on No. 141 of Pudong Avenue, which was always switched on, no doubt became the representative of a streamlined, efficient, honest, and pragmatic image. The red tiles and gray walls were so plain that it is hard to imagine today that it was once a place for sub-provincial leadership.

In China, almost all the large and small government departments had a kind of impulse of expansion and inflation and, with "Parkinson's Law" deeply rooted, rent-seeking phenomenon was also common. But why did developers in Pudong continue to limit their power and shrink the institution and staffing? What kind of courage and resilience did this require?

Unfortunately, Pudong's exploration of "small government, big society" was just like driving a small boat in the ocean of traditional administration. When the waves hit, there was always the danger of turnover. While China's traditional low-efficiency administrative system had not fundamentally changed, the micro-climate eventually had to adapt to the macro-climate.

The first man who put forward the theory of "small government, big society" was Liao Xun, a researcher at the Institute of Quantitative Economics and Technology Economics, Chinese Academy of Social Sciences. In March 1986, Liao Xun, who submitted a paper at the Symposium on the View of Economic System in the History of Socialist Thought, put forward the theory of "small government, big society", which was highly valued in the theoretical circle. Since then, "small government, big society" was widely publicized in a series of national conferences and media. This theory, which once attracted the attention of the decision-makers of the Central Government, won the "1977–1991 Excellent Achievement" award, the longest-spanning award of the Chinese Academy of Social Sciences.

But the theory is really valuable only through the application to practice. Since the reform and opening-up, China had carried out four large-scale reforms of the administrative system and institution, but it was still difficult to get out of the weird cycle of simplification, expansion, re-simplification, and re-expansion. Therefore, it was of national significance to practice the theory of "small government, big society" in Pudong.

After 2000, the administrative structure of Pudong was expanded. The Administrative Committee was turned into a district government, and the People's Congress and the CPPCC were established in succession. So far, Pudong became an administrative area of Shanghai with a traditional government structure, and with a slight increase in organizational setup. In 2009, when Pudong incorporated the neighboring Nanhui District, the number of institutions increased to 19, but it accounted for two-thirds of the average number of district and county organizations throughout the city and it was still very difficult to practice "small government, big society".

7.3 Reopening of the Stock Exchange

In the 1930s, Shanghai was known as the head of China's silver bank, storing most of the country's silver. Shanghai was also the financial heart of the country, into and out of which funds flowed. According to the recollection of Gong Haocheng, the former head of the Shanghai branch of the People's Bank of China, before the founding of New China, the inflow and outflow of funds through the Shanghai People's Bank of China accounted for 43% of the national capital flow. Unfortunately, from the 1950s to the late 1980s, this flow was virtually stagnant in Shanghai, accounting for only about 7% to 8%, since at that time there was no capital market at all.

As the mayor of China's largest industrial and commercial city, Zhu Rongji had a tight hand. On one occasion, he called a meeting of cadres of the banking system, and said, "You major in finance, so you should rack your brains to go to Beijing and collect more information to get some dry provisions." The dry provisions referred to money. The leaders of the Shanghai banks kept going to Beijing until the end of the year, but they could only get tens of millions of loans. In Shanghai there were so many enterprises, so how could they allocate the mere tens of millions? Not to mention the development of Pudong.

If you ask for fish from the superior, you might as well breed fish on your own. This idea of Zhu Rongji was becoming clearer and stronger.

At this time, several students back from abroad and domestic young scholars in Beijing were enthusiastically planning to establish China's securities market. They first thought of Beijing and hoped to set up a stock exchange in Beijing. They also organized a Joint Office for Research and Design of China's Securities Market, or "Joint Office", which was officially renamed as "China Research and Design Center of Securities Market", under the Commission of Structural Reform. Unfortunately, in those days, it was very difficult to make people understand stock trading and shareholding system in Beijing.

However, Pudong development gave these young people a light of hope. Shanghai planned to develop Pudong with a development budget of several hundred billion yuan. Since the founding of New China, most of Shanghai's income had been turned over to the Central Government, so it had not so much money left at all.

Gong Zhuming, the General Secretary of the "Joint Office", first noticed this point, and he knew that Shanghai had the most developed securities market in the Far East. With strong financial consciousness and tradition, Shanghai was more capable and hopeful to set up a stock exchange. Therefore, he wrote to Zhu Rongji and suggested that to develop Pudong, he would have to borrow money from all over the country. He wrote to Zhu Rongji to introduce the capital market in simple and plain language, and his introduction attracted Zhu Rongji's attention.

Gong Zhuming, a graduate from the People's Liberation Army (PLA) Military Institute of Engineering, served as the Chief Engineer of The Prediction Center of State Planning Commission at the age of 32 years old. He had successively worked as a member of the State Planning Commission, a member of the State Commission of Structural Reform, a member of the People's Bank of China (PBOC) Party Group, Director of the PBOC Structural Reform Office, Director of the PBOC Comprehensive Planning Department, and so on.

In 1978, Gong Zhuming ran errands at a panel of screening right wings in the China Planning Commission. One of those screened by him was named Zhu Rongji. In 1957, Zhu Rongji was branded a rightist for saying, "It makes sense for the workers in Yugoslavia to demand for autonomy." So, of course, they knew each other well. The question was where to find people who knew the business well if a stock exchange was to be built. Jing Shuping, Chairman of the "Joint Office", told Zhu Rongji, "We have a group of young people engaged in stock exchanges." Zhu Rongji said in a straightforward manner, "Well, just bring them in and I'll solve the problem of registered permanent residence for them."

Jing Shuping is a well-known industrialist in Shanghai. After the founding of New China, he became the General Manager of the Shanghai Cigarette Joint Production and Sales Company, Director of the Shanghai Cigarette Industry Association, and Deputy Secretary of the Shanghai Municipal Minjian Committee. Jing Shuping was very proficient in the capital market. In a certain year, the amount of government bonds the Central Government allocated to Shanghai was so large that it exceeded its tolerance, which Jing Shuping reported to the Shanghai Municipal Government. The Municipal Government sent him to Beijing to report the situation. Jing Shuping's ability and knowledge left a deep impression on Bo Yibo and other financial leaders of the Central Government. Chen Shutong, the first Director of the Industrial and Commercial Federation of China, admired him greatly. In 1956, he invited Jing Shuping to work in Beijing and said half-jokingly, "You may be wrongly treated to live here. Our four best rooms are for you to live. Of course, they are much smaller than the small building where you live in Shanghai." The whole family moved to Beijing without any hesitation.

In 1989, Jing Shuping suggested to Zhu Rongji that famous overseas entrepreneurs should be invited as consultants. Under his planning, 21 corporate giants from 11 countries in the world, which made up the "Shanghai Mayor International Entrepreneur Consultation Conference", offered advice and suggestions for Shanghai reform and opening-up, especially for the development of Pudong. Therefore, Jing Shuping's words were of significance.

In 1987, Zhu Rongji served as Assistant Director of the State Economic Commission, as well as Dean of the School of Economics and Management of Tsinghua University. As a PhD supervisor, he supervised four doctor candidates. Although most people were not clear about the role of stocks at that time, Zhu Rongji would have known and thought about it. More importantly, the establishment of stock exchange was, to certain extent, risky in politics, since stock came entirely from the west.

On December 2, 1989, Zhu Rongji, as both the Party Secretary and Mayor of Shanghai, held a conference on financial reform in the small auditorium of the Communist Party Committee on Kangping Road. The conference lasted a whole day, and Liu Hongru, Deputy Governor of the People's Bank of China, also came from Beijing to attend the meeting. Chen Biaoru, an international finance authority and Professor of the East China Normal University, was also invited.

The conference topic was how to speed up financial reform in the face of the withdrawal of foreign capital. There were two aspects: the introduction of foreign banks and the opening of the Shanghai Stock Exchange.

There was no objection over the introduction of foreign banks. The biggest debate at the meeting was over the establishment of the Shanghai Stock Exchange. Although they did not oppose it in principle, they all thought the conditions did not permit it, and some agreed to create conditions while doing so.

Zhu Rongji said with deep feelings, "Last year, I came to work in Shanghai on February 6. I got off the train in the morning and listened to the report made by the municipal Finance Bureau in the afternoon. Why? I don't think I can become a good mayor if I did not understand finance, so first of all, I had to figure out the financial situation. After a year of work, I felt that finance alone was not enough, and I was more and more aware of the importance of banking. Almost every day I encountered this problem." By this time, Zhu Rongji had realized that it was necessary to start with financial reform, namely, to set up the stock exchange and introduce foreign banks.

Finally, Zhu Rongji, who presided over the meeting, decided to officially open the Shanghai Stock Exchange in December 1990 at the latest. He told Gong Haocheng, President of the Shanghai Branch of the People's Bank of China, "Lao Gong, you just do it, and then it will expand slowly." After the meeting, a leading group was established, consisting of Li Xiangrui, Gong Haocheng, and He Gaosheng.

At that time, it was very risky to set up a stock exchange. A lot of people were afraid and said to Gong Haocheng, "Lao Gong, never do this, otherwise the Chinese bourgeoisie will emerge from here in the future." Some leaders had such doubts as to whether the establishment of a stock exchange would divert credit funds from banks, whether the shares issued by state-owned enterprises to individuals would be privatized in disguised form, whether the securities would cultivate a new bourgeoisie in Shanghai, etc.

In the early days after the founding of New China, all the people in the Shanghai financial system knew the story about the People's Liberation Army closing down the old Shanghai Exchange on Jiujiang Road. It is no wonder that most people's knowledge of securities trading was limited to the depiction of the old Shanghai Stock Exchange by the famous Chinese writer Mao Dun in his novel *Midnight*. The stock exchange was described as a crazy, cruel, and life-and-death place. The plots of constant tricks and bloody hunting left people a very deep impression.

At this time, just after the political turmoil of 1989, a number of "leftist" theorists controlling the ideological sector were expressing their remarks to the public. For example, the shareholding system was criticized as "sneaking privatization", the contracting of enterprises as "disintegrating the public economy", and the introduction of foreign capital as "willingness to become dependent on the foreign bourgeoisie".

Therefore, at that time, when Zhu Rongji proposed the idea of establishing a stock exchange, all the participants at the meeting were aware of the risks involved.

In an article, Li Xiangrui, then Board Chairman of the Bank of Communications, later a leading member who participated in establishing the Shanghai Stock Exchange, and the first Chairman of the Stock Exchange, recalled an interesting dialogue between Zhu Rongji and others. At the meeting, after Zhu Rongji put forward his idea, he first asked Li Xiangrui, "Lao Li, what do you think?" Li Xiangrui replied, "It is risky mainly in politics." Li Xiangrui hoped that the plan would not fall apart after doing revolutionary work for 40 years. Zhu Rongji turned his head and asked Gong Haocheng, President of the Shanghai Branch of the People's Bank of China, "What do you think, Lao Gong?" Gong Haocheng replied, "I don't think there is no political risk that Lao Li just talked about. Even if there were no political risks, a stock exchange can be established only when 100 to 200 large- and medium-sized enterprises enforce a stock-holding system, and 50 to 100 stocks are listed." Gong Haocheng, former Professor at the Shanghai College of Finance and Economics, had a deep theoretical background as a scholar-type official.

However, Zhu Rongji did not hesitate and made the final decision. "If anything happens, Liu Hongru and I will in charge. You guys are still on the second line." He immediately appointed Li Xiangrui, Gong Haocheng, and He Gaosheng, Director of the Shanghai Institutional Reform Office, to make up a three-member group to study the establishment of the Shanghai Stock Exchange.

At the crucial moment, the true quality of a hero was brought into play. Zhu Rongji, an orphan, once publicly told the representatives of the Shanghai Municipal People's Congress, "I wholeheartedly regard the Party as my mother, so I have no scruples about anything to say. As long as I think it good for the Party, I would speak it out. Even if I am wrongly treated, I don't care." In 1957, Zhu Rongji was labeled as a rightist, expelled from the Party, sent to the countryside for rural labor, farming, raising cattle, raising pigs, cooking, and so on. This experience and tribulation cultivated his intrepid courage and perseverance. He insisted, "My own character and my creed is to think independently. Whatever I think in my heart, I think I should say it accordingly."

It was known that since October 1949, the stock market had been viewed as something of a monstrous capitalism.

In 1985, American economist James Tobin, a Nobel laureate in economics, came to China to attend the famous "Bashan Cruise Conference". He said, "China should not rush to develop the capital market, because China's market economic system is not sound yet, and in such an environment it is risky to develop capital market." He suggested that China should wait another 20 years.

Tobin's suggestion was not unreasonable. At that time, neither the words "capital" nor "capital market" was allowed to be spoken about in China. In textbooks, "fund market" was used instead of "capital market", because capital markets were seen as capitalism.

But another 20 years was so long that Pudong development cannot wait.

There are always some similarities in history. In May 1916, Sun Yat-sen also planned to set up an exchange in Shanghai to raise funds for the national revolution. In the long-term revolutionary struggle, Sun Yat-sen realized that they should have both gun and purse.

He asked the Kuomintang Veteran Zhang Jingjiang to contact Yu Qiaqing and other Shanghai tycoons to prepare for setting up the "Shanghai Stock and Goods Exchange", which was submitted to the Agriculture and Commerce Ministry of Beijing Government for approval. However, the Agriculture and Commerce Ministry did not agree on the grounds that "securities and goods cannot be traded at the same time". Later, Sun Yat-sen was arrested under the Constitution Protection Movement and the plan did not go off. However, two years later, because of the lack of money, Dai Jitao, Zhang Jingjiang, and others thought of Sun Yat-sen's unfulfilled plan, so they contacted Yu Qiaqing and others, went around and sent representatives to repeatedly negotiate with the government. Finally, on July 1, 1920, the Shanghai Stock Exchange, the first official stock exchange in China, was established. Half a year after the opening, the profit earned was more than half a million yuan.

It was really a shortcut for raising funds and making money to set up exchanges, issue stocks, and list transactions. Profit-seeking businessmen rushed in, so that on Fuzhou Road, Hankou Road, and Jiujiang Road of Shanghai, the exchanges opened were as many as 140 at most.

Similarly, in the early 1990s, Chinese reformers faced a shortage of funds. Also, there was the additional difficulty of the resistance from the traditional ideology.

Shanghai was a lucky city. There was the enlightened and intrepid leadership, and more importantly, the exploration for a capital market in Shanghai was endorsed by Deng Xiaoping.

Gong Haocheng recalled, "One year after the establishment of the Shanghai Stock Exchange, I met Zhu Rongji and mentioned it again. Mr. Zhu told me that before setting up the exchange, he reported to Deng Xiaoping. And Deng Xiaoping said, 'Do it first, and then you can wait and see. If It's not a good job, we can change it again.'"

With the support of the top leaders of the Central Government and the fearlessness of local leaders, the Shanghai Stock Exchange was established with high efficiency. In June 1990, Zhu Rongji visited Singapore and revealed to the outside world that Shanghai would set up a stock exchange this year. This news not only shocked the western financial community, but also Shanghai's financial officials — the office building for the exchange had not been found yet. And Beijing's financial officials were also shocked, because they had not yet received a formal application.

On September 17 of the same year, the Shanghai Branch of the People's Bank of China submitted to the head office and the Shanghai Municipal Government the "Application for Establishing the Shanghai Stock Exchange". Two days later, the People's Bank of China and the Shanghai Municipal Government jointly reported to the State Council the "Application for Establishing the Shanghai Stock Exchange". The application went, "We believe the conditions and opportunities for establishing the Shanghai Stock Exchange are basically ripe. So we apply to the State Council for the approval so that we can further set up a good image of China's reform and opening-up, accelerate the development and opening of Pudong, and promote the further development of China's developed securities market and better serve the state and enterprises by financing construction funds."

On November 14, the head office of the People's Bank of China approved the application for the establishment of the Shanghai Stock Exchange. On November 26, Shanghai held the meeting of the establishment of Shanghai Stock Exchange.

Undoubtedly, the efficiency in the preparation and establishment of the Shanghai Stock Exchange carried out by the leaders of Shanghai is described by Deng Xiaoping's statement, "Shanghai is our trump card, and it is a shortcut to build Shanghai."

On December 3 of that year, Zhu Rongji visited the Shanghai Stock Exchange, which was under renovation in Pujiang Hotel, a 150-year-old building of European style, on the bank of the Huangpu River. It is said to have been the most luxurious hotel in China and even in the Far East and the first electric light and the first telephone in China showed up in the hotel. The magnificent Peacock Hall of the hotel was converted into the stock exchange hall.

At that time, the renovation had not been completed, and outside the hotel the construction site was still in a mess, so Zhu Rongji had a sulky look on his face. But as he walked into the hall, he noticed that the arrangement was ready and his face was eased. He asked Wei Wenyuan, the then head in charge of the establishment of the exchange, if there were any difficulties he needed to solve for them. Wei Wenyuan said that the round arched glass to be used to decorate the boxes was not available. Zhu Rongji suggested that he could go ask for Pilkington Yaohua for help, by saying it was Zhu Rongji who would like them to make it right away.

Later, Zhu Rongji challenged him, asking whether he dared to manage the stock exchange with boldness. 35-year-old Wei Wenyuan said, "Yes." As a result, he became the first General Manager of the Shanghai Stock Exchange, at the time known as the "youngest head of exchanges in the world". In fact, at that time, Wei Wenyuan did not know much about stock exchange. Until the eve of the opening, he was at a loss.

Eight months after the announcement of Pudong development, at 11 in the morning on December 19, 1990, the Shanghai Stock Exchange was opened. After Wei Wenyuan hit the opening gong with all his strength, with extreme excitement he nearly fainted and fell to the ground, but the Shanghai index stood up, soaring from the horizon of 100 points.

At this time, more than 500 Chinese and foreign guests witnessed the opening of the Shanghai Stock Exchange, with a strong echo at home and abroad. After all, in history, Shanghai was the financial center of the Far East, with the largest stock exchange and, after the political turmoil of 1989, the stock exchange that had previously been wiped out was reopened, demonstrating China's determination to continue opening-up to the outside world.

At the opening ceremony, Zhu Rongji said in his speech that the establishment of the Shanghai Stock Exchange "was a sign that China will unswervingly continue to carry out the policy of reform and opening-up". He spoke it first in Chinese and then again in English.

An elegant and beautiful woman, standing next to Zhu Rongji, stood out with her special identity. She was Deng Lianru, Chairman of the Hong Kong Trade Development Council. Her presence also signified that the Chinese government would be more open.

What is more interesting, some important figures witnessed the occasion, such as Liu Hongru, Zhou Daojiong, Zhou Zhengqing, and Zhou Xiaochuan, the future four chairmen of the China Securities Regulatory Commission; Zhu Rongji, Dai Xianglong, and Zhou Xiaochuan, the three future governors of the People's Bank of China; Huang Ju, future Vice Premier in charge of economic and finance; and Zhu Rongji, the future Premier.

7.4 Shanghai's Response to the Chief Designer's Request with Great Action

Five days after the opening of the Shanghai Stock Exchange, on December 24, 1990, Deng Xiaoping invited Jiang Zemin, Yang Shangkun, and Li Peng to his home. He specifically brought the topic to the market. "You should not think of the market economy as a capitalist road. This is not the case. Both the planned economy and market economy are necessary. Without the engagement in market economy, there would be no information about the world. This would lead to self-indulgence and backwardness." According to the research of some scholars, Deng

Xiaoping's understanding of the market economy can be traced back to his youth.

In October 1920, Deng Xiaoping, only 16 years old, and more than 80 other Chinese students took a ship to France for a work-study program. At that time, France suffered from economic crisis, hyper-inflation, soaring prices, and factory layoffs, with the price of bread rising nearly six times within a year. The international students were starving. Deng Xiaoping later recalled, "What we earned by working can hardly afford our livelihood, so how could we study in schools?" Deng Xiaoping left France on January 7, 1926, after five years and four months in France, which was the whole cycle of the French economy from crisis, depression, recovery, to upsurge. Living at the bottom of society in a country where the market economy mechanism was very mature, the young Deng Xiaoping personally experienced the operation of a market economy.

After leaving France, Deng Xiaoping came to study in Sun Yat-sen University in Moscow. He learned of the failure of the Soviet Union's wartime "communist policy", and the immediate implementation of the "new economic policy" in transition to socialism, such as replacing the system of collecting surplus grain with grain taxes, state-owned enterprises carrying out economic accounting and participating in market activities, granting small producers free trade and allowing private enterprises to start small businesses, allowing mineral resources that the state was temporarily unable to develop to be operated by foreign capitalists in the form of concessions, changing the practice of state monopoly trade, renewing the currency circulation and commodity exchange, abolishing the system of physical distribution, and so on.

It should be mentioned that his experience of studying in France for five years and staying in the Soviet Union for one year provided him with considerable materials for reflection to direct the great transformation of China from planned economy to market economy. In this respect, it is the experience that other Communist Party leaders, such as Mao Zedong, did not have. So, in 1985, Deng Xiaoping talked to African guests about the impression that his life in that very period had left him. "What does socialism really look like? The Soviet Union made attempts about it for many years, but it was not made entirely clear. Perhaps Lenin had a good idea, as he adopted the new economic policy, but later the Soviet model became rigid."

Italian scholar Lolita Napolioni provided a comment from a global perspective, "Deng Xiaoping witnessed the whole process of the first oil crisis in 1973–1974. The flexibility and ingenuity of the capitalist system in responding to the crisis convinced Deng that the Chinese Communist Party must make major adjustments to adapt to a changing world."

Hence, on November 26, 1979, he had a meeting with guests from the United States and Canada. When Lin Daguang, Director of the East Asian Institute at McGill University in Canada, mentioned the topic of "expanding the role of a non-capitalist market economy", Deng Xiaoping uttered some earth-shattering words: "It is certainly incorrect to assume that market economy exists only in capitalist society and there is only a capitalist market economy. Why can't socialism have a market economy? A market economy cannot only be regarded as part of capitalism. We mainly implement a planned economy, but at the same time we can have an experiment of a market economy. Anyway, this is a socialist market economy."

A market economy cannot be taken merely as part of capitalism, since it was geminated in the period of feudal society. Socialism can also implement a market economy. This was the first time the leaders of the Communist Party of China proposed the concept of a socialist market economy. But at that time, for most people in China's political and theoretical circles, the saying that "socialism can also take the road of market economy" was still a heresy, but Deng Xiaoping mentioned it to foreigners. However, it is interesting to note that this statement was not included *Selected Works of Deng Xiaoping(1975–1982)* published in 1983. Not until October 1994, when the revised version of the second volume of *Selected Works of Deng Xiaoping* was published, was it made known to the public. From 1979 to 1994, it remained unknown for 15 years. Was it out of strategic consideration?

Xue Muqiao, a Chinese economist, argued that the reason for its concealment for more than a decade was that he was unwilling to force the cadres to accept his views, but to patiently guide them to gradually reach consensus in practice.

Sometimes, it is true that outsiders see most of the game. American scholar and writer Thomas Kuhn believed, "Mao Zedong is an idealist, but Deng Xiaoping is a realist. He had a famous saying, 'It doesn't matter whether the cat is black or white as long as it can catch mice.' In China, subtle language can express rich meaning. No one will ignore the pragmatic message that comes from it, and no one will ignore Deng Xiaoping's impressive commentary on the black cat and white cat, which is a metaphor for two economic systems: planned economy and market economy." It is worthwhile to review Deng Xiaoping's thinking about market economy and planned economy in the 1980s.

In early February 1983, Deng Xiaoping came to the south of the Yangtze River. Along the way, Deng Xiaoping was most concerned about whether the goal of a well-off life can be achieved, and what method should be employed to achieve it. In Suzhou, Deng Xiaoping learned of the rapid development of local enterprises as a result of adopting flexible management mechanism. He said succinctly, "It seems that market economy is important."

The local enterprises Deng Xiaoping praised are the village and township enterprises that were later recorded in the history of China's reform and opening-up, called one of the four marginal forces of China's reform and opening-up by British economist Ronald Harry Coase.

On October 20, 1984, the Third Plenary Session of the 12th Central Committee of the CPC was held in Beijing. Chinese leaders took a step further in their understanding of the market economy. At the meeting, "Decision on Economic System Reform by the CPC Central Committee" was unanimously agreed. It held that to reform the planned economy system, first of all, we should break through the traditional concept of planned economy against commodity economy. It should be clearly recognized that the socialist planned economy, based on the application of the law of value, is the planned commodity economy on the basis of public ownership.

Previously, China had been adhering to the "planned economy, supplemented by market regulation".

Deng Xiaoping gave a high opinion on "Decision on Economic System Reform by the CPC Central Committee". He said, "I am deeply impressed by this first draft of political economy," and "some are new words, what our ancestors had never said before. I see this clearly. We could not have written such a document in the past, without the practice in the previous years. Even if it were written out, it would have been regarded as 'heresy'."

In the history of China's reform and opening-up, this is another landmark meeting since the Third Plenary Session of the 11th Central Committee in 1978.

On October 23, 1985, at a meeting with a delegation of senior executives of *Time* magazine and senior American entrepreneurs, Deng Xiaoping reiterated, "There is no fundamental contradiction between socialism and market economy. The question is what can be done to develop social productivity more vigorously. In the past we carried out planned economy, but for many years it proved that, in a sense, planned economy alone would hamper the development of the productive forces. If we combine planned economy with market economy, the productive forces would be liberated, so that economic development would be accelerated."

Many Americans appreciated Deng Xiaoping's ideas and marveled even more at the dramatic changes that Deng's market economy brought to China. This delegation of over 40 people, composed of the Senior Directors of *Time* magazine, the President of Ford Motor Company and other leaders of major American companies, visited Beijing, Shanghai, Guangzhou, Shenzhen, and so on successively. Shenzhen, in particular, was a barren small town a few years prior, and by 1985 it had become a modern city with a vibrant landscape that had a huge visual impact on visitors. Richard Holnick, the Beijing Bureau Chief of *Time* magazine, described, "Foreigners who travel back to China after only a few years can hardly believe it is the same country."

The group agreed that Deng Xiaoping's ongoing reform of China was more likely to change the course of history than all other events around the world in 1985.

Holnick recalled that in choosing Man of the Year of *Time* magazine, "The original top candidate was former Soviet leader Mikhail Gorbachev, but in October the sequence changed after the Senior Directors of *Time* went on a field trip to China."

In 1985, Deng Xiaoping was re-elected as Man of the Year in *Time*. "It doesn't matter whether the cat is black or white as long as it can catch mice." was written in *Time* magazine. The "Cat Theory" influenced the whole world.

In 1987, Deng Xiaoping was determined to put an end to the battle between planned economy and market economy. In a talk with several leaders of the Central Committee on February 6, he pointed out, "Why do we refer to market as capitalism and only planning belongs to socialism? Both planning and marketing are the ways for economic development. As long as it is beneficial to the development of productive forces, it can be used. When it serves socialism, it is socialist. If it serves capitalism, it is capitalist. It is wrong to always refer to planning as socialism. In Japan there is a planning office, and in the United States there is planning."

Deng Xiaoping, with his political authority, stressed, "We used to follow the Soviet Union and implement planned economy. Later on, we said we should focus on planned economy. Now we should not talk about it again."

Zhou Qiren, a Chinese economist, asked in a very strange way in a speech, "Economists usually go to great lengths to promote the market price mechanism. This is not surprising, given the strong support of the tradition of economics since Adam Smith. But why is Deng Xiaoping also fond of the 'invisible hand'? The politician, who once commanded millions of field armies and served as General Secretary of the Communist Party of China and Vice Premier of the State Council, clearly has a pair of 'visible hands'."

According to Zhou Qiren, "It is precisely because he had a personal experience of the overburdened cost pressure of the original system and was extremely dissatisfied with the operating efficiency of the original system that Deng Xiaoping understood the main result of excessive concentration of power more clearly than outside critics, that is, the inability to exercise state power effectively."

For the people who had no experience of that age, it is hard to imagine the low efficiency of the planned economy. Even a box of matches that would be priced two cents more had to be discussed and decided on the Standing Committee of the Provincial Committee of the People's Republic of China. Ren Zhongyi, leader of the Guangdong Provincial Party Committee, said helplessly, "The planned economy is like this. The party is in charge of everything, all the trifles, so it is impossible to manage them well."

China's agriculture is the most affected sector of the planned economy, which is the main reason why the distribution of farmland to households spread widely like wildfire in China. After the rural reform, the agricultural production developed at super-normal speed, with bumper harvests year after year, so the farmers no longer suffered from hunger.

Facts speak louder than words. In 1987, according to Deng Xiaoping's talk, the report at the 13th National Congress of the CPC no longer referred to the planned economy, but put forward a new overall operating mechanism, "The state regulates the market, and the market guides the enterprises", and pointed out, "The direct management mode based on directive plan cannot meet the requirements of the development of socialist commodity economy."

In 1989, with the drastic changes in the Soviet Union and Eastern Europe, the western sanctions, the domestic political turmoil, the economic downturn, and the bad situation, some people raised the problems of the planning and the marketing to a higher plane of principle and two-line struggle. The dispute over whether market economy should belong to capitalism or socialism arose again.

Therefore, in December 1990, Deng Xiaoping invited the principal leaders of the Central Committee to his home. He repeatedly stressing that the distinction between capitalism and socialism did not lie in the problem of planning or marketing. He made the thinking and understanding at the top of the Party reach an agreement. And in some subsequent talks on this issue, he made several statements. Especially during the "tour in the south" in 1992, he stressed again, "More planning or more marketing is not the essential difference between socialism and capitalism." Finally, the 14th National Congress of the Communist Party of China decided that the goal of China's economic system reform was to establish a socialist market economy system.

In November 1993, at the Third Plenary Session of the 14th Central Committee, "Decision of the Central Committee of the Communist Party of China on Several Issues Concerning the Establishment of Socialist Market Economy System" was agreed upon. It was pointed out at the meeting that the socialist market economy system was integrated with the basic socialist system. To establish a socialist market economy system, it is necessary to make the market play a fundamental role in the allocation of resources under the macro-control of the state.

Since then, the debate came to an end. The reform of China's economic system was carried out in an all-round way. Instead of the dodge and hide in guerrilla warfare, positional warfare was waged on a large-scale and in a pugnacious manner. Pudong development was launched at the right time. It was the great mission for Pudong to shoulder.

However, the Chinese Communists had no experience in how to establish the operational system and mechanism of the socialist market economy and how to give play to the basic role of resource allocation in the market. The leaders, experts, and scholars in Shanghai realized this point and naturally took the development and cultivation of the factor market as the key breakthrough point with the help of Pudong development.

History also proves that in Shanghai, the stock exchange, which was successfully set up, raised some of the necessary funds for Pudong development. Meanwhile, Pudong development also provided opportunities for the establishment of the capital market. This can also be said that Pudong development was launched in the favorable conditions of timing, location, and human relationship.

In his book *How China Became Capitalism*, Ronald Harry Coase, a British economist and winner of the 1991 Nobel Prize in Economics, analyzed the significance of developing market factors in the transformation in China: "Under the planned economy, the factors of production are owned by the state, and allocated in a unified way by central planning. Therefore, the key step in the transformation to a market system is to upgrade the position of the market factors and replace the allocation of resources by central planning. In China's transition to a market system, the rise of market factors started from the local, and with the increase participation of local governments, the competition gradually became regionalized."

Deng Xiaoping made a request to Shanghai: "I would like you to think about what can be done to make Shanghai become an example to show to the world that we carry out further reform and opening-up." Shanghai people responded to the request of Deng, the chief architect of reform and opening-up, with the development of Pudong and the establishment of the Shanghai Stock Exchange.

Perhaps that is why local leaders in Shanghai were attracting more attention from Deng Xiaoping?

Following the opening of the Shanghai Stock Exchange, the construction of the factor markets in Shanghai was also on the rise. For example, the Shanghai Futures Exchange, the Shanghai Joint Property Exchange, the China Financial Futures Exchange, and the Shanghai Diamond Trading Center were also established one by one. The establishment of these trading platforms initially set up a national financial system for Shanghai, so that Shanghai regained the status of a financial center in the Far East in the 1930s, with funds from both home and abroad flowing continually into this huge center of wealth. This also means that the construction of Shanghai's international financial and shipping center was launched, which laid foundation for the establishment of the China (Shanghai) Pilot Free Trade Zone.

In the history of China's reform and opening-up, two major events occurred in 1990: the development and opening of Pudong and the establishment of the Shanghai Stock Exchange.

7.5 Doubts from Foreign Scholars

Since the opening of Pudong development in 1990, a batch of builders and investors poured into Pudong, and Pudong witnessed flourishing development. Pudong shouldered the heavy responsibility of guiding China's reform and opening-up.

Therefore, at that time there was a popular saying, "In the 1980s there were big changes in Shenzhen, but in the 1990s the big changes were in Pudong." An official in Pudong believed that if the reform and opening-up in Shenzhen in the 1980s was the "ice-breaking journey" of China's reform and opening-up strategy, then the development of Pudong in the 1990s was the "uphill battle" of China's reform and opening-up, the overall upgrade of reform and opening-up.

History seems to put to test Shanghai people who were developing Pudong on a large scale. In 1997, the fast-growing Pudong was badly hit by the Asian financial crisis.

A billionaire named George Soros, with his huge amount of money, launched a violent financial attack on Asian countries and their currencies, which led to a financial storm in Asia. Following Thailand, the exchange market and stock market in the Philippines, Malaysia, Indonesia, and other Southeast Asian countries suffered from a plunge, with industrial and business sectors falling into grief and despair.

Pudong was also hit. As to building the Global Financial Centre, the foundation of which had just started, investors demanded divestment, so that the capital chain was broken, followed with a halt of the project and an empty construction site. Zhengda Plaza, the large-scale shopping and entertainment center in Lujiazui of the Pudong Area, invested by Thai businessmen, was suspended due to the financial crisis shortly after the start of construction. The Tomson group just got a piece of land in Lujiazui, but because of the crisis, they entreated the Pudong government to withdraw money.

Yaohan of Japan became bankrupt. The first Yaohan Building, the Sino-Japanese joint venture in Shanghai located in the busiest part of Pudong, suffered an unprecedented crisis when it opened within a year, leaving a loss of more than 200 million on the Chinese side.

A large number of investors retreated one after another. In the foreign media, there were some statements like "Pudong development failed", "the rate of office building occupancy was only 20%", and "Pudong's lights were not lit up". Yang Zhouyi, former secretary general of the Pudong Research Institute for Reform and Development, recalled that the situation was not optimistic, "The saying of 20% occupancy rate was exaggerated, but it was indeed depressing."

At that time, when one came to Lujiazui in Pudong at night, he must have such a feeling. A large number of commercial buildings had been built, but there were few companies to move in, with the buildings standing there silently, occasionally with few lights. Also there were few pedestrians on the roads, with the cold wind blowing unbridled through the empty roads.

Hu Wei, the former President of Pudong New Area, recalled that when people overseas visited Pudong at the time, all of them asked, "What impact does the southeast Asian currency crisis on have China? Can the development of Pudong proceed smoothly?"

This also made the local leaders Shanghai and Pudong highly nervous. Xu Kuangdi, former Mayor of Shanghai, said that he could not fall asleep without sleeping pills at that time, because the buildings in Pudong were not invested by the municipal government. The government did not borrow a penny of debt and all of them were built by foreign investors. The government promoted the development of Pudong and invited people to invest, and they were glad to make the investment, so they were the worthy friends, and their assets should be protected by all means.

But an article, written by a western scholar, was highly influential and controversial.

It was in 1998 that Joshua Cooper Remo, Senior Editor of *Time* magazine, published an article in Foreign Policy entitled "The Shanghai Bubble". Remo claimed that 70% of Shanghai's buildings were vacant, and that real estate prices had fallen 50% since 1995. He predicted, "In the economy, there will be the consequence of 'what the hell is wrong'."

Remo wrote at the end of the article, for the city, the iconic buildings, such as the Oriental Pearl TV Tower and the Yangpu Bridge, may soon become a symbol of the troubled real estate market.

But the builders of Pudong's development resisted the pressure and encouraged themselves with a phrase by Deng Xiaoping, "fighting a way out". Hu Wei recalled, as a result of the Asian financial crisis, the financial difficulties occurred when Century Avenue was constructed half way, and the leaders of Shanghai arrived at the spot to encourage the builders that no matter how difficult it was, they must overcome the difficulties and fight a way out.

About this, the westerners tended to be confused about why the Chinese were so tenacious. As a result, they had always turned negative on this.

Kobayashi, a Japanese economist who made in-depth research on China's economy and visited China more than 60 times, once expressed a wonderful point of view. In the countries and regions where the economy is developing rapidly, people use Chinese characters and chopsticks, which is a common phenomenon. But why does the economy of the countries and regions that use Chinese characters and chopsticks grow faster? He held the view that using Chinese characters and Chopsticks was a very harsh requirement for young kids. In his opinion, it took a strong memory to remember Chinese characters and it was difficult for children to learn how to use chopsticks, and because children of these ethnic groups had undergone strict training since childhood, they grew up with the ability to cope with even worse environments.

In view of the fact that a large number of buildings had been erected and various functional enterprises could not keep pace in their entry, Professor

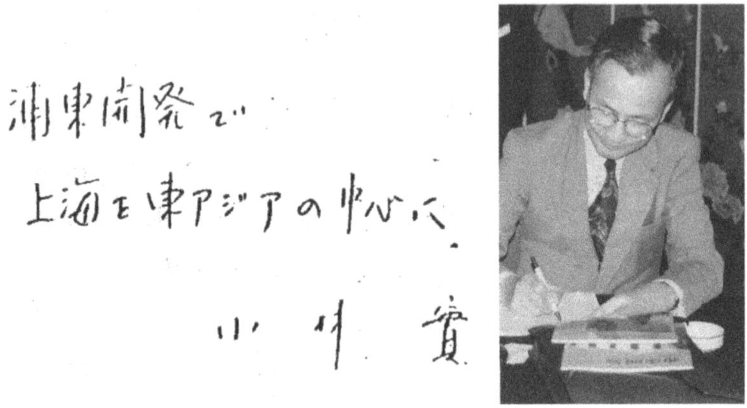

In October 1993, the famous Japanese economist Kobayashi wrote an inscription for Pudong development: "To build Shanghai into the center of East Asia through Pudong development."

Yao Xitang, who was President of the Pudong Reform and Development Research Institute, wrote a letter to Mayor Xu Kuangdi on November 23, 1995. He suggested that the Shanghai Real Estate Trading Center located in Puxi should be moved east to Pudong and promote the formation of the Lujiazui Central Business District by moving the factor market to the east. The proposal was personally approved by Xu Kuangdi, and was also actively cooperated by other government departments in Shanghai.

The letter also launched "the east movement" of Shanghai factor market from Puxi to Pudong. Soon, under the strong impetus of the Shanghai Municipal Government, the Shanghai Real Estate Trading Center in Puxi moved east to Pudong, and then seven state-level exchanges, such as the Shanghai Stock Exchange, the Shanghai Futures Exchange, and the Shanghai Property Right Exchange, successively moved to Pudong. The state-level Diamond Trading Center was also set up in Lujiazui.

It was under the agglomeration of the factor market that the Lujiazui Financial and Trade Zone in Pudong gradually took a shape, and the image as the international financial center began to build up.

Xu Kuangdi recalled, after a few years, especially in 2000, everything completely improved. Xiao Lujiazui was rented out, and the rental rate of office buildings in the whole city exceeded 80%.

At this time Xu Kuangdi could have sleep soundly.

After the financial crisis, the lights of hundreds of buildings in Lujiazui gradually lit up, and bright lights during the night became Shanghai's most charming scenery.

Before this, some foreigners criticized that too many buildings were built in Lujiazui and the vacancy rate was too high. Zhao Qizheng, Director of the Pudong New Area Administrative Committee, said that in China, smart mothers always make their children's trousers longer so that they can still wear them when they grow up.

In a few years, a large number of financial institutions gathered in Lujiazui, which proved the "longer trousers" theory. The "longer trousers" made in the past appeared to be shorter. By 2005, it became hard to rent a room in the 128 high-grade office buildings in the Lujiazui Financial and Trade Zone of Pudong, with an intelligent office area of 2.3 million square meters. The average occupancy rate reached nearly 90%.

According to a reporter, every skyscraper there was a "standing" financial street.

Remo, who later served as Vice Chairman of Henry Kissinger's board of directors, also revised his previous view that Pudong was a representative of "exceptionalism in China". In almost every corner, people could see the economic tools that the western politicians dreamed of were playing their roles. It was these tools that allowed China to succeed again and again despite their mistakes in the past three decades of reform.

By this, the Japanese Kazuo Wada was most deeply impressed.

During the Asian financial crisis in 1997, the core company of Japanese Yaohan Group went bankrupt, and President Kazuo Wada became impoverished overnight. However, in Pudong, the first Yaohan in Shanghai overcame the crisis and began to make profit in 2001. In 2004, it became the top-sale department store in China. Every day, 17 vertical elevators and 70 escalators carried customers to every floor of the mall.

On December 25, 2005, at the 10th anniversary of Shanghai First Yaohan, Wada received a "thank you letter" from Pudong. It was a beautiful scroll, with the signatures of all the staff in the store. The old man was moved into tears with the scroll in his hands.

Later, the old man was invited to Shanghai First Yaohan Mall to overlook the outside through the bright floor-to-ceiling glass windows. The farmland in the past had become a modern urban area bristling with tall buildings. He said with emotion, "I encountered some setbacks in my life, but the success of First Yaohan proved that it was not wrong for me to have chosen Pudong."

Perhaps because Remo had been living in China for many years, he had a deeper understanding of China than other foreigners. In 2004, he published a paper describing the "Beijing Consensus", China's unique development model, which aroused strong repercussions in the West, since this concept challenged the popular "Washington Consensus" in the West. Remo believed that the "Beijing Consensus" was characterized by hard work, initiative innovation and bold experimentation, resolute defense of national sovereignty and interests, gradual progress, and so on.

In Remo's view, China's experience based on the "Beijing Consensus" was valuable and can be used as a model for some developing countries to pursue economic growth.

7.6 Why Pudong Can Attract so much Foreign Capital

Boring numbers often tell more truth.

From 1990 to the end of 2013, Pudong introduced a total of 21,700 foreign investment projects from 123 countries and regions around the world, with a contractual foreign investment of US$78.1 billion. In other words, an average of 4.2 foreign investment projects landed in Pudong every day, with more than US$15 million invested in Pudong every day.

This current situation was interesting and doubting. Was there really so much overseas investment?

Looking back at the state of international capital flow in the early 1990s, it is easier to understand why Pudong development attracted so many foreign investors, which is an important reason for China's rapid economic growth.

According to International Monetary Fund, in the late 1980s, the net external financing for developing countries had been on the rise, with an average growth rate of 9.9% from 1986–1993. From 1990–1993, the average growth rate was 22.5%. International capital flows accompanied by large shifts in industry were not only accelerated, but also the flows to areas such as Latin America and Asia increased greatly. According to estimates made in the 1993 by the World Bank, from the mid-1980s to

1992, foreign direct investment flows to developing countries increased fourfold. Some scholars called it "the third wave of overseas investment".

This phenomenon is related to the reform in developing countries, the improvement of the investment environment, the opening of domestic capital markets, the gradual relaxation of the control of foreign exchange markets and capital markets by developed countries, and the financial markets' global integration, securitization, liberalization, and financial innovation, with the scale of global capital flows significantly expanded. This also makes it easier to achieve industrial transfer, so as to speed up the pace of industrial restructuring in developed countries. Therefore, in developing countries, economic growth can be achieved by means of more supporting policies to undertake industrial transfer.

Overseas investors with big money were also delighted to find the best place for their investment — a vast market with a rich and cheap labor force. Especially in Pudong, with Shanghai as the matrix, there were more technical staff, more industrial sectors, and more managers, making communication easier.

What is important is that a market economy was being implemented there. This means that they would invest in a market economy that they were familiar with and could reap lucrative profits. As a result, pension funds, life insurance funds, and so on that the developed world could not digest rushed to mainland China.

Pudong was naturally their first choice.

Terence Winter, Chairman of the Management Committee of United Kingdom-China Trade Group 48, said, "More than 20 years ago, I did not encourage foreign investors to invest in China, but now I would say, if you want a short-term profit, go to the United States and Europe. If you want to burn your finger, go to the former Soviet Union and Eastern Europe. But if you want long-term benefit, go to China, and the best place in China now may be Pudong New Area of Shanghai."

Pudong, once a neglected place name, began to heat up among foreign investors.

Li Weibo, former official of the Waigaoqiao Free Trade Zone Commission, recalled that after the establishment of the Waigaoqiao Free Trade Zone, a large number of investors rushed to Waigaoqiao immediately. "Those who came here for consultation, going through formalities, and requesting for land arrived in endless streams, and in the small offices, like tea shops, more than a dozen projects were processed every day. The projects were received during the day, and brought home at night for examination and approval, which was jokingly called 'doing homework'."

After the development of Pudong, groups of investors arrived at the Administrative Committee of the Pudong New Area. The picture shows the economic delegation of the United States visiting the Administrative Committee of the Pudong New Area.

The map publishers of the United States may be more sensitive.

In 1995, Zhao Qizheng, Director of the Administrative Committee of Pudong New Area, received a sub-volume world map sent by Robert Allen, Chairman and Chief Executive of AT&T of the United States. He saw the "Pudong sketch map" drawn separately on the page of the Shanghai map, which was newly published by an authoritative map publisher in New York.

Zhao Qizheng was also excited to find that the map was marked with "Lujiazui", "Waigaoqiao", and other place names of development zones.

However, at that time, Pudong was more like a large construction site, with wind blowing and dust flying, and on a rainy day, the road became muddy potholes, which made pedestrians suffer a lot.

The manager of the Japanese Bank of Fuji made an analogy to this: Pudong development was like playing the game of go. In other words, there were many central points in a wide area, and at the beginning of development, it seemed a little disorganized, but with the passage of time, it was like a game of go from middle game to decisive game, the mutual influence of many development centers gradually enhanced and at last, a magnificent picture was completed. This is different from the general development approach, that is, there is an existing center, and then gradually expands outward.

7.7 The Past of Shanghai Represented by the Bund and the Future of Shanghai Represented by Pudong

On September 27, 1999, more than 300 heads and representatives of transnational corporations, as well as 200 representatives of Chinese enterprises and officials, gathered at the Shanghai International Convention Center on the eastern bank of the Huangpu River to attend the "99 Shanghai *Fortune* Forum".

More than 40 privately-owned planes landed one by one on the runway at the Pudong International Airport. Disembarking the plane were the presidents and wives of transnational companies, as well as their entourages. They attended the "*Fortune* Forum" at the Shanghai International Convention Center on the east bank of the Huangpu River.

The fact that so many privately-owned planes arrived in Shanghai from overseas was of great interest to photographers, and they focused their cameras on the rows of planes, a very spectacular sight. It was also the first time in Pudong history that so many privately-owned planes landed.

A group of Chief Executive Officers (CEOs) of western multinationals said, "It felt like the Super Bowl and people were watching a classic game."

The topic for the meeting that year was "China in the next 50 years".

At the opening dinner of the forum, Jiang Zemin said fervently, "In Lujiazui of Pudong, Shanghai, where we are tonight, there were still some shabby houses and farmland six years ago, but now it is a thriving financial and trade zone with tall buildings."

Not only did great changes occur in Pudong itself, but Puxi was also greatly motivated. Like a horsepower engine, it drove the rapid development of Shanghai. In a short period of 10 years, there was no longer the division of backward Pudong and prosperous Puxi in Shanghai.

After the development of Pudong in 1990, Shanghai began to transform as a whole, achieving co-prosperity of the east and west side (Photo taken in October 2015 by Niu Yixin, Shanghai News Aerial Photography Alliance, China)

One year later, at the Asia-Pacific Economic Cooperation (APEC) Conference held in Brunei, Jiang Zemin invited heads of different states to meet in Pudong, Shanghai. He introduced Pudong New Area, where the next meeting would be held, "Pudong is the epitome of Shanghai's modernization, and also a symbol of China's reform and opening-up."

From October 20 to 21, 2001, the Ninth APEC Leaders' Informal Meeting was held in Shanghai. On the evening of October 21, at the Shanghai International Conference Center on the east bank of the Huangpu River, blazed with lights, the banquet for guests attending the APEC meeting was coming to a climax. Accompanied with the melody of "Auld Lang Syne", the host and guests came to the promenade, enjoying a big fireworks show. In the night sky, a cluster of red fireworks bloomed, and on both sides of the building, neon lights flew with laser beams, with the fireworks and colorful lights in the same color as the river water. All of a sudden, a burst of fireworks flashed, and in mid-air, the huge fireworks formed of the letters "APEC", which was quite eye-catching.

Exclamations came out of all their hearts. The guests did not know that 10 years ago, the land under their feet was still a crowded and noisy shantytown, where more than 3,000 households were living, and was called a "poor street" by Shanghai people.

During the conference, Pudong, Shanghai was given special notice in the Global Urban Meteorology News of CNN, USA. On the television screen, the Pudong New Area's panoramic beautiful scenery was showered in the morning sun. The reporter of CNN of the United States said, in the wave of reform and opening-up, Shanghai was reliving the "eastern Paris" charm.

More interestingly, at first some overseas investors did not take the development of Pudong into consideration. Zhao Qizheng, the first Director of the Administrative Committee of Pudong New Area, told reporters at an interview that initially, the international public was skeptical that this might be only a slogan rather than an action.

Milton Friedman, an influential American economist and winner of the Nobel Prize in Economics, mocked Pudong's development as a construction of the Russian-era "Potemkin" for the Empress. He also suspected that the new Yangpu Bridge was an expensive show for the government.

In order to impress Catherine the Great, with the great wealth of his territory, the Russian Marshal Potemkin built a set of beautiful villages that she was to pass by, which were named "Potemkin". They looked very beautiful, but they were all pieces of artificial settings, in which there were actually tattered thatched cottages. Thus, "Potemkin" became the synonym of fraud.

At that time, the officials in charge of attracting foreign investors for Pudong development often pointed to the colorful planning models to tell foreign businessmen which would be the Jinmao Tower, which would be the World Financial Center, and which would be the Shanghai Center. After listening, the foreign businessmen laughed, because at this time, outside the window, there were only cranes all around, ragged everywhere.

Shu Rongbin, General Manager of the Shanghai Waigaoqiao Group, remembered that moment freshly. “I remember guiding a South Korean businessman to visit Waigaoqiao of Pudong. When we arrived at Waigaoqiao port, we only saw a large range of reed marshes. The South Korean businessmen could not conceal his suspicion and ridicule. He asked me, did you really plan for the development? How many years will it take?”

Lujiazui in 1993, with only the lower section of the Oriental Pearl TV Tower just erected

But in the midst of questioning, ridicule, and even disdain, Pudong rose up rapidly. Only in several years, the world-famous economists “felt amazed at the changes that have taken place”.

Years later, Henry Kissinger, the former Secretary of State of the United States, said to Zhao Qizheng with deep emotion and confidence, “When Pudong announced its opening and development, almost all Americans thought it was just a slogan. But I think I was right. Many Americans didn’t know China. They didn’t know that as long as Chinese people want to do something, they will surely be able to do it, because they can do big things through the pooling of money, manpower, and material resources.”

With the passage of time, the wisdom of people can really be proved. As early as in August 1992, soon after Pudong development started, Jimmy Cruz, the Chief Correspondent of *Time* magazine of the United States stationed in China published a long cover article. The author wrote, “The Bund represents the past of Shanghai, and Pudong represents the future of Shanghai.” It was very influential at that moment. 10 or 20 years later, reliving his remark, I had to admit Jimmy’s wisdom.

Zhang Wuchang, a Hong Kong economist, also told a story about Pudong: “In 1993 when I guided Milton Friedman there, we saw only a row of high-rise shops that were said to have been built for show to Deng Xiaoping. Milton, of course, was opposed to doing so, pointing out that the government's development plans might generally fail. Eight years later, however, when I guided an American architect to the Pudong business district, he was stunned to say that the densely scattered commercial buildings there might be the best in the world."

At this time, there were 155 commercial buildings in Lujiazui, Pudong, 10 times as many as all the multinational buildings in the Bund of Puxi.

In 2001, the large-scale infrastructure construction in Pudong had been or was to be completed. The Yangpu, Nanpu, and Xupu Bridges, Metro Line No. 2, the Pudong International Airport, Century Avenue, and Yanggao Road were all completed.

Previously, in the eyes of the outsiders, Shanghai had a great strength in talent, scientific research, culture, and so on, but the infrastructure such as transportation, communication, and electric power was very weak. After the development and opening of Pudong, Shanghai carried out large-scale and high-starting-point infrastructure construction. By the year 2001, the infrastructure had been accomplished. Pudong could accept bigger-scale and higher-level investors for entry, and the multinational companies were just what Pudong craved for.

The great problem that especially troubled Shanghai for many years, that is, "the difficulty in crossing the river", had been overcome at that time. Previously, it usually took two hours for the ferry to go across the river, but now with the bridge, it only took seven minutes to reach the other side.

With the completion of the infrastructure construction, a Taiwan businessman said, "The threshold of Shanghai was suddenly raised. Previously, a 10-million-dollar project could be highly valued in Shanghai, but after that, a project less than a billion dollars can only be regarded as an ordinary investment. There were no preferential terms anymore, such as the opening ceremony with attendance of officials, special approval of the project, and so on."

News journalists are usually emotional. In June of that year, a journalist from Beijing was stunned, deeply impressed with what she saw in Pudong. She wrote, "It was a fine morning. I took a taxi to Pudong, and it was very quiet all around. Only our car glided across the elevated road. Suddenly when I looked up, I saw a round red sun leap out quietly from the high-rise building of Pudong. At a moment, the variety of high-rise buildings were all dyed with gold, like they were touched by a magic wand. In the middle of the air, we — the driver and I — were all 'stunned' in sight of the beautiful scene that cannot be seen on the ground, with the wind whistling in our ears and the tall buildings receding rapidly on both sides, and more high-rise buildings showered in the sunlight came into sight. Like this, we come up to 'hit' the mirage, and the driver who had been silent all the way blurted out, 'Pudong is so beautiful'."

The Huangpu River bends over on its way to the sea (Photo by Niu Yixin, Shanghai News Aerial Photography Federation, China)

At the beginning of Pudong development, the local officials expected the total gross domestic product (GDP) of Pudong would reach 50 billion yuan by the year 2000. But in fact, the total GDP of Pudong reached 9.23 billion yuan in 2000, 15 times more than that in 1990.

In just 10 years, the population of Pudong accounted for only 12% of the total population of Shanghai, but the GDP of Pudong accounted for 22% of Shanghai, with the total import and export accounting for more than 23%, and the amount of foreign direct contractual investment reaching 45% of that of the whole city. In that year, Shanghai's GDP accounted for about 5% of the country, fiscal revenue for more than 13% of the country, and total imports and exports for 23% of the country. These figures can show clearly the impact of Pudong development on Shanghai, the Yangtze River Delta, the Yangtze River Valley, and even China as a whole.

More importantly, the development and opening-up of Pudong, like a powerful engine, drove Shanghai out of its predicament. The economic operation of Shanghai changed greatly, and the growth rate accelerated. A single-function and super-huge industrial city turned into the center of international economy, finance, trade, and shipping. Like a leading wild goose, it led the entire Yangtze River Valley to co-experience the golden age of China's high-speed economic growth.

From a global point of view, a French scholar believed that the development of Pudong was the biggest project for contemporary China to participate in the process of economic globalization, and it is a new lever for China to enhance its international prestige in the future. In fact, Pudong has become the most prominent symbol of China's opening to the world economy. This futuristic city, which would resonate with all the new forms of economic development in the 21st century, is really promising. A few years later, Lanny Eppenstein, Friedman's biographer, said, he thought Fricdman might havc bccn wrong at thc timc and if hc wcrc still alive, he would readjust his point of view. Shanghai, even China as a whole, has demonstrated the strength of market forces.

Chapter 8

Big Experiment: Holding High the Banner of Pioneering

8.1 Pre-World Trade Organization (WTO) Previews

On April 18, 1990, when Chinese Premier Li Peng announced the development and opening of Pudong of Shanghai, investors were concerned with the remark that Beijing had approved Pudong to carry out the policies executed in economic and technological development zones and certain special economic zones.

In the eyes of those investors, "the policies of certain special economic zones" mainly referred to the preferential tax policies. When the special economic zones, such as Shenzhen, China, were established 10 years ago, Deng Xiaoping told the leaders of the south, "The Central Government has no money, but we can give you some policies and you can do it yourself." Since then, for quite some time, the special economic zones adopted preferential tax policies as the main means of attracting foreign investors, so that preferential policies almost equated to China's special economic zones. Special economic zones are defined as "areas where special preferential economic policies are implemented". This made government officials elsewhere feel quite envious.

The 10 initial policies that the Central Government gave to Pudong basically covered the policies given to the five special economic zones, which also included preferential tax policies.

Naturally, as a result of these preferential policies, groups of investors and investigators came into No. 141 of Pudong Avenue — the site of the

Administrative Committee of Pudong New Area. At peak time they had to wait in line for reception.

In the development of Pudong, the policies implemented mainly came from two sources: those given by the Central Government and the relevant state ministries and commissions, and those put forward by the Shanghai Municipal Government and the Government of Pudong New Area. The key words of these policies were decentralization and preferential policy. These policies were issued and formulated in a very short time, so we can see the determination of the Central Government in developing Pudong.

These policies were implemented in Pudong and can be divided into three stages:

The first stage was in 1990, with the policy of the China Central Committee (1990) No. 100 as the main policy, with fiscal and tax preferential policies as the core and with market access and other functional policies as the support, the main purpose of which is to reduce investment costs, improve the investment environment, and promote the rapid start-up of Pudong development and opening-up.

On March 10, 1992, Huang Ju, Mayor of Shanghai, announced to Chinese and foreign reporters that in order to further support the development and opening of Pudong New Area, the Central Government, at the beginning of 1992, gave Shanghai the right of approval for five more categories of projects and added the right for fund raising in five aspects.

Shanghai was given the approval right for expanding five categories of projects. Shanghai was authorized to examine and approve the China-invested and overseas-funded enterprises engaged in entrepot trade in the Waigaoqiao Free Trade Zone, the import and export operation right of the state-owned large and medium-sized enterprises in Pudong New Area, the non-productive projects in the new area of Shanghai, the relevant productive projects in the new area of Shanghai with a total investment of less than 200 million yuan, and the issuing of its own shares and bonds within the central quota, with shares issued throughout the country allowed to be traded in Shanghai.

The Central Government gave Shanghai the right to raise funds in five aspects. Shanghai was allowed to issue 500 million yuan of Pudong Construction Bond every year; on the basis of the original annual central loan of US$100 million to Shanghai, from that year there would be an annual increase of US$200 million in concessional interest rate loans; Shanghai was allowed to issue another 100 million RMB shares in addition to the original quota for Pudong development; Shanghai was allowed to issue US$100 million of RMB shares every year; on the basis of the previously allocated 200 million RMB, an additional 100 million yuan would be allocated to Shanghai that year. The above-mentioned five new fund-raising rights took effect from 1992 to 1995. If operated well, the fund-raising would be increased by 4 billion yuan every year.

This is the second stage. Shanghai and Pudong New Area were given a series of policies such as expanding the right to approve foreign trade and projects and increasing channels for raising funds, which basically reached and partially exceeded the policy scope enjoyed by the special economic zones.

The third stage, in 1995, focused on "Document No. 61" of the State Council, allowing Pudong New Area to open to the outside world in the service trade and other fields, which was not enjoyed by special economic zones and had the most far-reaching impact. The policy content in the document came from a closed-door meeting in 1995 at the Chuansha Hotel in Pudong.

Yang Zhouyi, former Secretary-General of the Pudong Institute for Reform and Development, recalled, "In the early 1990s, some leaders in Pudong thought about the issue: What will be introduced in the next round of development of Pudong? At that time, people were aware with sensitivity that there was little room for development in the manufacturing industry. And experts agreed that in the next round a modern service industry led by the financial sector should be developed."

According to Yang Zhouyi, Zhu Rongji, who already worked in the State Council, came to visit Pudong every year. In 1995, before Vice Premier Zhu arrived in 1995, they specially discussed the list of the next round of service industry which would be opened in Pudong, that is, the request for instruction. Thus, the "Chuansha Conference" was held.

In March 1995, about 30 government decision-making experts and scholars, such as Wang Zhan, Director of the Development Research Center of the Shanghai Municipal Government; Yao Xitang, Director of the Pudong Reform and Development Research Institute; and so on were "brainstorming" for three days and three nights in a hotel in Chuansha,

Pudong. Finally, a report was drafted and submitted to the Central Government, requesting for opening-up to foreign investment in the field of service trade in Pudong.

On April 18, 1995, Zhu Rongji visited Pudong and read the request for instruction, which had been discussed for three days and three nights. He was very satisfied with it. He immediately issued it to the State Council, and thus "Document No. 61" of the State Council was formed.

The key content of the report is a proposal for the Central Government to allow Pudong New Area to have a try to open up to foreign investment in certain sectors, such as service trade. It included: to allow foreign banks to run RMB business as a test in Pudong; to allow the establishment of Sino-foreign joint foreign trade companies in Pudong; to allow the establishment of Sino-foreign joint venture insurance companies in Pudong; to allow foreign trade companies in other provinces of Mainland China to set up subsidiaries in Pudong; and to implement the policy of some free ports in the Waigaoqiao Free Trade Zone.

Since 1978, China initially only opened the manufacturing industry to foreign investors, but kept the service industry closed. For example, at that time, some departments stipulated that the overseas-funded banks cannot handle RMB business. After the issuance of Document No. 61, foreign banks were allowed to conduct a pilot operation of RMB in Pudong, which promoted the opening-up of China's financial sector. This is a milestone event.

Considering the course of China's opening to the outside world, the first stage of the 1980s was represented by the establishment of 5 special economic zones and the opening of 14 coastal cities. The industry opened, which was mainly the secondary industry, and promoted the development of the secondary industry through the implementation of preferential policies. Of course, there were some tertiary industries (such as hotels and other services), but the core fields of tertiary industry, such as finance, trade, and commerce, were still not opened to the outside world. In the 1990s, the development of Pudong marked the second stage of China's opening to the outside world.

After the development and opening of Pudong, the industrial structure of Shanghai changed greatly. The proportion of the tertiary industry increased, and a new pattern began to take shape in which the secondary and tertiary sectors jointly promoted economic growth. A large number of foreign-funded enterprises, especially transnational corporations, entered Pudong and Shanghai, which greatly transformed Shanghai's industrial structure and system. This was completely different from the processing trade industry in Shenzhen development, which was characterized by processing the materials supplied by foreign businessmen, assembling the materials supplied by foreign businessmen, processing the samples supplied by foreign businessmen, and compensatory trade.

Therefore, both the builders, experts, and scholars of Pudong development believed that the development of Pudong should gradually be free of preferential tax policies to explore and implement functional policies. The so-called functional policies were to allow Pudong industry and operation and so on at that time, by breaking through China's restrictions on the introduction of foreign capitals, to experiment in Pudong in accordance with international practice and the current domestic situation. These functional policies made Pudong become the area with the highest degree of opening to the outside world and market access in China.

Because of the functional policies, in 1990s, in the process of China's reform and opening-up, Pudong played the role of a connecting link between the preceding and the following. Pudong promoted the upgrading of China's overall industrial structure and the enhancing of the level of reform and opening-up in the transformation from the initial processing industry and labor-intensive manufacturing industry to modern service and high-tech industries.

8.2 Pioneering under the Functional Policies

By the mid-late 1990s, officials in Pudong had discovered the drawbacks of some policies of excessive reliance on tax incentives, such as violating the principle of fairness, "siphoning effects", the vicious competition in attracting investment, and so on.

Therefore, on April 1, 1996, the preferential tariff policies executed in China's special economic zones were canceled. Pudong leader Zhao Qizheng proposed to consider preferential policies with a different mode of thinking.

He said, "The special features of the special zones in the future will mainly reflect the fact that it will take the lead and try out China's new economic operation before the rest of China. That is to say, due to China's vast territory, some international or certain new economic operation modes suitable for China cannot be started at the same time throughout the country. These new measures will be firstly carried out in the more mature 5+1 places (the 5 economic zones of Shenzhen, Zhuhai, Shantou, Xiamen, and Hainan, and the 1 Pudong New Area). Five special economic zones in Xiamen and Hainan plus the Pudong New Area will take the lead. For example, opening RMB convertibility to foreign banks would not be possible to be operated at the same time throughout the country, and it could only be tested in the 5+1 places."

Therefore, pioneering test became a banner of Pudong, as a means of promoting development. From the mid-late 1990s, Pudong, facing the future, began to get rid of its dependence on the policies of tax preferences, capital resources, and others, and turned to functional policies. As a result, it would become history to drive regional growth by depending on advantages of "preferential policies".

There are two larger contexts for this shift — the establishment of a market economy in China and China's application to join the World Trade Organization (WTO).

In October 1992, the 14th National Congress of the Communist Party of China was held, which clearly stated that the goal of China's economic system reform was to establish a socialist market economy system.

This is an epoch-making change in modern Chinese history. From the Third Plenary Session of the 11th Central Committee in December 1978 to October 1992, the Chinese Communists spent 14 years "crossing the river by feeling the stones". Finally, the goal of China's reform and opening-up was decided — to establish a socialist market economy system. Scholars of China's economic reform took 1992 as a dividing line. After 1992, China began to really speed up the pace of market-oriented reform, and more resolutely proceed towards the market economy system transition. This year is also known as the first year of China's socialist market economy.

In 1993, at that first session of the Eighth Session of the National People's Congress (NPC), the "socialist market economy system" was included in article seven of the amendment to the constitution, and the market economy was legalized in China.

In October that year, the Third Plenary Session of the 14th Central Committee of the Communist Party of China (CPC) passed the "Decision of the CPC Central Committee on Several Issues Concerning the Establishment of a Socialist Market Economy System". As a result, the market economy became a powerful motive force pushing China's economic train forward at high speed.

On May 11 of the same year, in Beijing, which was the first city to use grain stamps, the use of grain stamps was stopped, and all kinds of stamps were sent to the historical archives. As early as nine years ago, the food stamps were abolished in the Shenzhen Special Economic Zone.

In that year, 93.8% of retail commodities were market-priced, while in 1978, 97% were government-priced. This is a successful turn from the planned economy to market economy.

The situation in China changed greatly, and the situation in the world also underwent great changes.

During this period, many countries in the world were seriously rethinking the relationship between planning and marketing, and the relationship between government intervention and economic freedom. More and more scholars, government officials, and even the heads of major international economic organizations began to advocate the more frequent use of "the invisible hand". In the West, it was a reflection on Keynesianism, returning to the track of the market. In the East, it was the negation of a planned economy, complete denial of a planned economy, and transition to a market economy.

In developed countries, Britain's Margaret Thatcher, as an example, abandoned long-held Keynesianism to relive economic liberalism and deregulation. In developing countries, such as Uruguay, Chile, and Argentina in Latin America, they also accelerated their transition to a market economy. Even some of the former socialist countries such as Hungary and Russia also actively carried out the reform of the economic system. Market economy was surging in the world.

Pudong made a great leap forward in the exploration of improving the socialist market economy, taking the lead in adopting the functional policies in the field of modern service industry.

Maybe this is the kind of gene that Shanghai was born with. American scholar and old China Hand Rhoads Murphey made a profound research on the history of Shanghai from 1843 to 1949 and wrote the book *Shanghai: Key to Modern China*. He pointed out that as to China's economic transformation, the earliest roots and seedlings of the modern society grew fully along the Huangpu River.

Perhaps it is the rebound to the planned economy. As is well-known, in the era of the planned economy, Shanghai was the place where the planned economy of China reached the extreme. The reform aimed to transform the planned economy into the market economy, so Pudong development undertook the mission of exploring and perfecting the operation mechanism of the socialist market economy. Therefore, the development and opening-up of Pudong should be practiced not only in the industrial field, but also in the tertiary industry, such as finance and commerce, including the establishment of free trade zones, the establishment of stock exchanges, and the admission of foreign capital into the financial industry. This was a step taken in advance of the opening of China's modern service industry to the outside world and the establishment of a relevant market system, rules, environment, and other aspects.

The transition of Pudong development from preferential policies to functional policies was also motivated by China's accession to the WTO.

On January 1, 1995, the WTO began to operate, taking the place of the General Agreement on Tariffs and Trade (GATT) which was established in 1947. The main objective of this organization, known as the "United Nations" in global trade, was to promote open markets, achieve fair trade, and liberalize world trade.

The Chinese government had, since 1987, proposed to restore its seat in the GATT. Since the establishment of the WTO in 1995, China's negotiations for accession to the WTO had been under way. There were about 10,000 words in the Chinese version of China's WTO accession protocol, with "opening" as the core key word. The WTO accession protocol was an open commitment of the Chinese government to the outside world. The principles of national treatment, market access, and transparency ensured that China would change from policy opening to institutional opening.

Among the many rules of the WTO, there was a basic requirement of universal national treatment, that is, all kinds of preferential policies given to domestic enterprises should also be given to foreign-funded enterprises alike. Under this circumstance, it was obviously contrary to the principle of universal national treatment if China continued to enclose a piece of land and establish special economic zones under special policies.

Therefore, in Article 222 of "The Report of China Joining the Working Group" by the Chinese Government, there was such a statement:

> The Chinese representatives said they had no plan to establish any new special economic zones. The special preferential tariff policies applicable in special economic zones had been abolished, and with the development of China's economic reform and opening-up, China would implement the same tariff policies in its customs territory.

The "entry into WTO" also means, with the implementation of the idea of universalization, the preferential policies for special economic zones came to an end. Like all special zones, Pudong must face the reality of the disappearance of preferential policies.

Yang Zhouyi said, "The reform under the functional policies of Pudong at that time was the preview on the eve of WTO." This preview made Pudong once again stand at the forefront in a new round of reform and opening-up. Yang, who had studied the development and opening of Pudong for a long time, said, "The development of Pudong is inseparable from the support of functional policies made by the Central Government". It was these policies that helped Pudong complete the process of energy accumulation.

According to Yang Zhouyi, commitment to the reform and opening of the service industry, as one of the most successful experiences in Pudong development and opening-up, was an important exploration of China's opening-up to the service sector before China joined the WTO, which achieved the obvious demonstrative effect for the whole country.

In the larger context, after Zhu Rongji successfully achieved the "soft landing" of China's overheated economy in 1993, in 1994 he launched the reform in six aspects, that is, the fiscal and taxation system, the financial system, the investment system, the enterprise system, the housing system, and the pricing system. It was aimed to introduce the tax-sharing system, establish the modern banking system, abolish the dual-track system of the RMB exchange rate and domestic prices, and so on. So Pudong, in order to take the lead in furthering China's service sector to the outside world, naturally needed experimental policies.

This kind of functional policies was of more macro significance. When reform and opening-up had in-depth development, in some places the shortcomings of those policies merely relying on tax preferences came to the surface, so the innovation on the institutional level was required.

As for the functional policies, Zhao Qizheng gave a vivid explanation. It is through the functional policy that a military site at the seaside was changed into a coastal swimming site, that is, a change of function. Compared with the previous preferential policies, the greatest feature was that it had nothing to do with taxation, and nothing to do with the investment made by higher authorities.

The implementation of this kind of functional policy was an important strategy in China's reform and opening-up — continuously carrying out system experiments in a special area and successfully promoting it. Pudong people were the first to realize this, which may be one of the reasons for the first test area of free trade to settle in Pudong in 2013.

8.3 Great Experiment in the New Century

Pioneering test became a banner of Pudong, a method to promote Pudong to accelerate development when it gradually lost the effect of preferential policies. In the history of Pudong's development and opening-up, as a result of the pioneering test, Pudong achieved a number of firsts.

On July 26, 1992, Japan Itochu Commercial Co., Ltd., the first foreign company in China engaged in import and export trade in the bonded area of China, registered in the Waigaoqiao Free Trade Zone with the approval of the State.

In November 1993, the Waigaoqiao Free Trade Zone took the lead in setting up a bonded trading market — the Shanghai Bonded Capital Goods Market.

On December 20, 1995, No. 1 Yaohan Co., Ltd., the first large-scale Sino-foreign joint venture retail enterprise, opened its business with the approval of the State Council.

On January 1, 2000, it became the first place for foreign banks to handle RMB business.

What was most influential in society was the grand opening of the Shanghai No. 1 Yaohan Co., Ltd.

This is the first large-scale Sino-foreign joint venture retail enterprise approved by the State Council in China, jointly invested by the Japan Yaohan, Hong Kong Yaohan, and Shanghai First Department Store. On December 20, 1995, it opened a new building in Lujiazui, Pudong. Despite the cold wind, 1.07 million customers flooded into the mall, which was listed in the Guinness Book of World Records.

Kazuo Wada, the President of Yaohan Co., Ltd, said in surprise, "I was stunned by the arrival of 1.7 million customers all at once. At the opening of all the department stores in the world, there was never such a high record. It really deserves to be opened in China."

Previously, no foreign investors had gotten involved in China's domestic business, so No. 1 Yaohan in Shanghai was the first to break up the dominance of Chinese business and Chinese-funded operations, which made the Chinese business realize the huge appeal of overseas business to Chinese consumers.

But officials in Pudong tried to make experiments in broader, more comprehensive fields.

In July 2004, when Hu Jintao, General Secretary of the CPC Central Government, came to Pudong during his visit to Shanghai, he demanded "to continue to make great effort in the development of Pudong, to accelerate institutional innovation, raise the level of export-oriented economy, and strive to achieve rapid development at a higher starting point".

At the beginning of the development, Pudong experienced explosive growth and made great contribution to the development of the whole of Shanghai. But how can Pudong achieve rapid development at a higher starting point while gradually losing the effect of preferential policies?

Opportunities came quickly. In 2004, the concept of "comprehensive reform" emerged in the minds of certain officials of the National Development and Reform Commission, and discussions began on how to select pilot sites. The National Development and Reform Commission (NDRC), an important department of the Chinese government, was in charge of formulating economic and social development policies and guiding the overall economic institutional reform.

At this time, after more than 20 years of reform in China, the senior officials in Beijing noticed that some problems in the reform and development, such as the mismatch and the poor coordination between the reform of government administration system and social management system and reform of economic system, began to be exposed intensively. The contradictions caused by the monomial reform went beyond economic category, so the system and coordination of the reform must be valued so as to put the economic reform, the political reform, and the social reform in the frame of the harmonious development of man and society, man and nature. So the officials of the NDRC began to do research on the comprehensive reform.

Pudong soon learned this information. According to Zhang Xuebing, the then President of Pudong New Area, recalled, "Once, while we were eating in the canteen, a comrade from the National Development and Reform Commission of Pudong New Area showed me a document. He said that they had received a message from the NDRC that they were studying comprehensive and coordinated reform and selecting pilot sites throughout the country."

On September 24 of the same year, Jiang Huigong, Assistant Director of the Pudong New Area Development and Reform Commission, came to the China Development and Reform Commission to make a report on the reform and opening-up in Pudong.

Upon hearing this, Fan Hengshan, Director of the Institutional Reform Department, said, "Now, many places have carried out the pilot reform, but they all favor the individual reforms, and there is no comprehensive reform. Some time ago, several ministries and commissions such as the China Development and Reform Commission, appointed by Premier Minister Wen, made special investigations and their plan has been reported to the State Council."

Jiang Huigong seized the opportunity to report the advantages and conditions for Pudong to take the lead in the reform in the new century, and asked for advice on how to proceed next.

Fan Hengshan thought that the China Development and Reform Commission had been considering selecting the site for comprehensive reform pilot, and Pudong had the advantages for the pilot. What Fan Hengshan said made Jiang Huigong excited.

Fan Hengshan also suggested that the Institutional Reform Institute and Pudong New Area first draw up a plan, then make a demonstration, and when everything was relatively ready, they report to the Shanghai

Municipal Government, and then the Shanghai Municipal Government would report to the NDRC so as to make Pudong a reform pilot in the new era.

Pudong officials understood that this was an opportunity to be seized, that the Central Government would implement some major measures in Pudong such as opening up to the outside world and institutional innovation.

In October, it was the clear and refreshing autumn in Beijing, the best season for tourism. The top leaders of Pudong rushed to Beijing, without any intention of appreciating the scene, in hope of winning support from the central ministries and commissions for the reform pilot.

In an exchange with the official of the NDRC, there was the following communication:

Fan Hengshan said that as far as the whole country was concerned, the single-item reform was no longer effective, because it was a matter of connecting with the tendons in spite of the breaking of bones; you cannot move this item without moving that one, therefore, comprehensive and coordinated reforms must be carried out.

The Pudong official answered that Pudong was willing to take the first test, as Pudong itself was the product of reform and opening-up, and reform was a fundamental attribute of Pudong development.

Fan Hengshan said with encouragement that he also hoped Pudong could take the lead, because Pudong had been written into the reports of the recent National Party Congresses, but he hoped that Pudong would not focus on the preferential policies in the process of the comprehensive reform, but make a comprehensive plan for reform and submit it for examination and approval.

According to the recollection of a leader of Pudong New Area, at a meeting with the Director of the NCRC, Ma Kai, the Pudong side proposed to become a national comprehensive reform pilot, with the principle of "three NOs": no preferential policies, no projects, and no capital support. After listening with great interest, Ma Kai took out his notebook and asked for repetition, taking notes while listening.

In no time, the Pudong New Area completed "Proposals by Pudong New Area to Get Central and Municipal Support for Functional Policies (first draft)".

The NDRC, which attached great importance to this, sent a special research group to Pudong New Area for investigation and the investigation affirmed the "six transformations" proposed by Pudong New Area (marketization of economic operation, internationalization of business environment, regionalization of functional development, intensification of growth modes, socialization of public affairs, and legalization of government administration). So it was argued that a pilot made in such a local area as Pudong was less risky and it could be popularized on the ground of gaining experience.

At the beginning of 2005, based on this "proposal", the "Framework of Shanghai Pudong Comprehensive Reform Experimental Zone" was completed. This was an application for a national comprehensive reform pilot, and was formally submitted to the State Council.

At this time when Pudong development and opening-up had been advancing for 15 years, it was totally different. In that past 15 years, the gross domestic product (GDP) of Pudong increased by 19.2% annually on an average, reaching 179 billion yuan in 2004, about 30 times higher than that in 1990. Pudong, with one-eighth of Shanghai's population and one-tenth of Shanghai's land area, created a quarter of Shanghai's GDP and total industrial output value, half of its foreign trade and imports, and a third of its total foreign investment, equivalent to creating another Shanghai in just 15 years. At this time, Pudong was already an important economic pillar of Shanghai.

A Taiwan businessman, Wu Dazhong, said, "The high standard of planning and high-speed development in Pudong brought about the great results in only 15 years. It had taken one hundred or more years for the international metropolises such as Tokyo, New York, and London to achieve this effect."

In the high-speed development, Pudong people also encountered "the pains in growing". The marginal effect of preferential policies was diminishing, as the various regions in China competed with each other and foreign investors continued to study the preferential degree of the policies executed in various development zones. At the beginning of Pudong's development, investors flowed into Pudong to enjoy the preferential policies at that time, but then they found that the neighboring Kunshan of Jiangsu Province was more favorable, so they turned away from Pudong.

The rising business costs in Pudong also reduced its appeal to foreign capital. 3M Company of the United States was the first multinational company to enter Shanghai, but in 2005 it set up the factory in Suzhou because for the buyout of 50-year right of use, in Waigaoqiao of Pudong the price was US$110 per square meter, while in the Suzhou Industrial Park the public offer was only US$15 per square meter.

Pudong was also shouldering the heavy responsibility of structural adjustment and industrial upgrading. Shanghai scholars at the time were outspoken. From the perspective of foreign investment, the development of high-tech industries and other indicators, Pudong's economic operation was not satisfactory, so maintaining the momentum of development aroused great concern. In the past 15 years, the radioactive effect of Pudong on the economic development of the Yangtze River Delta and the Yangtze River Valley was not yet brought into full play, and the model of "small government, big society" was not yet improved. There were still many mismatches between the mode of economic operation and growth and socialist market economy, and the features of dualistic economic and social structure were still relatively obvious.

But in the exploration of "small government, big society" by Pudong, Pudong officials believed, "A lean government is just the beginning, and on this basis, Pudong meticulously outlined a modern embryonic form of public service-oriented government. This is exactly the requirement made by the pilot comprehensive reform that started in 2005 — the 'small government' needed to be further reformed to be more efficient."

This is the background against which Pudong officials hoped to carry out comprehensive reform.

In the history of China's modern regional economic development, since the establishment of the Shenzhen Special Economic Zone, the local governments always preferred the preferential policies, which had been widely disputed, especially after China joined the WTO in 2000.

At this time, all parts of China already stepped out of the stage of simply relying on policies for development and entered the stage of institutional innovation and system innovation. Pudong attempted to make major national initiatives of opening-up and system innovation by making pioneering experiment in Pudong and promoting comprehensive institutional innovation actively and prudently. Therefore, Pudong gained support from the Central Government in taking the lead in carrying out the institutional reform. At that time, Pudong was not the only one to apply to the Central Government for pilot reform, but also there were a number of competitors such as Shenzhen and the Tianjin Binhai New Area. As a result, Pudong became the first winner. In addition to the advantages of reform and opening-up over the years, the operability of Pudong's institutional reform plan was also an important reason for Pudong to take the lead.

Some economists attributed the development of Pudong to institutional innovation which was carried out at "the most appropriate time in the most appropriate place".

Pudong was chosen by history. In the early summer of 2005, on June 22, a telegraph of Xinhua News Agency made Pudong people experience the same excitement once again as that at the Pudong development and opening-up 15 years ago: "Premier Wen Jiabao presided over the State Council Executive Meeting on the 21st, which studied the issues of building a conservation-oriented society and developing a circular economy, and approved to make a pilot comprehensive reform in Pudong New Area of Shanghai."

The news was put like this:

> The Executive Meeting of the State Council demanded that the pilot program of comprehensive reform in Pudong focus on changing government functions, the ways of economic operation, and the dualistic economic and social structure. Pudong should organically combine reform with development, local practical problems with common problems on the whole, key breakthroughs with overall innovation, and economic system reform with other reforms, so that Pudong can take the lead in establishing a perfect socialist market economy system and play an exemplary role in promoting national reform.
>
> It was held at the meeting that China's reform, which was in the critical stage, should continue to do a good job in the pilot reform of the relevant special areas, and at the same time, should select the areas with conditions to carry out a comprehensive reform pilot to improve the socialist market economy so as to provide relevant experience. This was of great significance to realize the reform goal put forward by the Third Plenary Session of the 16th Central Committee of the CPC.

Once again, Pudong was at the forefront of China's reform and opening-up. It made pioneering tests in continuing the functional policies, and became the first comprehensive pilot reform zone in China.

Deng Xiaoping felt regretful about the fact that the Chinese government did not take Pudong into account in setting up the special economic zones. But in 2005, the Central Government first considered Pudong to see if Pudong could make a breakthrough in the comprehensive reform. This kind of breakthrough was of macroscopic meaning, because when the reforms went into the depths, what needed to be broken through was no longer a local problem, but the underlying problems which often involved a wider range of issues. It might have a demonstration effect on other local governments in China, which is one of the reasons why Pudong became the first comprehensive pilot reform zone.

In fact, in the areas like Shenzhen or Pudong as well as others where preferential policies were implemented, it was clear that the preferential policies would end sooner or later. The inclining policies would always be made up-right, but institutional innovation could continue to be explored. Yang Zhouyi, former Secretary-General of the Pudong Institute of Reform and Development, made an analogy: Preferential policies were like offering grain directly, while the comprehensive pilot reform zone obtained "production autonomy".

As early as September 18, 1995, after introducing the functional policies entrusted to Pudong by the Central Government, Zhao Qizheng, Director of the Administrative Committee of Pudong New Area, said that the focus of new policies was to take Pudong New Area as a comprehensive pilot zone for reform and opening-up, and as a leading zone in line with international practices.

In other words, as early as 10 years ago, Pudong had been thinking about comprehensive system experiments rather than just begging the Central Government for preferential policies.

For this, Zhao Qizheng explained, "This is Pudong, making pioneering tests to carry on the innovation in theory and practice ceaselessly."

The "second reform" of Pudong was supported by the Central Government. Of course, to make pioneering tests in such a new area with great economic contribution, the Central Government also considered the operability of the Pudong plan.

"The Framework of Pudong Comprehensive Pilot Reform Zone in Shanghai" proposed seven major tasks for the construction of the Pudong Comprehensive Pilot Reform Zone, which involved many aspects of political, economic, and cultural development. Three new contents were added to the framework after the approval of the NDRC, including cultivating and developing intermediary organizations to improve the degree of social organization of economic activities, exploring to establish the optimization of the accumulation mechanism for human capital and create a system environment to revitalize China through talents development, and establishing a scientific adjustment mechanism to improve the system of modern social income distribution and security in line with economic and social development.

Scholars shared the view that from the Shenzhen Special Economic Zone in the 1980s to the Pudong Development Zone in the 1990s, to the comprehensive pilot reform zone in the new century, it was a step-by-step reform experiment carried out by the Chinese government in various specific regions.

As the first pilot area of comprehensive coordinated reform, it was more difficult for Pudong to carry out the pilot comprehensive supporting reform. When Pudong was approved in 2005, the telegraph by Xinhua News Agency only briefly reported "three changes": changing government functions, changing patterns of economic growth, and changing the dualistic structure of economic society. The saying that came along with this was "three NOs", that is, in the comprehensive reform pilot in Pudong, no penny from the Central Government, no project, and no fiscal and tax preferential policies. The "three changes" referred to the requirements for the comprehensive pilot reform in Pudong. The "three NOs" is the prerequisite for the comprehensive pilot reform in Pudong.

Indeed, at the beginning of Pudong development, the Central Government gave preferential policies to Pudong and large projects, but since Pudong became a pilot of comprehensive reform, people in Pudong understood that the "greatest privilege" given by the Central Government to Pudong would be the priority of taking the pioneering test in institutional innovation. In other words, through early and pilot implementation and by means of the organic combination of reform with development, the solution of local practical problems with the common problem on the whole, the key breakthroughs with the overall innovation, and the economic system with other reforms, Pudong took the lead in establishing a perfect socialist market economic system and played an exemplary role in promoting nation-wide reform.

This means that the senior leadership in Beijing also paid more attention to the institutional innovation of Pudong in the comprehensive pilot reform. According to a leader of Shanghai, "Pudong can make a breakthrough, and it can be popularized in the whole city and followed in the whole country."

Therefore, after 2005, 23 state ministries and commissions conducted various policy experiments in Pudong in the name of comprehensive pilot reform projects, and more than 70 reform projects at the national level were executed as pilot projects in Pudong, such as the State Administration of Quality Supervision, the State Administration of Industry and Commerce, Customs, the Ministry of Commerce, etc. So it is not an exaggeration to say that Pudong had become the experimental area of the national new policies. These tests were small in motion, specific and scattered, and different subjects performed different tests for different purposes, which thus gave a sense of fragmentation.

On November 16, 2014, the Pudong New Area Market Supervision Bureau, which was integrated with the original Industrial and Commercial Department, Quality Supervision Department, and Food Supervision Department, was put into operation. This is the pilot project for Pudong to explore the reform of the giant-department system. (Photo by Zhang Xian)

In the early 21st century, in addition to Pudong's demonstrative function, regional reform experiments were also constantly fermenting. Gradually, local governments had no hope for regional preferential policies, so they began to pursue experimental policies. They believed that if an area was set up as a national comprehensive pilot reform zone, the policy environment would be greatly improved and more local autonomy would be brought into play. And a growing number of forward-thinking local officials realized that "first-rate governments need strategy, second-rate governments need policies, and third-rate governments need money". Therefore, the local governments applied to the Central Government for experiments in comprehensive coordinated reform.

The experiments in regional comprehensive coordinated reform blossomed everywhere, which can be regarded as the result of the leading function played by Pudong.

8.4 Dancing in Fetters

It was greatly related to the reform of the government itself for Pudong to become the pilot area for comprehensive coordinated reform. Since Pudong development, local officials had been breaking through a variety of cumbersome administrative approvals.

On September 10, 1990, the Shanghai Municipal Government held a press conference on Pudong development. A reporter from *Time Weekly* of the United States asked Zhu Rongji, Mayor of Shanghai, why the bureaucracy in Shanghai was as hard as the stones of the Great Wall, and how to change this situation, and how to make Pudong New Area more attractive to foreign investment.

It is recorded that at that time, if a project was to be carried out in Shanghai, they had to get as many as 126 stamps at the most, and the procedures were extremely opaque. Investors for a project had to run around for approval. They had to go to merely one administrative department several times for approval, waiting for half a year or more, which aroused particularly strong dissatisfaction from foreigner businessmen.

Therefore, Zhu Rongji frankly told reporters that he hated bureaucracy as much as they did, but it can also be said that bureaucracy was a common disease in the world. In the past, in Shanghai, a project could only be approved with more than a hundred stamps, so the Municipal Foreign Investment Committee was set up, in hope of approving foreign investment with only one stamp.

Zhu Rongji was once called the "economic tsar" by Western reporters after he became China's Premier. He was aggressive in his work and disgusted with prevarication. He hoped that the establishment of such a committee could solve the red-tape problem, so he was dubbed "one-stamp Zhu".

On January 31, 1991, in approving an internal investigation report on the lengthy process of the approval for investment, Zhu Rongji bluntly issued an instruction, "Alas, Shanghai! No reform, and it will be doomed". He ordered for the report to be distributed to the people involved. "If there are 10,000 people, 10,000 copies should be printed, and it will be paid by the Municipal Government."

At the Shanghai People's Congress in 1993, Zhao Qizheng, leader of Pudong New Area, pointed to the reform of Pudong's government functions, "The major issues that should be managed must be managed well, the issues that should not necessarily be managed can be handled by intermediary agencies, and those that should not be managed should be resolutely ignored."

It can be seen that both the leadership in Shanghai and the leadership in Pudong had the impulse to reform the traditional administrative system.

In 1992, the Ministry of Foreign Trade and Economic Cooperation of China accumulated the funds of national import and export companies to invest in Pudong to build the super-high-rise building Jinmao Tower, which may cost about US$400–500 million at that time. Such a large-scale investment must be submitted to the China Planning Commission for examination and approval by the State Council.

According to Jiang Huigong, who still worked in the Pudong Development Office at the time, they all knew that if they were to submit it to Beijing for approval, it would take a very long time and may greatly delay the completion of this landmark building.

As a result, Pudong took charge of the project approval at a risk, while Shanghai only pretended not to know. Once the Planning Commission of the state learned that Pudong made an ultra vires approval, Pudong would take the risk of being blamed.

Jiang Huigong said, "This is a reasonable practice, because the Pudong Development Commission had just been authorized for examination and approval, if it did not know the regulations well, it was reasonable for them to make minor mistakes, but it had to bear responsibility. Considering the influence of this project was too great at the initial stage of Pudong development and it was very helpful to set up the image of Pudong development and promote the investment in Pudong, I agreed without hesitation, even if I had to take responsibility later on."

Sure enough, a few years later, when the State Planning Commission learned that Pudong had built the nation's first super-high-rise building without their approval, they were ready to make a thorough investigation. Fortunately, the Chinese Ministry of Foreign Trade and Economic Cooperation (MOFTEC) was prepared in advance, and in addition, the attention paid by Zhu Rongji and Li Lanqing, two leaders of the State Council, made it a false alarm.

Fortunately, in the early 21st century, these procedures for approval were reformed. As long as the projects were not listed as restricted or prohibited projects in the national industry-oriented list, and did not rely on the national financial allocation, they can be approved by the local government itself.

Pudong became a pilot area of comprehensive coordinated reform against this background: since the reform and opening-up of China, the game rules played in the planned economy era were broken so as to keep in line with the market economy, such as dealing with the fake and shoddy, environmental pollution, and other problems. So all levels of government standardized the order, having issued a variety of standards and regulations. As a result, there were more rules and regulations, more regulators with official large caps, more fees, and more checks and penalties, but it became less and less efficient. There was a Chinese folk saying, "Seven or eight official big caps cannot control a broken straw hat". They could not control whoever they wanted to control. The rules and regulations were expanding continuously like the well-known Parkinson's Law.

This phenomenon was not understood by foreigners, especially foreign investors.

Reducing approvals became an important task of government reform. After the development of Pudong, Pudong took the lead in reforming the administrative examination and approval system. After six rounds of reform, by 2012, the approval items had been reduced from 724 items in 2001 to 242 items, and the time limit of approval was reduced from 22 working days to 8.4 working days, with a double drop of 60%.

Of course, these figures were not achieved easily. An official in Pudong once said to the media, "It is very difficult to negotiate one by one, to reduce items one by one. This is a very painful process."

Officials in government agencies felt, more directly, that the authority of the office remained the same from the top to bottom, but with fewer personnel and fewer procedures such that, to a large degree, the people left were much busier. Some students who wanted to apply for Pudong civil service were often reminded, "Our government is small, not easy to muddle along, so anyone who wants to be idle around should not come over here."

Reform was always accompanied by this type of pain. It was the dancing in iron fetters, because when it came to the later phase, almost all the items to be cut down were closely related to the distribution of benefits.

"The administrative efficiency should be the greatest, the administrative transparency should be the highest, and the administrative charges should be the lowest" — this was the goal of the comprehensive transformation of government functions in Pudong.

However, even if the items were reduced by more than 200, it was still time-consuming and laborious for an enterprise to complete the application for approval. One management official said, "We have all concentrated the services in one agency, but some of the national policies and regulations are mutually pre-conditional. For example, this regulation requires that department A should make decision first, and the other requires the department B to nod first. Who is the first? Applicants come back again just after turning away."

Without a fundamental breakthrough at the institutional level, the problems still remained. Li Jinming, Senior Manager of the Planning and Development Department of Shanghai GM Automotive, told the media the story about such a circle:

Shanghai GM planned to build a vehicle logistics flyover to connect the two plants. The project was reported to the Jinqiao Administrative Committee and then to the district management. All the officials of the Development and Reform Commission, Construction and Transportation Commission, Environmental Protection Bureau, and Land Bureau agreed to it, but the consent of other departments would be the prerequisite. As a result, the report went around several government departments, with no progress over the course of a year.

The ball was kicked around. The authorities were operated on the premise of each other, so that a ring was formed.

The problem lies in this ring. One project may involve several functional departments, and a lot of time was spent in the horizontal flow between departments, so no one would like to step forward to take the responsibility. It seemed that no one was wrong, but it was really inefficient.

Therefore, Pudong did not stop the steps, but continued to carry on the institutional innovation.

8.5 The Birth of a Community Service Organization

The pursuit of government efficiency and the mission of building a public service-oriented government contributed to the emergence of a new institution.

On the opposite of the government building of Pudong New Area, behind a lush green shade, it was a pale-yellow building, which was the Pudong Civic Center. It was translated into English as the "Public Service Center of Pudong, Shanghai". As one can see from the English name, it was an organization that provided services for the public.

On October 18, 2006, the sunshine of golden autumn witnessed the inauguration of four Pudong resident representatives at the Pudong Public Service Center, one of whom was a German businessman.

At first, passers-by took a curious look at the pale-yellow building: What does this organization do?

In fact, the idea of setting up such an institution was simple: most of the affairs that the public and businessmen would like the government to examine can be done in this one building, that is, through this "one-door" or "one-stop" service, the efficiency of administration could be improved.

For the first time, a community resident surnamed Huang walked into the spacious lobby of the Public Service Center. Under the guidance of volunteers wearing blue vests, he came up to the electronic screen and with a touch, it "spit out" a small piece of paper under the screen with numbers of the queue and window number written on it. Huang, who had been sent to the countryside for re-education more than 30 years ago, now

The facade of the Pudong Public Service Center

wanted to go back to Shanghai by going through the necessary formalities. He was happy to learn that all the formalities could be done by merely visiting the Service Center, where all the windows for the street-level and district-level management were assembled there, and there was no need to run to many places.

Huang had a fresh feeling as he looked curiously at the staff in various uniforms at the counter. When he came up to the counter, what was new to him was that with the low counter and no glass separating them, it was convenient to sit down and have a talk with the staff, and in less than 10 minutes, he finished all the formalities.

Huang was also surprised by the speed.

A special Complaint Center for Administrative Inefficiency was also set up in the Service Center. Once a matter was handled over the time limit, the screen of the Complaint Center would display "violation", and the Supervision Department would supervise and handle it.

The Pudong Public Service Center was also networking with the service centers of various community affairs to incorporate the investment, taxation, finance, health audit, talent introduction, and other aspects which the original Investment Promotion Center had handled. There were more than 370 service items in the 84 windows, and more than 140 special lines were set up at the central platform established by the commissions, offices, and bureaus of the Pudong New Area government.

Comprehensive information inquiry machines were provided from the first to the third floor of the Service Center. With the help of these inquiry machines, citizens could find all kinds of information about various government public information and information on public affairs, such as food, clothing, housing, transportation, employment, and education.

The service organizations closely related to the public were also allowed to enter the Service Center, such as the Pudong Marriage Registration Center and Legal Aid Center. In the center, there were also the public dining room, tea rooms, hall, living rooms, banks, post offices, the self-service ATMs, and so on.

The 17,000-square-meter Pudong Public Service Center, with a spacious and bright hall, made people's eyes bright up. The public leisure area next to the office hall was three to four times larger than the office area, with green shrubs dotted with round tables and chairs for the public to work or rest. In addition, wheelchairs for the disabled and the strollers for the kids were provided, as well as magnifying glasses, reading glasses, medicine boxes, first-aid bags, needle thread bags, and the like.

When the Public Service Center of Pudong New Area was officially opened, a special hotline was operated. When people encountered troubles, they could call this hotline. Even if a husband and wife quarreled, they could call the hotline for help.

Different social organizations and government departments could also hold various forums, lectures, seminars, and fund-raising activities in the Service Center. There was also a variety of exhibitions, such as collection exhibitions and painting exhibitions. Since there were so many activities that there was not enough space upstairs, the basement had to be put into use.

Many activities attracted the participation of foreigners. For instance, some foreigners would volunteer to teach English, and there were also some courses for foreigners' children or wives to learn Chinese and to practice brush calligraphy.

There was an English salon at 2 every Saturday afternoon in the public tea room on the ground floor of the Service Center. From 2006 to 2014, more than 10,000 people participated in the activities of the English salon. With the volunteer team composed of more than 20 foreigners, overseas Chinese, and other English masters, the Service Center became a paradise for local English learners.

Patrick, an American volunteer who had been teaching English for eight years, served the salon for 1,750 hours without pay. He said, "I came here to take part in volunteer service, and in fact, it is an interactive process of learning from each other. I also learned a lot of Chinese culture here. It was very helpful to me."

According to the official statement, the Pudong Service Center was the outcome of Pudong's transformation of government functions and comprehensive reform. It was called the citizens' world, the social platform, and the window of the government — the interactive trinity of government, market, and society.

The associations in Pudong held trainings and invited foreign experts to give lectures

8.6 Giving Full Play to Society

In the exploration of "small government, big society", in the contemplation of "what should be done and what should not", Pudong, on the one hand, carried out the system reform of greatly reducing the administrative examination and approval, and on the other hand, developed social organizations to allow the citizens to achieve autonomy.

On February 6, 1996, the Luoshan Civic Guild Hall, the community public service center that Shanghai first adopted the "civilian-run and government-supported trustee mode", was listed at No. 30, Lane 40, Boshan East Road, Pudong. The founder was Wu Jianrong. He was originally a high school music teacher in Shanghai and later worked at the Shanghai Young Men's Christian Association (YMCA).

In 1994, Wu Jianrong was sent to Yokohama, Japan, to study the management and operation of non-profit organizations. After returning to China, Wu Jianrong intended to promote the community management experience of Yokohama YMCA in Shanghai.

In the era of China's planned economy, the government was like a butler in charge of everything, in charge of every citizen from birth to death. The government took on all things and, as a result, it managed too much to manage well. Therefore, after China's reform and opening-up in 1987, the government began to let go gradually. Then came the question of how the citizens should manage themselves, and civil autonomy became a problem for the Chinese government and the people.

Wu Jianrong hoped to follow the experience of foreign countries for reference to answer this question by setting up the Luoshan Guild Hall. But in 1994, in the eyes of common people, Wu Jianrong was too forward-thinking.

Also forward-thinking was the Pudong New Area Administrative Committee. The Social Development Bureau of Pudong New Area followed the "small government, big society" model, trying to introduce new mechanisms into community construction and management and entrust government-invested public facilities to civil society for operation. The opportunity came in 1995. In a newly-built community, on Luoshan Street, there were some idle public supporting facilities. The Social Development Bureau made a bold institutional experiment — transforming the public infrastructure into a community public facility directly under the authority of the Social Development Bureau, launching social mechanism and seeking for a social organization to manage it. The Social Development Bureau enlisted agencies from the community who were voluntarily administer it.

This was in line with the wishes of the Director-General of YMCA, Wu Jianrong. Finally, the Social Development Bureau of Pudong New Area and Shanghai YMCA reached a consensus: a guild hall would be built on a street named Puxing in Pudong.

The new establishment was named Luoshan Civic Guild Hall to show the difference from the community service center which was single-functioned and operated by the government or government agency. This guild hall started up a new governance model of "government leading, all-party cooperation, citizen participation, and community management" after China's reform and opening-up to the outside world. It is also the first community public service center in Shanghai to adopt the "civilian-run and government-supporting trustee mode".

The "civic guild" is a kind of community organization peculiar to China and in the 17th century it originated from fellow society, which referred to the organization set up by people born in the same province, city, county, or town living in the capital, provincial city, or big commercial port. However, Luoshan Guild Hall, founded by Wu Jianrong, only borrowed this name, since the service objects were not the people from the same province, the same city, the same county, or the same town, but the community residents. It was a community public service center that provided community culture, education, sports, life, and other services.

At the beginning of its establishment, one-third of the people that the Luoshan Civic Guild Hall served were "people of old Pudong", that is, the local people who changed from the farmers to residents; one-third of the people were the intellectuals who moved in from the vicinity of Chengdu Road viaduct in downtown Puxi; and one-third of the people were workers who moved in from the Yangpu District. So in the Guild Hall, a "999 Help Center" was set up. On the wall of the 999 Help Center on the second floor of the Luoshan Civic Guild Hall, the two lines were particularly striking: "Here are your friends who share your worries, and here are your friends who share your happiness."

In the investment structure of the Luoshan Guild Hall, the Pudong Social Development Bureau, as the government investor, contributed 2.6 million yuan, accounting for more than 50% of the total investment, and offered an idle kindergarten; the non-governmental funding, the Pudong New Area Social Development Foundation, contributed 900,000 yuan, accounting for 20% of the total.

Professor Yang Tuan, Assistant Director of the Center for Social Policy Studies at the Chinese Academy of Social Sciences, researcher at the Institute of Sociology, remarked, "The Luosan Guild Hall is a stage of self-organized experimentation offered by the government to non-profit organizations such as the YMCA. At that time or at present, few non-profit organizations in China were able, like the YMCA, to independently manage and organize experiments within their communities according to their own will and understanding. Therefore, it can be said that the Luoshan Civic Guild Hall provided a model for the survival and development of community non-profit organizations, and also provided reference for the survival strategy of a large number of non-governmental organizations (NGOs) or non-profit organizations (NPO) in China. It also brought some illumination to promote the benign interaction between the government and NGOs and NPOs, so the government should provide a wider space for the development of NGOs and NPOs from the institutional perspective and allow them, in the loose system environment, to spontaneously have a benign interaction and cooperation with the government and jointly manage the public affairs of the community."

But because it was a premature baby, this social service center could not be formally registered in a government agency for the first five years. Fortunately, with the support of the Social Development Bureau of Pudong New Area, the Luoshan Civic Guild Hall was registered as a civilian-run non-enterprise organization in 2000 after the "Opinions on Dual Management of Social Organizations and Private Non-Enterprise Organizations" was issued in Shanghai. The registration number was 0001.

The Luoshan Civic Guild Hall did a good job in community service, which was well noticed by people. In November 2005, at the First China Charity Conference, the Luoshan Civic Guild Hall was introduced as an example of cooperation between NGOs and the government. By the end of 2013, the YMCA had already operated eight guild halls in Shanghai, with Luoshan Guild Hall as a good example.

In addition to the guild halls, Pudong also established more forms of NPOs. On February 28, 2003, Shanghai Lequn Social Work Service, the first non-governmental social work organization in mainland China, was born in Pudong. A woman named Liu Xiaofang proposed to set it up. She graduated from the Department of Social Work of China Academy of Youth Political Science, and later her dream was ignited up by the professors of social work in Hong Kong University when she attended the first master program of social work jointly held by the University of Hong Kong and Fudan University. She quit her job to become the director of the service center herself, the first professional social worker in China.

Liu Xiaofang's venture was also supported by Dr. Ma Yili, then Director of the Social Development Bureau in Pudong New Area. He visited Japan in the early 1990s and was one of the first junior officials in mainland China to understand the social work in developed countries.

Ma Yili constantly promoted social organizations and social work, bringing in talents and vigorously promoting social work in welfare institutions, hospitals, and schools in Pudong.

But these practices were so new in China that people were rather dubious. Many officials criticized her as a bookworm, being too academic and too idealistic: How can Shanghai do things like this? How can China do things like this?

But Ma Yili did not give up. She constantly called for it and she supported social work with her own power. She explained the benefits of social workers with examples. For example, there was a problem that people encountered in renting accommodation, that is, garbage pickers turned over garbage cans every day. If it had to be tackled, usually a report should be submitted for a grant from the superior government, namely, 500 yuan a month would be given to the cleaner. It did seem that there was no better way. But can you imagine the method applied by the social workers? They may hold a meeting with outsiders like the garbage pickers. Why? They may choose among them two people with a higher educational level, and sign an agreement with them on some conditions, then the neighborhood committee may manage to issue an entrance card, so that later they can pick up rubbish without furtive worry, but they need to sweep the ground and clean trash cans after collection. There would be no cost of a penny for the government, and everyone would be happy. Was such a vision and method, after all, professional or non-professional?

In January 2006, the Shanghai Pudong Non-profit Organization Development Center (NPI), the first social welfare organization incubator in China, came into being in Pudong. The founder Lv Chao, once Xinhua News Agency reporter, was awarded "one of the top 10 outstanding young people" of Pudong New Area in 2008.

Lv Chao built such an incubator to provide free venues, equipment, and even small subsidies to those who had the dream of creating social organizations and offer help in registration. Training courses were also offered such as how to set up an NGO board, how to raise money, how to manage volunteers, and how to make financial and human resources management. Every start-up NGO was located in the incubator for about a year.

Gradually, social work began to be accepted, and new social organizations emerged. There was a breakthrough in 2009. On December 15 of that year, in a cold winter, it rained in Shanghai, and in the old workshop of a handkerchief factory in Pudong, people were jubilant about the establishment of China's first public service park, celebrating like in a festival. Officials from China's Ministry of Civil Affairs also came for congratulation. Pudong hoped that the remodeled old factory building would become a base for the development of social organizations in Pudong, so that more social organizations would be incubated.

At the same time, hundreds of meters away, the Tangqiao Community Public Welfare Service Park emerged, and then the Pudong Foundation Service Park was opened.

Eshan Road connected the two parks. Pudong officials envisaged that the shops on the roadsides could also be vacated for social institutions, so that the public street could take shape for social organizations to flock together. In this way, on a common street in Pudong, all kinds of shops gradually quit, and various social organizations opened their "shops".

Social organizations constantly moved into and out of the public welfare park. On the yellow telephone book of Pudong, new social organizations were constantly added, such as the Pre-school Children Education

Center that provided education and psychological counseling for children, the Life Care and Development Center for carrying out hand-in-hand hospice care, and so on. And all these organizations were needed in the society, but were impossible to be managed by government departments due to lack of resources.

An official in the Pudong Civil Affairs Bureau cited a saying from the "Yellow-page Book" from Singapore. They hoped that as long as they looked up the telephones in the yellow-page book, they could get to know what the social organizations were doing, and the government would not have to do whatever the society could do.

It also turned out that when some social functions were separated and entrusted to the social organizations, they could do better with their professional advantages.

"If the public service of the government is a 'mountain', then the service of the social organizations is the 'sands' of the 'mountain', which may fill the gaps and make all parties attached," an official in Pudong said.

The factory was transformed into a public welfare park to provide services for public welfare organizations

The public welfare projects in Pudong invited public bidding from the society every year (Photo by Xu Wanglin)

By the end of 2013, various social organizations in Pudong had grown to more than 1,600, with more than 5,000 community groups on record, annually receiving over 500 million yuan of policy subsidies, policy incentives, and government purchase services. In 2014, Pudong New Area was also named the “National Innovation Demonstration Zone of Social Organization.”

But the officials of Pudong were not proud of the number. “If 5,000 social organizations were developed, that would be better. Now that’s nothing, far from enough.”

Chapter 9

Economic Transformation: Big Airplane and Disney

9.1 The End of the "Crane Economy" Because of the Financial Crisis

On August 28, 2008, a grand opening ceremony was held for the Shanghai World Financial Center Building, the tallest skyscraper in Pudong. Minoru Mori, the Japanese real estate magnate, Chairman of Japan Mori Mansion Co., was so excited as the protagonist of the opening ceremony that his soft and clear eyes were filled with tears.

Minoru Mori gave many reporters attending the ceremony copies of the book *Pudong Miracle* co-written by Zhao Qizheng and Shao Yudong. He said sincerely, "I am honored to be a player in one of the acts of Pudong miracle."

In the hot summer in Shanghai, it was hot and humid, and the whole city was like a big steamer. On the broad Century Avenue in Pudong, the long traffic was moving rapidly, with their shining bodies reflecting the sunlight into dazzling white light. The heat wave stirred up by traffic flow was almost suffocating, and there were few pedestrians on both sides of the avenue. It is said that this famous road was designed by a famous French architect, well-known for its spaciousness and tree shade.

Not far from the starting point of Century Avenue, the Shanghai World Financial Center Tower stood 492 meters high next to the famous Shanghai landmark Jinmao Tower, which took the title of "the tallest building in China" from Jinmao Tower.

But even in the scorching heat, as an entrepreneur with a global vision, he would have felt the chill of the financial crisis from the other side of the ocean.

In 2008, the sub-prime mortgage crisis that started from southern California of the United States turned into a global financial crisis, which spread around the world. After the Asian financial crisis in 1997, Pudong, which had always been proud of attracting a large amount of foreign capital, was facing a severe problem again. Overseas investors hesitated, suspected, and even planned divestment. Minoru Mori was the first to be questioned as an investor in the construction of the super-high-rise skyscraper in Pudong.

Half a month later, the news came from Wall Street that America's famous Lehman Brothers collapsed first and filed for bankruptcy protection.

When the Wall Street sneezed, the global economy caught a cold. The continuous bad news lingered in the high-class office buildings of Lujiazui in midsummer. Although the white-collars enjoyed the coolness brought by the air-conditioners, the cool feeling in the body did not erase the psychological panic of these white-collars, since the news began to circulate that the company would be out of business or downsizing. There is reason to question who would use such a super-skyscraper that this Japanese built in China.

There used to be a skyscraper index, put forward in 1999 by Andrew Lawrence, a securities analyst at Deutsche Bank. He found out that loose government policies and optimism about the economy often stimulated investment in big projects. However, when the bubble was about to endanger the economy, the government would adopt tight policies to deal with the crisis, resulting in a recession. This usually happened around the completion of skyscrapers.

The "skyscraper index" is also known as the "curse of Lawrence". Would the Global Financial Center fulfill this spell? Some reporters present at the ceremony expressed their doubts.

The global financial crisis hit Pudong like a tsunami. In 2008, the growth rate of the added value of finance in Pudong New Area dropped from 39% to 15%. Container throughput experienced a negative growth for the first time in history, and more than 1,000 enterprises were canceled in the whole year. In the Jinqiao Development Zone, where the manufacturing industry was concentrated, more than 80 enterprises moved out in one year. The news of relocation, shut down, and layoff continued to spread, which even resulted in some labor disputes. In the Waigaoqiao Free Trade Zone, there were more than 500 labor disputes in that year, nearly two cases handled every day on average.

The global financial crisis struck a heavy blow to the fragile model of relying on cheap exports to fuel economic growth.

Many economists believed that this resulted from the export-oriented economic model. In this model, capital, technology, and even raw materials come from abroad, and the sales market is also in foreign countries, but only labor and production are domestic. In order to maximize profits, the multinational companies kept a firm hold on research and development (R&D), investment, sales, and service with high value-added at both ends, but transferred the intermediate link of manufacturing to the developing countries. This is the so-called "two-ends-out" economy.

Wu Jinglian, a Chinese economist, said many times that China was at the very bottom of the industry's smiling curve.

Implementation of this economic model, which stimulated the local economy very fast, can help to achieve ultra-conventional development, so since the 1980s, local governments, especially those in coastal areas, preferred this economic model. The share of China's foreign capital stock in gross domestic product (GDP) had been much higher than that of other Asian countries, even 30 times higher than that of Japan. At the same time, the proportion of foreign direct investment of the total investment in social fixed assets in China was one of the highest in the world's major economies.

Despite high economic growth, economic strength was difficult to develop, because the core technology or sales channels were in the hands of other countries. And when this kind of economy developed too fast and productivity was too high, the troubles may come like foreign anti-dumping.

In 2008, this model fully exposed its disadvantages due to its high dependence on foreign countries. The advent of the financial crisis, the shrinkage of overseas markets, slow sales of products, and the shutdown of many enterprises resulted in the unemployment of a large number of workers.

In Pudong, it was not only because of the high degree of economic dependence on foreign countries that led to super-conventional development, but also because of the large-scale investment in fixed assets that resulted in the high-speed development of the economy.

Pudong's economic growth was once visualized as a "crane economy" — economic growth was stimulated through the investment in fixed assets such as the construction of bridges, roads, and houses. Some economists also pointed out that this kind of economy supported by the investment of extended capital cannot completely stimulate the internal and effective investment demand, and once the construction investment slowed down, the development would suffer from setback.

Zhang Jun, professor in the School of Economics of Fudan University, questioned the "crane economy" dominated by the powerful government: "Due to land leasing, relocation of downtown, and the Expo effect, it is out of the question for the development to last for another 10 years and 20 years. The question is: what will happen in 10 or 20 years?"

Since the development and opening-up of Pudong, the high-speed economic growth was mainly driven by large-scale investment. The average growth rate of GDP in Pudong New Area during the "Eighth Five-Year Plan" period (1991–1995) was 23%, and then it began to decline gradually. The average growth rate of the "Ninth Five-Year Plan" period (1996–2000) was 17.6%, and the "10th Five-Year Plan" period (2001–2005) dropped to about 15.7%, and in the "11th Five-Year Plan" period (2006–2010) it continued to decline, generally kept at about 14%.

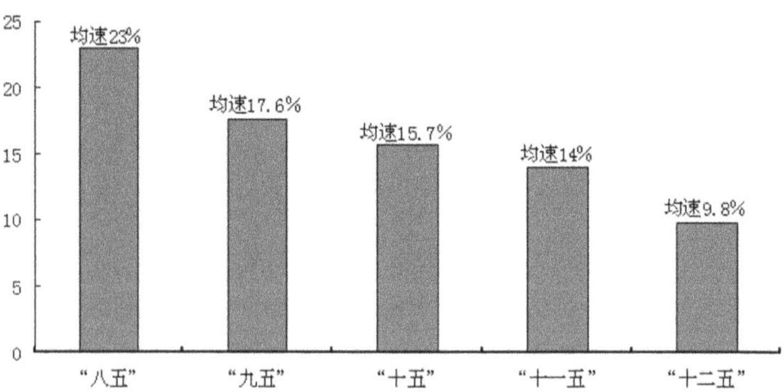

After the development of Pudong, GDP grew from high speed to medium-high speed

As to the contribution rate of scientific and technological progress, in 2007, in Pudong it was 62%, lower than the 70% in the innovative countries and regions. As a result, the law of diminishing marginal benefits in the regional economy played a role. Large amounts of construction investment could not keep the economy growing at a high rate.

As early as in 1993, the World Bank published a research report entitled "The East Asia Miracle", attributing the "East Asia miracle" to massive investments into capital and human resources and market-oriented reforms and policy interventions by governments in those countries. But at the end of 1994, Paul Krugman, a young American economist, published "The Myth of the East Asia Miracle" in *Foreign Affairs,* questioning the East Asia miracle. He argued that it was hard for this economic growth model, which relied too much on large amounts of capital, to achieve sustainable economic growth. The "sweat-based" economic growth in the early period was not sustainable in the long run.

Most economists were dismissive of Krugman's predictions. Many Chinese economists even considered Krugman an alarmist. Three years later, the "East Asian miracle", which was hit hard by the Southeast Asian financial crisis, seemed to confirm Krugman's judgment, and he was honored for predicting the crisis. As a result, he won the Nobel Prize in Economics in 2008.

Therefore, the "crane economy" should not be taken as the road of economic development in Pudong. The driving force of Pudong's development must be changed from factor-driven to innovation-driven. The Pudong government began to think about how to transform the economic structure from a catch-up economy to a leading economy. This kind of leading economy can be realized by developing strategic newly-emerging industries to promote the transformation of the economic structure.

This is the higher-level leading economy.

9.2 The Difficulty of Economic Growth due to Land Insufficiency

Land is the topic that cannot be skipped in the development of Pudong. At the beginning of the development of Pudong, the huge land differential between Pudong and Puxi brought a lot of funds to Pudong. But land is a limited and non-renewable resource. What if we're done with the land?

In fact, since the beginning of the 21st century, the decrease of land and the rise of land price had become the bottleneck of Pudong's development. In particular, a nationwide surge in land prices since 2003 greatly increased Pudong's business costs. The pace of foreign investment faltered, but foreign investment was the greatest engine of GDP in Pudong.

There was an example in Pudong. In the introduction of major foreign-funded projects, the relevant departments offered all preferential policies, and when the contract was about to be signed, the other party stopped it by giving a very simple reason: "in Pudong, the business cost is too high" and they had found an investment place with lower cost in business.

In the early stage of Pudong development, the Central Government and the Shanghai Municipal Government gave Pudong preferential policies, but little appropriation. Pudong took advantage of the policies and made the best use of land differential to attract as much capital by "finance idling and land leasing". In the early 1990s, when the financial resources were scarce and the infrastructure was seriously overdrawn, a "meal without rice" was made.

Land leasing built a bridge for the "east-west link" in Shanghai, and also found a shortcut for the development of Shanghai and the urban layout adjustment. Subsequently, the new system and the new mechanism, such as the build-operate-transfer (BOT) mode operation, intervention of capital market, and transformation of the enterprise's shareholding system, promoted Shanghai's economic development.

But many economists were critical of this land-for-investment model that eventually turned the development zone into workshops for multinational companies. The government authorized development companies to enclose land, to relocate and move residents, and to mortgage land to banks. Then with fund rolling on, added with the preferential policies, GDP went up. The question is: what do you do when you're done with land?

In terms of land resource, Hong Kong, like Pudong, is extremely limited. Hong Kong's land area is a little smaller than Pudong, but the most part is mountains, hills, beaches, and so on, so the land that can be used for production and living is even more scarce. But such a "tiny place" with scarce natural resources, with less than one-tenth of the world's area and one-thousandth of the world's population, created the world's second-largest per capita foreign trade value and the world's first total value of entrepot trade.

The continuous development of Hong Kong's economy can be mainly attributed to three strategic transformations. As Tang Yingnian, the former Financial Secretary of Hong Kong, said, "The economic transformation ability is the major factor for Hong Kong and Hong Kong enterprises to maintain the strong competitiveness."

Since the 21st century, it was difficult for Pudong to maintain the original scale and speed of the expansion of investment in fixed assets, because Pudong's per capita capital stock, including the saturation degree of the developed land and infrastructure, had been at a relatively high level. At the same time, in light of the experience of economic development in developed countries, the economic growth rate is inversely proportional to the degree of economic development. This is the "law of convergence" in economy.

The Zhangjiang High-tech Park is one of the four state-level development zones in Pudong. An official of the Zhang Jiang Group also admitted that the implementation of "land-selling economy" in the development zone was unsustainable. He believed, "The space for Shanghai transformation also cannot depend mainly on the supply of new land resource, but should instead solve the problem by improving the degree of urbanization like, in the original industry-concentrated areas, raising plot ratio, changing land use, changing dispersive afforestation to centralized afforestation, increasing the connection between buildings, improving inter-regional transportation, and promoting the low-carbon environment and human culture." He said that the park had no longer relied on selling land.

The land made Pudong's wealth grow rapidly, and growth became more difficult just because of the land.

Therefore, the transformation is a grand thought. In the various documents of Pudong government and the leaders' speeches after 2005, the wording of Pudong transformation can be seen or heard everywhere.

9.3 The Difficulty in Transformation and Upgrading

It can be said that the industrial starting point of Pudong is higher than that of the Shenzhen Special Economic Zone. That is to say, when Pudong began to develop, Shanghai people were greatly more far-sighted than Shenzhen people 10 years ago. They were not only satisfied with the workshop-type industry of "processing the materials supplied by foreign businessmen, assembling the materials supplied by foreign businessmen, processing the samples supplied by foreign businessmen, and compensatory trade", but wanted to undertake the development of higher-grade industry, and thereby drive the adjustment of industrial structure of Shanghai as a whole. This industrial upgrading is the opportunity for the future industrial development of Pudong New Area.

In 1980, Shenzhen and other special economic zones just started. Because Shenzhen, without an industrial foundation, was hungry for foreign investment, a number of "sweatshops" emerged and low-level industry and commerce was formed. After 1990, with the help of Shanghai's complete industrial system and high-quality human resource, Pudong naturally hoped to become a financial, trade, and shipping center and develop high-tech industries.

Yao Xitang, former President of the Pudong Institute for Reform and Development, described the historical process of industrial transfer 20 years before China's reform and opening-up, "In the 1980s, China's strategy of opening to the outside world was, first of all, to establish special economic zones in Guangdong, Fujian, and other southeast coastal areas so as to take advantage of preferential policies to attract foreign investment. In the 1990s, China needed to develop its opening-up to a new stage and level on this basis, that is, while attracting foreign investment in labor-intensive enterprises, China should expand into technology-intensive and capital-intensive industries such as automobiles, electronics, and so on and make full use of the opportunity of economic globalization to promote and accelerate the strategic upgrading of industrial structure. The opening-up of Pudong, Shanghai, and the Yangtze River Delta just met the need of this development."

Pudong development and opening-up started at the time of the adjustment of global industrial structure. In the world, in terms of industrial upgrading and industrial restructuring, the Asia-Pacific region was the most active. This kind of global industry transfer made Pudong seize the opportunity to achieve the high-speed economic growth.

According to gradient theory prevailing at that time, Pudong undertook the industrial transfer from developed countries.

Integrated circuit was an industry worthy of pride in Pudong. Taking the opportunity for the global chip industry to shift to China, Pudong supported and fostered the chip industry as a strategic pillar industry. As a result, Pudong's micro-electronics industrial belt with chip manufacturing as its main body was well developed, which gathered nearly 100 enterprises of chip R&D, design and manufacture, packaging and testing, and other supporting enterprises of semiconductor materials, equipment, devices, and so on. Pudong became the first key area of China's chip industry.

But Beijing's high-level administration also demanded Pudong to develop the modern service industry. In April 2008, Li Yiping, Director of Pudong New Area said, "At present Pudong is in the important stage of industrial structure transformation. It is an important task for us to develop the service economy, innovation economy, and circular economy, and strive to develop a new industrial structure dominated by the modern service industry and high-tech industry."

Developing the modern service industry was a bigger ordeal for local government.

The modern service industry creates higher demand for the institutional environment. Professor Chen Zhiwu of Yale University in the United States pointed out that in manufacturing and service industries, the requirements for the institutional environment were very different. According to him, the manufacturing industry deals with tangible objects and is relatively weak in dependence on institution and mechanism, while the service industry deals with people and is highly dependent on the system environment. The service industry, which trades the invisible and intangible "services" or "promises", increases the likelihood of moral hazard and adverse selection.

For example, the supply chain management of the modern logistics industry requires that the links are well connected, such as zero storage, the "on-time supply system" of parts supply, etc. In the market environment where contracts cannot be strictly enforced, this system cannot work properly. Therefore, in a society with an imperfect system, the service industry can only develop slowly and suffer from stagnation.

In fact, one of the original intentions of Pudong development lies in this — providing a good environment for the service industry through institutional innovation.

In the history of China's reform and opening-up, the opening-up in the 1980s was mainly in the secondary industry. By the early 1990s, most of the service sectors were closed to the outside world. One of the missions of Pudong development and opening-up was to make a breakthrough in the tertiary industry and push China's reform and opening-up into a new stage with the goal of establishing a socialist market economic system. Therefore, at the beginning of Pudong development, the concept of financial priority was put forward.

Unfortunately, Pudong still considerably lagged behind in terms of the speed and depth in this aspect. This is why, since 2005, Pudong leaders constantly repeated "transformation" as a key word.

In April 2005, Shanghai reoriented Pudong according to the "Shanghai Outline for the Implementation of Accelerating the Development of the Modern Service Industry". Pudong New Area planned to increase, through a three-year effort, the proportion of modern service industry to about 55%.

In 2007, Pudong's economic structure underwent a significant change. The added value of the primary, secondary, and tertiary industries was 606 million yuan, 300.49 billion yuan, and 143.521 billion yuan, respectively. The tertiary industry exceeded the secondary industry for the first time. However, with the advent of the world financial crisis in 2008, the pace of transformation and upgrading of this industry slowed down. It was a challenge for the local government to both stimulate GDP and to achieve transformation and upgrading.

Singapore's Senior Minister, Lee Kuan Yew, had deeper insight about the significance of the transition and upgrading.

In May 2006, he visited Shanghai and after hearing about the plan of transformation and reform in Pudong New Area, he asked Zhang Xuebing, then Director of the New Area, whether he had made the same introduction of the plan to the visiting Japanese guests. His answer was "Yes." Lee Kuan Yew said, "Then they must feel worried when they hear about it," because of the limited development space of Tokyo as a financial center and the saturation of international airport development. "If your plan can be carried out on time, it will change the pattern of East Asia as a whole."

After all, he is a famous statesman in the world with an international vision.

9.4 The Coming of Big Plane

During the financial crisis, Pudong began to reflect deeply. Shen Rong, General Manager of the Jinqiao Development Company, said, "With painful reflection, we decided to advance the development zone into the future by leading the industry to the higher end."

On the afternoon of February 26, 2009, the project by the China Commercial Aircraft Design and Development Center (CCADDC) was officially settled in the Zhangjiang High-tech Park. Prior to this, the company's headquarters had settled in the Lujiazui Financial and Trade Zone, Pudong.

CCADDC mainly worked on the research and development of large airliners and two series of regional aircrafts and the research on the relevant design technology of civil aircrafts. This center was put into operation in 2012 and hired 3,000 employees working in the center.

The General Assembly and Manufacturing Center based in the Shanghai Commercial Aircraft Design and Development Center, Zhuqiao, Pudong (Photo by Zhu Quanchun)

This made Pudong people exultant. In China there was a huge demand market for aircrafts. According to the 2011–2030 Annual Forecast Report on the China Market for Civil Aircrafts issued by the China Aviation Industry Group, Chinese civil aircrafts would reach 5,118 by 2030, which would require 4,583 more civil airliners. But the Chinese could not yet make civil aircrafts.

Chinese officials also knew clearly that aircraft manufacturing was known as "the crown of manufacturing". A large aircraft consists of 3 million to 6 million components and involves thousands of suppliers, related to almost all industrial sectors such as materials, electronics, machinery, vehicles, energy, and construction, which would undoubtedly make the manufacturing industry chain greatly expanded and extended.

In fact, several hundred enterprises and institutions had been engaged in the development of made-in-China large aircraft. Each segment needed to be tested, and the tests were made hundreds of times, like a "collective test" for the country's manufacturing industry.

One Chinese scholar said, "Without this big plane project, it would have been so hard for us to know how much we're lagging behind."

China is a big country, but not yet a powerful country in manufacturing industry. As a result, the Chinese government hoped to take the chance of developing large aircrafts to improve the country's industrial manufacturing level.

On November 18, 2009, the Pudong New Area Government signed a cooperation agreement with the China Commercial Aircraft Corporation (CCAC) on the project of the General Assembly and Manufacturing Center. Pudong would like Shanghai to become the most successful city in international aviation like Seattle, Toulouse, and Montreal.

The Chinese local governments were more interested in such projects, because the introduction of such large projects could often lead to the formation of an industrial base, industrial cluster, and pillar industry, so that a large number of high-tech supporting projects would follow.

That is to say, with a registered capital of 2 billion yuan and an area of 4000 mu (1 mu = 0.000667 square kilometers), the General Assembly and Manufacturing Center of the CCAC settled in Pudong, which meant that the industrial chain of aircraft manufacturing would be developed in Pudong.

According to Zhang Qingwei, Chairman of the CCAC, the total investment would reach 200 billion yuan. As much as 30 billion yuan would be invested in the three major centers and one headquarter in Shanghai alone in three to five years.

Pudong officials believed that another important feature of the transformation in Shanghai as a super-large city was the introduction of capital and major projects, instead of dependence on land sales, but rather through capital markets and inter-firm mergers and acquisitions, as well as headquarters plus holding companies, R&D center, sales center, and service-oriented investment.

Therefore, Pudong held a very high expectation for the development of the aviation industry. In accordance with the "12th Five-Year Plan and the Vision Plan of Civil Aviation Industry in Pudong New Area", in Pudong, a civil aviation industry cluster would be established with an output value of more than 150 billion yuan in 15 to 20 years, so that Pudong might become the largest civil aviation industry base in Asia and one of the three famous civil aviation industry bases in the world.

However, at the beginning, with the settlement of the CCAC in Pudong of Shanghai, Zhang Jiazhen, Senior Director Designer of the Shanghai Aircraft Design Institute of the CCAC, also felt somewhat surprised.

Zhang Jiacheng remembered that when he was 10, he went to Shanghai for a tour with his father. In a small park in Pudong, stood a stone statue of the Chinese peasant uprising during the late Qing Dynasty. His father also told him about the history of Pudong and the story of the well-known people. He was deeply impressed with the pastoral scene in Pudong. But by 2009, when Zhang arrived at the Pudong Airport, he was surprised to see that farmland and reed marshes in the past had already been replaced by modern urban area. The changes in merely 20 years made him believe that Pudong could create a miracle.

Of course, this kind of miracle also had much to do with individual dream and struggle for it.

For Chen Yingchun, Executive Vice-Chief Designer of the Research Institute of the CCAC, developing a big plane was a dream in his heart. He said, "It is the dream of the generations of Chinese to fly in the blue sky. As members of this generation and this group, we have been working for 20 or 30 years in hope of China's big plane to fly in the blue sky and realize the dream of several generations."

This dream also had something to do with his experience of being sent to Germany in the 1980s for joint design. He was paid 45 yuan a month at that time. He said, "At that time the Germans were paid a few thousand marks, a few dozen times more. They laughed at us, because the Chinese were so poor, but had a dream of big planes. When people donated money, they were definitely unwilling to donate to the Chinese. So I felt offended."

This kind of offence also made Chen Yingchun think every day about what were still their disadvantages then, what they should do then, and how they could catch up in a short time. Chen Yingchun said, "That's what I think about every day. It's not a big talk."

Time soon proved that the dream could come true.

On the morning of November 2, 2015, in the workshop of the newly-built General Assembly and Manufacturing Center of the CCAC based in Pudong, as the two curtains were slowly opened, a new commercial aircraft with "Comac Blue" and "Comac Green" coating was fully presented. The C919 passenger aircraft independently developed by China was officially off the line after the seven-year design and development.

The C919 big aircraft was officially off the assembly line (Photo by Zhang Anchao)

The C919 is a commercial airline aircraft that China has independent intellectual property rights and is the second type of China-made large passenger aircraft designed and developed independently by China after the invention of the Yun-10. The standard air-range designed is 4,075 kilometers, but the range designed was increased to 5,555 kilometers.

The good news ensued one after another.

On November 29 of the same year, the Chinese manufacturing industry went into another beautiful stage, that is, the ARJ21 new regional aircraft made by Comac set sail.

It was 10 in the morning. The ARJ21 regional plane, printed with the red and white "Sunbird" logo, took off from Shanghai. The developers of China Comac affectionately called the plane "Lovely Baby Girl", watching her growing up from a toddler to flying over the mountains and rivers. Their affection for it was like their baby daughter. Around 1 in the afternoon, "Lovely Baby Girl" flew to Chengdu.

A reporter of Xinhua News Agency said that this was another major breakthrough in China's aviation industry after the completion of the general assembly of the C919 airliner on November 2, which marked that China had completed the whole process of design, trial-production, testing, test of flight, evidence collection, production, and delivery related to jet regional airliner, and China had possessed the development capability and airworthiness certification capability in terms of the regional jet airliner. On domestic airlines, for the first time, China had its own regional jet planes.

Thereafter, the State Post Office issued commemorative stamps of the ARJ21 new regional aircraft.

9.5 The Following-up of Chip Manufacture Giants

Since the 21st century, the theory of industrial chain and industrial cluster was very popular in some local governments in China. The theory refers to the aggregation of related industries in a certain region such as the higher and lower ends of an industry. Industrial clusters determine the competitiveness of an industry in a region.

Pudong is no exception. In August 1999, Shanghai launched the strategy "Focus on Zhangjiang" — mobilizing all the resources of Shanghai to advance the Zhangjiang High-tech Park in Pudong to make it the model of technological innovation and the leader of high-tech industry in Shanghai and even China. In the short period of 20 months after the implementation of the strategy, Zhangjiang introduced 189 projects, with foreign investment worth US$3.9 billion and domestic investment worth 3 billion yuan. All economic indicators exceeded the sum of the previous seven years.

Zhangjiang was given the title of Hi-tech Park in 1992. It was originally a farmland with sparse villages, and seven years after being operated as a high-tech zone and before the "Focus on Zhangjiang" strategy, its fiscal revenue was "only enough for food".

These changes would not have taken place without the power of the Shanghai Municipal Government, the concentration of driving elements, and the formation of industrial clusters.

American economist Michael Porter put forward the theory of industrial agglomeration in his great book *Competitive Advantage of Nations*, arguing that the economic world today is characterized by industrial agglomeration. Industrial agglomeration refers to the overall combination of related industries and institutions, from suppliers to universities to government agencies, and it has unprecedented competitive advantages in specific fields. Silicon Valley and Hollywood are well-known examples.

Generally speaking, there are two models for the formation of industrial clusters. Firstly, a large enterprise settles in the local place, which thus drives the upstream and downstream small and medium-sized enterprises to form an industrial chain around it. Secondly, the cluster germinated by the local industry continuously extends the industrial chain to the upstream and downstream by technology upgrading, and among the numerous small and medium-sized enterprises, the big leading enterprise gradually comes into being.

But most local governments in China preferred to attract one or more big companies and form an industrial cluster to make the industry chain shaped there. In such a process of attracting investment, in order to attract one or more large enterprises that can play a decisive role, local governments would spare no expense. It can even be said that in the introduction of individual projects, local governments made no profits, but ran the business at great loss such as extremely low land prices and tax preference.

For example, Pudong became the winner of the integrated circuit industry, which can be attributed to the role the Pudong government played at the key time. The Semiconductor Manufacturing International Corporation was the first giant in the integrated circuit industry introduced to the Zhangjiang High-tech Park, with an investment of up to US$1.5 billion in the first phase. In order to introduce this project, all the people from Shanghai leaders to the staff in charge of investment were generally mobilized and officials of the Shanghai Municipal Government and the Pudong New Area Government went to the construction site to hold coordinative meetings. According to a Senior Executive of the Semiconductor Manufacturing International Corporation, "When we visited Shanghai for the selection of the construction site, the Mayor of Shanghai and the Vice Mayor in charge of science and technology were all there, and then immediately decided to go to Zhangjiang for site selection and told us we can get whichever piece of land we wanted."

On August 24, 2000, with an investment of nearly US$1.5 billion, Zhongxin International IC Manufacturing Co., Ltd. settled in Zhangjiang. Three months later, Hongli Semiconductor Manufacturing Co., with an initial investment of US$1.64 billion, also moved to Zhangjiang. Subsequently, Hua Hong NEC with investment worth US$1.2 billion and Shanghai Belling with investment worth US$300 million settled down in Zhangjiang one after another.

Pudong took advantage of a law about the semiconductor industry, that is, wherever the chip factory is located, the upstream and downstream enterprises related to chip design, manufacturing, production, and so on must follow up quickly. Therefore, while vigorously introducing high-end chip companies, Zhangjiang also created an industrial chain composed of hundreds of upstream and downstream enterprises such as wafer manufacturing, chip design, package testing, equipment installation, and supporting services which could match with Zhongxin and Hongli.

Pudong became the main place of integrated circuit industry cluster in Shanghai. In 2015, the sales market of Pudong's integrated circuit industry accounted for 63.8% of that of the whole Shanghai. Of the sales of the integrated circuit industry worth 360.98 billion yuan in mainland China, Pudong accounted for 16.8%.

Some scholars believed that as to the industrial innovation of Pudong, the greatest achievement did not lie in car manufacturing, but in wafer and chip manufacturing, the greatest contribution to the country. According to Moore's law, the chip products all over the world upgraded very fast, but China did not kept pace. Zhangjiang of Pudong made considerable contribution in this aspect. By means of a joint venture with NEC, Huahong was established, which successfully executed the strategy of exchanging market for technology, so that China began to be able to make chips, which was very meaningful. In the era of the information technology revolution, Zhangjiang of Pudong, which strived to make it, played a great role in China's industrial innovation.

By the 25th anniversary of Pudong development, the transformation and upgrading was even more urgent. Facing the ocean, Pudong, with the harbor in its most eastern end, also gathered advanced manufacturing industry. At the press conference of the Shanghai Municipal Government on October 15, 2015, the Shanghai Municipal Government announced that it would mobilize all the resources of the whole city to promote intelligence manufacturing in the port area of the Pudong New Area, in hope that in 2025 the harbor area would become an "International Center of Intelligence Manufacturing" to export key technologies and services in this sector to the world and gather global resources to incubate innovation in intelligent manufacturing.

The harbor covered an area of 315 square kilometers, with abundant land resources as its biggest advantage in developing intelligent manufacturing. In the harbor area, Shanghai would give impetus to the demonstration park of professional intelligent manufacturing clusters such as integrated circuits, civil aviation, optoelectronics, and so on, and foster the development of intelligent manufacturing services. Therefore, Shanghai planned to set up a leading team of intelligent manufacturing centers at the city level, and the Finance Bureau allocated 5 billion yuan to set up an industry guiding fund. The enterprises that would invest in intelligence manufacturing in the harbor area could gain support of up to 100 million yuan.

In 2015, the Chinese government launched "Made in China 2025", proposing to elevate Chinese manufacturing to the top level of the world through a three-step process in 30 years. Under this background,

Shanghai planned to rely on the harbor to build the intelligent manufacturing center, which conformed to the global trend and echoed the national strategy.

Pudong shouldered the responsibility of executing the national strategy once again. The manufacturing industry had always been the dominant industry in Shanghai and should provide important support for the construction of a scientific and technological center with global influence. Pudong, too, was greatly entrusted.

9.6 Why it Took More than 10 Years for Disney to Settle in Shanghai

The introduction of the American Disneyland project to Pudong was another important means to seek transformation.

On the morning of November 5, 2010, Xinhua News Agency issued a newsflash: the Walt Disney Company and Shanghai Shendi Group signed a cooperative agreement of the Shanghai Disneyland Project. This was the largest modern service project introduced by China.

In 2009, on March 7, Shanghai Mayor Han Zheng told reporters frankly at the Shanghai Hall of the Beijing Great Hall that they came up with the idea of building Disney in Shanghai decades ago, and since then, the communication, exchange, and negotiations between the two teams went on constantly. Then the reporter asked about the progress. "We are still in love, and when to marry, there is no timetable." The reporter was amused by Han Zheng's answer.

In other words, the "love" between the two sides began in the 1990s.

After China's reform and opening-up, Disney, as a multinational entertainment group, was first allowed to enter the Chinese market. In 1986, China Central Television signed a license agreement with Disney, and *Mickey Mouse and Donald Duck* cartoon began to broadcast in China, which was welcomed by the Chinese audience, especially children. The hot showing of the cartoon also initiated Shanghai leaders into the idea of building Disneyland in Shanghai.

According to the recollection of Lu Weisi, former head of the Investment Promotion Agency of the Hong Kong Special Administrative Region, Zhu Rongji, then the Communist Party Secretary and Mayor of

Shanghai, was the first to propose to build Shanghai Disneyland. After visiting Disney World in the United States, Zhu Rongji believed that Shanghai was very suitable for the construction of Disneyland, and Disney happened to be looking for a second site in Asia. So the two sides began to show great interest in cooperation.

It was on March 1, 1994 that Zhao Qizheng, Vice Mayor of Shanghai and Director of the Administrative Committee of Pudong New Area, visited Disney's headquarter in Los Angeles. For the meeting of the day, President Frank Wells postponed his original trip abroad.

The meeting was held in a spacious VIP room. Wells put on a dark suit and red tie with black spots solemnly and decorated the long table carefully with several bundles of flowers with red five-pointed stars.

After Wells's welcome speech, Zhao Qizheng said, "Disney is a big company. In terms of investment, a large company does not value the short-term interests, but the overall background — if you can prepare the projector, I will introduce the development of Shanghai and Pudong to you."

It took Zhao Qizheng 15 minutes to present to Wells the panorama of reform and opening-up in Shanghai and Pudong. After that, Zhao raised four questions: "Why is it necessary to build Disneyland in Shanghai? Why is it possible to build Disneyland in Shanghai? How can Disney culture be integrated with Chinese culture? How will the two sides continue to discuss this project?"

Zhao also said jokingly, "For the latter two questions, President Wells need not answer for the time being. They can be taken as a 'home assignment'."

Wells answered, "As for the first question, we think Disneyland has been very successful in the United States. If it will get into China, the best site is Shanghai."

Wells also said that Vice Premier Zhu had already suggested that Shanghai could be chosen if it was to operate in China. As for the third question, Wells decided to send a team to Pudong, Shanghai to make a survey immediately. At that time, Wells, who had spent more than the scheduled half-hour meeting time, took the initiative to introduce the Disney Theme Park in Florida, and said that he would send the video to Zhao Qizheng.

Finally, Wells said in an appreciative tone, "You are the only delegation I've ever seen to enter Disney but not have a tour in Disney, and the most persuasive delegation I've ever received."

Zhao recalled, at the time, the first motivation for Disney was to boost Pudong's popularity and influence: "At that time, Pudong was not well known at all in the world, not even popular at home. If Disney is introduced, it will have a good demonstrative effect on the large international enterprises, especially the American enterprises. People may say, even Disney has gone to Pudong!"

Wells' strong interest in Shanghai excited Zhao and others. An advance team had been sent to Pudong by Wells before their return to China. The "first love" heated up in this way.

Unfortunately, on April 3, Wells passed away in a plane crash, and the matter cooled down. Zhao Qizheng recalled, because of the accident, Wells's wish to build Disneyland in Pudong did not come true in time, but his enthusiasm and yearning for Pudong was unforgettable.

The death of Wells was a big loss for the Disney Company. Wells used to be a famous lawyer in Hollywood and he was cool-headed and good at dealing with complicated relationships. It was pointed out that if Wells were still alive, Disney would probably not have made so many mistakes.

Since then, in contact with Shanghai, Disney made six visits to Zhuhai, Guangdong, and showed great interest in Hengqin Island at the intersection of Macau and Zhuhai at the Zhujiang River estuary.

It was not until October 1998 that Disney announced the plan to build Asia's second Disneyland in Hong Kong or Zhuhai. In the following year, Disney announced that its first theme park in China would be officially opened in Hong Kong in 2005.

At this time, in the eyes of the outsiders, the "love" between Disney and Shanghai was fruitless.

In March 1999, when Xu Kuangdi, Mayor of Shanghai, attended the plenary session of Shanghai delegation of the National People's Congress (NPC) in Beijing, to the Chinese and foreign journalists he proactively mentioned the issue of the competition between Shanghai and Hong Kong in building Disneyland, and pointed out the two major advantages of Shanghai. He told reporters that Shanghai had a great advantage in geography, located in the Yangtze River Delta with a population of 100 million in the surrounding area. So he believed that as long as Disneyland was opened in Shanghai, it would be full of tourists every day, just like the current Town God's Temple in Shanghai.

When talking about Shanghai's second advantage, Xu Kuangdi pointed out that Shanghai had more land for option, while Hong Kong, on the whole, had less land, more mountains and islands, and it was somewhat difficult in transportation and other aspects.

Xu Kuangdi revealed that in fact, Shanghai had been making the feasibility study for more than three years. Four years prior, Disney sent someone to Shanghai specially for the cooperation, and the company had compared Shanghai with Guilin and Zhuhai as well.

Xu Kuangdi also disclosed that Disney had invited Zhou Yupeng, Vice Mayor in charge of Pudong New Area, to visit the headquarters in the United States a week before to discuss the feasibility of building Disneyland in Shanghai.

But nearly 10 years passed since the initial talk was conducted.

During this period, the news that Disney would settle in Shanghai was widespread, and as a result, the stock concerned with Disney in the stock market also went up and down, bearish and bullish.

The "love" between the two sides was time-consuming. As outsiders saw it, it resulted not only from the cumbersome details, but also from Disney's long-term plan to expand in China. According to a man in charge of Disney in China, Disney was very optimistic about the development of China, so Disney adopted the principle of "prolonging the negotiation cycle to get the biggest discount".

For example, Disney's profit model did not only lie in the theme park, but also the industry chain of the entire theme park, with intellectual property as the core. So Disney's entry meant not only a park, but also the industry chain of the whole cultural communication.

For another example, when the park opened, Disney would need a television channel that tells stories to Chinese children every day, because the main channel for Disney's earnings would come from television channels and related derivatives. While there were no restrictions on joint venture filmmaking and the opening of Chinese websites, setting up television channels would fall within the category of strictly restricted "broadcasting".

In addition, according to the "Guidance Catalogue of Industries with Foreign Investment" formulated by the State Economic and Trade Commission, the construction and operation of large theme parks were included in the scope of industries restricted in foreign investment. That was a problem Disney had never met in Japan or France before.

Different cultural backgrounds between China and the United States made this "love" suffer from twists and turns.

The prolonged "love" made Disney Company also miss the best opportunity for entry. Many years ago, Chinese children were most familiar with Mickey Mouse and Donald Duck, but now they fall in love with Pleasant Goat and Big Big Wolf, Japanese Doraemon, and more fashionable cartoon characters.

An opportunity emerged in 2008, that is, the global financial crisis. At that time, the Disney Company showed a positive attitude. Since the fourth quarter of 2008, sales of the park and resort business rose 6.5% year-on-year, but profits fell 4.2%. As profits continued to fall and domestic consumption in the United States was expected to remain under pressure for some time, Disney attached more significance to developing overseas markets, particularly in fast-growing China. There were frequent high-level mutual visits, and at that time, the negotiations entered the substantive stage. Therefore, some insider said, "Disney took advantage of the financial crisis. Shanghai at that time urgently needed to stimulate the confidence of the economy and the Central Government hoped to stimulate domestic demand, so the project examination and approval were unprecedentedly loose."

Like the engagement before marriage, on January 8, 2009, Disney and Shanghai officially signed a framework agreement for establishing the theme park in Shanghai.

On January 9, Disney issued a statement acknowledging that it had worked with the Shanghai Government to prepare for the application and would submit it to the Central Government for approval. Once it was approved, Pudong would build the world's sixth Disneyland at an estimated cost of 24.48 billion yuan.

One newspaper commented that while the terms were less harsh and the negotiations were not as tough as they used to be, Disney grasped the good chance when China desperately needed to "boost domestic demand".

More interestingly, when the overall situation had settled, as to the "love" of the two sides, small episodes also appeared.

On February 3 of that year, in Dongyi Hotel of Pudong, the experts from the State Development and Reform Commission, the Culture Ministry, the Land Ministry, the Tourism Ministry, and other state ministries, and the Shanghai tourism sector and transport sector made the final examination and review of the feasibility report about the Shanghai Disneyland project that was to be submitted to the relevant departments of the State. At the final review meeting, there were still many different voices.

For example, the cultural issue was argued. At the meeting, some experts questioned whether the invasion of "foreign culture" would have an impact on Chinese traditional culture. Some people argued that the entry of foreign culture should be restricted, and the settlement of Disney of the United States in China would have a great impact on Chinese culture. In contrast, some other experts insisted that Chinese culture should be introduced to the world market and it was beneficial for "the sea to refuse no river", that is, to have cultural tolerance.

At the moment of confrontation between the two viewpoints, Disney Vice President Disney Leslie A. Goodman emphasized Disney's cultural characteristics: healthy, optimistic, and positive, and Disney aimed to give full display to the innocence, beauty, and wonder in human childhood and input integrity, courage, care, creation, and other qualities in order to show the meaning of "universal value". His statement finally dispelled the oppositions.

The location of Disney was also argued. Some experts suggested that Disney should be constructed in the west in order to boost the Chinese economy. But from the perspective of traffic, some people preferred it to be located in Hongqiao of Puxi, because it was obviously more convenient for the tourists from the Yangtze River Delta to arrive in Hongqiao than Pudong.

From the perspective of the economy, the market in the Yangtze River Delta was undoubtedly larger than other candidates, and the convenient traffic and perfect facilities in Chuansha of Pudong became an advantage, because it was only a 10-minute drive from Chuansha to the Pudong International Airport. So foreign visitors can visit Disney within 48 hours without applying for a visa. After three days of brainstorming, Pudong won with its comprehensive advantages in the economy, land, and transportation.

The road to happiness is always strewn with setbacks.

Thanks to the Shanghai World Expo, in 2010, the number of visitors to the Expo was over 70 million as expected, which made the whole world amazed and made Disney deeply "impressed" and more confident about going to Shanghai and becoming "part of the great city". At the same time, the success of the Expo also enhanced people's confidence in the success of the Disneyland project in Shanghai.

In the autumn of 2010, on the plot of land for the Shanghai Disneyland project, the golden rice was swaying with the wind, which indicated a harvest season was to come. The "long-distance running of love" of both sides reached the end.

On the morning of November 5, 2010, the Walt Disney Company and Shanghai Shendi Group formally signed the cooperation agreement of the Shanghai Disneyland Project. At the same time, the Shanghai International Tourist Resort Management Committee and Shanghai Shendi (Group) Co., Ltd. which were responsible for the project management and development of Shanghai Disney, were inaugurated. The total investment for the project was 34 billion yuan.

This indicated that the Shanghai Disneyland project officially began to operate.

In releasing the news, a newspaper in Shanghai used the headline: Shanghai and Disney got their marriage license.

Disney and Shanghai were finally "married", and Donald Duck began to build a new home in Shanghai. However, the transformation and upgrading was a dynamic process. In the new century, more and more people with insight believed that although Pudong was opened at a high starting point, from the high-end processing industry in the early 1990s to the later advanced manufacturing industry, to the modern service industry in the early 21st century, there was still room for its transformation.

For the ordinary people, it is really hard to understand why it took more than 10 years of negotiations for Disney to settle in Shanghai. Is it just for building a theme park? In fact, the Shanghai Disney project was far more than a theme park. For Disney, it was a march into China's film,

In 2010 the World Expo was a great success. This is the most popular Saudi Pavilion. It usually took several hours to stand in line to get in, and as long as eight hours at most. (Photo by Xu Wanglin)

entertainment, media, and various derivative industries, namely, the entire industrial chain with its intellectual property as the core.

For Shanghai, it also carried a mission of transforming the economy through Disney's drive to upgrade the industries, especially the service industry. The development of the service industry could accelerate the strategic adjustment of Shanghai's economic structure, and the Disneyland project could provide more opportunities for the development of the service industry in Shanghai, and could also gain more competitive advantage for Shanghai.

Development economists also applied the history of modern economic development to prove that dominant sectors of a country with strong growth and innovative industries often congregate in large cities with the agglomeration and diffusion function and innovation function in talent, capital, commodity, technology, and information, which can help it become the "growth pole" of the surrounding areas. The development of such an economic center with strong attraction, radiation, and competitiveness would surely drive the economic development of its surrounding areas.

On April 8, 2011, the construction of Shanghai Disneyland started. This is the performance at the commencement ceremony. (Photo by Zhang Xian)

Shanghai Disneyland held a grand opening ceremony (Photo by Niu Yixin, Shanghai News Aerial Photography Alliance, China)

The concept of "growth pole" has two meanings: First, in the industrial sense, it refers to propulsive dominant industrial sectors; second, in the geographical sense, it refers to areas with superior geographical conditions. Pudong is such an area. The introduction of the world-famous entertainment Disney to this area played an exceptionally significant role in the economic transformation of Pudong and Shanghai.

Chapter 10

New Pudong: "Two Centers" and the Merging of Two Districts

10.1 The Priority of Finance

After Pudong development started, the manager of a Japanese bank was keenly aware that, unlike other development zones in China, Pudong put forward "finance first" at the outset. In fact, this was also the hope of Chinese leaders — to restore Shanghai's status as the Far East financial center in the past, and to win the right to speak in the world.

In the spring of 1974, Deng Xiaoping attended the Sixth Special Session of the United Nations in New York. On Sunday, Deng was not busy, and his men asked him what he wanted to do. Deng said, "Let's go to Wall Street to have a look." Despite the closure of the American financial center on Sunday, he took a walk into what had been hailed as a symbol of Western capitalism. Wall Street was short, narrow, cold, and not eye-catching at all. No one could tell Deng's feelings as he strolled down the street.

In history and tradition, Shanghai, as a financial center, radiated across the country.

In 1847, the first foreign bank, Liru Bank (also known as Oriental Bank), landed in Shanghai, the first bank in Shanghai and the first modern commercial bank in China to issue banknotes. In 1897, at the initiative of the Westernization faction, the China Trade Bank was established in the Shanghai Bund, which was the first commercial bank run by the Chinese. In 1905, China's first national bank, the Revenue Ministry Bank of the Qing Dynasty was also set up in the Bund, which is the predecessor of the famous Bank of China established after the Republic of China was founded.

In the 20th century, the development of Shanghai as a financial center began to speed up.

In 1928, the Central Bank was established in Shanghai. At the same time, Bank of China and Bank of Jiaotong moved their head offices from Beijing to Shanghai. In the eyes of the financiers, the Beiyang regime had collapsed, and the Nanjing National Government became the central government, so it was inevitable for China's political center to move to the south. If the headquarters of Bank of China and Bank of Jiaotong were not moved in accordance, it would be likely for them to lose out in competition with other commercial banks for that part of the financial business that was directly linked to the new central government.

At that time, the two banks were the strongest, the most extensive, and the most influential banks. The moving of their headquarters to Shanghai made a decisive change in the status and influence of the north and south financial centers. Shanghai's status as a national financial center began to be established.

Several other banks in the north also moved to the south. In 1930, Zhongfu Bank and China Industrial Bank moved from Tianjin to Shanghai. In 1931, Xinhua Commercial Bank and China Agricultural and Industrial Bank moved from Beijing to Shanghai. In 1933, Donglai Bank moved to Shanghai from Tianjin.

The National Government also set up a state-controlled Chinese State Bank in Shanghai in November 1929, under the chairmanship of Kong Xiangxi, Minister of Commerce and Industry. In April 1937, another government bank, China Farmers Bank, was moved to Shanghai from Hankou.

The National Government also set up a series of non-banking financial institutions in Shanghai, such as the Central Mint, the Postal Savings and Money Exchange Bureau, China Construction Corporation, the Central Trust Bureau, and the Central Savings Association. This further strengthened Shanghai's position as a financial center.

Local private banks sprung up as well. In Shanghai, the financial framework was shaped by the famous "four northern banks" of China's banking industry: Jincheng Bank, Salt Bank, South China Bank, and

Mainland Bank, and "three southern banks": Shanghai Commercial Savings Bank, Zhejiang Xingye Bank, and Zhejiang Shiye Bank.

At that time, Shanghai's financial market covered a complete range, including the credit market, the interbank lending market, the bill market, the domestic exchange market, the foreign exchange market, the gold market, the silver market, the bond market, the stock market, and the commodity futures market. It provided adequate financial support and financial services for the development of economic activities and trade throughout the country.

The banks' buildings rising from the intoxicating crescent-shaped shoal on the Huangpu River fully record the vicissitudes of the financial center. The picture shows the Shanghai Bund in the 1930s.

Shanghai was then called the central treasury of China. The trade volume of the Shanghai gold market was only less than that in London and New York. The funds flowed in and out of the center, and the buildings of banks that erected from the intoxicating crescent-shaped shoals on the Huangpu River recorded the vicissitudes of the financial center.

At that time, Shanghai had already been the financial center of China, the Far East, and even Asia.

Unfortunately, history does not always develop as expected.

In 1937, the Anti-Japanese War broke out in an all-round way, and on August 9, Shanghai was occupied by enemies, so that Shanghai's financial business began to be battered by wind and rainstorm. According to historical data, in the first three months of the Anti-Japanese War, the total deposit balance of the famous Shanghai Commercial Savings Bank reduced from 201.94 million yuan before the war to 129.21 million yuan, a decrease of 40%. The outbreak of the Pacific War completely ended the short-lived financial glory of old Shanghai. According to the post-war statistics of 1946, the total capital of Zhejiang Industrial Bank alone lost five-sixths in just eight years.

The war led to the decline of the Shanghai financial center.

After 1949, China adopted the planned economy, and various kinds of financial institutions, such as banks, big and small, and money shops were merged and reshaped to establish a highly centralized state banking system, namely, a "unified" banking system. And in 1953, the planned management system of centralized and unified comprehensive credit was established. Since then, all capital flows had to be carried out as planned without the need for capital markets, and the latter was even seen as illegal. Shanghai was no longer an international financial center, but an oversized industrial manufacturing center.

In the 1980s, a consensus took shape among Shanghai people. If the economy of Shanghai was to continue to develop greatly, the urban functions of Shanghai was to be brought into full play; if Shanghai was to re-establish itself as the hub and center of China's exchanges with the world, major measures and big actions must be taken to search for the new point of growth.

Although Shanghai lost its core economic function under the planned economy system, in terms of talents and management knowledge necessary for the market economy such as finance and insurance, Shanghai remained the most powerful city to become another major financial center besides Hong Kong. That may be one of the reasons why the head office of the newly-established Jiaotong Bank, the state comprehensive bank, was not based in Beijing in accordance to tradition, but in Shanghai in 1986.

Therefore, it is natural for Shanghai to rebuild its financial center which would radiate across the Yangtze River Delta and the Yangtze River Valley. In 1990, after the official launch of Pudong development, Shanghai put forward the "finance first" strategy.

Because of the strategy of "finance first", Deng Xiaoping put forward his famous remark that "finance is very important as the core of modern economy".

On the morning of the fourth day of the new lunar year of 1991, Deng Xiaoping listened to the report on Pudong development in the revolving hall on the 42nd floor of Shanghai Xinjinjiang Hotel. Huang Qifan, Assistant Director of the Pudong Development Office, who was present at the meeting then, recalled, "When Comrade Zhu Rongji reported to Comrade Xiaoping, he said that our strategy of Pudong development was 'to put finance first, to prosper the city with trade, and to pave the road of development with infrastructure and industrial linkage'. After hearing this, Comrade Xiaoping said, 'Finance is very important and is the core of the modern economy. Once the finance is done well, we can activate the whole game. Shanghai used to be a financial center, a place where currencies were freely convertible, and so will be the case in the future. The first step for China to gain an international position in finance is to rely on Shanghai. It will be realized in many years, but we must do it now.'"

One year later, the report of the 14th National Communist Party of China stated, "With Shanghai playing the leading role, the cities along the Yangtze River will be further opened. Shanghai will be developed into one of the international economic, financial, and trade centers as soon as possible, so as to promote the economic leap of the Yangtze River Delta and the entire Yangtze River Valley."

Many years later, Huang Qifan recalled what happened in that year, "The great old man made his famous remark after 'finance first'. Without this strategy of Pudong development and without Comrade Zhu Rongji's opening report, the old man might not have had the opportunity to make this great, guiding remark on finance. This statement is of great significance to China's current financial development. Therefore, we cannot overestimate the strategy of Pudong."

10.2 Meanings of Gifts

As for the implementation of "finance first", Pudong builders believed that in the process of China's transformation to the market economy system at the beginning of Pudong development, the factor market should be established first. Therefore, the builders vigorously introduced the financial institutions of symbolic significance in attracting investment in order to activate the cohesive force of the market.

The significance can also be seen from the landing of Chinese and foreign financial institutions and the different gifts given by Pudong.

On June 28, 1995, the headquarters of the Shanghai Branch of the People's Bank of China moved from Puxi to Pudong, the first state-level bank branch to move into Pudong. At the opening ceremony, Zhao Qizheng, Director of the Pudong New Area Administrative Committee, presented a lively and lovely white sheep to the other party as a gift on behalf of Pudong, signifying that the Shanghai Branch of the People's Bank of China took the lead in entering Pudong as a "leader" of the financial industry. The lamb wore a red ribbon that read "Financial Head". This drew applause from the whole audience, and even all the reporters who came for interviews praised the brilliance and shrewdness of the Pudong people.

The Pudong New Area Administrative Committee presented a lively and lovely white sheep as a gift to the Shanghai Branch of the People's Bank of China (Photo by Zhu Lan)

On September 28, the Shanghai branch of the Fuji Bank of Japan opened its business in Pudong, the forerunner of foreign banks to directly participate in the financial development of Lujiazui. The Pudong Government presented a running horse carved with rosewood as a gift, wishing the foreign banks entering Pudong to take the lead like the horse. In receiving the gift, Takahashi Langfu, President of the Shanghai Branch of the Fuji Bank, felt too excited to speak, forehead sweating.

On December 28, the Shanghai Merchants Building was inaugurated in Pudong. At the ceremony, Pudong officials presented a wooden eagle as a gift to the leaders of Shanghai Merchants, implying that with an eagle-like eye for Pudong they could fly like an eagle. In 1872, under the management of Li Hongzhang, the China Merchants was established in Shanghai and was the earliest shipping enterprise in China. More than 100 years later, the China Merchants became an aircraft carrier business group.

On September 28, 1995, the Fuji Bank of Japan first settled in Pudong. Zhao Qizheng gave a rosewood running horse as a gift for congratulations, which meant "taking the lead". (Photo by Li Zili)

In August of the following year, Taihua International Bank, the first foreign sole-capital bank in China, moved from Shantou to Pudong, which became the first head office of foreign banks in Lujiazui. Pudong presented a rosewood sculpture of a group of elephants, meaning "everything takes on a completely new look". Later, on December 19, 1997, the Shanghai Stock Exchange officially moved to Pudong for opening, and the Pudong New Area Government invited an Italian artist to make a statue of a cow and a bear made of glass fiber reinforced plastics, which was inscribed with "Bull Market".

It can be said that these gifts successively presented signified Pudong kicking off the construction of the core functional area of the Shanghai International Financial Center.

The Shanghai Branch of HSBC in Lujiazui located in Pudong was the first to be allowed to do RMB (renminbi) business. On the opening day, Tang Weilun, the British Consulate-General in Shanghai, came to HSBC to deposit RMB 888.88. The number eight is usually regarded as good financial fortune and best wishes. This Consulate-General became the first customer to deposit RMB in a foreign bank in Shanghai.

At the same time, with the settlement of domestic and foreign financial institutions, a number of state-level financial factor markets also settled in Pudong.

By the end of 2014, more than 6,000 financial institutions had settled in Pudong. These financial institutions gathered in the buildings in Lujiazui of Pudong, and with the lights of the skyscrapers twinkling at night, it was a very beautiful landscape.

A media compared Lujiazui of Pudong to the eastern "Manhattan", with the "flow" of thousands or even trillions of dollars a day in this 1.7 square kilometer area. Manhattan, New York's financial center, had been synonymous with international financial center for nearly a hundred years.

As a media overseas wrote, "China's banking center, China's stock market accelerator — in Shanghai, in Pudong, you can even feel money was flowing in the streets."

Huang Qifan believed that Pudong development and opening-up marked the opening-up of China's central cities and tertiary industry, and the core of this openness was represented by the revival of the financial industry, the lifeblood of the modern state.

One Taiwanese once talked about the development of Pudong. He insisted that the success of Pudong was in attracting the tide of finance and keeping the tide from retreating, so that Pudong became the seaman in the waves of Mainland economic development.

Zhao Qizheng, the first Director of the Administrative Committee of Pudong New Area, said that it was correct for them to have followed Comrade Xiaoping, that is, "finance is the core of modern economy", and always adhered to "finance first". Up to now, people in Pudong are still aware that doing well in finance is indeed the "punchline" to "win the whole game with one good move in chess".

10.3 The Objective of Establishing "Two Centers"

In 2009, Shanghai again accelerated the construction of the international financial center and shipping center. The biggest impetus came from the two documents issued by Beijing: "Opinions on Accelerating the Development of the Modern Service Industry and Advanced Manufacturing Industry in Shanghai and the Construction of the International Financial Center and International Shipping Center" and "Application for Canceling Nanhui District and Transferring Nanhui District into Pudong New Area".

These two documents are of historic significance to Pudong.

On March 25, 2009, the Executive Meeting of the State Council adopted "Opinions on Accelerating the Development of the Modern Service Industry and Advanced Manufacturing Industry in Shanghai and the Construction of the International Financial Center and International Shipping Center", also known as Guofa Document No. 19 [2009].

This document followed the sub-prime crisis in southern California that had turned into a global financial crisis in 2008. The financial crisis made Chinese officials and scholars realize that the American Federal Reserve started dollar printing to rescue the market, which made the investment of Chinese foreign exchange become less profitable and exposed to investment risks. These problems had become a trouble for China.

Asian countries' over-reliance the on dollar and United States financial markets hurt China. This further strengthened Chinese government's strategic awareness of strengthening finance, promoted the Chinese government to accelerate structural adjustment and industrial upgrading, in particular, the establishment of a safe, efficient, and open financial system, and accelerate the transformation of China's financial industry from a large one to a strong one.

In fact, by 2009, China had become the world's largest producer and the second largest consumer of resources, so the trend of internationalization of RMB emerged, with the RMB stock of about 200 billion yuan overseas.

China needed to establish a center that was compatible with it and can serve it and allocate resources around the world. Thus the internationalization of RMB and the construction of a resource allocation center were put on the agenda at the national strategic level. Shanghai, with its indisputable advantages, was the best choice for an international financial center.

So on March 23 of the same year, Zhou Xiaochuan, Governor of the Central Bank, wrote an article calling for expanding the use of the Special Drawing Rights (SDR) of the International Monetary Fund to create a super-sovereign international reserve currency. In other words, the Chinese wanted to rebuild a "world currency" other than the dollar.

If these two things are put together, it means that the dollar's dominance in the world was coming to an end and RMB's status would be elevated. To achieve this, a platform was required and Shanghai was the best choice.

As for the advantages of Shanghai, Lian Ping, Chief Economist of Jiaotong Bank, pointed out three points. First, China's capital market was in Shanghai. Second, the inter-bank bond market was in Shanghai, as well as the gold futures exchanges and foreign currency exchanges. Third, Shanghai's financial market was opened to the outside world at quite a high degree, and most domestic and foreign financial institutions were concentrated in Shanghai, among which the capital market was the most important. In addition, Shanghai had the advantage of linking up with other financial markets around the world. Previously, the capital markets in Hong Kong, London, New York, and Tokyo were jointly interlinked. All of these proved the good conditions of Shanghai to become an international financial center.

While proposing to build Shanghai into an international financial center, the State Council stressed that Shanghai should also be built into an international shipping center with the allocation capacity of global shipping resources. The development of the international shipping center cannot be separated from the support of finance, and the development of financial centers mostly resulted from the shipping center. The famous international shipping centers like New York, London, Tokyo, and so on are also famous international financial centers. The juxtaposition of "finance" and "shipping" conveyed the government's emphasis on the deep interaction between the two industries.

History chose Shanghai. Shanghai was duty-bound and Pudong assumed the great responsibility.

On January 16, 2010, Han Zheng, then Mayor of Shanghai, said at a press conference held by the Shanghai Municipal Government that the goal of building the Shanghai International Financial Center was clearly set, that is, by 2020, it would be built into an international financial center commensurate with the economic strength of the country and the international status of the RMB.

As a western proverb goes, the chance of success is only for those who are prepared. Five years later, Zhou Xiaochuan's wish was realized.

On December 1, 2015, in the early morning Beijing time, the board of the International Monetary Fund (IMF) voted to include the RMB in the IMF's SDR currency basket.

In that morning, the People's Bank of China held a news briefing. At the conference, Yi Gang, Deputy Governor of the Central Bank, expressed his joy, and described his own mood in several words like "joy, calmness, and modesty".

He said that the RMB's accession to the SDR was a milestone event, greatly significant and quite beneficial in the long term. It meant that the international community had approved of China's economic development and the achievements of reform and opening-up, especially the internationalization of the RMB. This, a win-win result for China and the world, was certainly a happy and fulfilling event.

According to regulations, the SDR currency basket is examined every five years. Two conditions must be met: the exporting trade in the currency-issuing country is large enough and the currency can be used freely.

The next day, Ben Bernanke, former Chairman of the American Federal Reserve, wrote that the RMB's "basket-entry" was symbolic, like "a golden five-pointed star given for a pupil's excellent homework".

This American said the actual use of the SDR was very limited except for the IMF's internal accounts, and that the RMB's entry into the SDR did not bring China any significant additional power or privilege.

Then why was the IMF's announcement of the inclusion of the RMB so reverberating? Bernanke remarked that because the Chinese government was eager to make China recognized as a global economic power, it was very concerned about this symbolic significance.

Indeed, the RMB's entry into the SDR meant that the international monetary system was broken by the Bretton Woods System which was developed after World War II. In the past, the international monetary system was dominated by Western currencies, but now the currency that represented emerging markets and eastern forces came into being, so that the structural changes took place in the international financial monetary system.

With the internationalization of the RMB, Shanghai, as the International Financial Center, was to play a greater role. Shanghai hoped to become a global center for innovation, trading, pricing, and clearing of RMB products.

10.4 The Development of Shipping and the Economic Significance of Proximity to the River

In this process, Shanghai was also committed to the construction of an international shipping center.

Shanghai was a typical commerce-driven city in modern China. The initial impetus for the start of the urban economy in modern Shanghai was the rapid development of foreign trade when Shanghai was forced to open to the outside world, namely, foreign trade was the forerunner of urban economic development in modern Shanghai.

By the 1980s, for every additional US$100 million in foreign trade exports from Shanghai, the export volume of 100,000 tons of foreign trade goods would be increased. For every 1 billion yuan of industrial output value produced in Shanghai, a berth of 600,000–700,000 tons per year was required to match it. For completing every 10,000 tons of "local" throughput, the Shanghai Port provided conditions for Shanghai to create an industrial output value of 15 million yuan.

Shanghai developed as a port city, so Shanghai officials knew better than officials elsewhere about the importance of a good port to a city, but one of Shanghai's disadvantages was there was no deep-water port.

After Shanghai opened its port in 1843, it took advantage of the natural conditions of "relying on the rivers for life". The Huangpu River was used as the route for foreign shipping. From Shiliupu to Wusong Port, the docks were densely distributed, and gradually extended from Nanshi of the old urban area of Shanghai to the lower reaches of the Huangpu River.

From the end of the Qing Dynasty to the first decade of the Republic of China (1921), Shanghai dredged the Huangpu River, which made water eight meters deeper at most. But because the silt kept silting, the river must be continuously dredged. Sometimes, "the relatively deep-drawing ships can only be berthed at the Huangpu River estuary, so that the cargoes cannot be unloaded. The loading and unloading all relied on the shallow-water boats for connection, so it was time-consuming and labor-costing."

In general, the closer the port transit was to the seaport, the more obvious the comprehensive benefits that human utilized water to develop water transport capacity. Therefore, Sun Yat-sen first chose Zhapu in Hangzhou Bay when he sketched the oriental big port. He believed, "If you want to choose a deep-water port for China's future business, the former planned port (namely, a port was planned to be built in Zhapu) must be taken into account and Shanghai should not be chosen doubtlessly."

After the founding of New China, the new large-scale port area was built near Wusong Port. After the development of Pudong, the Shanghai Municipal Government hoped to get rid of the restriction of the river port of the Huangpu River by building the Waigaoqiao new port area at the end of the Yangtze River estuary, but Waigaoqiao was not a deep-water port in the real sense.

The center of the port must be shifted to the seaport, which was the consensus of all shipping experts, not only because of the backward-flow of a large amount of sediment carried by the Yangtze River into the sea with the tide resulting in the siltation at the waterway, but also because the ships were getting larger and bigger and the draft became deeper and deeper.

Previously, Shanghai had been searching for a suitable port with water depth of more than 10 meters. However, the water depth of the Huangpu River was only about 10 meters, and the Yangtze River estuary at the throat of Shanghai Port was even shallower, only 7.5 meters. In the mid-1980s, the fifth-generation container ship that appeared in the world required the water depth of more than 14 meters.

Shanghai is China's largest coastal port city. Since the 1980s, China's economy developed rapidly, so that Shanghai's geographical advantages became increasingly prominent. Shanghai was not only equidistant from Japan, South Korea, North Korea, Taiwan, the Russian Far East, Hong Kong, and Macao, but also nearly equidistant from Guangdong in the south, Tianjin, Dalian, Qingdao, Yantai, and Yingkou in the north.

What's more important, the economic hinterland of Shanghai, located at the mouth of the Yangtze River known as China's "golden waterway", is very extensive. The Yangtze River is one of the largest navigable rivers in the world, with a total length of 6,300 kilometers, flowing through 11 provinces and cities, covering an area of 1.8 million square kilometers and accommodating thousands of tributaries. There was a large amount of transportation transit services at Shanghai Port, with its transit throughput accounting for half of total throughput. The economic hinterland was the life source of the port. Of course, this geographical advantage can be fully demonstrated only when shipping is developed. Therefore, some scholars said, "Only with the development of shipping, the proximity to the sea is meaningful; only with the development of shipping, the proximity to the river is of economic significance."

Hu Wei, former Director of Pudong New Area, stated, "The formulation of Shanghai's coastal development strategy is the key to the new round of overall planning of Shanghai, and is the inherent requirement for the evolution of Shanghai as a famous international city, from the development of the Suzhou River to the development across the Huangpu River and then to the cross-sea development. If Shanghai is to achieve the goal of 'one leader and three centers', the key lies in the development of modern ports and the construction of deep-water ports as the core." ("One leader" means Shanghai development and opening-up. "Three centers" refer to economic center, financial center, and trade center.)

The Huangpu River cannot carry the new generation of container ships, so shipping must be entrusted to the sea. Therefore, in the urban master plan of the 1980s, Shanghai raised the question of the construction of the seaport and airport. Shanghai proposed at least seven or eight options about the site of the deep-water port.

He Pengnian, former Assistant Director of the Transportation Office, recalled, "There was no deep-water port in Shanghai, and it was a very difficult problem to solve at the time. There is a mouth bar at the Yangtze River estuary, where the water was usually about 8 meters deep, and at high tide up to 11–12 meters at most, so deep-draft ships could not enter the port. In order to overcome this bottleneck that restricted the development of Shanghai, Wang Lao (Wang Daohan, former Mayor of Shanghai) proposed a research in 1982, namely, the feasibility of selecting a site for a deep-water port in the coastal and inland area near Shanghai."

In 1986, Yuan Suishan, member of the Shanghai Chinese People's Political Consultative Conference Committee, made a proposal, "Shanghai's Port Development should Face the World". It pointed out that Shanghai was an important port city in China, but the big ships could not get into Shanghai Port and only ships of less than 25,000 tons could wait for the tide to rise for entrance. There were as many as 176 ships waiting for the tide and unloading every day in 1984 and there were still 97 ships in January of 1985 and 1986. As a result, every year the country lost nearly US$100 million in foreign currency. With the reform and opening-up, the number of ships coming to Shanghai was still increasing. Without a long-term vision, the Shanghai Port might lose its advantage to become a big port in the world. The proposal suggested that the port construction in Shanghai should be oriented to the world, instead of being limited to the site selection in the Huangpu River. In line with the shipping trend, by means of technological democracy, a long-term comprehensive plan should be formulated to make Shanghai a true big port in the world.

In fact, when planning the development of Pudong, Shanghai leaders considered to construct docks outside the Huangpu River. Zhu Rongji once told World Bank officials, "We already have a huge plan for the development of the infrastructure construction in Pudong. First of all, a new port will be built in Waigaoqiao, Pudong. ... In total, more than 40 berths of 10 thousand tons will be built, equivalent to the number of berths in the present Shanghai Port. Now the docks are all located inside the Huangpu River. When the new port is completed, many transport ships will not have to enter the Huangpu River."

In August 1995, Shanghai leaders carried out special research on the site selection of the deep-water port. Municipal Party Secretary Huang Ju emphasized that the deep-water port was one of the most important infrastructure projects when Shanghai moved towards the 21st century. The construction of the deep-water port was the key to the construction of the Shanghai International Shipping Center, and whether Shanghai could become an international shipping center was the key to whether Shanghai could be built into a city of "one leader, three centers".

On December 8 of the same year, the leaders of the Central Government proposed that building Shanghai into an international shipping center was the key to developing Pudong to make it become the economic center of the Far East, and thus to developing the entire Yangtze River. The construction of the Shanghai International Shipping Center was an important strategic plan of the Communist Party of China Central Committee and the State Council.

In December 1995, Xu Kuangdi, Mayor of Shanghai, introduced the general plan of the future development of the Shanghai Port at the International Maritime Technology Academic Conference. With a focus on developing and constructing a deep-water port that can accommodate the third and fourth generations of international container ships, the Shanghai Port would be built into a modern international deep-water hub on the west coast of the Pacific Ocean and become a huge combined port with a port cluster in the Yangtze River Delta. It would take 20 or 30 years to execute the plan in three steps: in 2000, the construction of the international shipping center would be fully started; in 2010, the region-level international shipping center would be completed; in 2020, the intercontinental-level international shipping center would be completed.

In January 1996, the leaders of the State Council held a meeting among leaders from Jiangsu, Zhejiang provinces, and Shanghai, and officially launched the construction of the Shanghai International Shipping Center with the Shanghai deep-water port as the main body and with the sea ports and river ports in Zhejiang and Jiangsu as two wings. The meeting pointed out, "from the overall perspective, the construction of the Shanghai International Shipping Center is of great significance, since it was not only the need of China's economic development, but also the requirement of international political and economic competition."

In May of the same year, the Leading Group and the Office for Shanghai International Shipping Center was established. Vice Mayor Xia

Keqiang was appointed as the leader of the leading group to carry out the work relevant to the construction of the Shanghai International Shipping Center.

In August of the same year, the Ministry of Transportation issued "Letter on the Demonstration of the New Port Site of the Shanghai International Shipping Center". In September, the demonstration of the new port site and some preliminary preparations started. Since then, in total, more than 100 professional research institutions and 2,500 people from institutions of higher learning participated in this work, and 329 well-known experts participated in the evaluation of achievements in various special research.

Experts demonstrated the harbor-building schemes such as going-north (Luojing), going-east (Waigaoqiao), and going-south (Jinshanzui), but all of them were given up due to the insufficient water depth, the shortage of shorelines, and so on. Finally, the islands such as Dayangshan and Xiaoyangshan, 32 kilometers away from Luchao Port, Nanhui, Shanghai, attracted the attention of experts and thus the consensus was reached in the demonstration. The island was only 45 nautical miles from the international shipping route. It was the closest deep-water port to Shanghai. A 32.5-kilometer cross-sea bridge was planned to be built to connect the islands and the mainland, and the islands were to be built into deep-water ports.

In November 1997, Shanghai submitted to the Ministry of Transportation the "Demonstration on the New Port Site of the Shanghai

The spectacular night view of Donghai bridge, the 32.5-kilometer cross-sea bridge (Photo by Wu Huiquan)

International Shipping Center", which pointed out that it was technically feasible to construct the deep-water port outside the mouth bar of the Yangtze River estuary, and the overall economic benefits would be good.

On June 26, 2002, the builders drove the first pile into the earth for the cross-sea bridge. Thus the Yangshan Deep-water Dock became China's first port to be built on the tiny island.

Since then, the construction of the shipping center increasingly speeded up. On December 10, 2005, the Yangshan Deep-water Port was officially opened. In a short period of 10 years, the throughput of the Yangshan Port grew from the initial 3.24 million twenty-foot equivalent units (TEUs) to more than 15 million TEUs by 2015, with a total container throughput of 108 million TEUs in 10 years. With the support of the Yangshan Port, in 2007, the container throughput of the Shanghai Port exceeded 20 million TEUs, which surpassed Hong Kong for the first time and rose to second place in the world. Three years later, its throughput exceeded that of Singapore and became the largest port in the world and also the largest island-type deep-water artificial port in the world.

History proved that the decision was a successful one. Although the throughput in Chinese ports generally declined after the global financial crisis in 2008, Shanghai's Yangshan Port continued to grow at a rate of 20%. Among the vast seas, a small nameless island, in 10 years, became the shinning landmark in the world's shipping map.

10.5 New Pudong with the Merging of Two Districts

Shortly after the Chinese government announced the document to promote the construction of the "two centers" in Shanghai, Chen Qiwei, spokesman for the Shanghai Municipal Government, announced at a press conference on the afternoon of May 6, 2009 that the State Council had formally approved of Shanghai's "Request for Instructions on the Cancellation of the Nanhui District Establishment and Merging the former Nanhui District Administration into Pudong New Area", and had agreed to revoke the Nanhui District and merge its administration into Pudong New Area.

That was the season when the large area of peach blossomed in Nanhui.

The area covered by Pudong New Area surged from 569.57 square kilometers to 1429.67 square kilometers, more than twice of that of the original. It was hoped that Pudong would become the international financial center and shipping center in 2020.

Obviously, Nanhui was merged into Pudong, which was in line with the interactive development of the Shanghai International Financial Center and International Shipping Center. The main location of the "two centers" belonged to two districts: Pudong and Nanhui.

Three years prior, experts from the Pudong Reform and Development Research Institute embarked on the project "Research on the Interactive Development of Pudong and Nanhui", in which although there was no proposal for the two districts to be administratively merged, it was proposed that the various policies of the "pioneering test" in the comprehensive supporting reform of Pudong should cover the modern service industry and high-tech manufacturing industry in both Nanhui and Pudong, so that through the interaction of the two districts' policies, planning, and industry, the "integration" in the economic development of the big Pudong golden triangle would be promoted.

Previously, Nanhui, with an area of more than 600 square kilometers, was called "cloth pocket", which meant traffic dead end. However, since the construction of the Pudong International Airport and the Yangshan Deep-water Port, Nanhui began to have the geographical and position advantage of the "first hinterland" and "first station". Moreover, in spite of the shortage of land resources, Nanhui's planned industrial land was up to 187 square kilometers, ranking first in the city, and thus the rich land resources would spur a huge space for industrial development.

After 19 years of development and opening-up, Pudong had accumulated strong economic strength and leading industrial clusters. But meanwhile, the resources such as exploitable land and other resources were increasingly tight such that the continuously rising regional comprehensive business cost and the adverse effects brought about by the international financial crisis were increasingly becoming the bottleneck that impeded the further development of Pudong.

The study at that time suggested that the geographical distribution of big Pudong should start from Baoshan District in the north wing of Shanghai and the coastal zone from Pudong New Area, Nanhui, and

Fengxian to coastal Jinshan District of Hangzhou Bay. With the organic combination of the developed financial and trade centers and advanced manufacturing industry, the development efficiency and production level in the area should be further improved. Inside the manufacturing industry, the reasonable division of labor in the industrial structure and layout should be achieved to improve the intensive degree of the industry in the whole region. Inside the tertiary industry, from Lujiazui to the airport and the Yangshan Deep-water Port, a hierarchical and efficient gradient division of labor should be realized.

This was also related to the Central Government's "Opinions on Speeding Up the Development of the Modern Service Industry and Advanced Manufacturing Industry and the Construction of the International Financial Center and International Shipping Center", which required Shanghai to accelerate the development of the modern service industry and advanced manufacturing industry and to build the "two centers". Yang Zhouyi, former Secretary-General of the Pudong Reform and Development Research Institute, said, "After the merging of Pudong and Nanhui, the problems of policy radiation, overall planning of land resource, and industrial transformation will be gradually solved. After the merging of Pudong and Nanhui, big Pudong's modern service industry and advanced manufacturing industry can be re-planned in the layout of the whole area, and the urbanization process of the original Nanhui District will be accelerated."

Professor Zhou Zhenhe of the Chinese Historical and Geographical Center of Fudan University believed that the structure of administrative division was very rigid, while the economic zone should be elastic and economic development should not be affected by any administrative boundary. But in China, with its own special circumstance, the administrative region and economic zone had usually been in a state of integration. If the Nanhui District were not merged with Pudong, the laws, decrees, and measures related to the "pioneering test" for the comprehensive reform in Pudong New Area would not be implemented in the Nanhui District. ... In short, it was necessary to adjust the administrative divisions appropriately to adapt to and promote the development of economy so that the economic zones and the administrative divisions can be made consistent with each other again.

Li Jianeng, who had participated in the planning of Pudong New Area since the development of Pudong, recalled a historical detail:

> On July 15, 1988, principal consultant Wang Daohan led the members of the research team for investigation, driving to the Luchao Port, Nanhui, located in the Yangtze River estuary and the north bank of the Hangzhou Bay. In those days, there was only the Dapu Road Tunnel for crossing the river. Roads and highways in Pudong were at a lower grade. After the car went across the river, they had a bumpy ride all the way through Zhou Zhou Highway and Hunan Highway. Comrade Daohan was aged, but good in spirit. People were talking and laughing all the way. From time to time, Comrade Daohan talked about his plan for the development of Pudong. From the perspective of large-scale Pudong, the east part to the Huangpu River and the Jinhui Port and the north part to the Hangzhou Bay were spacious, so it was the best place for the merging of the river and sea. From the perspective of middle-scale Pudong, the area of 'three districts' and a county east of the Huangpu River was relatively moderate. From the perspective of small-scale Pudong, the east part to the Huangpu River and the north part to the Chuanyang River, 350 square kilometers, was more suitable and realistic for development, with less impact on the existing administrative division.

20 years later, the conception of big Pudong finally came true. According to the overall goal of the Shanghai International Shipping Center Construction, by 2020, Shanghai would become an international shipping center with the capacity of global shipping resource allocation. The merging of the two regions first solved the management problems arising from the boundary of the administrative division, especially the Waigaoqiao Free Trade Zone and the golden industrial belt of the Port Area, the Pudong Airport, and the Yangshan Port, which belonged to two districts.

As a result, people give Pudong a new title: "Big Pudong", "New Pudong". The New Pudong enjoyed a quiet "turning around", from the Lujiazui Financial Center to the Waigaoqiao Free Trade Zone to the Pudong International Airport, the Yangshan Deep-water Port, and the Lingang New Town, which covered almost all the fields of Shanghai construction, such as finance, shipping, trade, and others. The Yangshan Deep-water Port, the Cross-sea Bridge in Hangzhou Bay, the Yangtze

River Tunnel, and the Sutong Bridge also became the hardware from "New Pudong" directly to the Yangtze River Delta, which would enhance the level of Shanghai to serve the Yangtze River Delta, the Yangtze River Valley, and the whole nation.

In the meantime, under the national strategies such as the development and opening of Pudong, the comprehensive reform, and the construction of the Shanghai International Financial Center and International Shipping Center, a number of pioneering policies of reform were executed in new Pudong so that Pudong exhibited its advantage as the "pioneer" and the national strategic capacity increased significantly.

In terms of economic scale, in 2008, the gross domestic product (GDP) of Pudong New Area reached 315.099 billion yuan, accounting for about one quarter of that of the city. The GDP of Nanhui was 54,803 million yuan. After the merging of the two districts, "New Pudong" developed synergistically in the aspects of system innovation and opening-up, and the value created by the new area was more than "1 + 1 = 2". In the second year after the merging, the GDP of New Pudong reached 470.7 billion yuan in 2010.

According to the planned objective of New Pudong, by the 30th anniversary of Pudong development and opening-up in 2020, Pudong New Area would strive to increase the proportion of GDP from more than one quarter to more than one third of the whole city, and strive to achieve a higher target, $30,000 GDP per capita.

10.6 Building the Global "Pricing Center"

In 2011, two years after Beijing approved of the construction of Shanghai's "two centers", Pudong New Area set a five-year goal, that is, to achieve good and rapid development in changing the way of economic development and to become a new node in global resource allocation.

A reporter once described a scenario in which Pudong became a new node in global resource allocation:

"At 9.15 in the morning Beijing Time every weekday, a set of data spread around the world from the China Foreign Exchange Trading Center, based in Pudong, Shanghai, as traders tapped their keyboards. A quarter of an hour later, another set of interesting figures came from the Shanghai Stock Exchange in the Lujiazui Financial Zone of Pudong.

"Thousands of financial institutions, foreign-exchange traders, importers, exporters, and investors around the world were waiting for data from Pudong in Shanghai at this time." A reporter of Xinhua News Agency called these data "Pudong price".

From Monday to Friday, with the opening of the major factor markets, the prices of various factors of production flew rapidly from the whole country and all over the world to Pudong every day, and then to the whole country and all over the world through the quick feedback of the major factor markets there.

In October 2005, Yao Xitang, former President of the Pudong Reform and Development Research Institute, told reporters, "At present, the minister of the economy of Chile is concerned about the copper futures in Pudong, and the minister of the economy of Malaysia is concerned about natural rubber futures in Pudong. More and more financial institutions and multinational companies held the board meetings in Pudong."

Zhuang Ling, once researcher of the Pudong New Area Administrative Committee, recalled an episode in 1995 with strong emotion.

In the early summer of 1995, a group of guests from Pudong visited the London International Financial Futures and Options Exchange. A. Albert, the Assistant President, stood outside the gate, smiling, to greet them.

The London International Financial Futures and Options Exchange is Europe's largest, and the world's third-largest futures and options exchange. Albert told the guests, "Britain was the world's largest producer of copper in the mid-19th century. Since the beginning of the 20th century, the London Metal Exchange publicly announced the transaction prices, and then was widely used as a benchmark for world metal trade. So far, 70% of the world's total copper production has been traded at the price announced by the London Stock Exchange."

Suddenly, the smiling Albert shrugged his shoulders and changed his topic, "I heard that Pudong had also begun trading copper and other commodities. What impact may Pudong's rise have on London Exchange? Perhaps only God knows."

In just over a decade, Albert's presentiment came true.

China became the world's largest importer of copper, with nearly 40% of global consumption. In 2013, the market of the Shanghai Futures Exchange accounted for about 60% of the futures market of the whole country, and in copper transaction it became the world's second-largest copper pricing center after the London Exchange, so it had greater right to speak in the international market.

The so-called new node of global resource allocation meant that Pudong was becoming one of the "pricing centers" in the world.

Pudong's leaders held the view that China had already become a trading power, an investment power, and a power in absorbing investment, but there was still an insufficiency in its ability to allocate global resources. In the construction of the "four centers", especially the construction of the financial and shipping centers, it was important to enhance the ability to allocate resources across boundaries. What was to be built was an international financial, trade, shipping, and economic center, so without such a function, it would become, at best, a domestic and intra-regional center. If it was aimed to become an international center, its ability to allocate resources across boundaries was highly required.

Chapter 11

Prying up the Fulcrum: Pilot Reform Zone (Version 3.0)

11.1 Small Fulcrum with Great Effect

Years ago, Zhao Qizheng, leader of Pudong, compared Pudong to a "beautiful teenager". But by 2013, the teenager had grown up. The area of Pudong expanded to more than 1,400 square kilometers, with a permanent population of more than 5 million.

Richard Stanley, President of Citigroup in China, said that compared with some places abroad, Pudong might be deficient in several aspects, but the developing Pudong had never disappointed us, because every day in Pudong, there were new hopes, that is, the people living there had the feeling that the sun was new every day.

This feeling came from Pudong's continuous pursuit of greater openness and deeper reform through institutional experimentation.

On the morning of October 1, 2013, the five-star red flag fluttered in the wind at Building 9, Jilong Road, Pudong New Area, adjacent to the Yangtze River estuary. In front of the new exterior wall was a nameplate decorated with gold with both the Chinese and English words of "China (Shanghai) Pilot Free Trade Zone", which many people took photos of.

A BBC reporter also came to the Shanghai Free Trade Zone, where he noticed three tall chimneys in the distance. He wrote that the chimneys of a power plant were emitting exhaust gases into the sky, a reminder of China's existing model of growth.

Just two days prior, the Shanghai Free Trade Zone was inaugurated. At 10 that morning, Ralph Haupter, Microsoft's global Senior Vice President and Chairman of Greater China, took over a registration certificate of foreign-invested enterprise from Han Zheng, Shanghai's Party Secretary, and both sides smiled. The number of the registration card was "001".

Just as Pudong's development and opening-up marked the opening-up of China's central cities and tertiary industry, represented by the revival of the financial sector as the lifeblood of a modern nation, the Shanghai Free Trade Zone was characterized by developing service trade so as to achieve the transformation and upgrading of China's economic structure.

This free trade zone was only 28 square kilometers, equivalent to 1/226 of the size of Shanghai, but it was highly expected by Chinese leaders to become the pivot of a new round of China's reform and opening-up.

More than 2000 years ago, Archimedes, the ancient Greek scientist, discovered a secret and wrote excitedly to the king, "Give me a fulcrum and I can pry up the whole earth." This is an exaggeration, but Archimedes had solid basis — the principle of the equilibrium of leverage.

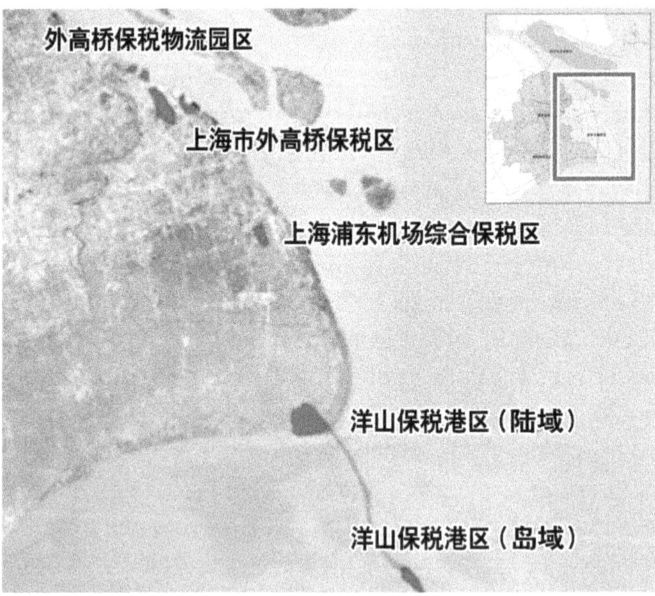

The Shanghai Pilot Free Trade Zone, 28 square kilometers, included the previous Special Surveillance Zone of Customs

Local media reported that the Shanghai Free Trade Zone, just like a fulcrum, would pry up China's new round of reform and opening-up. Judging from the history of China's reform and opening-up, prying up the overall reform and opening-up at the fulcrum was one of the most important experiences of China's high-speed economic growth for 30 years. In 1980, the Chinese government set up four special economic zones in the south, which were small-scaled in both area and population, but they acted as a small fulcrum for promoting China's reform and opening-up, especially as the frontier to open windows to the world.

According to the leverage principle, the fulcrum is small, but the effect is huge, because of the great power of the fulcrum. In as early as the late 1980s, Deng Xiaoping put forward the strategic envision of "rebuilding several 'Hong Kongs'" in mainland China. Hong Kong, a typical free port, was characterized by its mature market economy system, the management and the rule of law in line with the international standard, the entrepot trade of global leading position, and efficient commercial service platform. Therefore it played an important role in the international financial and trade market, the most open and transparent place in the world. Deng Xiaoping said, "We must build several more 'Hong Kongs' in the mainland, that is, we should be more open in order to achieve our strategic objectives in development."

In the history of China's reform and opening-up, the topics of free trade parks, free ports, special customs zones, pilot free trade zones, and so on were constantly raised and discussed by Chinese officials and scholars. It is clear that the Chinese government was attempting to reinvent "Hong Kong" to promote China's wider opening and deeper reforms.

Ancient China used to be so enclosed and arrogant, and so intoxicated with and indulged into the ego that China suffered from backwardness and attacks. Karl Marx, founder of scientific socialism, once made a detailed description:

> As soon as the prestige of the Qing Dynasty met with the guns of Britain, it was wiped out. The superstitious belief in their eternal imperial empire was fatally struck, and the barbarous and enclosed state and the isolation from the civilized world was broken up. ... What followed must be the process of disintegration, just like the mummy, which, though carefully preserved in a sealed coffin, must disintegrate upon exposure to fresh air.

Therefore, since 1978, the Chinese Communists tried to break up the rigid system by opening to the outside world, that is, the reform forced by opening to the outside world.

In 1980, the Shenzhen Special Zone became the first experimental field for China to open up, introducing the market economy, subverting the planned economic system, and forcing the continuous reform of the system and mechanism — the implementation of the shareholding system, the reform of the price system, the innovation of the labor and personnel system, etc. In just 30 years, a small country town was developed into a modern big city.

In 1990, as the pioneer in the second round of China's reform and opening-up, Pudong attracted a large number of multinational corporations to settle down with a more open mind and better development prospect, which forced the government to make comprehensive coordinated reform in service conception, administrative efficiency, open information, legal conditions, and so on. In particular, in the course of building a socialist market economic system, Pudong took the lead in the market-oriented allocation of production factors and the opening-up of the service industry, and thus it became one of the most attractive and popular places for overseas investors, especially transnational companies.

China's entry into the World Trade Organization (WTO) in 2001 promoted China's all-round opening-up. Shi Guangsheng, former Foreign Trade Minister who participated in the negotiation, said that more than 3,000 laws and regulations were amended after China's entry into the WTO. As a result, profound changes took place in the fields of economy, politics, culture, and society. The all-round opening brought about the rapid economic development of China for more than 10 years, and China became the number one trading country in the world.

To the world, China had been constantly opening its own windows and doors one by one and adjusting its own systems to keep in step. This also made Chinese people taste the sweetness, in Chinese words, the dividend brought by the reform and opening-up.

On the contrary, at the same time, some countries did not develop after their entry into the WTO, since they made no corresponding reform of the domestic economic system, while China cleaned up old laws and regulations on a large scale to establish an economic system and market environment that were both in line with international rules and national conditions.

In 2013, the new Chinese government came into being, and the new government began to pursue a higher level of openness. On March 28, Li Keqiang, as the new Premier of the State Council, made his first stop in Shanghai for investigation.

Li Keqiang said, "30 years ago, the spectacular reforms were first and foremost driven by the opening of special economic zones along the coast. Today, it seems that there is still much room and impetus for promoting a new round of reform through opening-up. The reform will unleash a huge institutional dividend."

Li Keqiang put great hope on Shanghai. He encouraged Shanghai officials, "China must not be afraid of opening-up and must move forward step by step. At this stage, it is time for China to select a new pilot place for opening-up. Shanghai has all the conditions and the foundation for this experiment, that is, promoting reform by opening-up to the world."

It is the historical experience of China's reform and opening-up to enforce reform with opening-up and stimulate "reform dividend". It is on the basis of this experience that the Shanghai Free Trade Zone was open at a higher level. The Chinese government was full of expectations of this small fulcrum. Although it accounted for less than 0.3% of the territory of Chinese land, it was expected to create an "upgraded version" of the Chinese economy.

Opening-up was of extraordinary significance to Pudong. According to Zheng Shao, researcher at the Shanghai Institute of Development and Reform, opening-up was the gene of Pudong. The essential experience of Pudong's success in the past 20 years was opening-up, and future development would still depend on opening-up. Pudong's opening-up should be so all-rounded and deep as to make all market participants regard it as a "paradise". It was the task of the government to create a "paradise" with an open mind.

Considering the history of opening-up to the outside world, Zhao Qizheng believed that the first batch of 14 opened coastal cities in China could be called the pilot reform zones of version 1.0; Shenzhen and other special economic zones and the development of Pudong were the pilot reform zones of version 2.0; and the China (Shanghai) Pilot Free Trade Zone was the pilot reform zone of version 3.0.

11.2 The Debate over the Translation of the Name into English

According to the research by Zhong Jian, a Professor at Shenzhen University, the free trade zone and free port were different types of special economic zones. In 1228, the Marseilles Free Trade Park was considered the world's first special economic zone. In 1547, the Genoa Free Port of Italy was the first special economic zone officially named as a free port in the world. Hong Kong and Macao of China were declared as free ports in 1841 and 1845, respectively.

In the history of China's reform and opening-up, thanks to the example of the Hong Kong Free Port, the construction of China's special economic zones involved the activities of learning, following, and innovating. Therefore, at the beginning of Pudong development, Shanghai proposed to establish a free trade zone in Pudong with the aim of a "free port".

From June 8 to 15, 1990, Zhu Rongji, Secretary of the Municipal Communist Party Committee, headed the Shanghai Economic Delegation to visit Hong Kong. At the "Seminar on Shanghai Economic Development in the 1990s: Prospect of Economic Cooperation between Shanghai and Hong Kong", he made a long speech: "Compared with the existing special economic zones and economic and technological development zones, the development and opening-up of Pudong had four characteristics. First of all, with the aim to establish a 'free port', Pudong planned to establish a free trade industrial zone with free access that would guarantee tariff exemption for commodities, personnel, and merchant ships. In this zone, foreign businessmen would be allowed to carry out entrepot trade and develop wholesale business. This was not the case in other special economic zones."

But the word "free" was too sensitive in the era when people had to ask whether whatever people did was "capitalism or socialism". According to the recollection of Wu Nansheng, Secretary of the Guangdong Provincial Party Committee in charge of preparing for the establishment of the special economic zone in the late 1970s, at that time there was a great debate over the name given to the three places in Shenzhen, Zhuhai, and Shantou that took "the lead". If the name "export processing zone" were given, it would be the same as that of Taiwan. If the name "free trade zone" were named, people would feel afraid of being considered as practicing capitalism, a big charge of crime at that time. Of course, in the end, Deng Xiaoping decided to call it "special zone".

Therefore, on November 1, 1991, at the "Seminar on Hainan Foreign Strategy" held after the establishment of the China (Hainan) Institute of Reform and Development, the participants unanimously called for the establishment of a "special tariff zone" in Hainan instead of a free port and free trade park as named.

Zhu Rongji openly proposed to establish a free trade zone, which exhibited his insight and courage.

However, local leaders, at first, did lack experience in how to set up a free port and free trade park. For example, on June 29, 1985, the State Council approved of the Fujian Provincial Government's "Report on the Implementation Plan of the Xiamen Special Economic Zone", which agreed to the expansion of the Xiamen Special Economic Zone to Xiamen Island and Gulangyu, and the gradual implementation of some policies of a free port. Among them, "the gradual implementation of some policies of a free port" was regarded as a unique "effective weapon" by people in the Xiamen Special Economic Zone at that time. Unfortunately, in the specific practice, it was full of twists and turns.

But the smart Chinese came up with a way to set up a free trade zone, a term with Chinese characteristics. In December 1987, Shenzhen founded the earliest free trade zone in China — the Shatoujiao Free Trade Zone. In June 1990, taking advantage of the development and opening-up of Pudong, the State Council officially approved the establishment of the Waigaoqiao Free Trade Zone in Pudong New Area.

Interestingly, for the English name of the Shanghai Waigaoqiao Free Trade Zone, there were twists and turns. Chen Binghui, former Director of the Foreign Affairs Office of the Pudong New Area Administrative Committee, recalled that the Waigaoqiao Free Trade Zone was translated as Free Trade Zone: "In 1991, Mayor Zhu Rongji told me on the train that there was no bonded zone in the world. There was only bonded warehouse. If the name of a bonded zone was used, foreigners could not understand. Then it can only be translated into Free Trade Zone. So the name used now was given by Zhu Rongji."

Pudong also proposed to change the Chinese name of Bonded Zone to Waigaoqiao Free Trade Zone. After thinking for a long time, Zhu Rongji finally asked his secretary to make calls to inform others concerned that the Chinese name for the zone should not be changed, and the English name should be Shanghai Waigaoqiao Free Trade Zone.

However, this translation was strongly opposed by the relevant departments. Some people also asked, "What is your translation based on? Who made the translation?" At that time it was easy for people to confuse economic liberalization with political liberalization.

In September 1992, the "First National Conference on Free Trade Zone" was held in Tianjin, at which Pudong proposed a special policy of "three freedoms" — freedom of trade, freedom of currency, and freedom of import and export of goods, and suggested to develop the free trade zone according to international practice by taking trade as the breakthrough. Therefore, as the representative of Pudong, Ruan Yanhua, the first general manager of the Waigaoqiao Development Company, believed that the translation into Free Trade Zone was beneficial in terms of publicity and integration with the world, and it was easily accepted. After all, the name free trade zone was more internationally acceptable.

Pudong's proposal resonated with representatives of the 14 bonded zones. The host, however, suggested that the "three freedoms" be replaced by other words. Customs, which they were also against, recommended that it should be translated into Bonded Warehouse Zone.

The representative of Pudong further explained that the translation had been decided after consulting many international experts and taking the overall international situation into consideration. Moreover, the translation had been agreed by Zhu Rongji.

Immediately after that, Vice Mayor of Shanghai Zhao Qizheng made a speech. Zhao stressed that in order to keep in line with international practice, it should be translated into Free Trade Zone, and he cited many examples to provide further explanation. Many years later, Ruan Yanhua recalled, "His speech clarified the concept of free trade zone, and 20 years ago, there was little theoretical research in this regard."

Ruan Yanhua recalled, "After Vice Mayor Zhao backed me up, there was a strong reaction. After the meeting, Zhao Qizheng still felt worried, so they went to meet the host to provide further explanation about the translation. Free trade zones, in which goods were imported and exported freely according to international conventions, would be connected with trade globalization. In short, Shanghai hoped to play the role of an international free port like Hong Kong, as opposed to trade protectionism."

In the end, Pudong people insisted on it, and all other bonded zones changed their English translation to Free Trade Zone.

Of course, the foreigners, who do not understand Chinese, may not find the problem of such a translation. However, a shrewd Japanese who was proficient in Chinese and English discovered the problem. According to Zhao Qizheng, the Japanese asked him about the underlying reason why the Chinese and English names of Waigaoqiao Free Trade Zone were not consistent with each other.

Zhao Qizheng could only give such an answer: because most Chinese people were not very clear about the meaning of free trade zones, but they knew very clearly about bonded warehouses, and when goods entered bonded warehouses, they did not need to pay taxes, and only if goods were taken out, then they had to pay taxes. Many bonded warehouses gathered together would make up a free trade zone.

This explanation, indeed, was the only answer he can give. It also helped to understand why it would take nearly 30 years for China to develop a free port into a pilot free trade zone.

If we stand beside the globe and look at China, the special economic zones, and the free trade zones, we can more profoundly understand Deng Xiaoping's context of strategic conception and the historical value from "implementing certain policies of free port" to "rebuilding Hong Kong on the mainland".

In the late 1980s, Deng Xiaoping proposed to "rebuild Hong Kong" on the mainland. In May of the following year, in a talk with the leaders of the Central Government, Deng Xiaoping reiterated, "I said in the past that we should rebuild several 'Hong Kongs'. I meant that we should be open, more open to the outside world. If there were no opening, there would be no development."

The construction of special economic zones was undoubtedly one of the conceptions of "rebuilding Hong Kong".

In contrast to Hong Kong's rule of law, market openness, economic transparency, free-flowing capital system, and free currency system, the mainland was characterized by a fragile system environment such as imperfect legal system, complex and volatile regulations, outdated accounting systems, opaque business practices, and so on.

Therefore, in 1992, in Shenzhen, Deng Xiaoping demanded, "We must boldly absorb and draw lessons from all the achievements of civilization created by human society, and absorb and draw lessons from the world today, including all advanced modes of operation and management that reflect the laws of modern socialized production in the capitalist developed countries."

At that time, Pudong studied the different types of free trade zones in the world and found that in foreign countries, laws were first formulated to determine what can be done, that is, there were rules first and then people would do things accordingly. Therefore, it was very important to legislate in the free trade zones, so Pudong people boldly made a leap forward in the legislation.

In the 1990s, in China, local legislation was like "Arabian Nights", a fantasy story, because both the tax system and the legal system were unified in the overall nation. Pudong tried to persuade the Municipal People's Congress to conduct research. Since 1994, headed by the Financial and Economic Committee of the Municipal People's Congress, a research group was created, consisting of the Legal Affairs Office of the Municipal Government, the Administrative Committee of Pudong New Area, the Municipal Foreign Economic Affairs Committee, and other departments. They conducted research and investigations in 12 domestic free trade zones and more than 10 foreign free trade zones. In six years, they collected texts of laws and regulations of more than 100 free trade zones in the world.

In drafting legislation, Pudong hoped to make a breakthrough, "so some problems were not yet included". Hu Wei, former Director of the Administrative Committee of the Waigaoqiao Free Trade Zone, recalled, "After it was done, we felt very satisfied, but the agreement of the Central Government was still needed. After discussions by Beijing's relevant departments, there was no progress and no breakthrough. As to whether the legislation was necessary, there was some controversy. In the end, however, we believed that, since some policies were constantly changing, it must be progress if our perceptions at that time can be determined in the form of law."

In December 1996, the first Chinese local law on Free Trade Zones was formally passed.

Unexpectedly, the effect greatly exceeded the expectation. A lot of multinational companies came one by one, firmly confirming that this first Chinese law and regulation on free trade zones proved that Shanghai would follow the law and regulation, in which they had a high sense of confidence.

Hu Wei said, "This is really a great legal education to me, and also strengthened our courage to have trials constantly and to 'meet setbacks'."

This was the local economic law in the region of the highest degree of development and opening-up at that time. There were several firsts for it: the first creative local law formulated by the Standing Committee of the Municipal People's Congress for the development of Pudong, the first law passed unanimously in the first deliberation by the Standing Committee of the National People's Congress, the first law that required the National People's Congress deputies to go abroad with relevant government departments for investigation to make the law conform to international practice.

Because Pudong people had the courage to have trials with legal protection, by the end of 2012, in the 10-square-kilometer Waigaoqiao Free Trade Zone, the total amount of trade reached 1 trillion yuan, the total import and export worth more than 100 billion dollars, the tax revenue 100 billion yuan, with an average tax of 10 billion yuan per square kilometer, which surpassed the busiest Nanjing Road in Shanghai. The function of the free trade zone was brought to full play such that it became a resource allocation node for Shanghai to serve the Yangtze River Delta, the whole country, and the world.

The legislation in the Waigaoqiao Free Trade Zone demonstrated that since the market economic system had been officially decided as the goal of China's reform, based on the successful experience of Hong Kong, it was necessary to build a free port and a free trade zone as an important driver.

11.3 The First Case in China and the Pioneer in the World

At the end of 2003, the establishment of a free trade zone was formally proposed by Chinese scholars.

On December 9 of that year, Cheng Siwei, Vice Chairman of the Standing Committee of the National People's Congress, put forward a very sensitive proposal at the "Seminar on the Management and Development of China's Free Trade Zone" held in Qingdao. Transition to a free trade zone was the target of the development of the Chinese bonded zone. At that point in time, it was the right time to launch the pilot reform of transition from a bonded zone to a free trade zone, so the site for pilot reform should be selected as early as possible.

Cheng Siwei was also an economist, known as "the father of Chinese venture capital". Previously, he managed to carry out a special research of the transition from a bonded zone to a free trade zone.

Cheng Siwei said that from 2003 to 2006, the pilot reform site should be selected so that the task of pilot reform could be completed in 2006, that is, a free trade zone in line with the target pattern should be preliminarily completed, and then, by means of constant adjustment and consolidation, they should strive to establish two to three world-class free trade zones in China by 2015.

In fact, even earlier, Pudong made a conception about the transition of a bonded zone to a free trade zone. On September 22, 1993, Hu Wei, Director of the Administrative Committee of the Waigaoqiao Bonded Zone, proposed at the Working Conference of the Waigaoqiao Free Trade Zone, "As to the medium- and long-term development objectives of the Waigaoqiao Free Trade Zone, after five to six years worth of effort, by the year 2000, the Waigaoqiao Free Trade Zone will be built into an international free trade zone. It will operate in accordance with international practices, in line with the international market, and in line with the domestic market, and it will be capable of radiating the policy to the Yangtze River Valley and even the whole country."

With China's entry into WTO, many officials of bonded zones, including those of the Waigaoqiao Bonded Zone, put forward the proposal of transforming into free trade zones. According to the China Securities Journal on May 31, 2001, "The Waigaoqiao Bonded Zone of Shanghai had reported to the State Council for approval to transform into China's first free trade zone, which aroused the concern of all parties."

The newspaper also reported the explanation by Zhong Weilin, Assistant Director of the Administrative Committee of the Waigaoqiao

Free Trade Zone: "The bonded zone was established as the initial model for China's development of free trade zone, so it is essentially transitional in nature. The establishment and development of a free trade zone is an effective means adopted by all countries in the world to share the benefits of global free trade and enhance international competitiveness." Therefore, they thought they could take the bonded zones that started earlier and developed faster as pilot bases for China's entry into the WTO, which would gradually be transformed into free trade zones to be integrated with the WTO.

It should be said that Pudong officials were bold enough to say so, because officials who spoke openly about free trade zones were few at the time.

In 2005, the Yangshan Deep-water Port was opened in Shanghai. Despite continuous new records in throughput, it was still restricted by the fact that Shanghai was not a duty-free port or a free trade zone, and the goods overseas could not be transferred in Shanghai.

Officials in Shanghai believed that the international hub not only needed deep water, but also must be integrated with the financial center, trade center, and free trade zone. And Pudong was at this junction. Therefore, after the completion of the Shanghai Yangshan Deep-water Port, it was hoped that Shanghai would set up a free trade zone in Pudong.

In 2007, Li Youwei, former Secretary of the Shenzhen Municipal Committee, suggested in the capacity of a member of the Chinese People's Political Consultative Conference that in due time, the Shanghai Pudong New Area, Tianjin Binhai New Area, and Shenzhen Special Zone should be built into bonded special zones. The concept of bonded zone he described was nearly like a free trade zone, but he avoided using the word "free".

In 2009, organized by the China Productivity Association, a group of experts headed by Professor Li Boxi, a famous domestic expert on development strategy management, came to Shanghai for investigation and research. At that time, the Chinese government issued a document entitled "National Development and Reform Commission's (NDRC) Opinions on Deepening the Economic System Reform in 2009, Approved and Forwarded by the State Council". In Article 11 of the document, that is, "Deepening the Foreign-related Economic System Reform and Improving the Open Economy System", "actively and properly carrying out the Strategy of the Free Trade Zone" was demanded.

About half a year later, the experts team headed by Li Boxi drafted a research report to recommend the construction of a free trade zone in Pudong. The Review Committee gave a high appraisal of the research report and reported it to Premier Wen Jiabao. The report, entitled "Research on the Establishment of a Free Trade Area in Pudong New Area of Shanghai", was submitted by the China Productivity Society. After analyzing the feasibility of building a free trade zone in Shanghai, the report continued, "On the whole, it is feasible to establish the first free trade zone in Pudong New Area of Shanghai."

At that time, Pudong, as the core of the Shanghai International Trade Center, contributed half of the \$270 billion worth of foreign trade of export and import of Shanghai in 2009, of which the port trade accounted for 88% of the city. The trade was mainly concentrated in the 10-square-kilometer Waigaoqiao Free Trade Zone of Pudong New Area, and the professional trading platform of 10 high-tax industries was developed, including car, clock, watch, medicine distribution, liquor, and so on.

On March 1, 2010, Premier Wen Jiabao of the State Council commented on a report, "Comrade Keqiang and Qishan, please read this report. Then the NDRC may, together with the Ministry of Commerce, make in-depth study and put forward suggestions."

In 2011, Shanghai clearly stated the necessity to build a "free trade zone". At the "2011 Conference of Enterprises in the Comprehensive Bonded Zone of Shanghai" held on April 7, Yang Xiong, Executive Vice Mayor of Shanghai and Director of the Administrative Committee of the Shanghai Comprehensive Bonded Zone, claimed that the Shanghai Comprehensive Bonded Zone should actively explore the transformation and upgrade to the internationalized free trade zone.

In November 2011, the 11th Conference of the World Free Trade Zone was held in Pudong. Li Boxi, head of a research group on "Research on the Establishment of a Free Trade Area in the Pudong New Area of Shanghai", was invited to give a special report on "Innovative Thinking on the Functions of the Development of the Free Trade Zones in China", and he also introduced the research on the development of a free trade zone in Pudong New Area of Shanghai.

Shanghai hoped that the free trade zone to be built might cover the entire Shanghai Comprehensive Bonded Zone. The free trade zone was completed on November 18, 2009 under the unified management of the Yangshan Bonded Port Area, the Waigaoqiao Bonded Zone (including the Waigaoqiao Bonded Logistics Zone), and the Pudong Airport Comprehensive Bonded Zone with an area of more than 20 square kilometers.

But Shanghai believed that compared with the 99 special supervised areas approved by the General Administration of Customs, the Shanghai Comprehensive Bonded Zone included the Gaoqiao Port, the Pudong International Airport, and the Yangshan Port. This meant that the advantages were obvious in the process of the transition to free trade zones if the sea, the land, and the air transports were connected.

Nevertheless, at that time, Shanghai still viewed the free trade zone from the perspective of boosting the local economy, instead of a national strategy.

In his keynote speech, Cheng Siwei, the economist who first promoted the study of China's free trade zone, stressed that it was imperative to set up free trade zones in China, and it would be better to build at least five or six more.

At that time, while some local governments in China were actively applying for the free trade zone, the Central Government was also challenged by the United States.

From November 8 to 13, 2011, in Hawaii, the United States, the Asia-Pacific Economic Cooperation (APEC) summit was held as scheduled, with the topic being "closely-connected regional economy".

At the meeting, Barack Obama announced to the world that the Trans-Pacific Partnership (TPP) pushed by the United States was unanimously agreed in the United States and eight other countries. He said the deal would double United States exports and create millions of jobs.

For a time, the topic of the TPP was frequently discussed in the world media.

The TPP, originally launched by Brunei, Chile, New Zealand, and Singapore in 2005, was named a Free Trade Agreement (FTA). In 2009, after the United States joined, it was renamed TPP.

The United States and the European Union were also engaged in the Transatlantic Trade and Investment Partnership (TTIP).

There was also the Trade in Services Agreement (TISA), the members of which covered 70% of the world's trade in services. China made an application to join the TISA in September 2013, but was rejected, since China's service industry had yet to be opened enough.

The TPP, TTIP, and TISA, that is, the 3T, were all led by the United States.

Some scholars believed that in the 3T, China's participation in the TISA was of most strategic significance. First, the member states of the TISA were the most influential, so only by participating in it could China gain a right to speak in formulating the rules for international trade in services. Second, China's entry could open a channel to joining the "BRICS". Third, after China's entry, higher standards of investment and trade could be adopted to promote the reform and further opening-up of the domestic service industry. Fourth, market access to other members of the TISA would provide more space for the development of China's service trade, and change China's long-term trade deficit in service. Therefore, China's joining in the TISA can be taken as an optimal choice. The premise for this optimal choice to be carried out was the degree of openness of the Shanghai Free Trade Zone in the service industry.

China became the largest trading country in the world in 2013. With the slow progress of the round of negotiations of WTO in Doha and trade protectionism gaining ground, the WTO dividends gradually disappeared. So the United States took three major steps to gradually make the WTO impracticable: to establish a TPP alliance with the Pacific Rim countries in the Eastern Hemisphere, to forge a TTIP trade alliance with the European Union in the Western Hemisphere, and through the TISA, dominate the future of global service trade with more than 50 member countries. All these three steps excluded China, the world's second-largest economy.

The Chinese came to understand that Americans were reformulating the game rules of global free trade. Secretary of State Hillary Clinton said that in the 21st century, the United States would focus on the Pacific, and that the TPP would get engaged in not only developing the economy but also sharing values system, that is, to unify the Asia-Pacific region with American values.

"If we don't set the game rules for Asia, China will," Gary Horlick, attorney agent of the trade lawsuits for the United States government and big companies, reporting what President Obama said.

Under this background, China faced new challenges and choices. Being marginalized by the WTO posed a crisis for China. More Chinese scholars believed that, just as China joined the World Trade Organization, China must "re-enter the WTO" to participate in the formulation of the rules of international free trade.

Therefore, one of the measures China had to take was to establish a free trade zone in Pudong, Shanghai to safeguard China's leading position in the global trade competition, which would also facilitate the integration of the Chinese economy with the global economy.

Opportunity once again arose in Pudong, Shanghai.

In March 2013, after Li Keqiang became the Premier of the State Council, the first stop of his survey was Shanghai. One of the most important things on his agenda was to give a positive signal to the establishment of a free trade zone in Shanghai. At that time, it had been more than half a year since the plan of establishing the Shanghai Free Trade Zone was submitted to the State Council, but there was no reply yet. After Li Keqiang's trip to Shanghai, Shanghai quickly resubmitted the proposal.

Some media reported at the time that at the joint hearing, the China Banking Regulatory Commission and the Securities Regulatory Commission did not agree to the establishment of a free trade zone in Shanghai, and the Ministry of Treasury had certain reservations.

On July 3, the State Council approved the establishment of the Free Trade Zone in Pudong, Shanghai, named as the China (Shanghai) Pilot Free Trade Zone.

At this time, the fifth round of China-United States Strategic and Economic Dialogue was being held in Washington. The dialogue had been going on for more than five years since it began in 2008.

China's announcement of the establishment of a free trade zone also exhibited the attitude of Chinese people. China also announced that substantive negotiations on an investment agreement with the United States would be conducted on the basis of the "pre-entry national treatment and negative list", which became the breakthrough of the Shanghai Pilot Free Trade Zone in the future.

In China's own words, the Shanghai Free Trade Zone was established as a result of forced reform, which was similar to the establishment of the special economic zones in southern China more than 30 years ago, that is, "fighting the way out" in spite of the different backgrounds.

In August of the same year, Yang Xiong, Mayor of Shanghai, revealed at the Seminar in Shanghai of "The 50-person Forum on China's Economy" that when Li Keqiang conducted investigations in Shanghai in the first half of the year, he asked Shanghai's top leaders whether Shanghai wanted preferential policies or reform. "He asked me again and again, is Shanghai going to reform? I answered yes, with a firm tone. I said we do not want policy, but we want reform."

Wang Xinkui, the major participant in the overall design of the Shanghai Free Trade Zone and director of the Advisory Office of the Shanghai Municipal Government, pointed out three significant changes that were taking place in global trade and investment at that point in time. First, due to the combination of technological revolution, intelligent manufacturing, and digital services, the new industrial form and business model were promoted. Second, with the rapid development of service trade, service had become an important trade product instead of finished goods. Third, there were some changes in global trade rules. In the past, the focus was on trade rules, but now on investment rules; in the past, it was multilateral, but now more and more bilateral, regional, and multilateral. "This requires that we must have a new way of thinking of opening-up to the outside world."

As to why the Free Trade Zone was first settled in Pudong of Shanghai, on September 29 of the same year, Gao Hucheng, Minister of the Ministry of Commerce who attended the opening ceremony of the Free Trade Zone of Shanghai, explained that Shanghai was selected as the pilot site mainly out of three considerations. First, Shanghai had a good foundation. Shanghai could be experimented at a high starting point because of the large-scale open economy, extensive internal and external economic ties, high concentration of international enterprises, and relatively strong ability to bear risks. The Shanghai Pilot Free Trade Zone, composed of the four existing special supervision areas of customs, had good infrastructure conditions. By that time, this area had attracted 12,000 investment enterprises of various types, among which the top 500 enterprises in the world invested 230 projects, with import and export trade of US$113 billion in 2012. Second, the regulatory system and management experience was relatively mature. In 2009, the Shanghai Municipal Government established the Administrative Commission for Comprehensive Bonded Zones. The higher standard and efficiency in management and more experience in managing higher-degree open areas helped to innovate the model of supervision service to promote the free flow of all kinds of factors. Third, Shanghai possessed better regional advantages. Shanghai, located in the Yangtze River Delta, with vast economic hinterland, can drive development and opening-up in a wider range and a wider region by giving play to the radiation effect.

As for the English name of the China (Shanghai) Pilot Free Trade Zone, there were some doubts. Why is it named the "pilot"?

In fact, the name of the free trade zone was not a new one. More than 2,300 free trade zones had been established in 119 countries around the world, with exports totaling more than US$200 billion, offering 100 million direct and indirect jobs.

It is said that the leaders of the Central Government added a word to the official name, and it was translated into English as "pilot". "Pilot" means both experiment and leading. This name clearly told people at home and abroad that a different name may mean a different historical mission and role to be undertaken. The China (Shanghai) Pilot Free Trade Zone was named with brackets added in the front, and followed by the word "pilot". This meant that, in contrast to the free trade zones of other countries in the world and various forms of special supervision areas of customs in China, it was intended to break through the traditional concept of a free trade zone and highlight the function of institutional innovation. Moreover, this "pilot", by no means an isolated experiment, would play the role of demonstration and can be replicated and popularized.

The China (Shanghai) Free Trade Pilot Zone is an innovation, the first in China and the first in the world.

Therefore, in this pilot zone, it is by no means possible to "enclose a place to open casinos and red-light district" or to make a series of preferential policies for inviting foreign investment as some people imagined naively. In the early years of the development of the Shenzhen Special Zone, local leaders once urged the special-zone currency to be issued, but it was eventually suspended by the Central Government, because the special zone was required to play the demonstrative function. But in China, the independent currency intended to be issued by the special zone cannot display an exemplary effect of promotion and replication. It was well known that the establishment of the special zone by the Central Government aimed not only to use barbed wire to enclose an area for special development, but to become a window and test field. Without this function, this special economic zone would not function in the big chess game of China's reform and opening-up. This is what people in the special zone gradually learned from the practice many years later.

Shen Xiaoming, Party Secretary of Pudong New Area, insisted, "What we are doing is an experiment, so what we do will not necessarily always be successful. Some people told me that what people in Pudong are doing are very meaningful, but I am afraid they will not necessarily succeed. I say it doesn't matter as we are experimenting. But if these experiments can be made successfully, it is of great result. If these experiments do not work, there will be less detours elsewhere. Pudong should have a broad mindset that 'success does not necessarily result from my very effort' in the reform."

11.4 Institutional Experiment in Specific Zones

In the grand experiment of China's reform and opening-up, another big difference from the Shenzhen Special Zone was that in the Shanghai Free Trade Zone there was a judicial guarantee mechanism at the beginning.

Some scholars once told such a background: "After the 1990s, our country entered the high tide period of legislation. Most of the legislation in our country is drafted by interested parties, and the interests of many departments are consolidated through the legislation. Along with the deepening of reform, it is inevitable to encounter more problems in collision with current laws and regulations."

In particular, in the establishment of the China (Shanghai) Pilot Free Trade Zone there were more collisions with the current laws and regulations. Therefore, on August 30, 2013, on the eve of the establishment of the Shanghai Free Trade Zone, at the Fourth Meeting of the Standing Committee of the 12th National People's Congress held in Beijing, the attendees voted to agree to "speed up the transformation of government functions, innovate the model of opening to the outside world, and further explore the experience of deepening reform and opening up", and the State Council was authorized to temporarily adjust the administrative examination and approval of relevant laws and regulations in the China (Shanghai) Free Trade Experimental Zone.

Obviously, the Chinese government realized that the pilot reform of the Shanghai Free Trade Zone would conflict with the relevant laws, and the reform should not "run a red light" or break the law, but modify the "signal system".

Market access can be taken as an example. The laws like the Act on Sino-foreign Joint Ventures, Act on Sino-foreign Contractual Joint Ventures, and Act on Foreign-funded Enterprises all proposed advance examination and approval procedures. According to international practice, the current practice of administrative examination and approval should be changed to develop an open, fair and square environment with clear standard and high transparency. However, since the urgency of the launching and operation of the Shanghai Free Trade Zone, it was impossible to wait for the laws mentioned above to be perfected. As a result, China's leaders first abolished the relevant laws in the particular zones, then began to experiment with reforms and even conducted stress tests for three years. This is a more pragmatic and smarter approach, so the Shanghai Free Trade Zone can be bold enough to conduct a series of institutional innovation experiments with less risk and resistance.

More importantly, the Shanghai Free Trade Zone sent this message to the outside world: All the tests would be carried out in the framework of the rule of law — the law that is not authorized does not work; the law that is not prohibited can be executed.

Professor Zhou Hanmin, Vice Chairman of Shanghai Chinese People's Political Consultative Conference, said, "We must either suspend or revise the existing laws, and remove the parts of the existing laws that do not meet our reform so that we can move forward. This practice is advanced at least all over China." As a legal expert, he once participated in the formulation and translation of nine laws at the beginning of Pudong development. He insisted that "the Shanghai Pilot Free Trade Zone should not go forward regardless of the existing laws, but should consider whether what is to be done conforms to the law, and if necessary, they should change the law before doing".

On this basis, some scholars believed that the Shanghai Free Trade Zone today was different from the Shenzhen Special Zone in the past in that the institutional experiment in the Shanghai Free Trade Zone emphasized the precedence of the legal system.

"The rule of law is the highlight in the reform of the Shanghai Pilot Free Trade Zone," said Luo Dongchuan, head of the Judicial Guarantee Group of the Free Trade Zone, Supreme People's Court.

Xu Lin, one of the leaders of Pudong New Area, made an analogy: Reform was not running red lights, but creating a new signal system. He said, "Some people simply identify reform with going against regulations, like running 'red lights', which usually results in 'traffic accidents'. In fact, reform should not run red lights, but focus on creating a new system. Then the new system should be tested to see whether it is in line with the objective demanded. If it is well applicable, it will be popularized. If it is no better than the original one, it should be stopped and restored to the original. This is also the duty of Pudong as the first pilot area."

This is just one of the important features of a new round of reform and opening-up launched by China's new leaders after taking office in 2013, and the Shanghai Free Trade Zone undertook the national mission — creating a new signal system.

As for whether the three-year limit can bring about the investment risk for the foreign-funded enterprises in the pilot zone, according to the interpretation of the officials of the Administrative Committee of the Shanghai Free Trade Zone, the Shanghai Pilot Free Trade Zone was a process of continuous and gradual opening-up and reform, and the three-year limit referred to the time period for the system exploration. The three-year exploration may be used to verify the effectiveness of the new system of rules. If effective, the next step would promote revisions in the relevant systems and laws.

In addition to the Central Government's adjustment of relevant laws, Shanghai, by following "the creation of a new signal system", also formulated an important local regulation — the Regulations of the China (Shanghai) Pilot Free Trade Zone.

On the morning of July 25, 2014, the 14th Meeting of the 14th Session of the Standing Committee of the People's Congress of Shanghai deliberated and approved the "Regulations of the China (Shanghai) Pilot Free Trade Zone". The regulation consisted of 9 chapters and 57 articles, covering the management system, investment opening, trade facilitation, financial services, tax administration, comprehensive supervision, the rule of law, and so on, which was referred to by the media as the "Basic Law" of the Shanghai Free Trade Zone.

Investors found that in the regulations, many items had recently started undergoing tests in the Pilot Free Trade Zone, such as the management mode of the negative list, innovation of industrial and commercial registration system, innovation of trade supervision system, financial innovation, innovation of government supervision mode, etc. Despite the limited time of test, they had been verified and improved by local laws and regulations.

Before the agreement of the regulations, the Legal Affairs Commission of the Shanghai Municipal People's Congress declared: The construction of the Pilot Free Trade Zone was a national strategy, with system innovation as the core. As the framework regulation for the construction of the Pilot Free Trade Zone, the regulations should reflect the demand for "bold breakthroughs, bold trials, and independent reform". All the reform experiments should be consolidated by legislative regulations and meet the requirements of environmental norms under the rule of law, namely, "to legislate in accordance with the law" within the framework of the socialist legal system with Chinese characteristics.

Investors also found that the regulations clarified that "if the local regulations of this city are not applicable to the development of the Pilot Free Trade Zone, the city government may request the Municipal People's Congress and its Standing Committee to make corresponding provisions on its application in the Pilot Free Trade Zone; if the city's regulations are not applicable to the development of the Pilot Free Trade Zone, the Administrative Committee may request the Municipal People's Government to make corresponding provisions on its application in the Pilot Free Trade Zone."

In fact, this practice is what Chinese people learned from the reform and opening-up for more than 30 years. According to Zhou Qiren, Professor at Peking University and a Chinese economist, the bottom-level and local spontaneous improvement and reform was legally acknowledged, protected, improved, and promoted so that it was made into policy and the national system. Without this, reform would not succeed and reform at the bottom would be self-contained and difficult to be integrated into a great force of system reform.

Professor Zhou Qiren believed that over 30 years of reform and opening-up in China, more importantly, two forces were linked together to open up the channels and make great changes in China's economy. The joint force to bring about institutional change was created between the force of spontaneous efforts at the bottom and the force of the application of state authority so that the integration of decentralized interests resulted in great power to develop China's economy. He referred to the two forces as those at the bottom and from the top.

The experiment reform carried out in the Shanghai Free Trade Zone became a grassroot force, which constantly struggled to break through the old rules and establish new ones.

However, it is certain that once the new rules were legally acknowledged, protected, improved, and promoted by the Central Government to become a policy and a national system, it can be popularized nationwide. According to the Wall Street Journal of the United States, the Shanghai Free Trade Zone possessed the potential to become China's "rule changer".

Some scholars believed that more than 30 years ago, the Shenzhen Special Economic Zone opened the first episode of China's market economy, and the Shanghai Free Trade Zone was expected to become the second episode of China's market economy reform.

From the Shenzhen Special Zone to the Shanghai Free Trade Zone, China went through more than 30 years of reform and opening-up. At first, a border town was chosen from the perspective of political risk to "fight a way out", and then from the perspective of economic principle, China's largest industrial and commercial city was chosen for system experiment which was more efficient, more typical, and more open to the outside world. After all, in China, a country with a vast territory, a large population, and great regional differences, coupled with thousands of years of autocratic rule and accompanying traditional culture, any change is tremendously challenged. Lu Xun once said angrily and sadly to the students, "It is so hard for China to make a change that even moving a table and refitting a stove may almost cause bleeding."

In response, the Communist Party of China tried hard to emancipate their minds and seek truth from facts, like crossing the river step by step by feeling the stones — continuously executing system reform in specific areas. Whether in the first or the second episode, it is the major strategy in reform and opening-up in China, just like a red line guiding through all the time.

11.5 Offering Convenience Instead of Preferential Tax

At first, though the real function of this pilot free trade zone was not entirely well-known, despite the daily influx of people into the service hall of the Shanghai Free Trade Zone, just as in the late 1970s when the Chinese government set up the special economic zone in the border town of Shenzhen.

On September 29, 2013, at the official opening ceremony of the China (Shanghai) Pilot Free Trade Zone, an old man in a light gray suit named Wang Maolin showed up, who had once been the Secretary of the provincial Communist Party and retired as Director of the China Productivity Association. Four years ago, he was invited to organize a group of experts and scholars to make a survey about the establishment of a free trade zone in Pudong, and wrote a report to the Prime Minister.

Wang Maolin explained the context at that time that in 2008, 18 years after the opening and development of Pudong, Shanghai was unable to complete the mission of constructing an international economic, financial, trade, and shipping center, mainly because of the limited space for independent reform in Shanghai, namely, the economic and financial reform had to be approved by the ministries and commissions and the progress was very slow.

Chang Xiuze, researcher at the China Economic Research Center at Tsinghua University, believed, "China's reform can be divided into two types. One is the 'endogenous' reform, such as the rural reform with the responsibility system of household contract as the core. The other is the 'exogenous' reform, that is, the forced reform and opening-up. Since

1978, policy makers have tried to break up the rigid institutions by opening up to the outside world."

Historically, Pudong had conducted a comprehensive pilot reform since 2005, which, as an endogenous reform, was not successful in some key areas of Pudong, especially the reform of the government itself. Therefore, according to past experience, reform can only be forced to make progress by exogenous reform, that is, further opening-up.

On April 11, 2008, Yu Zhengsheng, then Secretary of the Shanghai Municipal Party Committee, arrived at the office hall of the Pudong Civic Center to learn about the efficiency of the government. One investor told Yu Zhengsheng, "It will take as long as three months to go through the procedures of industrial and commercial department, tax department, banks, and others." After hearing this, Yu Zhengsheng answered in regret, "We should change our thinking, to make bold experiments and make up our mind to improve the examination and approval system to enhance working efficiency."

The new situation of opening-up to the outside world also required China to make deeper reform, a more institutional reform. This is different from both the former special economic zones and the various development zones later on. Therefore, in a period of time, the people who paid attention to the Shanghai Free Trade Zone, especially investors, slowly learned that in the Shanghai Free Trade Zone, there was no preferential policy at all.

Wang Xinkui, a participant in the overall design scheme of the Shanghai Free Trade Zone, recalled that some people came to ask about the pilot zone after the Shanghai Free Trade Zone was approved, and they walked away with disappointment when they learned that it was a zone mainly institutional innovation instead of preferential policies.

Wang Xinkui said, "Over the past 20 years, people became accustomed to the special supervision guided by preferential policies and special policies."

Indeed, in people's mind, preferential policies were usually given to most special economic zones, development zones, high-tech zones, and so on. This impression can be traced back to the time before the establishment of China's special economic zones.

At the Working Conference of the Central Government in April 1979, Guangdong leaders boldly allowed Shenzhen, Zhuhai, and Shantou to mark out a place for independent management to serve as an investment area for overseas Chinese, compatriots from Hong Kong and Macao, and foreign businessmen, where the production was to be organized to meet the needs of the international market. They were first named as the "Trade Cooperation Zones". The leaders of the Central Government present at the meeting agreed to the proposal. Deng Xiaoping encouraged the leaders of Guangdong, "The Central Government has no money, but we can give some policies, and you can do it yourself."

Therefore, a special economic zone was born in the southern border. According to Professor Su Dongbin, a Chinese economist, the special zone was a short form for "a zone where special preferential economic policies are implemented". At that time, several leaders of the Central Government repeatedly stressed to the people of the Shenzhen Special Economic Zone that instead of money, only policies would be given. Even after a decade, the development of Pudong was the same. In other words, with only preferential policies and without monetary support, the special zone builders were forced to carry on, with Deng Xiaoping's encouragement kept in mind, "to fight a way out", so that they created the "Shenzhen miracle", which can be taken as a great historic initiative.

Therefore, in quite a period of time, preferential policies were equated with China's special economic zone. But with the deepening of reform and opening-up, the disadvantages gradually appeared, such as violating the principle of fairness, effecting "siphon effect", resulting in vicious competition in inviting investment, and so on. As Wang Xinkui said, "If the special and preferential policies continue to carry on, the situation will indeed get worse and worse, like snatching for investment, and in the end there will be no benefit."

Xing Houyuan, Vice President of the Institute of International Trade and Economic Cooperation of the Commerce Ministry, explained, "The connotation of the Pilot Free Trade Zone is the facilitation in trade and investment instead of preferential policies. The Third Plenary Session of the 18th Central Committee of the Communist Party referred more to system dividends than to policy dividends. This round of reform aims not to provide tax and other preferential policies, but offer more convenience to enterprises in market access, examination and approval, management, and so on so that enterprises can enjoy more freedom. So it is called a free trade zone."

However, Xing Houyuan said regretfully, "In some places people do not understand this, but think that the free trade zone is a new round of land enclosure, and after that there will be preferential policies and local development can be promoted with policy dividends."

As a result of this misunderstanding, the craze for the free trade zone quickly heated up. The media reported this with the headline, "The Hidden Misconception behind the Hustle and Bustle of 23 Provinces Applying for Building the Free Trade Zone".

As a result, when investors came to the Shanghai Free Trade Zone, they found that it was different from others. Officials repeatedly declared that there were no preferential policies, which, though they looked very beautiful, can impede the efficient flow of all kinds of factors, and they were "like driving on highways, and if there are depressions, accidents are likely to occur".

11.6 Investment Blacklist

Similar to all free trade zones in the world, the Shanghai Free Trade Zone must facilitate enterprises, but unlike all the other free trade zones in the world, the Shanghai Free Trade Zone carried out a pilot reform for the country, the most important of which was the reform of the government. But it was not an easy job.

Among them, the most concerned is the "negative list", a very technical term, which frequently appeared in the mass media in China after the establishment of the Shanghai Free Trade Zone.

According to the "Notice of the General Plan of the China (Shanghai) Pilot Free Trade Zone (No. 38, 2013)" issued by the State Council on September 18, 2013, "the Shanghai People's Government should carefully manage the implementation of the plan." Efforts should be made to explore the management model of national treatment and the negative list prior to the investment access, deepen the reform of the administrative examination and approval system, accelerate the transformation of government functions, and comprehensively promote the level of supervision in and after the event."

In the early morning of September 30 of the same year, the Shanghai Government published China's first "negative list" for foreign investment — "Special Administrative Measures for Foreign Investment Access (Negative List) in the China (Shanghai) Pilot Free Trade Zone (2013)". Thus China became the 78th country in the world to implement negative list management.

The negative list was first used by the United States government and gradually became an international practice. But previously in China, positive lists had been mainly used. In other words, the Chinese government had regularly issued the "Catalogue for Guiding Foreign Investment in Industries", which listed the categories of encouraging, restricting, and prohibiting foreign investment. Foreign investment was required to get approval from the Ministry of Commerce, the National Development and Reform Commission, the Ministry of Industry and Commerce, the Department of Taxation, and other departments in accordance with this catalogue.

The negative list, in contrast, presented the industries and fields that were prohibited, which was, in fact, the government-issued blacklist in investment. Once negative list management was implemented, as long as the foreign investment projects were not in the blacklist, they could be directly registered by the industrial and commercial department, free of the trouble of getting approval from the National Development and Reform Commission, the Ministry of Foreign Trade, and other Chinese departments in charge.

This means, for government officials, "they cannot do what the law did not authorize", and for enterprises, "they can do what the law did not prohibit".

As a result, the black box operation that the foreign businessmen felt most frustrated about would no longer be put into practice. Shen Xiaoming, Director of the Shanghai Free Trade Zone Management Committee and Party Secretary of Pudong New Area, said frankly, "I communicate with many foreign friends, and they are very confused or even dissatisfied with the traditional way our government manages the economy. For example, though we have the 'Catalogue for Guiding Foreign Investment in Industries', in fact, the industries listed in the encouraged category in the catalogue are not necessarily approved, and those listed in the restricted category are not necessarily unlikely to be approved, so many foreign investors feel very confused."

The Director of a foreign company in charge of the Chinese Branch said, "In fact, efficient, transparent, and impartial administrative services can be more effective. So changing the backward mode of management would be helpful to arouse the enthusiasm of investors."

It turned out that in the seven months since the Shanghai Free Trade Zone was established, 826 enterprises were invested by foreigners, 90% of which were directly registered in the industrial and commercial departments instead of applying to the relevant departments for approval.

For the industry, the significance of a negative list was not just a list of prohibited or restricted investment fields, but more importantly, the evolution from controlled openness to free openness.

Graham Mather, President of the World Free Zone Convention, said, "Foreign investors look at the negative list from a different perspective, that is, they understand that the negative list means the end of the bureaucratic phase, and the examination and approval is gone and replaced by a simpler and clearer registration system."

Some Chinese scholars even pointed out that the "Catalogue for Guiding Foreign Investment in Industries" implemented by the Chinese government marked the overall turn to negative list management. It is as significant as China's accession to the WTO. This practice is precisely the implementation of "the decisive role of market" in resource allocation, which was demanded by the Third Plenary Session of the 18th Communist Party of China Central Committee.

In 2013, after the first introduction of the negative list management mode in the Shanghai Free Trade Zone, according to the industries of the national economy, 18 categories were identified, consisting of 89 broad sorts, 419 medium sorts, and 1069 minor sorts, totaling 190 management measures, accounting for about 17.8% of the industries. In other words, more than 80% of the industries did not need to be examined and approved by the governmental departments from the lower to the higher levels. For the general foreign-invested projects that were not listed on the negative list, the business license, organization code, and so on could be obtained within four days at the earliest.

This negative list is known as the 2013 version. Microsoft was the first beneficiary of this version.

The joint venture between Microsoft and Chinese companies planned to produce and sell entertainment equipment in China, but due to the restrictions on articles issued by the Ministry of Culture and others in June 2000, Microsoft's plan was not carried out. After the establishment of the free trade zone in 2013, the production and sales of foreign-funded game entertainment equipment were not included in the negative list, so according to the regulations of the negative list management mode, the filing system should be implemented instead of the examination and approval system. According to the reform of industrial and commercial registration system, the joint ventures were required to file in the free trade zone, that is, after obtaining a business license, Microsoft may apply to the departments in charge for permission of production and operation, and the filing and registration formalities can be completed within three working days.

From as long as 13 years to as short as 3 days, Ralph Haupter, Chairman of Microsoft Greater China, was certainly greatly delighted.

A year later, on June 30, 2014, Shanghai released a second version of the negative list, also known as the 2014 version. Compared with the 2013 version, the list was cut down from 190 to 139 items, 51 items fewer.

On April 8, 2015, the third version was issued, and the publisher changed from the Shanghai Government to the General Office of the State Council. The 2015 version was further reduced to 122 items, and the scope of application was expanded to the four free trade zones in Fujian, Guangdong, Tianjin, and Shanghai.

The change of numbers reflects the gradual maturity of the Shanghai Free Trade Zone from the prudence at the beginning as it advanced the negative list and a series of system innovations that followed.

11.7 Surprise for Investors

As the pilot was widely spread, the administrative examination and approval system was also undergoing major changes. The Shanghai Free Trade Zone adopted the new policy of "handling all the necessary formalities at a one-counter service" for enterprise-invested projects.

Walking into the spacious comprehensive service hall in the China (Shanghai) Pilot Free Trade Zone, we can see the staff sitting behind the counters in a line, representing more than 20 departments of industry and commerce, customs, inspection and quarantine, quality supervision, public security, as well as greening, urban construction, urban planning, environmental protection, and so on to "handle all the necessary formalities at a one-counter service" in the service hall.

On October 8, 2013, on the first working day after the National Day holiday, it rained cats and dogs in the morning. Chen Shu, founder of the Ariel (Shanghai) Network Technology Co., Ltd., arrived at the comprehensive service hall early and submitted the application materials to the counter.

"I happened to stand in the first place." What made Chen Shu more surprised was, different from the service halls in other places, the nameplates were not hung at the numerous windows and there was no indication of the names of departments, thus all necessary formalities were handled at the one-counter service. Except for some enterprises specially listed, most enterprises only needed to submit materials to the all-service window, then those materials would be circulated in various departments such as industry and commerce and taxation and finance, and the enterprises did not need to run to one department after another for approval, which was more convenient.

Three days later, the company received a notice for the business license. "I expected to get my license on October 25, but I didn't expect it to be so much earlier. It took only four working days to complete all the procedures, like at lightning speed," said Chen Shu, who was lucky enough to open the first Internet company with a license in the free trade zone, and his company was engaged in Internet finance.

The shrewd investors found out about the low cost of registration there. According to the regulations on enterprises' access to the Pilot Free Trade Zone, in addition to banking, securities, funds, insurance, direct selling, and other industries, most enterprises should register with the paid-in capital instead of subscribed capital and the provision for minimum capital investment was canceled. This regulation, in the eyes of many people, equated to "zero-cost registration".

Therefore, investors swarmed to Pudong, so enterprise registration in the Free Trade Zone reached its climax. Since October 8, 2013, enterprises streamed into the comprehensive service hall of the Shanghai Free Trade

The first investor to get a license from the Shanghai Free Trade Zone (Photo by Xu Wanglin)

After Pudong practiced "all the necessary formalities handled at a one-counter service" for foreign investment, the applicant got the license happily (Photo by Liu Sihong)

Zone for consultation and registration every day. Thousands of people came to handle business every day, with a maximum of 3,800 people.

Gu Xiaohua, a clerk of the Industry and Commerce Bureau in charge of data entry, every day constantly inputted and printed small and big licenses for each of the newly registered businesses. In a day there could be about 200 copies, which meant in her hands a hundred enterprises were born every day. On one side of the lobby, the photocopier in the business center was working non-stop to make copies of all kinds of materials and documents for investors.

The head of Microsoft, who obtained the joint venture registration number "001" in the free trade zone record, once bluntly pointed out that, of course, companies would like to have preferential policies in taxes or others, but in contrast, the convenient business environment, open and transparent system, and complete facilities were what the enterprises needed most urgently. "Enterprises' registration can be reduced from 29 days to 4 days, and the dividends of this change are unimaginable."

Such a dividend filled the comprehensive service hall in the Shanghai Free Trade Zone with a mood of optimism.

On the afternoon of November 12, 2015, the extended function of the newly-launched "one-counter service" for enterprises' access to the Shanghai Free Trade Zone also surprised the famous football coach Xu Genbao. Chen Xuejun, director-general of the Shanghai Administration of Industry and Commerce, issued him the license of Shanghai Genbao Investment Co., Ltd. — this included the Record-keeping Certificate, Business License, Registration Form for Foreign Trade Businessmen, Registration Certificate for Customs Declaration and Record Form of Enterprise for Inspection Application, Seal Casting Permit, and Digital Certificate for Juridical Person. It took only 10 working days to finish all these certificates and licenses.

This Chinese coach planned to buy Spanish Lorca Football Club, and this investment company was just what Xu Genbao set up for acquisition.

Xu Genbao said, "Two months ago, I wanted to buy the club, but I only drafted a contract and other procedures had not been done yet. There were too many formalities for overseas investment in the past. It might have taken at least 3–4 months and at most half a year to complete the feasibility report, capital verification, audit, and form-filling. If it had really taken half a year, everything would have become late over there."

Xu Genbao once built the "Genbao Soccer Base" on Chongming Island of Shanghai, which cultivated five current national players and dozens of players of the Chinese Football Association Super League. The 70-year-old coach wanted to create another "Genbao Base" in Europe, which aimed to send the elite Chinese players to Spain for training and competition.

Xu Genbao came to the Shanghai Free Trade Zone, and the reform facilitating business access made him quickly complete the purchase of the Spanish Lorca Football Club. People also learned that the extended function of the "one-counter service" for enterprise access and the experiment for centralized registration of enterprise residence made it more convenient for enterprises to handle their affairs in the free trade zone.

According to an official in the free trade zone, after the "one-counter service" function was extended, newly-established enterprises could generally complete, within nine working days, all the formalities of enterprise record filing certificate (foreign investment), business license, registration form for foreign trade businessmen, and so on.

That very night, Xu Genbao flew to Spain.

By November 2015, 23,236 newly-established enterprises and 625 overseas investments had been handled through the "one-counter service" for enterprises' access to the bonded sector of the Shanghai Pilot Free Trade Zone. In this sector, nearly 10,000 enterprises had been introduced in the past 23 years, that is to say, in more than two years, it had more than doubled.

11.8 All Efforts for Making the Market More Efficient

The Shanghai Free Trade Zone began to allow enterprises to enjoy the convenience and efficiency of the experiment.

In the past, the Joint Development Co., Ltd. of the Shanghai Free Trade Zone was troubled with the high financing cost. On February 21, 2014, the company received good news. The Shanghai Headquarter of the People's Bank of China issued the "Notice on Supporting the Expansion of the Cross-border Use of RMB in the China (Shanghai) Pilot Free Trade Zone", and enterprises in the zone could apply for the use of RMB abroad. Interest rates on RMB loans abroad were often lower than those at home. But previously it had been difficult for companies to borrow RMB from abroad.

As a result, the Joint Development Co., Ltd. of the Shanghai Free Trade Zone smoothly borrowed 100 million yuan from abroad through the Bank of China, saving a large expense.

"Using the free trade zone platform, we can bring in low-cost funds from overseas, which can greatly help to reduce the financial cost of enterprises in China. Once the financial cost is reduced, it means that the competitiveness of Chinese enterprises is improved. This is of far-reaching significance in the process of RMB internationalization," said Zhou Hehua, President of the Shanghai Free Trade Zone Branch of the Bank of China.

For Hony Capital, a Chinese private equity investment institution, the relevant departments of the free trade zone completed all the formalities so quickly that it became one of the first group of companies to settle in the Shanghai Free Trade Zone, and the first to invest in an overseas enterprise through the free trade zone with US$170 million. Because a feasibility study report was not required to be submitted for general overseas investment projects of less than US$300 million in the free trade zone where the examination and approval system had been replaced by a filing system, the certificate of registration for overseas investment projects could be obtained within five working days. Previously, it might have taken at least eight months. "Eight months later, it would have been too late," Zhao Jinhuan, President of Hony Capital, said with a smile.

For Chenxun Electronics, a mobile phone manufacturer, raw material procurement and finished product sales were all done abroad, but because a free trade account had been opened in the free trade zone Branch of the Pudong Development Bank, banking services like cross-border settlement, financing, and guarantee could be directly handled and the currency could be freely exchanged in the account, which increased the efficiency of the use of funds.

It was hard to imagine such a phenomenon more than 30 years ago in China.

In 1980, China's reform and opening-up was just launched. Milton Friedman, an American economist and Nobel laureate in economics, was invited to visit China. At a banquet, he was asked a question by the vice minister of the Ministry of Materials and Equipment who was going to visit the United States. "Which department is responsible for the distribution of goods in the United States?"

This master economist responded with a shock, "I guess no one in the United States, no matter how ignorant he is in economics, would ask such a question."

Friedman originally suggested for him to visit the Chicago Mercantile Exchange Holdings, where many commodities, such as wheat, cotton, silver, and gold were traded.

But such a response puzzled the other side, and Friedman continued patiently to tell him that no one in the United States — not even a person in committee — was in charge of the allocation of materials. The Ministry of Commerce and the Ministry of Internal Affairs were concerned with the production and allocation of materials in a completely different way. In the United States, no individual or no political group was "in charge of the allocation of materials" in the sense of what China or the Soviet Union referred to. Indeed, western economists like Friedman could not imagine that the government was "in charge of materials allocation" — the production and sale of every pair of leather shoes or every piece of underwear was allocated by the government.

In this dialogue, it is really difficult for them to understand each other because of their different economic context, China being a planned economy, and the United States being a market economy.

Such a story of dark humor is unbelievable. It turned out that the failure of the planned economy taught the Chinese government how much it could do, and the dividends of the market economy allowed the Chinese to find it more efficient to hand over most of the government's functions in running the economy to the market. The Chinese people often say that reform brought about dividends, but in fact, it was the transformation of the market economy that brought about dividends, or the "invisible hand" that played the role in bringing about dividends.

The so-called "invisible hand" was created by Adam Smith, the founder of modern economics. In 1776, his book *The Wealth of Nations* was published. The title page of the book reads: "Your Majesty, please do not interfere in the national economy. Go home! What does the country do? Just be a night watchman. When night comes, go and ring the bell. As long as there is no theft on the street, you just go home. As long as you ignore the economy, the economy can develop."

Adam Smith believes that the free market, which seems to be haphazard, has a self-regulating mechanism, that is to say, the "invisible hand" plays the role of regulating, so the government can govern by non-interference.

In the understanding of this "invisible hand", the Chinese paid a great price.

More and more Chinese people realized the role of the market economy and demanded a thorough turn to the market economy.

Naturally, the new Central Government hoped to establish a fair, just, and orderly competitive market system as an experiment in the Shanghai Free Trade Zone to create a dynamic and ever-changing ecological environment of market economy for the "invisible hand".

A columnist of the *Financial Times* (Chinese Network) of Great Britain wrote, perhaps, for modern metropolises like Shanghai, the government did not need to stand at the front line, but simply to bring together the best companies, offer them full freedom, urge them to abide by the rules of fair and free competition, and conduct its services well. "If the Shanghai Free Trade Zone serves to provide a positive upgrade to China's economic transformation, the best orientation is to reshape the duties of local governments from a strong government to a service government."

All these were aimed at making the market more efficient.

11.9 Exporting Experience

To the outside world, the Shanghai Pilot Free Trade Zone plays an important role, that is, an experienced wholesaler. The Pudong people took advantage of their favorable position, copying the experience of the Shanghai Free Trade Zone of 28 square kilometers.

On the afternoon of March 26, 2014, the Pudong New Area Government issued the new policy of the "one-counter service" for foreign investment. This policy stipulated that foreign investors only needed to submit all the application materials to the "one-counter service" window set by the government, and all the certificates should be issued by the "one-counter service" window.

So, on the first floor of the Pudong Civic Center hall was the "one-counter service" window, with the number of the applicants displayed on the electronic screen above.

This enhanced the working efficiency of the government. Foreign investment projects in Pudong (including the establishment and modification of projects) were approved within the original timeframe of two to four working days, 90% shorter than the state's statutory time of 20 working days.

Chen Guoshan, Vice President of Business Development in China of Worldpay Marketing Consulting (Shanghai) Co., Ltd, said, "The certificate processing is much faster than expected, nearly a week or so, and the time saved can be spent hiring people and doing business. Time is money."

When Chen Guoshan received the documents for approving foreign investment, business license, certificate of organization code, tax registration certificate, and others from the Market Supervision Bureau, Business Committee, and Tax Bureau in Pudong, he said gladly, "We are lucky to enjoy the new policy of the 'one-counter service'. It is unimaginably fast to set up the company."

In countries with a developed market economy, such a practice does not count for much, but in the transformation of China it is of great significance. Foreign investors frequently complained about the cumbersome process of examination and approval in China, and it is hard even for the students returning from overseas, who want to start their own businesses, to understand. A French student who returned home to start a business complained to an official of the Pudong Commerce Commission that all the formalities for his business registered in Lyon to be moved to Paris had been completed within a week, but in Shanghai, all the paperwork had not been completed in three months for his business to move from one district to another.

According to Xin Yachen, Director of the Pudong New Area Business Committee, this reform was the first innovative measure taken for the integration of the Pudong pilot comprehensive reform and the construction of the Shanghai Free Trade Area.

At the same time, the experience and practices of the Shanghai Pilot Free Trade Zone started to be taken as example to follow all over China, especially the model of negative list management.

Because of the practice of "entry and exit in batches for centralized declaration" in the Shanghai Free Trade Zone, in the Pingtan section of the Fujian Free Trade Zone, Chen Hong Technology (Pingtan) Co., Ltd. saved nearly five days in customs clearance every month. Due to the multiple batches and the large amount of mobile phones and computer touch panels produced by the company, according to the traditional mode, ticket-by-ticket declaration was required, and the transportation vehicles had to run at night when the customs clearance was delayed, which was unsafe and clients who were unwilling to work overtime for goods complained, but now, all the ticketed goods would be collected together for a one-time customs declaration only once a week.

As for the replication of institutional innovation and experience in the Shanghai Free Trade Zone, Han Zheng, the leader of Shanghai, made an analogy. It was not "planting bonsai", but "planting a nursery". That is to say, all the rules and reform measures in the pilot zone should be popularized and replicated in accordance with the demands of the Central Government.

"On the other hand, whatever can't be popularized and replicated like 'planting bonsai' is not what the Shanghai Pilot Free Trade Zone should plan to do. Even if we have some immediate interests, we will not do it. They should be reproducible, figuratively referred to as "planting a nursery," Han Zheng said.

On the afternoon of May 23, 2014, General Secretary Xi Jinping of the Communist Party of China Central Government came to the Waigaoqiao Comprehensive Service Hall of the Free Trade Zone to listen to the report on the progress of the overall construction of the pilot zone and communicated with the staff from the industry and commerce, customs, inspection, and quarantine departments. Xi Jinping was pleased to learn that since the establishment of the free trade zone eight months prior, more than 16,000 investment enterprises and 280,000 employees were assembled to make great progress in building a more open and transparent investment management system, improving trade facilitation, and deepening the innovation of the financial system. As a result, more than 30 items of reproducible reform projects were initially advanced. Then he stressed that the Shanghai Pilot Free Trade Zone, as a large experimental field, should be sowed with seeds, carefully cultivated and carefully managed in hope of a good harvest, which would promote such an experience.

This metaphor illustrates the national strategy and historical mission of the China (Shanghai) Pilot Free Trade Zone. At the beginning of China's reform and opening-up, the Central Government conducted a reform experiment in the southern border town of Shenzhen and other places. At that time, many people argued over what these zones should be called: "export processing zones" or "trade cooperation zones" or "export special zones". In the end, Deng Xiaoping, with his global vision, decided on the name "special zones". It took years for people to come to terms with what it really meant and why it was named "special zones" instead of "export processing zones" or alike. Some scholars held that this change of name clarified the main tasks and functions of the special economic zones, that is, the change from export trade and export processing to reform experiments, and also they were raised to the higher level of national strategy of reform forced by opening-up. A fundamental change in nature took place. The Central Government greatly reduced the probability of choosing an invalid system.

On the occasion of 35 years of reform and opening-up, the Chinese Government set up the Free Trade Zone to provide a model for China's further reform and participation in establishing a new international economic order by trial and error.

In fact, this is the national strategy that the Shanghai Free Trade Zone must shoulder after more than 30 years. And it is an inevitable result of the historical logic of China's reform and opening-up, or an upgraded version of China's economy.

Obviously, this is at a different level from the special economic zones before. The so-called special economic zone means special policies are enjoyed in certain zones. Once out of the special zones, the enterprises cannot enjoy the special policies, and without the special policies for support, the special economic zones would make no sense. In contrast, the policies tested in the free trade zone would be replicated in the near future and can be enjoyed in other places. If the experience were not replicated and generalized, the pilot free trade zone would not assume any significance.

The Shanghai Free Trade Zone followed some examples in doing so.

Boston is an important center of shipping and manufacturing and a center for higher education and healthcare in the United States with world-renowned universities such as Harvard and Massachusetts Institute of Technology, and is also considered as a globalized city. But more than 400 years ago, it was a barren beach. Because Boston, as a port, rapidly developed free trade, especially the early development of trade with China which made the United States quickly accumulate a large amount of funds needed for economic construction, it broke the blockade imposed by Britain and France on the newly-born United States. As such, Boston is known as the starting point of free trade in the United States.

Boston also creatively integrated the experience of free trade with the development of higher education, healthcare, technology, and finance so that now it has become a center of intelligence, technology, and political thoughts.

Boston's experience was rapidly reproduced in the United States into as many as 260 free trade zones, covering the major port cities across the United States. This created a strong hematopoietic system for American economy.

Therefore, for the construction of the Shanghai Free Trade Zone, Shanghai repeatedly stressed the measures and the rules of reform implemented in the free trade zone should be reproducible. This is obviously different from the practices adopted after the establishment of the Shenzhen Special Economic Zone in 1980. In this sense, the free trade zone was more promising, that is, even if there were just a little progress, the role of promotion would be played in more than the 28 square kilometers, and the impact of its regulatory measures would also outstrip that in the Shenzhen Special Zone, which developed only within the barbed wire fence. In fact, the importance of the Shanghai Free Trade Zone does not lie in the concept of entity, but the concept of rules. Instead of being built into a special zone with special policies, it would become a new example of "crossing the river by feeling the stones" shared all over China through step-by-step trial and error.

When the regulatory measures in the Pilot Free Trade Zone can be implemented not only in the fields of trade and finance, they can also be replicated in other fields, that is, in light of Boston's experience, they can be reproduced in the fields of higher education, healthcare, and science and technology. As a result, the significance of free trade is not only limited to the field of trade. As an American scholar once put it, if free trade is to bloom like a flower, then all the petals need to open at a time. That is to say, the free trade zone assumes its significance not only in free trade itself, but also in the fields of technology, education, healthcare, community, and so on.

A spokesman of the Ministry of Commerce expressed this more specifically. At the press conference of the Seminar entitled "Construction of the Free Trade Zone" on December 4, 2013, Yao Jian, spokesman for the Ministry of Commerce said, some tentative policies were adopted in the Shanghai Pilot Free Trade Zone, such as simplifying the industrial and commercial registration, expanding the opening of the service industry, and facilitating investment including negative lists, which were all problems encountered in the negotiations of the free trade zone. If these policies were fully implemented and approved by the enterprises in the Shanghai Pilot Free Trade Zone, and the ability of the government management and the level of modern management can be adapted, then they could be further popularized and reproduced to provide the foundation and experience for the country to sign free trade agreements overseas and build free trade zones so that their confidence in further opening-up could be highly enhanced.

Of course, in the long term, it is harder and greater to accomplish. What is really difficult is not the implementation of reform measures within the free trade zone, but how to reproduce them outside the zone.

Just as Ding Jianping, Director of the Center of Modern Finance Studies at the Shanghai University of Finance and Economics, said, "The process of reproduction is actually a process of overcoming resistance, a process of breaking certain interest monopolies. To reproduce them in other local places, it is inevitable to affect the interests of certain financial institutions and local governments. So it may depend on their willingness to simplify procedures like merging institutions."

11.10 The Expansion of the Free Trade Zone

On April 8, 2015, the State Council issued "Notice on the Plan of Further Deepening the Reform and Opening-up of the China (Shanghai) Pilot Free

Trade Zone", which decided the scope of the Shanghai Free Trade Zone to be 120.72 kilometers, which covered four special customs supervision zones and the Lujiazui Financial Zone, the Jinqiao Development Zone, and the Zhangjiang High-tech Zone.

That is to say, the free trade zone was expanded from the original 28 square kilometers to 120 square kilometers.

The notice required that after the expansion, the Pilot Free Trade Zone should become a leader in reform and opening-up, act as the pioneer in innovation and development to continue to take institutional innovation as the core, implement the national strategy of the development of the Yangtze economic belt, and take the lead in bringing out the potential for reform and solving problems of reform in building a new system of an open economy, exploring new models of regional economic cooperation, and creating a law-based business environment. In the Free Trade Zone, people should actively explore the management mode of national treatment and negative list before the entry of foreign investment, deepen the reform of administrative management, and enhance the ability and level of supervision in and after events.

It is a great opportunity for Pudong. As Shen Xiaoming, Director of the Administrative Committee of the free trade zone and party secretary of Pudong New Area, put it, "If the greatest opportunity for Pudong in the first decade of the 21st century is the comprehensive reform, it is no doubt that the greatest opportunity in the second decade is the Pilot Free Trade Zone."

A reporter of Xinhua News Agency revealed that Shanghai, as the pioneer in China to explore the pilot free trade zone, formally stepped into a new era of the free trade zone (version 2.0).

On April 27 of the same year, the Shanghai Free Trade Zone Expansion Area was opened by the Pudong New Area Government. After the expansion, the Shanghai Government set up the Free Trade Zone Leading Group of Promotion and its office at the municipal level. At the level of the Pudong New Area, the Shanghai Free Trade Zone Management Committee and the New Area Government shared their offices, with three functional bureaus like the Comprehensive Coordination Bureau set up inside the Management Committee, five regional bureaus such as the Free Trade Zone and Lujiazui set up at the district level, in which the

Free Trade Zone Bureau was in charge of 28.78 square kilometers of administrative affairs in the former Free Trade Zone.

As expected, the expansion brought more conveniences to more enterprises.

The Pharmacopoeia Committee of the United States set up a regional headquarter in China at the Zhangjiang High-tech Park in Shanghai, an institution with global influence in formulating and promoting public standards for food and medicine. Thanks to the expansion of the Shanghai Free Trade Zone, the United States Pharmacopoeia Committee's strategic project of "Global Center of Food Excellence" also settled in the Shanghai Free Trade Zone in 2015.

Before the launch of the new policies for the free trade zone, it had been more demanding to handle the examination and approval procedures and relevant documents for the samples used for the United States Pharmacopoeia research and development, so it had taken at least more than two weeks for the samples to be conveyed from the airport to the laboratory, which forced most of the samples to China to be transferred to other countries for research and development.

Feng Bingbing, Vice President and General Manager of the United States Pharmacopoeia Committee and General Manager of the China Branch, said that according to relevant regulations, for each sample of healthcare product imported from abroad for research, they had to carry out complicated registration procedures in the same way as the import and sales enterprises did, but after entering the free trade zone, the situation improved fundamentally, which can be said to be "twice the result with half the effort".

Feng Bingbing gave an explanation, "'Half the effort' refers to the time for customs clearance for imported research and development samples reduced by half, because the examination and approval of certificates was more scientific and more convenient. 'Twice the result' means, with our booming business, the total number of standard research and development projects completed by the China regional laboratory of the United States Pharmacopoeia Committee in 2015 was twice of those in 2014."

It is really exciting that the time for customs clearance was only three to five days, and as a result total cost was cut down nearly a quarter and most of the samples forced to transfer to other countries gradually returned to the Chinese laboratory.

On October 8, 2015, the Ministry of Commerce held a regular press conference, at which press spokesperson Shen Danyang remarked that the Shanghai Pilot Free Trade Zone made remarkable achievements in four aspects in the past two years: the foreign investment management system was basically established with negative list management as the core; the trade regulation system focusing on trade facilitation was effectively operated; the innovation of the financial system with the aim of capital account convertibility and opening of financial service was promoted in an orderly way; and the supervision system during and after the event was preliminarily developed with the government function transformation taken as the core.

The Shanghai Free Trade Zone was expanded in less than two years, which resulted from the strong expectations of the Central Government.

A month later, on November 25, 2015, Li Keqiang paid a visit to Shanghai again to inspect the latest progress of reform and opening-up in the Pilot Free Trade Zone. This was the third time in three consecutive years for him arrive for inspection. This was a rare case.

When Li Keqiang visited the free trade zone the year prior, he encouraged the free trade zone to actively explore the establishment of free trade accounts between domestic and foreign currencies. That year, Li Keqiang was happy to learn that nearly 39,000 free trade accounts had been opened in the free trade zone so far, and that the cross-border revenue and expenditure of the financial reform had reached 3.8 trillion yuan, which effectively reduced the financing cost of enterprises. He said that the reform of free trade accounts was an important measure to make better use of two markets and two resources, and on the one hand, the experience should be learned to be reproduced wherever conditions were suitable, and on the other hand, the supervision should be improved to build up the "anti-seepage wall" to prevent the abnormal flow of cross-border capital from affecting the stability of China's financial market.

Li Keqiang insisted that the Shanghai Free Trade Zone was the first state-level free-trade demonstration zone, an icebreaker for opening-up and an excavator of reform, so it would be expanded after the icebreaker. In the free trade zone, more effort should be made in simplifying administration and decentralization, and the management of three lists should aim to stimulate the enthusiasm of enterprises to start new businesses and the vitality of innovation.

Li Keqiang arrived in the bright administrative service hall of the free trade zone, and the person-in-charge introduced the progress of reform in the Shanghai Free Trade Zone. He pointed out that the reform of "license first and then permit" greatly stimulated the market vitality, but in the market research some enterprises reflected that even if the business license was given first, in the absence of the business permit issued by relevant departments, the enterprise still could not operate. Therefore, it was hoped to carry out the pilot reform of "the separation of license and permit".

Li Keqiang expressed his agreement to the idea on the spot and suggested that the pilot reform should be carried out in a number of easily operable and manageable fields. He demanded for Shanghai to submit the application of "separation of license and permit" to the State Council as soon as possible. Three weeks later, the report on the overall plan for Shanghai to carry out the pilot reform of "separation of license and permit" was placed on the table of the executive meeting of the State Council for discussion.

On December 16, 2015, deliberated and approved at the executive meeting of the State Council, the pilot reform of "the separation of license and permit" that Pudong New Area took the lead in executing would be valid in the following three years from the date of approval.

Li Keqiang visited the Shanghai Free Trade Zone three times in three years. At the beginning of the Pudong development in the 1990s, Zhu Rongji, one of the leaders of the State Council, also visited Pudong every year.

When the new Chinese Central Government was established in 2013, the first step to be taken was to streamline administration and delegate power. "The aim of the reform is to shift the focus of management from 'examination and approval' in the past to the 'regulation' at present. The reform of the Shanghai Free Trade Zone based in Pudong met the strategies of the new government, which meant that the state leaders were highly concerned about the changes taking place in the delta where the Yangtze River enters the sea."

The outside world noticed that every time Li Keqiang made his statement in the Shanghai Free Trade Zone, a strong signal was sent out about the follow-up measures of reform. Clearly, the Central Government hoped that the Shanghai Free Trade Zone, as the test field, would produce more "experience in breeding seeds".

Chapter 12

Fulfillment of a Dream: 500 Meters up and down, 100 Years to and fro

12.1 The Great Story of Our Age

In 1990, a government official named Ruan Yanhua came to Waigaoqiao, Pudong, where Shanghai planned to set up a free trade zone near the Yangtze River estuary, but what caught his eyes was the blockhouse left by the war, farmland, and desolate reed marshes, with no man but the cold wind in sight.

The municipal construction in Pudong was backward, with poor transportation and almost no cultural facilities. "It's too backward!" Puxi people in Shanghai talked about Pudong contemptuously. At that time, population congestion led to poor housing in Puxi, but the Shanghai people said, "A bed in Puxi is better than a room in Pudong."

On December 19, 1992, at the invitation of a Chinese journalist, Fujida Ichi, a Japanese tycoon who invested in Jinqiao in Pudong, wrote an essay. "It will take a long time for the development of Pudong to be completed. Our generation may not see the beauty of the Pudong New Area. But we wish to create a beautiful city that the next generation can be proud of. I feel very honored to be able to make a little contribution."

However, since 1990, Pudong developed greatly with unprecedent economic explosion. In 1990, Pudong's economy totaled 6 billion yuan, but in 2014 it increased to 710.9 billion yuan. From 1990 to 2014, the total economy of Pudong increased 119 times, the total fiscal income 290 times, and the general public budget 136 times.

It seems that Rome was built in one day. Although the waves of the Huangpu River remained the same, the water flows into the sea day by day.

A guest from New York once landed at the Pudong International Airport and walked through the spacious, bright aisles in the airport, listening to the soft Chinese, English, and Japanese broadcasting. On the tarmac, planes from all over the world took off every minute on average. Outside of the airport, he took the world's fastest ground transport — the maglev train, with a top speed of 417 kilometers per hour. It took only seven minutes to arrive in the city from the airport. Deeply impressed by all of these, he wondered which was the third world country, China or the United States? The LaGuardia Airport in New York was no match for the Pudong International Airport, let alone the maglev train.

Pudong literally means the east to the Huangpu River, a very common name and a very common place. It is so common in the history of China that no Central Government ever highlighted it. Until 1992, no complete administration was ever established in Pudong.

It is very interesting that 100 years ago in Shanghai, a doctor and novelist named Lu Shi'e wrote a novel entitled *New China*. The hero of the novel had a dream of holding a World Expo in Pudong, but because "in Shanghai there was no place for building a venue, new houses were built in Pudong". In order to facilitate Shanghai people to come over, people also set up a big iron bridge, cross-river tunnel, and tram tunnel across the Huangpu River from Puxi to Pudong. Because of the expo, "Pudong flourished almost as much as other places in Shanghai, and the Chinese National Bank opened a branch in Pudong".

At that time, no one took Lu's dream seriously, and it was just taken as a fantasy novel.

But 100 years later, the dream in the novel came true in Pudong. It is so incredible that readers who ever read *New China* made such a reaction: "It's amazing, the coincidence is so amazing!"

On a sunny day in May 2010, Zhao Qizheng, the host of the NHK and the former Director of the Administration Committee of Pudong New Area, walked along the newly built embankment west to the Huangpu River in Shanghai. The focus of the camera slowly turned from Wanguo complex on Shanghai Bund to the modern complex across the river in Pudong.

17 years ago, in 1993, the Japan Broadcasting Association sent a camera crew to Pudong, Shanghai, to make a follow-up film entitled "A Day of Zhao Qizheng". At that time, for the vast majority of foreigners, Pudong was a strange geographical name. Returning to Pudong, Zhao Qizheng was deeply impressed by the great changes. The host asked him about the differences between the opening this time and the opening of Shanghai to foreigners 160 years ago.

Zhao Qizheng replied that in 1843, the government was forced to open out of incompetence and also allowed an additional "concession", while today it was an autonomous opening under China's full sovereignty and foreigners must act in accordance with Chinese laws and regulations.

The host nodded and said, "I understand!"

In 1892, looking at Pudong from the watchtower of the fire-fighting station, there were a number of docks and warehouses in Lujiazui

They crossed the Huangpu River to arrive at Lujiazui, where there were many Chinese and foreign financial institutions. A jungle of skyscrapers soared into the sky, among which there was an antique bungalow, with carved railings, red walls and black tiles, all particularly conspicuous. In 1914, Lujiazui on the bank of the Huangpu River was a barren land. A businessman named Chen Guichun built a mansion with Chinese and Western styles combined, which became the most luxurious landmark in Pudong. During the day, people could enjoy the scene of the open land in the south of the Yangtze River, and at night listen to the waves of the Huangpu River.

100 years later, on the opposite side of the mansion, the 632-meter Shanghai Central Building, the tallest building in Shanghai, rose from the ground. Beside it, two skyscrapers — the 88-story Jinmao Tower and the 495-meter-high World Financial Center — became new landmarks of Shanghai. The contrast gave people a strong visual impact and inner agitation.

Zhao Qizheng was so much inspired as to ask the cameraman to shoot the Chinese eaves of the old house together with the two skyscrapers. With camera lens raised and a long close-up, Zhao Qizheng blurted, "500 meters up and down, 100 years to and fro!"

The three super-high skyscrapers in Lujiazui, scattered in the shape of a triangle, all experienced and witnessed Pudong's reform and opening-up (Photo by Niu Yixin, Shanghai News Aerial Photography Alliance of Shanghai, China)

This scene and this sentence touched the host very deeply.

The height of 500 meters embodied the 100-year change of Pudong. In 1910, Lu Shi'e wrote the novel *New China* and in 1914, Chen Guichun built his own large mansion, both of which inadvertently became the witnesses of Pudong's vicissitudes. Coincidentally, there was the legend of Pudong.

On December 10, 2008, the magazine *Time* published a review of China's reform and opening-up for 30 years. At the end of the article, the author put it, "This is the great story of our age, the story of all of us, not only about China."

12.2 From "Ghost City" to Hot Land

In 2011, a reporter of *The Wall Street Journal* came to Pudong and interviewed Yao Wei, Executive of a real estate company. This Shanghainese had long believed in the old saying, "A bed in Puxi is better than a room in Pudong."

The reporter put it, "When Yao Wei arrived in Pudong for the first time in 1994, she persuaded a client out of renting an unfinished restaurant on the top floor of the Oriental Pearl Tower. She advised her client that it was too early. 10 years later, she gave the same advice to another client. At that time, however, Yao Wei owned a modern-style apartment beside the river in Pudong. Looking out from the balcony, the guest was strongly fascinated with the dazzling scene of Shanghai. She said, when they came upstairs, they sighed, 'Oh, this is Shanghai'."

The author described an interesting phenomenon.

Experts once mocked Pudong New Area. In their eyes, this specially-rebuilt Manhattan was historical evidence of the housing bubble because this steel-glass tower had a complex design and was largely uninhabited. Milton Friedman, a visiting economist, called it "a monument erected for the late pharaohs lying in the pyramid".

Today, at a time when the worry about the possible collapse of China's property market is renewed, Pudong was surprisingly a highlight to counter that worry.

The Wall Street Journal issued the article at a time when short-sellers such as James Chanos on Wall Street were talking down China. The story of "Pudong from a 'ghost city' to 'hot land' is undoubtedly the most classic case of refuting the talking down.

In turn, it is understandable that in this ancient country, the economy and society, which developed as slowly as a snail in the past, exploded in the more than 30 years after reform and opening-up. In more than 20 years, Pudong witnessed the same degree of industrialization and urbanization as that in the developed regions of Europe that took two centuries to complete. Why? It is hard for westerners to understand, and even Chinese themselves sometimes fail see the truth.

Only 20 years later it sounds funny to mention the popular saying and long-established traditional thinking that "A bed in Puxi is better than a room in Pudong". This echoed a popular saying that the world changes so fast that one can hardly understand.

12.3 Dreams Fulfilled

Since the 21st century, every early morning Pudong began its busyness and tension with taking the subway.

In Lujiazui, known as "Eastern Manhattan", crowds of people streamed out of the subway station. A young man named Yu Hui hurried to the Jinmao Tower with his red tie fluttering from side to side on his chest. In front of him and behind him the young men walked in a hurry like him into the rows of skyscrapers.

He came to the building and looked up at the 88-story building. As an Assistant to the President of a lease finance company, he had a desk on the 35th floor of the building, with a panoramic view of both sides of the Huangpu River.

In Zhangjiang, China's "Silicon Valley", a design assistant named Xia Jing squeezed out of the subway with other young men who were pouring out of the subway train and soon went out of sight in a pink building in the shade. Soon after she graduated from college, she began to work for a software company. Beside the building, there was a beautiful artificial lake. In this full spring, the sun was shining on the magnolia trees by the lake.

Almost at the same time, these young people did the same thing, that is, switching on their computers, clicking their computer mouses with their fingers, and starting the day's work.

It is the most common scene in Pudong in the early 21st century: eight subways across the river carried people to and fro Pudong and Puxi every day.

The scenes and pictures in this booming city filled with modern facilities and vibrant young people displayed the vitality of this piece of land.

We might as well go back to 1990, when the whole western world was full of suspicion and hostility to China, and investors abroad hesitated again and again. China's economic growth slowed down, and some radical reforms were halted. However, Deng Xiaoping insisted on the opening-up to the outside world. He said, "We must do a few things to show that our policy of reform and opening-up remains unchanged and that further reform and opening-up will be carried out."

In September 1990, a reporter from British Reuters asked Zhu Rongji, Mayor of Shanghai, about the political stability and legal protection of the rights of foreign investors: Since last year these two aspects suffered from setback. Will this setback affect the development and opening-up of the Pudong area?

12 years later, when the Reuters' reporter came to Pudong again, he wrote down the answer: Shanghai — a city that the whole world might admire!

In 1993, Taiwan launched a plan to build an "Asia-Pacific Operation Center". Zhao Qizheng, once director of the Administrative Committee of Pudong New Area, recalled that the "Asia-Pacific Operation Center" plan in the Taiwan region was somewhat similar to the policy of Pudong development. The plan, made for Taiwan by the famous Mckinsey Corporation of the United States, was arguably quite comprehensive. Taiwan's announcement of the plan was a sensation at that time.

But over the past few years, the "Asia-Pacific Operation Center" plan still stayed on paper, but Pudong's rise on the west bank of the Pacific was an indisputable fact. Today, the skyline of the skyscrapers in Pudong has become the most beautiful landscape in Chinese stories.

At the beginning of Pudong development, Li Jianeng, Assistant Director of the Management Committee received an "overseas returnee" and accompanied him to inspect Waigaoqiao. In the plan, Waigaoqiao was a free trade zone, but the "returnee" was shocked to see the reed marshes all over. In more than a decade, the reed marshes became China's largest free trade zone. Li Jianeng recalled, "Walking through the reed marshes, what can we see? There was nothing to see except a water tower left from the bathing place on the beach. Recalling the past, we seemed to have a dream. What dream? The Chinese Dream!"

On an evening in the early summer of 2014, Shen Ruqun, known as the "living map of Pudong", leaned cozily against the parapet, watching the fishes swimming merrily in the clear river, and beside the river was a Starbucks which was fully occupied. His heart and lungs were refreshed by the soft wind.

"This river is called Zhangjiabang. It used to be a smelly river. From far away, the rotten smell of the river could be smelled even before the river came into sight." He said that when he drew the map of Pudong, he was reluctant to put the river on the map, but now the 22-kilometer-long scenic river is like a beautiful green ribbon around Pudong.

Just opposite the river was the spectacular Shanghai Science and Technology Museum, where more than 10 heads of states gathered for the PACE conference in 2001. An 84-year-old man said with a smile, "In the past it was not wide at all, but now it is so wide and there is no smell at all."

Before Pudong development, in Shanghai there was such a saying, "A bed in Puxi is better than a room in Pudong." Time can change everything. 20 years later, Shanghai's most tasteful houses are located in Pudong. "Pudong plate" has become the highlight of Shanghai real estate. More than 100,000 international talents with international education backgrounds came to Pudong to start their business and living, including more than 30,000 foreigners. Among them, William Keller, General Manager of Roche Pharma, received the "China Green Card" No. 000002 in Shanghai. After his retirement, he and his family chose to stay in Pudong, and his son and daughter attended an international school.

Yu Ning, Assistant President of Zhongxin International who returned from the United States, said, "In Pudong, the modern atmosphere and cultural atmosphere as well as the investment environment, living environment, and ecological environment are all world-class. The choice of Pudong means not only the choice of success, but also a new way of life. Pudong is place suitable for both start-up and living. It can always bring you freedom, passion, and inspiration."

Shen Ruqun, a Pudong locale, said that when Pudong was developed in 1990, he served as a teacher in the secondary school of the Pudong Public Transport Company and when he once described the future plan of Pudong to the young people, there was a burst of laughter, "Planning is just drawing on a piece of paper and hanging it on the wall, so do you believe in this?"

Shen Ruqun argued, "I certainly believe that the development and opening-up of Pudong is what was decided by the state."

But no one believed what he said, and some people even laughed at him with suspicious eyes, "It is just a dream!"

The background of multi-dimensional internationalization made foreigners readily integrated into Pudong. The picture shows the 10th Long-distance Running Competition of the Biyun International Community in the Jinqiao Development Zone, which is the most popular running event among Chinese and foreign friends in Shanghai. (Photo by Xu Wanglin)

In the Biyun International Community located in the Jinqiao Development Zone, the foreign residents exercise in the bicycle lane. Pudong builders put forward that although Jinqiao was targeted as an industrial zone, it must be built according to urban planning.

When he retired in 1991, he thought he might as well draw a map of Pudong by himself to make people see what Pudong looked like just by looking at the map. He measured Pudong with his feet during the day and drew maps at night. Unexpectedly, on the ground in Pudong, new high-rise buildings started or completed almost every week and new roads were put into use every month. Shen Ruqun exclaimed, "Pudong changed so quickly that sometimes you could not know your way if you stayed at home for several weeks." He drew a new map almost every year, such that he was known for "chasing after Pudong with a map". On the map he used to mark the more than 450 newly-built buildings with more than 20 floors in Pudong one by one.

By 2007 he had completed 15 versions of the Pudong map. He was gratified by the fact that he had used a map to document the history of a dream fulfilled.

As a reporter for The Wall Street Journal in China, Feng Qiang visited Shanghai several times from 1981 to 1988. More than 20 years later, with regard to Pudong, the former Deputy Editor of the South China Morning Post first associated it with New York: "Looking across the river from the Bund, it was like standing at the foot of the Statue of Liberty in New York Harbor, overlooking Wall Street."

At the end of the novel *New China* written by Lu Shi'e, when the author woke up from a dream, he had a dialogue with a lady, which was even more interesting:

"I told the lady the dream in detail, then she said, 'You have held the crazy dream for such a long time that you just have this strange dream.' I said, 'It may not be a dream. By then, the sight would have come true.' The lady answered, 'You and I are still in our youth, so in the long run, we will find out.' I said, 'I want to record this dream as proof in the future.'"

Dreams can become true, so a dream is not necessarily a dream. This is the characteristics of the Chinese dream, which occurred in Pudong.

12.4 Trial and Error: Rebounding and Advancing Step by Step

In telling the story of China's reform and opening-up, the British economist and Nobel laureate Ronald Coase mentioned Pudong. He put it like this:

> This tiny area, across the river from Shanghai downtown, successfully turned a paddy field into an economic pillar by drawing lessons from the Shenzhen model, and became the focus of China's opening to the outside world in the 1990s. If Shenzhen is the symbol of China's opening to the outside world in the 1980s, Pudong is a model of opening to the outside world in the 1990s. Soon, the Yangtze River Delta around Shanghai will become the second engine of China's economic growth, advancing shoulder to shoulder with the Pearl River Delta in the south.

This is the story of Pudong's success. "Experiment" is the key word of the story. So, Coase said, "The story of reform varies from place to place, but there is one thing in common, that is, trying to find the best way for their own economic development, and the whole country has become a big lab, with a variety of different experiments being conducted everywhere. 'Crossing the river by feeling the stones' is the Chinese way of thinking about making experiments."

At the beginning of the reform, China did not have a clear strategy and plan. If any, it was partial and controversial, which could be said to be "felt". People did not know where they were going. As a result, Professor Ezra Feivel Vogel, an American scholar, China expert, former Director of the East Asia Center at Harvard University, and author of *Deng Xiaoping and the Transformation of China*, prefers to refer to Deng Xiaoping as the "General Manager" rather than the "Chief Designer" of China's reform and opening-up. He thought, for the work of "design" there must be a blueprint, with a clear plan about how to go, but Deng Xiaoping was to give a test to see what would follow, and if it does work, it could go ahead. "I do not think of it as a 'design'. He was 'crossing the river by feeling the stones'. He was a political leader, the general leader of the country, so he was a 'general manager'."

According to Wu Jinglian, a famous Chinese economist, "The strategy of 'crossing the river by feeling the stones', in the absence of theoretical guidance, contains an inherent rationality, namely, allowing the scattered micro-subjects to explore the directions of social development in their own way. And once these explorations have been proven successful, the society as a whole can share its achievement."

Some western scholars ignored this. Years later, Chinese economist Lin Yifu questioned: China's economic reform made a lot of substantial achievements in the 1980s, but why were some mainstream economists in the world not optimistic about China? Professors at Harvard University and the Massachusetts Institute of Technology, including Jeffrey Sachs, Irving Fisher, Oliver Blanchard, Andrei Shleifer, Robert Vishiny, Rudi Dornbusch, Paul Krugman, Richard Layard, and Lawrence Summers, who were involved in the Soviet Union and Eastern European reforms, were all master economists, who developed many cutting-edge theories. But why were they unable to predict and explain the predicament brought about by "shock therapy", and why were they not optimistic about China's economic transformation?

Both the prestigious scholars and the officials in some developing countries did not understand why China was able to achieve the miracle of economic growth. Joshua Cooper Remo, the famous Editor of *Time* once met with the development minister of a Southeast Asian country. He recollected, the minister "put down the teacup and asked a colleague of mine, an experienced development economist straight away, 'Why is our experience so different from that of China? We're so much alike. We also have a low-cost of labor and our political system is very strong. Did we do anything wrong?' The question sounds familiar. Across Asia, and across the world, there are anecdotes about some countries studying the rise of China and trying to find out what similar miracles they can achieve at home."

History is not a joke. The miracle took place under the guidance of the idea of "crossing the river by feeling the stones" without any theoretical value in the eyes of the great scholars. China developed from a planned economy to a market economy step by step. In particular, the large-scale transformation of the market economy was realized by constantly carrying out various system tests in a specific region.

In 1982, the London Institute of Economic Affairs in Britain published a pamphlet by the Hong Kong economist Zhang Wuchang, *Will China Take the Road of "Capitalism"?* At that time, Zhang Wuchang was Dean of the School of Economics and Finance of the University of Hong Kong. In the book, Zhang Wuchang put forward a startling prediction: "China will move towards a market economy," and "this transition is a slow process". Almost all of western academia was skeptical of his view.

Even Zhang himself was cautious in his own formulation of his view, arguing that "this transition is a slow process".

Four years later, in 1986, Zhang Wuchang's pamphlet was reprinted, in which he revised his previous views, admitting that he had "underestimated the speed of transition" and deduced that "the pace of economic reform in China will be significantly slower than that in the previous five years". In fact, however, the pace of transformation was accelerating.

History proved Zhang Wuchang's prediction and made him revise his prediction. The speed of China's move to a market economy was greatly beyond his expectation, which was an absolute shock to western academia.

In February 2008, someone asked Lin Yifu, Professor at Peking University who just assumed the new post of the chief economist of the World Bank, what ideas he would contribute to the development of the World Bank. He answered readily, "Emancipate our minds and seek truth from facts." His reply drew a burst of laughter from the audience.

In fact, Lin Yifu was serious. As an economist who had made great achievements in development economics, agricultural economics, and institutional economics, he knew that, after World War II, unrealistic development policies were carried out not only in China, but also many other developing countries, which afforded us too many lessons. Therefore, someone asked, why was it so difficult for governments in many developing countries to emancipate their minds and seek truth from facts? Lin Yifu wrote, "This is obviously a very important question, but unfortunately social scientists have yet to give a good answer."

In fact, the Chinese Communists truly recognized the importance of these several words, but also paid a very high price, and these words also became the ideological guideline of China's reform and opening-up.

As for the historical process of China's reform, Yao Yang, professor at Peking University and a Chinese economist, stated that China's reform was a gradual process, and in terms of time, each reform was carried out in stages, rarely in one step, and in terms of space, the advancement of reform was regional, that is, regional tests preceded all-round popularization. He called the former "regional reform" and the latter "partial reform".

Taking the path of China's gradual reform, the central and local governments adopted a constant "trial and error" approach. Xiao Gongqin, a Chinese scholar and Professor in the History Department of Shanghai Normal University, believed that Deng Xiaoping's idea of "crossing the river by feeling the stones", which was based on the limitation of human rationality and information knowledge, was fundamentally the empiricism thought that aimed to discover the path to China's modernization through the rebounding of trial and error.

Deng Xiaoping, he commented, was a pioneer of thought who broke away from dogmatism and constructed rationalism by the approach of trial and error. His way of thinking was closer to empiricism and, in his view, the concrete goal of socialism could be constantly revised and changed in practice. As long as there was a guiding value, through "taking small steps, steady steps, and constant steps", our goals can be gradually achieved. At present, the empirical thinking of "path obstacle, trial and error, and step by step" is still the spiritual heritage of our nation.

Because of the way of thinking of trial and error, every five years since 1990, the Central Government and the Shanghai Government entrusted a strategic task to test Pudong. In 1990, Pudong was announced to embark on the development and opening-up in 1990 to become the first new area. In 1995, it launched the first functional development strategy trial in line with international practice. In 1999, with the "focus on Zhangjiang", the strategy of high-tech development was implemented. In 2005, the implementation of the national comprehensive reform strategy made it become an experimental area for comprehensive reform. In 2009, New Pudong was established, with the construction of the "two centers" approved. In 2013, the China (Shanghai) Pilot Free Trade Zone was established in Pudong.

12.5 Whether the Golden Age can be Extended

On August 3, 2014, the Shanghai Tower, the tallest building under construction in Shanghai, had its top tower crown just completed, and this building of 632 meters became the "first high-rise" in Shanghai.

It became the first high-rise in China, and the second high-rise in the world, only 828 meters lower than the Khalifa Dubai Tower of the United

The sightseeing floor of the first high-rise building, as high as 632 meters in Shanghai, was put into test operation at the beginning of July 2016 (Photo by Xu Wanglin)

Arab Emirates. Designed by the Gensler Architecture Office in San Francisco, the construction cost was about US$2.4 billion, and the main building was composed of 118 floors.

It is reported that its lift, which could run 18 meters per second, could reach the building's sightseeing platform on the 119th story in 55 seconds. The building's distorted streamline shape could reduce wind load up to 24% during typhoons. But Arthur Gensler, a designer of the Shanghai Tower and the Chief Architect at Gensler Architecture Office, and Construction Director Uhler, told Agence France-Presse that the spiral was an icon that symbolized the Chinese people looking into the future. Some people likened it to a spiral pattern of genes, and also a spot for connecting the earth to the heaven.

The building is located in the Lujiazui Finance and Trade Zone of Pudong New Area, and next to it, the Jinmao Tower, completed in 1998, is 420-meter high and the Shanghai World Financial Center is 492-meter high. These three buildings, which take the shape of a triangle, witnessed or underwent the Asian financial crisis in 1997, the September 11 terrorist attacks in 2001, and the global financial crisis in 2008.

Henry Kissinger, former United States Secretary of State, visited Pudong many times. When he learned that China and Japan had invested in two of the three super-high-rise buildings planned in the small Lujiazui, he suggested, "The third high-rise building should be invested by Americans to reflect the world pattern. If another Asian country invested in this tall building, it would only reflect the Asian pattern." He really introduced an American investor. No doubt, in the eyes of the former diplomat, Pudong belongs to the world.

But the third tallest building was eventually invested and built by the Chinese themselves.

On July 23, 2015, with the last piece of steel spliced in place, the 12th bridge on the Huangpu River, Chenta Bridge, was completed smoothly. Since 1976, after the first bridge for the highway and railway was built in the west of Yexie Port in Songjiang County, the Nanpu Bridge, Yangpu Bridge, Fengpu Bridge, and Xupu Bridge were constructed and put into operation in the 1990s. Since the beginning of the 21st century, the Lupu Bridge, No. 2 Songpu Bridge, Minpu Bridge, No. 2 Minpu Bridge, No. 3 Songpu Bridge, and the Jinshan Railway Bridge were completed and put to use one by one. Among them, the Lupu Bridge was the largest-spanning arch bridge in the world at that time, with the largest main arch in the world, the largest hoisting weight in the world, and the largest amount of steel for a single arch bridge.

Under the bridges, thousands of boats and ships crossed the waves of vast water. The difficulty of crossing the river on both sides of the Pujiang River has completely become a past story.

On December 10, 2015, the 10th anniversary of the opening of the Yangshan Deep-water Port, a "Mediterranean Zoe" cargo ship with a full load of 19,000 international standard containers smoothly docked at the Phase 1 terminal of the Yangshan Deep-water Port. 10 years ago, thousands of twenty-foot equivalent units (TEUs) of container ships had to wait for high tide to enter the Waigaoqiao Wharf. The Yangshan Port made Shanghai become the largest port in the world for six consecutive years.

Under the sun, on this previously-isolated island in the sea, along the 5.6 kilometer dock shoreline, with 16 container berths in a row, many large cargo ships shuttled around. It is a spectacular scene.

On December 29, 2015, as the first pile of the Satellite Hall of the Shanghai Pudong International Airport was slowly driven into the earth, it not only indicated that the world's largest single satellite hall would be located in the Shanghai Pudong International Airport, but it also marked the beginning of the third-phase expansion of the Pudong Airport, which was a milestone in the construction of Shanghai's aviation hub. The total investment of the project was about 20.6 billion yuan. Upon its completion in 2019, the support capacity of annual passenger throughput in the Pudong Airport would reach 80 million.

On the morning of December 14, 2015, the annual number of arrivals and departures in the Pudong International Airport exceeded 30 million, the largest airport in China for 12 consecutive years. Demarchi Henri, a French passenger who arrived on flight SU208, became the lucky 30 millionth passenger at the Border Inspection Station of the Shanghai Airport that year. He received a beautiful and delicate souvenir "Sunshine Gate of China Border Inspection".

No one can deny the great changes in Pudong. More people admit that Pudong has entered the golden age of development since 1990.

At the end of the 20th century, after writing *Cities of Tomorrow*, British urbanist Peter Hall wrote another book *Cities in Civilization*.

Lujiazui in 2015 (Photo by Niu Yixin, Shanghai News Aerial Alliance, China)

The sun is new every day here. Lingang New Town under construction. (Photo by Liu Sihong)

Selecting 21 cities in the history of civilization of 2500 years, he reviewed the characteristics of their development, culture, and urban construction. Then he put forward the concept of "Urban Golden Age", that is, in some specific periods, cities can highlight their unique creativity and become beacons for the construction of human civilization.

Known as a "world-class master of urban planning", Hall served as a Special Adviser to the British Deputy Prime Minister's Action Group on Urban Development, as well as guided urban and regional development strategies in various countries and regions.

Hall found that these cities changed dramatically over the course of 10 to 20 years of development, the "golden age of the city" as he termed it, such as Athens in the 5th century B.C., Florence in the 14th century, London in the 16th century, Vienna in the 18th–19th century, Paris at the end of the 19th century, and so on. From the perspective of the history of human civilization, these cities in the so-called "golden age of cities" were all world cultural cities and prominent landmarks on the map of world culture. They all had their own culture and roots, but at the same time they were international cities with a high degree of openness. On the one hand, they could absorb all kinds of excellent culture in the world. On the other hand, they could make the essence of their culture known, accepted, and loved by the world.

Shanghai is a prominent landmark of modern China. But anyone who asserted in the 18th century that Shanghai would become a landmark in China in the future was seen as a daydreamer. Because at that time, in the administrative division, Shanghai only belonged to a county of Songjiang Prefecture, far inferior to Shanghai's neighbor Suzhou. Even among the five ports for trading determined after the Opium War, Shanghai was ranked behind Guangzhou, Fuzhou, and Ningbo, and only ranked in front of Xiamen which was not even a county at that time.

However, only 100 years later, and only after more than 50 years from the opening of Shanghai as a port, Shanghai became an international city with a high degree of openness. But in the process, it is with regret that Pudong was not eye-catching. After the development and opening-up of Pudong in 1990, this regret began to be erased, because Pudong entered the golden age. Then how long can this golden age last?

Afterword

I had an urge to write this book in 2010, when my first book on Pudong, *The Test of Wealth Growth: Pudong as an Example,* was published. A Shanghai historian who once worked as a visiting scholar at Harvard University suggested that I translate the book into English and introduce to overseas readers the changes that had taken place in Pudong, Shanghai, China, located at the Yangtze River estuary on the East Sea. He said, overseas readers would be interested in the story of Pudong. In the thousands of years since Pudong became land, there seemed no change at all, but in the last 30 years, unprecedentedly, Pudong's wealth grew so rapidly that it seemed that Rome were built in one day. Such a truly-realized dream not only belonged to Pudong, but should be shared to all.

I remembered what he said, but I was just a journalist, not a university graduate of history, and without professional academic training. Fortunately, I gained some experience. In 2015, my second book *The Story of Pudong: A Dream Come True* was translated into English by experts of the National Bureau of Foreign Languages and then published, which made me more confident. Thus I was encouraged to begin to typing on the computer, taking time to visit the libraries, archives, and museums. It took me as long as seven years intermittently for writing and revising.

But when I finished the last sentence of the book, I did not feel ecstatic because it was not easy to get it published as an academic book, though I tried to tell Pudong's story in a more colloquial style, hoping to make it acceptable to more readers. In fact, this is the distress for all scholars after the writing. At the time of distress, Mr. Zhou Zheng of Shanghai People's Publishing House took the initiative to contact me and said that Shanghai People's Publishing House was willing to publish the book. In fact, he and I never knew each other. The Editor-in-Chief Wang Weisong also put forward some constructive suggestions on the publication of the book. Only at that moment did I feel so ecstatic and relieved that finally I was able to leave a textual record of the "primitive history" for the development of Pudong.

Finally, the book was published in Chinese in 2017. Now it is planned to be published in English with the help of Shanghai People's Publishing House.

For both the Chinese and English versions, I would like to express my deep respect and gratitude to all these people.

First of all, I would like to thank Mr. Zhao Qizheng, the respectable old leader of the Pudong New Area, whose thoughts, ideas, insights, and stories about Pudong development has benefited me greatly. He, like an instructor, encouraged and guided me to make great effort in researching Pudong history and the study of Pudong so as to tell the world the story of China and the story of Pudong. I invited him to write a preface to this book. He also proactively promoted the translation of this book and the publication of the English version. He said this book should be available in university libraries in the United States in the future.

I would like to thank Xiong Yuezhi, a great historian. I have always greatly admired Mr. Xiong, for his works and articles are constantly studied in my writing. Especially *General History of Shanghai*, edited by him, is an important reference for my writing. And he gladly wrote a preface for this book, which added luster to it.

I would like to thank the Publicity Department and the Cultural Development Fund of Pudong New Area. With their great help, the English version of the book was successfully published.

I feel very grateful to Chai Zhiguang, Director of the Party History Office of the New Area. He took time to read the manuscript in his tight schedule and put forward his suggestions, as well as provided me with a lot of books and other materials.

I feel very grateful to the leaders of the New Area Archives and the Pudong Society for Literature and History. They provided me with information, suggestions, and opinions with their own advantages in resources.

I feel very grateful to my leaders and my colleagues, the editors and reporters, since their reports were also an important source of information in my writing.

I owe my thanks to my friend Niu Yixin and his news photograph team, since they provided many high-quality pictures for this book. He is also trying to use pictures to describe Pudong's past and present.

I owe my thanks Li Ying and Xiong Jie, Editors of Shanghai People's Publishing House, as they worked hard to make this book published.

Finally, I owe my thanks to Madam Li Zhang for her translation of the book from Chinese into English. The great effort she made can be imagined, so I would like to express my respect to her.

I have always believed that the story of Pudong's development and opening-up is a great story not only for China, but also for our time. So I hope more overseas readers have the chance to read the story that took place on the piece of land in Shanghai, China, located at the Yangtze River estuary of the East Sea.

Xie Guoping
Shanghai
January 2019

Lightning Source UK Ltd.
Milton Keynes UK
UKHW020657221220
375671UK00004B/310

9 789811 221699